America Firsthand

VOLUME TWO

Readings from
Reconstruction to
the Present

TENTH EDITION

America Firsthand

VOLUME TWO

Readings from Reconstruction to the Present

Anthony Marcus
*John Jay College of Criminal Justice of
the City University of New York*

John M. Giggie
University of Alabama

David Burner
*Late of the State University of
New York at Stony Brook*

bedford/st.martin's
Macmillan Learning
Boston | New York

For Bedford/St. Martin's

Vice President, Editorial, Macmillan Higher Education Humanities: Edwin Hill
Publisher for History: Michael Rosenberg
Senior Executive Editor for History: William J. Lombardo
Director of Development for History: Jane Knetzger
Developmental Editor: Jennifer Jovin
Production Editor: Louis C. Bruno Jr.
Senior Production Supervisor: Lisa McDowell
Executive Marketing Manager: Sandra McGuire
Copy Editor: Kathleen Smith
Senior Photo Editor: Christine Buese
Photo Researcher: Bruce Carson
Permissions Managers: Jennifer MacMillan and Kalina Ingham
Text Permissions Editor: Eve Lehmann
Senior Art Director: Anna Palchik
Cover Design: John Callahan
Cover Photo: CPL Archives/Everett Collection
Composition: Achorn International, Inc.
Printing and Binding: LSC Communications

For information, write: Bedford/St. Martin's, 75 Arlington Street, Boston, MA 02116
   (617-399-4000)

ISBN 978-1-319-02968-5

Acknowledgments

Preface

From its inception, *America Firsthand* has proved to be a favorite among students and instructors alike. Its unique collection of personal views of how Americans lived, witnessed, and made history has resonated with students, while its breadth of coverage and blend of fresh and familiar primary sources have been welcomed by instructors. As a tool for student learning, *America Firsthand* is more vital today than ever before. For while the Internet and the ongoing digitization of the humanities have revolutionized access to historical documents, they have created fresh problems of quality, credibility, and contextualization. Instructors now have access to an unprecedented number of documents online, but many find selecting the most teachable sources to be a frustrating and time-consuming endeavor. Students surfing the Web can easily and quickly come across a series of "hits" on any given topic, but it is not so easy for students to judge the reliability of these sites, assess the accuracy of their information, and detect bias and point of view. Reading primary sources gathered on the Web, students lack the tools to test their veracity, question the perspective of the authors, and situate documents in their proper historical milieu. *America Firsthand* meets these challenges because it provides teachable and engaging documents that instructors can rely on, presented within an organization and pedagogy designed to help students develop their skills of historical analysis and draw their own conclusions.

We aim to offer students a broad array of carefully vetted documents and introduce them to the core skills of the historical profession — skills useful for students who choose a wide range of majors and careers. Our goal for instructors is to offer a dependable resource that fits easily into a range of classroom activities and teaching styles and in a format that guarantees students will succeed. We have merged documents from earlier editions with a robust collection of new ones to create a type of laboratory wherein students and professors alike can examine slices of the past, connect them to their cultural settings, and test how they affirm or challenge the mores and values of their day. When studied collectively, the documents arranged in *America Firsthand* reveal patterns of continuity and change throughout United States history and, when used in conjunction with the supporting pedagogical apparatus, evoke habits of inquiry and critical reflection that lie at the heart of historical analysis.

NEW AND ENDURING FEATURES IN THIS EDITION

This tenth edition continues *America Firsthand*'s emphasis on individuals making and living history, adding newly uncovered and rediscovered selections with more of the voices and topics that reviewers have asked for and that reflect enduring and new themes and topics that American history instructors teach today. We have added more on early nineteenth-century religion and gender, opposition to slavery, the Korean War, sexism in the workplace, and the intersection of race and the criminal justice system. With twenty percent new selections, the tenth edition supplies a rich diversity of perspectives for students to explore. In Volume One, students meet William Strachey, an Englishman who was shipwrecked on Bermuda on his journey from England to Virginia in 1609. They also hear from Major John Norton about his command experience in the War of 1812; they read two women's reflections on the consequences of following their religious faiths; they view contemporary sketches and cartoons portraying controversial issues such as the domestic slave trade and women's rights; they see the Civil War's toll on the American landscape; and they consider one Northerner's observations of his fellow countrymen at the end of the war. Among the new selections in Volume Two, students read the testimony of a craftsman who observed the ways in which industrialization had reduced the quality of manufactured products. They also learn about the fight against the "white slave trade," a thinly veiled attempt to keep white women away from foreign-born men; they discover how new technologies like helicopters and antibiotics enabled Mobile Army Surgical Hospital (MASH) doctors to save lives in Korea; they read a female scientist's account of inequality and discrimination in academia in the 1960s; they witness the destruction of the Berlin Wall that signaled the beginning of the end of the Cold War around the world; and they read about an African American man's experience of "walking while black" in America in the early twenty-first century.

The tenth edition retains the popular **Points of View** part-opening features that juxtapose readings on a specific event or topic, providing students with contrasting perspectives from the past. Critical thinking questions at the close of each Points of View set help students sift through the evidence, make connections, and analyze the readings. The tenth edition includes two new Points of View: one on the Great Depression, which combines letters to the Roosevelts with an image of Americans seeking food relief and Morey Skaret's account of his homelessness as a teenager in the 1930s; and one on the public debate surrounding Somali immigration to Lewiston, Maine, in the early 2000s that originally appeared in the seventh edition of *America Firsthand*.

This edition features more **stand-alone visual documents**, sources that are treated the same as the textual documents, with headnotes and questions to help students interpret these images as evidence. For example, Volume One gives students the opportunity to savor the rough-

and-tumble life of a gold miner through a period daguerreotype and analyze a Mathew Brady photo of a soldier in the trenches, and Volume Two features photographs of a Woolworth's sit-in and a gay rights demonstration in the 1960s as well as a photograph of a Guantanamo Bay detainee.

As in previous editions, carefully written **headnotes** preceding the selections prepare students for each reading and help to locate personalities in their times and places. **Questions to Consider** following the headnotes offer students points on which to reflect when reading and encourage in-depth analysis of the evidence.

To equip students with the tools for working with all the sources—visual as well as textual—in this collection, we have updated the **Introduction: Using Sources to Study the Past**. This edition also features checklists for analyzing written and visual sources on the inside of the back cover.

This revision of *America Firsthand* has afforded us a wonderful opportunity to rethink core ideas about American history and how to present them to our students. It has also strengthened our conviction that, in the current technological age, *America Firsthand* is an essential instrument aiding students and instructors alike to work through judiciously selected and annotated documents with the overall goal of improving the teaching and learning of history. Indeed, we hope that this edition will provide a rewarding intellectual space for students, one in which they can develop a personal interest in firsthand sources to deepen their own historical knowledge and ultimately bring it to bear in the classroom and in the world beyond.

ACKNOWLEDGMENTS

We would like to thank all the instructors who graciously provided helpful and constructive comments for improving *America Firsthand*: George Cooper, Lone Star College–Montgomery; Petra DeWitt, Missouri University of Science and Technology; Thomas Anthony Greene, Elmhurst College; Vance Kincade, Arcadia University; Ann K. Lupo, SUNY Buffalo State College; Philip M. Montesano, City College of San Francisco; Stanley Rose, Nashville State Community College; Michael Sokolow, Kingsborough Community College, CUNY; Paul Swendson, El Camino College; Sharon Vriend-Robinette, Davenport University; and Valdenia C. Winn, Kansas City Kansas Community College.

We are also grateful to the members of the Bedford/St. Martin's staff and their associates who have made this edition of *America Firsthand* the best that it can be. Thanks to photo researcher Bruce Carson for implementation of the book's visual program; to John Callahan for creating the wonderful new book covers; to Kalina Ingham for expertly coordinating the text permissions; and to Louis Bruno for turning the final manuscript into a book. We also thank Michael Rosenberg and William

Contents

ix

PART TWO
The Gilded Age:
Industrial Growth and Crisis   47

POINTS OF VIEW
The Rise of Labor Unions

PART THREE
A Society in Flux:
Preparing for an American Century 95

POINTS OF VIEW
Suppressing the "Dreadful Curse of Liquor" (1890–1919)

PART FOUR
A New Society: Between the Wars   147

PART FIVE

"The American Century":
War, Affluence, and Uncertainty   199

POINTS OF VIEW
Building and Using an Atomic Bomb (1942–1945)

PART SIX
Awakenings: Authority and Liberty in the Modern Age   249

PART SEVEN
Between History and Tomorrow:
Into a New Century   303

Introduction: Using Sources to Study the Past

The study of history offers us a way of knowing who we are, where we have come from, and where we are headed. Perhaps because we live in the present, it is sometimes easy to assume that people of the past were basically like us, only with different clothing and hairstyles, as in many Hollywood history movies in which the characters are also made appealing to contemporary audiences by evincing modern goals and desires. In such "historical dramas" people fight for their nation, even if neither it nor the very idea of a nation yet exists; they make great sacrifices for romantic love, even if this concept has not yet been invented; they struggle to protect the innocence of children, even if there is not yet a concept of childhood; and they demand personal freedom in societies where the greatest goal is to have a defined place in the social order. Such usage of dramatic license to place modern motivations and values into the past is called historical anachronism, and it usually leads to good movies but a rather poor understanding of how our ancestors made decisions and took actions. History is a systematic attempt to study the differences and similarities between the past and the present, in order to understand how we got from there to here and how we may craft our future.

How, then, do we, as students of history or historians, approach the study of our past? A first step is to pose a research question about the past. For example:

- What were social relations like between African Americans and white Americans in colonial Virginia?

Asking this type of question is important because so much of our vision of race relations before the civil rights movement of the 1940s–1960s is built on visions of the hardened institutionalized slavery of the mid-nineteenth century and the Jim Crow segregation that followed. Some historians, among them Edmund Morgan, have argued that relations between whites and blacks were more fluid and equal in the first century of the British colonization of North America, when slavery was not hereditary or restricted to African Americans, who, if they were male, could still testify in court, cohabit with white women, buy their own freedom, and even own slaves—all provided that they had converted to Christianity.

Knowing something about how the nineteenth-century horrors of industrial-scale slavery, laws against literacy among slaves, and finally segregation emerged from an earlier time can help us understand the nature of race relations in America and tell us something about the potential for changes in the future. Whatever our motivation for posing questions such as the one above, the first step in trying to address them is to find relevant sources that may provide answers. These come in two broad categories: *primary sources* and *secondary sources.*

PRIMARY SOURCES

Primary sources are documents and artifacts directly produced by the individuals and groups that participated in or witnessed the situation, event, or topic being researched. They are a lot like the evidence and testimony that lawyers use in a courtroom to present different versions of what happened and why. Often answering the "why" question is just as important as figuring out what actually happened. For example, if it is known that a defendant shoved his brother off a roof to his death, it matters to the judge, jury, and district attorney whether the action was self-defense or an accident or occurred in the heat of anger. If the court can establish that the killer had invited his brother to the roof two days after learning that the brother had named him as sole beneficiary in a life insurance policy, the results are likely to be very different than if the court discovers that the dead brother had set up the rooftop meeting and that neither sibling stood to benefit from the death.

All the sources included in *America Firsthand* are primary sources, but the foregoing is only one example of what is possible in primary source research. Indeed, the types of primary sources are as limitless as the imagination of the historian. Human records of all kinds leave useful information for scholars and students. From a drawing done by an eighteenth-century child showing what was taught to young elites, to DNA evidence suggesting that Thomas Jefferson had children with his African American slave Sally Hemings, to a colonial New York candlestick holder made by a Portuguese Jew with designs borrowed from Native Americans, to oral history interviews—every primary source leaves behind clues for the historian. The problem is often sorting out which clues are useful and which are not. This may change depending on what questions are being asked and what techniques are available at the time of research.

Not only do science and technology make many old primary sources newly important; social and political change also opens up new possibilities for asking different *kinds* of questions of the evidence. Consider, for example, that Thomas Jefferson's DNA had little value before modern advances in genetics—but also consider that until the study of slavery and black–white sexual relations had advanced to a certain stage of intellectual development, few historians would have dared to ask questions about Jefferson's potential fathering of children by a slave woman. Similarly, historian James Lockhart probably never would have crossed the globe to bring together Nahua descriptions of the conquest of Mexico (Volume One, Document 2) if, when Lockhart was in school in the 1960s and 1970s, there had not been an indigenous civil rights movement that drew attention to the native point of view. And certainly the political growth of the women's movement and feminism in the last decades of the twentieth century fueled scholarly and popular interest in the diaries of women like Rebecca Cox Jackson (Volume One, Document 35), who found in religion a power to slip social strictures of race and gender in the early 1800s. Sometimes, forgotten documents, like Manuel Gamio's interviews with Mexican migrants in the Midwest in the 1920s (Volume Two, Document 36), become newly relevant and can be read differently in the face of contemporary debates around immigration (Volume Two, Documents 55 and 56) and the politics of ethnicity (Volume Two, Document 63). The changes of the present prompt historians to revisit old sources with new perspectives and to search for undiscovered new sources on old questions.

With respect to our question about the social relations between African Americans and white Americans in colonial Virginia, the relationship between Sally Hemings and Thomas Jefferson might tell us something important. Although Hemings was born at the end of the colonial period, the world that she and Jefferson inhabited may have been as much like the seventeenth century as the nineteenth century. Now that, thanks to DNA testing, it is widely accepted that Hemings bore Jefferson a child, much of the controversy revolves around how equal, unequal, voluntary, or coerced the sexual relationship was between an aged former president and the teenage girl who was his legal property. For some analysts, the inequality of race and age and the fact that Jefferson owned Hemings are decisive proof that it was a highly coercive relationship. For others, who argue that men and women of every race had legally unequal marriages at that time, the fact that Hemings signed legal documents for Jefferson, traveled with him, and chose to remain with him—even though they lived for a time in France, where she was legally a free woman and may have had offers of marriage from eligible Frenchmen—is proof that this relationship was somewhat mutual.

What kind of evidence do you think would show that this relationship was coercive and unequal? What kind of evidence would show that Hemings was her own woman? Does the fact that she was the half-sister of Jefferson's deceased wife say anything about the mixing of races among colonial American elites? For some commentators, "the bottom line" is that Jefferson never married Hemings and could not do so, by law. However, the existence of such key primary sources as laws allows a variety of interpretations. The mere fact that courts started to pass miscegenation laws (laws addressing marriage between people of different racial backgrounds) in the eighteenth century is a good sign that (a) there were such interracial marriages, (b) blacks and whites were increasingly being allocated different positions in society, and (c) inequality was becoming increasingly fixed. The historian may find clues in primary sources as complex as philosophic essays and autobiographies and as simple as shopping lists, photographs, and Hemings's signature on Jefferson household payments for animal feed.

SECONDARY SOURCES

Secondary sources are books and articles in scholarly journals that bring together collections of evidence in order to interpret and build arguments around what happened. They offer answers to research questions and provide stories that link together all the evidence into coherent and interesting narratives. Secondary sources provide background about a particular subject, include important references to primary sources through footnotes and bibliographies, and raise questions, topics, and debates that form the foundation for additional research. To carry the courtroom analogy a step further, it is the lawyer's job, like the historian's, to take the evidence (primary sources) and build a case (secondary source). It is impossible to build a case, however, unless you have some idea of what the other lawyers are saying, what their evidence is, and how they plan to structure their case.

This is why courts have a "discovery" process that requires lawyers to share their evidence with opposing counsel before trial. And it is why history teachers assign students to read secondary sources before giving them the difficult task of going through birth records or ship manifests looking for fresh evidence, trying to rearrange the old evidence, or combining the two to create a new understanding of what happened. The exciting part of history is coming up with your own questions about the past and finding answers that create knowledge and spark new ways of understanding the past, the present, and even the future.

APPROACHING SOURCES CRITICALLY

In any courtroom trial, opposing lawyers try many ways to poke holes in each other's argument, but at the end of the day, the jury must decide what evidence is most relevant, whose testimony is most reliable, and which argument is most convincing. The same standard applies to historical sources. In investigating whether slavery was economically inefficient, do we trust the tax office's records or the plantation owner's financial records, his complaints to his congressman about how much tax he was paying, or his boastful letters to his sister about cheating on his taxes? Is there a good reason why some or all of these sources may be lying, stretching the truth, or simply misleading? Who is a more reliable witness to slavery, the slave or the slaveholder; the Northern abolitionist or the Southern politician; the poor white farmer who hates the slaveholders or the English gentleman visiting his Georgia cousins? Every person has a unique point of view, set of beliefs, and reason for giving testimony; and we must critically analyze and evaluate everything—and assume nothing.

These factors constitute the bias of the source. Because all sources are biased, it is important to develop a set of questions for interrogating documentary sources. Some useful questions to ask are:

- What is the historical context for the document? When was it produced, and how does it relate to important events of the period? (Note: The headnotes for the sources included in this book provide you with background information.)
- Who is the author? What can you tell about that person's background, social status, and so on?
- What can you infer about the purpose of the document? Who was its intended audience?
- What do the document's style and tone tell you about the author's purpose?
- What main points does the author seek to communicate or express?
- What does the document suggest about the author's point of view and biases? Consider whether the author misunderstood what he or she was relating or had reason to falsify the account.
- What can you infer about how typical for the period the views expressed in the document are?

Additional thought must be given to visual sources. When working with visual material, ask the following questions along with those above:

- How is the image framed or drawn? What does the image include? What might the creator of the work have excluded? What do the creator's decisions regarding the content tell you about the event, person, or place you are analyzing?
- What medium (drawing, painting, photograph, or other) did the creator employ? What constraints did the medium impose on the creator? For example, photographic technology in the nineteenth century was very rudimentary and involved large, bulky cameras with very slow shutter speeds. This technological context tells us something about why people often posed stiffly and without a smile for early photographs. Likewise, although there are numerous Civil War battlefront photographs, most were posed or

created after battles because the camera's shutter speeds did not allow for action photography.

- Do you know if the work was expensive or cheap to produce? Where was the work intended to be displayed—in a museum, a courthouse, a private home, a grocery store, or elsewhere? What might these considerations suggest about the event, person, or place you are analyzing?

Historians strive not to use the standards of the present to make judgments about the past. When working with both primary and secondary sources, the question of historical context must always be considered. For example, the decision to drop atomic bombs on Hiroshima and Nagasaki is often said to have been made without the same taboos, sociopolitical fears, and ecological concerns that are today tied to nuclear energy and nuclear weapons. It was largely assumed, during the entire process of developing atomic weapons, that they would be used. At the time, there was little serious discussion of not using this new war technology to hasten the end of the conflict with Japan, beyond a few last-minute letters and petitions from the very atomic scientists who had spent years and vast sums of money working to develop these new tools of war. This was the historical context in which the decision to drop the atomic bomb was made. To bring in more modern concerns, such as nuclear proliferation and environmental impact, when analyzing evidence from the period would be moving beyond this decision's historical context.

In this example, one should be wary, however, of reducing history to "the way people viewed things back then"—and, consequently, wary of absolving those who made the bomb, gave the orders, and carried out the mission. It is difficult enough to figure out today's social contexts and popular world views; the past is even more challenging to sort out. Many respected and influential people during the pre–World War II years had argued passionately against the dropping of bombs (then a relatively new technology, originating in the late nineteenth century) on civilians. They claimed that such a drastic measure was ethically unforgivable and not a particularly useful or effective practice; they argued that bombing might in fact strengthen a civilian population's will to fight rather than soften up the people for conquest. These commentators might have had no true understanding of the potential devastation of atomic weapons, but in the context of the times in which they lived, they certainly would not have viewed the bombing of Hiroshima and Nagasaki as acceptable acts of warfare. Consider, too, that several international conventions attempted to eliminate the bombing of civilians from modern warfare, and thousands of journals, letters, autobiographies, movies, novels, and popular songs suggest that throughout the twentieth century, many politicians, generals, and bomber pilots were uncomfortable with this peculiarly abstract and violent form of warfare against civilians.

There are therefore no easy answers to the question, "How did people view things back then?" Like the present, the past contains a multitude of contested and contradictory norms, values, and perspectives held by a variety of people with different understandings of the context in which individuals and groups took action and made history. These are the most complicated aspects of historical inquiry and interpretation—taking evidence, finding the right context, and telling a story about the similarities and differences between past and present. Returning to the first question in this introduction, we cannot know whether blacks and whites were once equal in seventeenth-century Virginia unless we know something about the values, rules, and social expectations of that time.

What did it mean to be equal? If being a member of the Church of England was the key marker of belonging in seventeenth-century Virginia, it may be that African converts to Christianity had more rights than Irish, Jews, and Native Americans. Such a situation would suggest that a fully formed code of caste/color inequality had not yet developed, and we might look for clues later in colonial history.

Because all sources—both firsthand primary accounts and secondary works by historians—have unique points of view and reasons for presenting things as they do, it is essential to question and to critically analyze everything. Read all historical documents with skepticism; take into account the "fit" of their authors' perspectives into the context of the time, the voices of their contemporaries, and the way the authors might have imagined themselves being remembered historically. This last consideration, people's own sense of how they make history, has always been important. But it may have become even more so in the contemporary world that artist Andy Warhol characterized as providing everybody with "fifteen minutes of fame." Ultimately, the craft of history is as subjective as a trial verdict.

Whether inquiring into the historical past or probing the unfolding of a crime, we can never know for certain what actually happened. Whether dealing with historical sources or with criminal evidence, we can establish a fair trial, one with relevant evidence, good witnesses, sound procedures, and brilliant insights. This process will get us closer to the truth—but never fully beyond a shadow of a doubt. Fortunately, practitioners and students of history have the ability to reopen any "case" at any time and to work to overturn a "verdict" that does not sit right. It is just a matter of getting in there, studying or restudying the sources, and developing new interpretations that will be subject to future analysis and research—and so the process of doing history continues.

PART ONE

After the Civil War

New South and New West

Although slavery effectively ended in April 1865, the Union victory in the Civil War did not resolve questions about the roles that African American men and women would play in American society. White Southerners like Caleb Forshey refused to accept the realities of the Yankee victory and the legal change in the status of former slaves, while black Southerners like Felix Haywood rejoiced in their newfound freedom, even as they continued to face racism and prejudice on a regular basis.

The first attempts to secure rights for the former bond servants, which occurred during the postwar Reconstruction period, produced three new amendments to the Constitution but no lasting consensus about how to treat blacks in daily life. Despite federal laws mandating economic freedom for blacks, violent opposition from white Southerners blunted the radical edge of Reconstruction. In part, this resistance took legal forms, such as marshaling public opinion, applying economic power, and organizing politically. But a resort to terror came early and continued for generations. The Ku Klux Klan, arising soon after the war, was an extralegal group that intimidated, whipped, and killed African Americans and their white allies who dared speak out for freedom. Ida B. Wells, a black journalist from Mississippi, took on the Klan. In print and on the stump, Wells denounced lynching and demanded federal intervention on behalf of blacks. Her efforts and those of countless other protesters, however, failed to eliminate racial violence, as demonstrated by the rise of lynching as a public spectacle.

In the end, three institutions replaced slavery in the postwar South: segregation in social affairs, a whites-only Democratic Party in politics, and sharecropping and tenant farming in the economy. Southern farmers developed arrangements such as the Grimes family's sharecrop contract, which offered participants land and supplies in exchange for a large portion of their crops, while in the North parallel restrictions on free labor, such as the Swindell Brothers' contract, appeared.

At the same time that the former slaves' hopes for freedom were being dashed in the South, the West drew capital and immigrants from far and wide and stirred the American imagination. However, this renewed attention to the region and the opportunities it presented brought disastrous consequences for many Native Americans.

The completion of the first transcontinental railroad link in 1869, which accelerated newcomers' movement to the West, along with the collapse of the buffalo herds that fed and sheltered the Plains Indians, helped to decimate the remaining independent Native American peoples. The Battle of Little Bighorn (1876), remembered here in accounts by the Italian soldier-for-hire Charles DeRudio and by two Native Americans, She Walks with Her Shawl and One Bull, was the last Native American victory in centuries of sporadic warfare with settlers over ownership of land and natural resources. As Native Americans were shunted to reservations often far from their ancestral homes, their young people were placed in boarding schools for education in the ways of the settler society. The struggles of Zitkala-Sa, a Sioux from the Yankton reservation in South Dakota, to find her place in both the Sioux and the white worlds reveal the complexities behind the stereotypes.

POINTS OF VIEW
The Battle of Little Bighorn (1876)

1

SHE WALKS WITH HER SHAWL AND ONE BULL

Victory at Greasy Grass

Americans vividly remember the Plains Indians, whose last great victory came at Little Bighorn in 1876, as the "feather-streaming, buffalo-chasing, wild-riding, recklessly fighting Indian of the plains," as one historian describes their young male warriors. In most American imaginations, they are the archetype of the American Indian.

Jerome A. Greene, ed., *Lakota and Cheyenne: Indian Views of the Great Sioux War, 1876–1877* (Norman: University of Oklahoma Press, 1994), 42–46, 54–59.

The reality is far more complex, however. The Plains peoples' religion, elaborate warrior code, fierce grief for the dead, and stunning rituals and visions of other worlds were largely borrowed from the many Indian cultures these nomads had briefly conquered as they swept across the Plains in the eighteenth and nineteenth centuries on horses first brought to the Americas by the Spanish conquistadors. The rifle, acquired from French, English, and, later, American traders, was one of their most cherished cultural symbols, though, as noted in this account, the less expensive and easily crafted tomahawk was also employed in battle. And their beads were all from Europe. To describe the culture of nomadic Plains Indians like the Lakota Sioux, anthropologists use the term syncretic, *meaning that the culture represented an amalgam of all the peoples the Plains Indians had encountered. The Plains Indians were indigenous, surely, but in this syncretic quality, they were also quintessentially American.*

The horse and rifle brought wealth and military might. The Plains became a terrain of ritual hunting and warfare, and prosperity permitted extensive trade and the elaboration of Indian cultures. For about a century, competing powers hindered conquest of the Plains Indians. But over time, migrants to the West Coast, wasteful white buffalo hunters, ambitious miners, the railroads, rushes of settlers, and a determined U.S. Army all disrupted Indian life. A series of Indian wars, beginning during the Civil War, rapidly pushed all but a few Plains Indians onto reservations.

By 1876 the great Western saga appeared to be about over. That year, thousands of Sioux and Northern Cheyenne, still living off or escaping from the reservations, gathered briefly at the Little Bighorn River, which they called the Greasy Grass, to enjoy religious rituals and to hunt, in defiance of the U.S. Army. General George Armstrong Custer and his premier Indian fighters, the Seventh Cavalry, found them there and promptly attacked.

In this excerpt, we see the ensuing battle through the eyes of a Hunkpapa Lakota woman, She Walks with Her Shawl, and a Minneconjou Lakota man, One Bull, the adopted son of Sitting Bull. Keep in mind that both accounts are filtered through white interviewers.

QUESTIONS TO CONSIDER

1. What was the role of She Walks with Her Shawl in battle? How does this role fit with popular representations of Native American women during the late nineteenth century?
2. The account of She Walks with Her Shawl was given many years after the battle. What evidence do you find that she was arguing with historical representations?
3. On the basis of these accounts, how accurate is the popular characterization of the Battle of Little Bighorn as an Indian "massacre" of brave federal troops led by General Custer? Why does the "massacre" label persist today?

SHE WALKS WITH HER SHAWL (HUNKPAPA LAKOTA)

Account given to Walter S. Campbell in 1931

I was born seventy-seven winters ago, near Grand River, [in present] South Dakota. My father, Slohan, was the bravest man among our people. Fifty-five years ago we packed our tents and went with other Indians to Peji-slawakpa (Greasy Grass). We were then living on the Standing Rock Indian reservation [Great Sioux Reservation, Standing Rock Agency]. I belonged to Sitting Bull's band. They were great fighters. We called ourselves Hunkpapa. This means confederated bands. When I was still a young girl (about seventeen) I accompanied a Sioux war party which made war against the Crow Indians in Montana. My father went to war 70 times. He was wounded nearly a dozen times.

But I am going to tell you of the greatest battle. This was a fight against Pehin-hanska (General Custer). I was several miles from the Hunkpapa camp when I saw a cloud of dust rise beyond a ridge of bluffs in the east. The morning was hot and sultry. Several of us Indian girls were digging wild turnips. I was then 23 years old. We girls looked towards the camp and saw a warrior ride swiftly, shouting that the soldiers were only a few miles away and that the women and children including old men should run for the hills in an opposite direction.

I dropped the pointed ash stick which I had used in digging turnips and ran towards my tipi. I saw my father running towards the horses. When I got to my tent, mother told me that news was brought to her that my brother had been killed by the soldiers. My brother had gone early that morning in search for a horse that strayed from our herd. In a few moments we saw soldiers on horseback on a bluff just across the Greasy Grass (Little Big Horn) river. I knew that there would be a battle because I saw warriors getting their horses and tomahawks.

I heard Hawkman shout, Ho-ka-he! Ho-ka-he! (Charge.) The soldiers began firing into our camp. Then they ceased firing. I saw my father preparing to go to battle. I sang a death song for my brother who had been killed.

My heart was bad. Revenge! Revenge! For my brother's death. I thought of the death of my young brother, One Hawk. Brown Eagle, my brother's companion on that morning, had escaped and gave the alarm to the camp that the soldiers were coming. I ran to a nearby thicket and got my black horse. I painted my face with crimson and unbraided my black hair. I was mourning. I was a woman, but I was not afraid.

By this time the soldiers (Reno's men) were forming a battle line in the bottom about a half mile away. In another moment I heard a terrific volley of carbines. The bullets shattered the tipi poles. Women and children were running away from the gunfire. In the tumult I heard old men and women singing death songs for their warriors who were now ready to attack the soldiers. The chanting of death songs made me brave, although I was a woman. I saw a warrior adjusting his quiver and grasping his tomahawk. He started running towards his horse when he suddenly recoiled and dropped dead. He was killed near his tipi.

Warriors were given orders by Hawkman to mount their horses and follow the fringe of a forest and wait until commands were given to charge. The soldiers kept on firing. Some women were also killed. Horses and dogs too! The camp was in great commotion.

Father led my black horse up to me and I mounted. We galloped towards the soldiers. Other warriors joined in with us. When we were nearing the fringe of the woods an order was given by Hawkman to charge. Ho-ka-he! Ho-ka-he! Charge! Charge! The warriors were now near the soldiers. The troopers were all on foot. They shot straight, because I saw our leader killed as he rode with his warriors.

The charge was so stubborn that the soldiers ran to their horses and, mounting them, rode swiftly towards the river. The Greasy Grass river was very deep. Their horses had to swim to get across. Some of the warriors rode into the water and tomahawked the soldiers. In the charge the Indians rode among the troopers and with tomahawks unhorsed several of them. The soldiers were very excited. Some of them shot into the air. The Indians chased the soldiers across the river and up over a bluff.

Then the warriors returned to the bottom where the first battle took place. We heard a commotion far down the valley. The warriors rode in a column of fives. They sang a victory song. Someone said that another body of soldiers were attacking the lower end of the village. I heard afterwards that the soldiers were under the command of Long Hair (Custer). With my father and other youthful warriors I rode in that direction.

We crossed the Greasy Grass below a beaver dam (the water is not so deep there) and came upon many horses. One soldier was holding the reins of eight or ten horses. An Indian waved his blanket and scared all the horses. They got away from the men (troopers). On the ridge just north of us I saw blue-clad men running up a ravine, firing as they ran.

The dust created from the stampeding horses and powder smoke made everything dark and black. Flashes from carbines could be seen. The valley was dense with powder smoke. I never heard such whooping and shouting. "There was never a better day to die," shouted Red Horse. In the battle I heard cries from troopers, but could not understand what they were saying. I do not speak English.

Long Hair's troopers were trapped in an enclosure. There were Indians everywhere. The Cheyennes attacked the soldiers from the north and Crow King from the South. The Sioux Indians encircled the troopers. Not one got away! The Sioux used tomahawks. It was not a massacre, but [a] hotly contested battle between two armed forces. Very few soldiers were mutilated, as oft has been said by the whites. Not a single soldier was burned at the stake. Sioux Indians do not torture their victims.

After the battle the Indians took all the equipment and horses belonging to the soldiers. The brave men who came to punish us that morning were defeated; but in the end, the Indians lost. We saw the body of Long Hair. Of course, we did not know who the soldiers were until an interpreter told us that the men came from Fort Lincoln, then [in] Dakota Territory. On the saddle blankets were the cross saber insignia and the letter seven.

The victorious warriors returned to the camp, as did the women and children who could see the battle from where they took refuge. Over sixty Indians were killed and they were also brought back to the camp for scaffold-burial. The Indians did not stage a victory dance that night. They were mourning for their own dead. . . .

ONE BULL (MINNECONJOU LAKOTA)

Account given to John P. Everett in the 1920s

I was in Sitting Bull's camp on [Little] Big Horn River, One Horn Band Hinko-woji [Minneconjou] Tepee. They were called that because they planted their gardens near the river. Itazipco (Without Bow [Sans Arc]) was another band. Ogalala [Oglala] was the Red Cloud band. Another band, Schiyeio means Cheyenne. They were a different tribe, not Lakota. They were friends of Lakota.

Pizi (Gall) had another band. All the different bands camped together. There were many other chiefs with their bands. Four Horn and Two Moon and many others. Whenever the chiefs held a council they went to Sitting Bull's camp because he was a good medicine man.

Lakota and Cheyennes had gone to this camp to look after their buffalo and so young men and women could get acquainted. White men had driven our buffalo away from Lakota land. So we went where buffalo were to take care of them and keep white men away.

I was a strong young man 22 years old. On the day of the fight I was sitting in my tepee combing my hair. I don't know what time it was. About this time maybe. (Two P.M.) Lakota had no watches in those days. I had just been out and picketed my horses and was back in my tepee. I saw a man named Fat Bear come running into camp and he said soldiers were coming on the other side of the river and had killed a boy named Deeds who went out to picket a horse. Then I came out of my tepee and saw soldiers running their horses toward our camp on same side of the river. We could hear lots of shooting. I went to tepee of my uncle, Sitting Bull, and said I was going to go take part in the battle. He said, "Go ahead, they have already fired."

I had a rifle and plenty of shells, but I took that off and gave it to Sitting Bull and he gave me a shield. Then I took the shield and my tomahawk and got on my horse and rode up to where the soldiers were attacking us. They were firing pretty heavy. They were all down near the river in the timber. Lakota were riding around fast and shooting at them. I rode up to some Lakota and said, "Let's all charge at once." I raised my tomahawk and said, "Wakontanka[1] help me so I do not sin but fight my battle." I started to charge. There were five Lakota riding behind me. We charged for some soldiers that were still fighting and they ran to where their horses were in the timber. Then the soldiers all started for the river. I turned my horse and started that way too

---

1. **Wakontanka:** Sioux name for the Great Spirit.

and there was a man named Mato Washte (Pretty Bear) right behind me and he and his horse were shot down. I followed the soldiers. They were running for the river. I killed two with my tomahawk. Then the soldiers got across the river. I came back to where Pretty Bear was and got him up on my horse. He was wounded and covered with blood. I started my horse toward the river where the soldiers were trying to get across.

Then I let Pretty Bear get off my horse and I went across the river after the soldiers. I killed one more of them with my tomahawk.

Then I saw four soldiers ahead of me running up the hill. I was just about to charge them when someone rode along beside me and said, "You better not go any farther. You are wounded." That was Sitting Bull. I was not wounded but I was all covered with blood that got on me when I had Pretty Bear on my horse. So I did what Sitting Bull told me. Then Sitting Bull rode back but I went on. Another Lakota went after these four soldiers. He had a rifle and shot one of them off his horse. One of the soldiers kept shooting back but without hitting us. The man that was with me was a Lakota but I did not know who he was. Now the soldiers were getting together up on the hill and we could see the other soldiers coming with the pack mules a long way off.

Then I went back across the river and rode down it a way, then I rode with the man who was shooting at the four soldiers and we crossed the river again just east of Sitting Bull's camp. We saw a bunch of horsemen up on a hill to the north and they were Lakotas. We rode up to them and I told them I had killed a lot of soldiers and showed them my tomahawk. Then I said I was going up and help kill Custer's soldiers, but Sitting Bull told me not to go so I didn't go but we rode up where we could see the Lakotas and Cheyennes killing Custer's men. They had been shooting heavy but the Indians charged them straight from the west and then some rode around them shooting and the Indians were knocking them off their horses and killing them with toma- hawks and clubs. THEY WERE ALL KILLED. There were a lot of Sioux killed. The others were picking them up on their horses and taking them back to camp.

Then we had a war dance all night and in the morning we heard that the soldiers with the pack mules were up on the hill and the Sioux started up after them. I went with Sitting Bull and volunteered to go help kill these soldiers but Sitting Bull said no. So we watched the fight from a hill. I didn't have my rifle with me then, just my tomahawk. The Sioux surrounded them and they fought that way all day. The soldiers had ditches dug all around the hill. Then along towards sundown the Sioux broke camp and went [south] to the mountains.

The Sioux did not take any prisoners that I know of. I didn't see any. I don't know how many Indians there were, but it was a very big band. Many bands together. The Indians had rifles with little short cartridges. I didn't use mine.

After the fight we all stayed in the Big Horn Mountains about ten days. After that they broke camp and went north following along the Tongue River. Then we went to the Little Missouri, and we found a place where there must have been some soldiers for we found a lot of sacks of yellow corn piled up. Then some of the bands went one way and some went another. One little band went to Slim Buttes and they were all killed by soldiers.

I was with Sitting Bull all the time we were in camp on the [Little] Big Horn and saw him during the battle. He was telling his men what to do. The first I knew of any soldiers was when they killed the boy who went to picket his horse across the river from Sitting Bull's camp. Before we broke camp that night we saw the walking soldiers coming from down the river but my uncle said, "We won't fight them. We have killed enough. We will go. . . ."

2

CHARLES DeRUDIO

Witness to Custer's Last Stand

The Battle of Little Bighorn was not the U.S. Army's biggest defeat at the hands of Native Americans, but it was the most famous. On June 25, 1876, the Seventh U.S. Cavalry rode into battle in Eastern Montana Territory, led by Civil War general George Armstrong Custer. When the smoke had cleared the next day, 268 members of the U.S. Army lay dead, including Custer and his entire battalion. Though it is known historically as Custer's Last Stand, Little Bighorn (or Greasy Grass, as the Plains Indians called it) was in many ways the last stand for Native Americans on the Great Plains. It would be the last time Native Americans posed a significant threat to the U.S. military.

Historians have long argued about the legacy of Little Bighorn. There are thousands of works debating what happened on that summer day in Montana, what went wrong, whether it was Custer's fault, and why the battle ended so disastrously for the U.S. military. Nearly every person connected to Little Bighorn published an account, including Custer's widow. The narrative that follows was written and sent to the New York Herald *by Charles DeRudio, who witnessed the activities of Lakota women also described by She Walks with Her Shawl.*

Born in northern Italy in 1832, Count Carlo Camillo di Rudio, or Charles DeRudio as he called himself in the United States, was one of the many foreign-born soldiers who fought under Custer. He began his strange journey to Little Bighorn as an antimonarchist who fought for a unified and free Italy (then under the control of Austria). After the antimonarchists were defeated, DeRudio went into exile in London, where he became involved in a failed plot to kill Emperor Napoleon III at the opera in Paris. Sentenced to life imprisonment at the French penal colony on Devil's Island, DeRudio

The Custer Myth: A Source Book of Custerania, written and compiled by Colonel W. A. Graham (Harrisburg, PA: Stackpole, 1953), 76–78.

escaped and found his way to New York City on the eve of the Civil War. There he joined the army and, owing to his swarthy complexion, became an officer in an all-black regiment. DeRudio continued in the army after the war and was assigned as a lieutenant in the Seventh Cavalry, under Custer. Perhaps because of the Italian's radical politics, Custer disliked DeRudio, who at forty-four was the oldest officer under his command. Just before the attack, Custer moved DeRudio to another company—ultimately saving DeRudio's life and enabling him to write his account of the Battle of Little Bighorn.

QUESTIONS TO CONSIDER

1. In what ways might the fact that DeRudio was a foreigner, a radical, and an enemy of General Custer have influenced his account of the battle?
2. What might have motivated Lakota women to act in the way that DeRudio describes?
3. In what ways does DeRudio's account contribute to determining what went wrong for the U.S. Army at Little Bighorn?

Camp on N. side Yellowstone, July 5, '76

I had a narrow escape at the battle of the Little Bighorn on the 25 & 26 of June and I will endeavor to give you my experience of Indian fighting. At about 10 A.M. on the 25th June, Gen. Custer's scouts returned and reported that they had discovered an Indian village about 15 miles distant, on the Little Bighorn, and that from what they had seen, they supposed the Indians to be retreating before our advance. We continued our march two or three miles farther when a halt was ordered and Gen. Custer began preparations for attacking the enemy. He detailed Co's. H, D & K, under the command of Col. F. W. Benteen to take the left of our route, with orders, so I hear, to sweep everything in his way: Co's. M, A, & G were put under the command of Col. Reno; and being temporarily attached to Co. A, I found myself with this division. Gen. Custer took Co's. E, I, F, L & C, and occupied the right of the line of attack. The remaining Company, B, was left to guard the packtrain. After marching two or three miles, our command, the center, was ordered to trot and hold the gait until we reached the river, six or seven miles distant. Having reached the river, we forded, and on reaching the plain beyond the opposite bank, we were ordered into line of battle.

Everything being as was ordered, we started on a gallop and for two miles pursued on the verge of an immense and blinding cloud of dust raised by the madly flying savages ahead of us. The dust cloud was so dense that we could distinguish nothing, so Col. Reno halted the battalion and after dismounting, formed a skirmish line—the right flank resting on the edge of a dry thickly wooded creek. While the horses were being led to shelter in the wood, the Indians opened a galling fire on us which was immediately responded to, the skirmish continuing for about one-half hour. It was now discovered that on the other side of the creek, in a park-like clearing, there were a few lodges, and the whole line crossed the creek to find the lodges deserted, and be received by about two hundred yelping, yelling redskins. The fire from the numerically superior force necessitated a retreat which was almost impossible, as we were now surrounded by warriors. When we entered the engagement we were only 100 strong and the fire of the enemy had made havoc in our little band. When we were half way over the creek, I, being in the rear, noticed a guidon[1] planted on the side we had left and returned to take it. When coming through the wood, the guidon entangled itself in the branches and slipped out of my hand. I dismounted to pick it up and led my horse to the south bank of the creek. As I was about to mount, my horse was struck with a bullet, and becoming frightened, he ran into the Indians, leaving me dismounted in the company of about 300 Sioux not more than 50 yards distant. They poured a whistling volley at me, but I was not wounded, and managed to escape to the thicket near by, where I would have an opportunity of defending myself and selling my life at a good high figure. In the thicket I found Mr. Girard [Fred Gerard], the interpreter; a half-breed Indian; and Private O'Neill [Private Thomas F. O'Neill], of Co. "G," 7th Cav. The first two of the quartet had their horses, while O'Neill like myself, was dismounted. I told the owners of the horses that the presence of the animals would betray us, suggesting at the same time that they be stampeded. They declined to act on the suggestion and I left them and crawled through the thick underwood into the deep dry bottom of the creek, where I could not easily be discovered, and from whence I hoped to be able under cover of darkness to steal out and rejoin the command. I had not been in this hiding place more than 10 minutes when I heard several pistol shots fired in my immediate vicinity, and shortly thereafter came the silvery, but to me diabolical voices of several squaws. I raised my head with great caution to see what the women were at and to discover their exact location. I found the women at the revolting work of scalping a soldier who was perhaps not yet dead. Two of the ladies were cutting away, while two others performed a sort of war dance around the body and its mutilators. I will not attempt to describe to you my feelings at witnessing the disgusting performance. Finally the squaws went away, probably to hunt for more victims and I employed the time thinking of my perilous position.

While thus engaged, I heard a crackling noise near me, which upon investigation I found proceeded from burning wood, the Indians having ignited a fire. The wood being very dry, the fire made rapid headway, and I was forced from my hiding place. I crawled out of the creek bottom the same way I had approached, and as I was about to ascend the bank, I heard a voice calling "Lieutenant, Lieutenant." I could see no one, but the call was repeated, and advancing a few yards in the direction from which it proceeded, I found all three of the party I had left a short time before, hidden in the bottom of the creek. Mr. Girard told me he had left the horses tied together, where

---

1. **guidon:** A military flag or battle standard.

I had seen them, and followed down after me. I found that the party, like myself, was afraid of the progress of the fire; but fortunately for us, the wind subsided, and a little rain fell which, thank God, was sufficient to arrest the flames. . . . Finally the time came when under the protection of night (it was very cloudy) we were able to come out of our hiding places and take the direction of the ford, which was two miles to the south, through an open plain. Mr. Girard and the scout mounted their horses and the soldier and myself took hold, each one, of a horse's tail, and followed them. . . . During our transit through the open plain we passed many Indians returning to their village and could hear but not see them as the night was very dark. We reached the wood near what we took to be the ford we had passed in the morning, but we were mistaken and had to hunt for the crossing. Once we forded the stream but found it was at a bend and that we would have to ford it again. When we recrossed the river, we ran full into a band of eight savages. The two mounted men ran for their lives, the soldier and myself jumped into the bushes near us. I cocked my revolver and in a kneeling position was ready to fire at the savages if they should approach me. They evidently thought, from the precipitate retreat of the two mounted men, that all of us had decamped; and began to talk among themselves. In a few minutes to my surprise they continued their course, and soon after went out of hearing. I raised up from my position, approached the bank of the river and called to the soldier, who immediately answered. We then saw that all the fords were well guarded by the savages, and it would be very dangerous to attempt to cross any part of the river. The night passed and in the dim dawn of day we heard an immense tramping, as of a large cavalry command, and the splashing of the water convinced us that some troops were crossing the river. I imagined it was our command, as I could distinctly hear the sound of the horses' shoes striking the stones. I cautiously stepped to the edge of the bushes to look out (I was then no more than three yards from the bank of the river), and thought I recognized some gray horses mounted by men in military blouses, and some of them in white hats. They were, I thought, going out of the valley, and those that had already crossed the river were going up a very steep bluff, while others were crossing after them. I saw one man with a buckskin jacket, pants, top boots and white hat, and felt quite sure I recognized him as Capt. Tom Custer[2] which convinced me that the cavalrymen were of our command.

With this conviction I stepped boldly out on the bank and called to Capt. Custer, "Tom, don't leave us here." The distance was only a few yards and my call was answered by an infernal yell and a discharge of 300 or 400 shots. I then discovered my mistake and found the savages were clad in clothes and mounted on horses which they had captured from our men. Myself and the soldier jumped into the bushes (the bullets mowing down the branches at every volley), and crawled off to get out of range of the fire.

2. **Capt. Tom Custer:** Tom Custer was the brother of General George Custer and a two-time Medal of Honor winner.

In doing so we moved the top branches of the undergrowth, and the Indians on the top of the bluff fired where they saw the commotion and thus covered us with their rifles. We now decided to cross a clearing of about twenty yards and gain another wood; but before doing this, I took the precaution to look out. The prospect was terribly discouraging for on our immediate right, not more than fifty yards distant, I saw four or five Indians galloping toward us. . . . [But they] had not seen us and when the foremost man was just abreast of me and about ten yards distant, I fired. They came in Indian file, and at my fire they turned a right-about and were making off when Pvt. O'Neill fired his carbine at the second savage, who at that moment was reining his pony to turn him back. The private's eye was true, and his carbine trusty, for Mr. Indian dropped his rein, threw up his paws and laid down on the grass to sleep his long sleep. The gentleman I greeted rode a short distance and then did likewise. The rest of the party rode on, turned the corner of the wood and disappeared. During all this time the fire from the bluffs continued, but after we had fired our shots, it ceased, and we retired to the thicket. From our position we could see the Indians on the bluffs, their horses picketed under cover of the hill, and a line of sharpshooters, all lying flat on their stomachs. We could hear the battle going on above us on the hills, the continued rattle of the musketry, the cheering of our command, and the shouting of the savages. Our hopes revived when we heard the familiar cheer of our comrades, but despondency followed fast for we discovered that our wood was on fire and we had to shift our position. We crawled almost to the edge of the wood, when we discovered that the fiends had fired both sides. We moved around until we found a thick cluster of what they call bulberry trees, under which we crept. The grass on the edge of this place was very green, as it had been raining a little while before, and there was no wind. When the fire approached our hiding place it ran very slowly so that I was enabled to smother it with my gauntlet gloves. The fire consumed all the underwood around us and was almost expended by this time. There we were in a little oasis, surrounded by fire, but comparatively safe from the elements, and with the advantage of seeing almost everything around us without being seen. We could see savages going backward and forward, and one standing on picket not more than 70 or 80 yards from us, evidently put there to watch the progress of the fire. At about 4 o'clock P.M. this picket fired 4 pistol shots in the air at regular intervals from each other and which I interpreted as a signal of some kind. Soon after this fire we heard the powerful voice of a savage crying out, making the same sound four times, and after these two signals, we saw 200 or more savages leave the bluffs and ford the river, evidently leaving the ground. About one hour after, the same double signals were again repeated, and many mounted Indians left at a gallop. Soon the remainder of those left on the bluffs also retired.

Hope now revived, the musketry rattle ceased and only now and then we could hear a far off shot. By 6 o'clock everything around us was apparently quiet and no evidence or signs of any Indians were near us. We supposed the regiment had left the field, and all that remained for us to do was to wait for the night and then pass the river and take the route for the Yellowstone River, and there construct a raft and descend to the mouth of the Powder River, our supply camp. Of course during the 36 hours that we were in suspense, we had neither water nor food. At 8 P.M. we dropped ourselves into the river, the water reaching our waists, crossed it twice and then carefully crawled up the bluffs, took our direction and slowly and cautiously proceeded southward.

After marching two miles, I thought I would go up on a very high hill to look around and see if I could discover any sign of our command; and on looking around I saw a fire on my left and in the direction where we supposed the command was fighting during the day, probably two miles from us. Of course we made two conjectures on this fire: it might be an Indian fire and it might be from our command. The only way to ascertain was to approach it cautiously and trust to chance. Accordingly we descended the hill, and took the direction of the fire. Climbing another and another hill, we listened a while and then proceeded on for a mile or more, when on the top of a hill we again stopped and listened. We could hear voices, but not distinctly enough to tell whether they were savages or our command.

We proceeded a little farther and heard the bray of a mule, and soon after, the distinct voice of a sentry challenging with the familiar words "Halt; Who goes there?" The challenge was not directed to us, as we were too far off to be seen by the picket, and it was too dark; but this gave us courage to continue our course and approach, though carefully, lest we should run into some Indians again. We were about 200 yards from the fire and I cried out: "Picket, don't fire; it is Lt. DeRudio and Pvt. O'Neill," and started to run. We received an answer in a loud cheer from all the members of the picket and Lt. Varnum. This officer, one of our bravest and most efficient, came at once to me and was very happy to see me again, after having counted me among the dead.

My first question was about the condition of the regiment. I was in hopes that we were the only sufferers, but I was not long allowed to remain in doubt. Lt. Varnum said he knew nothing of the five companies under Custer and that our command had sustained a loss in Lts. McIntosh and Hodgson. It was about 2 A.M. when I got into camp, and I soon after tried to go to sleep; but though I had not slept for two nights, I could not close my eyes. I talked with Lt. Varnum about the battle and narrated to him adventures and narrow escapes I had had. Morning soon came and I went to see the officers, and told them that the Indians had left.

At 8 o'clock we saw cavalry approaching, first a few scouts and then a dense column and soon learned it was Gen. Brisbin's command coming up to our relief. Presently a long line of infantry appeared on the plain and Gen. Gibbon came up. Ah! who that was there will ever forget how our hearts thrilled at sight of those blue coats! And when Gens. Gibbon and Terry rode into our camp, men wept like children.

Yours truly,
CHARLES C. DeRUDIO

FOR CRITICAL THINKING

1. The U.S. Army lost many battles to Native Americans. Why did the Battle of Little Bighorn catch people's imagination?
2. Both Native American documents were published in the twentieth century, many decades after Little Bighorn. Why might Native Americans have wanted to tell a different story half a century later? What evidence do you find in the passages that suggests a desire to correct or change the record?

3

FELIX HAYWOOD ET AL.

African Americans during Reconstruction

After the Civil War, freedmen struggled to define their freedom. Some left the planta-tions to which they had been bound and found family members from whom they had been separated by slavery and war. Many—perhaps most—saw freedom in the owner-ship of land, a dream encouraged by a field order issued by General William Tecumseh Sherman in January 1865 that assigned some vacant lands to former slaves. As a black soldier told his white officer, "Every colored man will be a slave and feel himself a slave until he could raise his own bale of cotton and put his own mark upon it and say, 'Dis is mine!'"

Yet soon after the first jubilee of freedom, the Andrew Johnson administration, fall-ing under the influence of former Confederates, revoked Sherman's order assigning land to former slaves. The administration stood by as white Southerners began to force the freedmen back into old patterns—assigning them work under coercive labor contracts and allowing states to govern their daily activities by "black codes" that denied them their civil rights. When these policies provoked a political reaction in the North, Repub-licans in Congress took control of Southern policy through a series of Reconstruction acts. While restoring civil rights and providing military protection, these laws failed to provide land to the freedmen.

The Thirteenth (1865), Fourteenth (1868), and Fifteenth Amendments (1870) to the U.S. Constitution came into being in the aftermath of the war. Although the so-called civil rights amendments decreed equality between the races, equal status did not become a reality in African Americans' daily lives in either the North or the South. For about a

---

"African Americans React to Reconstruction," in B. A. Botkin, ed., *Lay My Burden Down: A Folk History of Slavery* (Chicago: University of Chicago Press, 1945), 65–70, 223–24, 241–42, 246–47.

decade, the federal government made vigorous efforts to help freedmen gain education, legal and medical services, reasonable employment contracts, and a measure of political power. But those efforts were abandoned once the Northern public, tired of disorder in the South and wary of government intervention, abandoned the former slaves to their old masters. African Americans were soon left to respond however they could to the social revolution brought about by emancipation, the war's impoverishment of the South, and the violence of groups like the Ku Klux Klan.

Historians have pieced together the story of the freedmen's actions from a multiplicity of sources. Interviews with former slaves collected in the 1930s, a sample of which you will read here, are an important source for comprehending the lives of those freed, and then abandoned, after the Civil War.

QUESTIONS TO CONSIDER

1. Judging from these accounts, what major problems did former slaves face after the war?
2. What did these former slaves expect of freedom?
3. Why did some freedmen continue to work for their former masters?

FELIX HAYWOOD

San Antonio, Texas. Born in Raleigh, North Carolina. Age at interview: 88.

The end of the war, it come just like that—like you snap your fingers. . . . How did we know it! Hallelujah broke out— . . .

Everybody went wild. We felt like heroes, and nobody had made us that way but ourselves. We was free. Just like that, we was free. It didn't seem to make the whites mad, either. They went right on giving us food just the same. Nobody took our homes away, but right off colored folks started on the move. They seemed to want to get closer to freedom, so they'd know what it was—like it was a place or a city. Me and my father stuck, stuck close as a lean tick to a sick kitten. The Gudlows started us out on a ranch. My father, he'd round up cattle—unbranded cattle—for the whites. They was cattle that they belonged to, all right; they had gone to find water 'long the San Antonio River and the Guadalupe. Then the whites gave me and my father some cattle for our own. My father had his own brand—7 B)—and we had a herd to start out with of seventy.

We knowed freedom was on us, but we didn't know what was to come with it. We thought we was going to get rich like the white folks. We thought we was going to be richer than the white folks, 'cause we was stronger and knowed how to work, and the whites didn't, and they didn't have us to work for them any more. But it didn't turn out that way. We soon found out that freedom could make folks proud, but it didn't make 'em rich.

Did you ever stop to think that thinking don't do any good when you do it too late? Well, that's how it was with us. If every mother's son of a black had thrown 'way his hoe and took up a gun to fight for his own freedom along with the Yankees, the war'd been over before it began. But we didn't do it. We couldn't help stick to our masters. We couldn't no more shoot 'em than we could fly. My father and me used to talk 'bout it. We decided we was too soft and freedom wasn't going to be much to our good even if we had a education.

WARREN MCKINNEY

Hazen, Arkansas. Born in South Carolina. Age at interview: 85.

I was born in Edgefield County, South Carolina. I am eighty-five years old. I was born a slave of George Strauter. I remembers hearing them say, "Thank God, I's free as a jay bird." My ma was a slave in the field. I was eleven years old when freedom was declared. When I was little, Mr. Strauter whipped my ma. It hurt me bad as it did her. I hated him. She was crying. I chunked him with rocks. He run after me, but he didn't catch me. There was twenty-five or thirty hands that worked in the field. They raised wheat, corn, oats, barley, and cotton. All the children that couldn't work stayed at one house. Aunt Mat kept the babies and small children that couldn't go to the field. He had a gin and a shop. The shop was at the fork of the roads. When the war come on, my papa went to built forts. He quit Ma and took another woman. When the war close, Ma took her four children, bundled 'em up and went to Augusta. The government give out rations there. My ma washed and ironed. People died in piles. I don't know till yet what was the matter. They said it was the change of living. I seen five or six wooden, painted coffins piled up on wagons pass by our house. Loads passed every day like you see cotton pass here. Some said it was cholera and some . . . consumption [tuberculosis]. Lots of the colored people nearly starved. Not much to get to do and not much houseroom. Several families had to live in one house. Lots of the colored folks went up North and froze to death. They couldn't stand the cold. They wrote back about them dying. No, they never sent them back. I heard some sent for money to come back. I heard plenty 'bout the Ku Klux. They scared the folks to death. People left Augusta in droves. About a thousand would all meet and walk going to hunt work and new homes. Some of them died. I had a sister and brother lost that way. I had another sister come to Louisiana that way. She wrote back.

I don't think the colored folks looked for a share of land. They never got nothing 'cause the white folks didn't have nothing but barren hills left. About all the mules was wore out hauling provisions in the army. Some folks say they ought to done more for the colored folks when they left, but they say they was broke. Freeing all the slaves left 'em broke.

That reconstruction was a mighty hard pull. Me and Ma couldn't live. A man paid our ways to Carlisle, Arkansas, and we come. We started working for Mr. Emenson. He had a big store, teams, and land. We liked it fine, and I been here fifty-six years now. There was so much wild game, living was not so hard. If a fellow could get a little bread and a place to stay, he was all right. After I come to this state, I voted some. I have farmed and worked at odd jobs. I farmed mostly. Ma went back to her old master. He persuaded her to come back home. Me and her went back and run a farm four or five years before she died. Then I come back here.

LEE GUIDON

South Carolina. Born in South Carolina. Age at interview: 89.

Yes, ma'am, I sure was in the Civil War. I plowed all day, and me and my sister helped take care of the baby at night. It would cry, and me bumping it [in a straight chair, rocking]. Time I git it to the bed where its mama was, it wake up and start crying all over again. I be so sleepy. It was a puny sort of baby. Its papa was off at war. His name was Jim Cowan, and his wife Miss Margaret Brown 'fore she married him. Miss Lucy Smith give me and my sister to them. Then she married Mr. Abe Moore. Jim Smith was Miss Lucy's boy. He lay out in the woods all time. He say no need in him gitting shot up and killed. He say let the slaves be free. We lived, seemed like, on 'bout the line of York and Union counties. He lay out in the woods over in York County. Mr. Jim say all the fighting 'bout was jealousy. They caught him several times, but every time he got away from 'em. After they come home Mr. Jim say they never win no war. They stole and starved out the South. . . .

After freedom a heap of people say they was going to name theirselves over. They named theirselves big names, then went roaming round like wild, hunting cities. They changed up so it was hard to tell who or where anybody was. Heap of 'em died, and you didn't know when you hear about it if he was your folks hardly. Some of the names was Abraham, and some called theirselves Lincum. Any big name 'cepting their master's name. It was the fashion. I heard 'em talking 'bout it one evening, and my pa say, "Fine folks raise us and we gonna hold to our own names." That settled it with all of us. . . .

I reckon I do know 'bout the Ku Kluck. I knowed a man named Alfred Owens. He seemed all right, but he was a Republican. He said he was not afraid. He run a tanyard and kept a heap of guns in a big room. They all loaded. He married a Southern woman. Her husband either died or was killed. She had a son living with them. The Ku Kluck was called Upper League. They get this boy to unload all the guns. Then the white men went there. The white man give up and said, "I ain't got no gun to defend myself with. The guns all unloaded, and I ain't got no powder and shot." But the Ku Kluck shot in the houses and shot him up like lacework. He sold fine harness, saddles, bridles — all sorts of leather things. The Ku Kluck sure run them outen their country. They say they not going to have them round, and they sure run them out, back where they came from. . . .

For them what stayed on like they were, Reconstruction times 'bout like times before that 'cepting the Yankee stole out and tore up a scandalous heap. They tell the black folks to do something, and then come white folks you live with and say Ku Kluck whup you. They say leave, and white folks say better not listen to them old yankees. They'll git you too far off to come back, and you freeze. They done give you all the use they got for you. . . .

TOBY JONES

Madisonville, Texas. Born in South Carolina. Age at interview: 87.

I worked for Massa 'bout four years after freedom, 'cause he forced me to, said he couldn't 'ford to let me go. His place was near ruint, the fences burnt, and the house would have been, but it was rock. There was a battle fought near his place, and I taken Missy to a hideout in the mountains to where her father was, 'cause there was bullets flying everywhere. When the war was over, Massa come home and says, "You son of a gun, you's supposed to be free, but you ain't, 'cause I ain't gwine give you freedom." So I goes on working for him till I gits the chance to steal a hoss from him. The woman I wanted to marry, Govie, she 'cides to come to Texas with me. Me and Govie, we rides the hoss 'most a hundred miles, then we turned him a-loose and give him a scare back to his house, and come on foot the rest the way to Texas.

All we had to eat was what we could beg, and sometimes we went three days without a bite to eat. Sometimes we'd pick a few berries. When we got cold we'd crawl in a brushpile and hug up close together to keep warm. Once in a while we'd come to a farmhouse, and the man let us sleep on cottonseed in his barn, but they was far and few between, 'cause they wasn't many houses in the country them days like now.

When we gits to Texas, we gits married, but all they was to our wedding am we just 'grees to live together as man and wife. I settled on some land, and we cut some trees and split them open and stood them on end with the tops together for our house. Then we deadened some trees, and the land was ready to farm. There was some wild cattle and hogs, and that's the way we got our start, caught some of them and tamed them.

I don't know as I 'spected nothing from freedom, but they turned us out like a bunch of stray dogs, no homes, no clothing, no nothing, not 'nough food to last us one meal. After we settles on that place, I never seed man or woman, 'cept Govie, for six years, 'cause it was a long ways to anywhere. All we had to farm with was sharp sticks. We'd stick holes and plant corn, and when it come up we'd punch up the dirt round it. We didn't plant cotton, 'cause we couldn't eat that. I made bows and arrows to kill wild game with, and we never went to a store for nothing. We made our clothes out of animal skins.

4

IDA B. WELLS

African American Protest

Like few Americans of her day, Ida B. Wells (1862–1931) not only spoke out against the lynching of blacks but also orchestrated a vigorous public campaign to end the lynchings. Born during the Civil War in Holly Springs, Mississippi, to slave parents, she attended Shaw University (now Rust College) in her hometown. As an adult, she relocated to Memphis, Tennessee, where she worked first as a schoolteacher and later as a journalist. In 1889 she became an editor at the Free Speech and Headlight, *an anti-segregationist newspaper. Wells focused her reporting on contemporary Southern politics and wrote movingly about the steady decline of African American liberties and the rise of violent white supremacy groups like the Ku Klux Klan. The fierce attacks against the lynching of black citizens that she first mounted from her editorial chair continued throughout her life.*

One of Wells's most famous writings is Southern Horrors: Lynch Law in All Its Phases, *published in 1892. In this pamphlet, excerpted here, Wells undercut the growing white rationalization for the lynching of black men—that they had raped white women. She argued that the real cause of the rise in extralegal racial violence was the growing economic power of African Americans. In the pamphlet, Wells also encouraged fellow blacks to respond aggressively. Gone were the days, she wrote, when an African American might simply ignore politics and hope that a studied indifference to the white-ruled Democratic Party would eventually end the escalating violence. Instead, she asserted, blacks must arm themselves and be willing to put their rifles and revolvers to use in self-defense.*

QUESTIONS TO CONSIDER

1. In Ida B. Wells's view, who was to blame for the rise in the number of lynchings in the late-nineteenth-century South?
2. What were the various solutions to the decline of black civil rights, according to Wells?
3. What was religion's role in Southern society in the late 1800s?
4. How would you describe the tone of Wells's writing? Was she hopeful for positive change for black citizens? Explain.

Ida B. Wells-Barnett, *Southern Horrors: Lynch Law in All Its Phases* (1892; Project Gutenberg, 2005), http://www.gutenberg.org/files/14975/14975.txt.

One by one the Southern States have legally(?) [*sic*] disfranchised the Afro-American, and since the repeal of the Civil Rights Bill nearly every Southern State has passed separate car laws[1] with a penalty against their infringement. The race regardless of advancement is penned into filthy, stifling partitions cut off from smoking cars. All this while, although the political cause has been removed, the butcheries of black men . . . have gone on; also the flaying alive of a man in Kentucky, the burning of one in Arkansas, the hanging of a fifteen-year-old girl in Louisiana, a woman in Jackson, Tenn., and one in Hollendale, Miss., until the dark and bloody record of the South shows 728 Afro-Americans lynched during the past eight years [from 1884 to 1892]. Not fifty of these were for political causes; the rest were for all manner of accusations from that of rape of white women, to the case of the boy Will Lewis who was hanged at Tullahoma, Tenn., last year for being drunk and "sassy" to white folks.

These statistics compiled by the *Chicago Tribune* were given the first of this year (1892). Since then, not less than one hundred and fifty have been known to have met violent death at the hands of cruel bloodthirsty mobs during the past nine months.

To palliate this record (which grows worse as the Afro-American becomes intelligent) and excuse some of the most heinous crimes that ever stained the history of a country, the South is shielding itself behind the plausible screen of defending the honor of its women. This, too, in the face of the fact that only one-third of the 728 victims to mobs have been charged with rape, to say nothing of those of that one-third who were innocent of the charge. A white correspondent of the *Baltimore Sun* declares that the Afro-American who was lynched in Chestertown, Md., in May for assault on a white girl was innocent; that the deed was done by a white man who had since disappeared. The girl herself maintained that her assailant was a white man. When that poor Afro-American was murdered, the whites excused their refusal of a trial on the ground that they wished to spare the white girl the mortification of having to testify in court.

This cry has had its effect. It has closed the heart, stifled the conscience, warped the judgment and hushed the voice of press and pulpit on the subject of lynch law throughout this "land of liberty." Men who stand high in the esteem of the public for Christian character, for moral and physical courage, for devotion to the principles of equal and exact justice to all, and for great sagacity, stand as cowards who fear to open their mouths before this great outrage. They do not see that by their tacit encouragement, their silent acquiescence, the black shadow of lawlessness in the form of lynch law is spreading its wings over the whole country.

Even to the better class of Afro-Americans the crime of rape is so revolting they have too often taken the white man's word and given lynch law neither the investigation nor condemnation it deserved. They forget that a concession of the right to lynch a man for a certain crime, not only concedes

---

1. **car laws:** Laws passed in the 1890s assigning whites and blacks separate railway cars.

the right to lynch any person for any crime, but (so frequently is the cry of rape now raised) it is in a fair way to stamp us a race of rapists and desperadoes. They have gone on hoping and believing that general education and financial strength would solve the difficulty, and are devoting their energies to the accumulation of both.

The mob spirit has grown with the increasing intelligence of the Afro-American. It has left the out-of-the-way places where ignorance prevails, has thrown off the mask and with this new cry stalks in broad daylight in large cities, the centers of civilization, and is encouraged by the "leading citizens" and the press. . . .

[The South's] white citizens are wedded to any method however revolting, any measure however extreme, for the subjugation of the young manhood of the race. They have cheated him out of his ballot, deprived him of civil rights or redress therefore in the civil courts, robbed him of the fruits of his labor, and are still murdering, burning and lynching him.

The result is a growing disregard of human life. Lynch law has spread its insidious influence till men in New York State, Pennsylvania and on the free Western plains feel they can take the law in their own hands with impunity, especially where an Afro-American is concerned. The South is brutalized to a degree not realized by its own inhabitants, and the very foundation of government, law and order, are imperiled.

Public sentiment has had a slight "reaction" though not sufficient to stop the crusade of lawlessness and lynching. The spirit of christianity of the great M[ethodist] E[piscopal] Church was aroused to the frequent and revolting crimes against a weak people, enough to pass strong condemnatory resolutions at its General Conference in Omaha last May. The spirit of justice of the Grand Old Party asserted itself sufficiently to secure a denunciation of the wrongs, and a feeble declaration of the belief in human rights in the Republican platform at Minneapolis, June 7. Some of the great dailies and weeklies have swung into line declaring that lynch law must go. The President of the United States issued a proclamation that it be not tolerated in the territories over which he has jurisdiction. Governor Northern and Chief Justice Bleckley of Georgia have proclaimed against it. The citizens of Chattanooga, Tenn., have set a worthy example in that they not only condemn lynch law, but her public men demanded a trial for Weems, the accused rapist, and guarded him while the trial was in progress. The trial only lasted ten minutes, and Weems chose to plead guilty and accept twenty-one years sentence, than invite the certain death which awaited him outside that cordon of police if he had told the truth and shown the letters he had from the white woman in the case.

The strong arm of the law must be brought to bear upon lynchers in severe punishment, but this cannot and will not be done unless a healthy public sentiment demands and sustains such action.

The men and women in the South who disapprove of lynching and remain silent on the perpetration of such outrages, are participant criminals, accomplices, accessories before and after the fact, equally guilty with the actual lawbreakers who would not persist if they did not know that neither the law nor militia would be employed against them. . . .

In the creation of this healthier public sentiment, the Afro-American can do for himself what no one else can do for him. The world looks on with wonder that we have conceded so much and remain law-abiding under such great outrage and provocation.

To Northern capital and Afro-American labor the South owes its rehabilitation. If labor is withdrawn capital will not remain. The Afro-American is thus the backbone of the South. A thorough knowledge and judicious exercise of this power in lynching localities could many times effect a bloodless revolution. The white man's dollar is his god, and to stop this will be to stop outrages in many localities.

The Afro-Americans of Memphis denounced the lynching of three of their best citizens, and urged and waited for the authorities to act in the matter and bring the lynchers to justice. No attempt was made to do so, and the black men left the city by thousands, bringing about great stagnation in every branch of business. Those who remained so injured the business of the street car company by staying off the cars, that the superintendent, manager and treasurer called personally on the editor of the *Free Speech*, asked them to urge our people to give them their patronage again. Other business men became alarmed over the situation and the *Free Speech* was run away that the colored people might be more easily controlled. A meeting of white citizens in June, three months after the lynching, passed resolutions for the first time, condemning it. But they did not punish the lynchers. Every one of them was known by name, because they had been selected to do the dirty work, by some of the very citizens who passed these resolutions. Memphis is fast losing her black population, who proclaim as they go that there is no protection for the life and property of any Afro-American citizen in Memphis who is not a slave.

The appeal to the white man's pocket has ever been more effectual than all the appeals ever made to his conscience. Nothing, absolutely nothing, is to be gained by a further sacrifice of manhood and self-respect. By the right exercise of his power as the industrial factor of the South, the Afro-American can demand and secure his rights, the punishment of lynchers, and a fair trial for accused rapists.

Of the many inhuman outrages of this present year, the only case where the proposed lynching did *not* occur, was where the men armed themselves in Jacksonville, Fla., and Paducah, Ky, and prevented it. The only times an Afro-American who was assaulted got away has been when he had a gun and used it in self-defense.

The lesson this teaches and which every Afro-American should ponder well, is that a Winchester rifle should have a place of honor in every black home, and it should be used for that protection which the law refuses to give. When the white man who is always the aggressor knows he runs as great [a] risk of biting the dust every time his Afro-American victim does, he will have greater respect for Afro-American life. The more the Afro-American yields and cringes and begs, the more he has to do so, the more he is insulted, outraged and lynched.

The assertion has been substantiated throughout these pages that the press contains unreliable and doctored reports of lynchings, and one of the most necessary things for the race to do is to get these facts before the public. The people must know before they can act, and there is no educator to compare with the press.

The Afro-American papers are the only ones which will print the truth, and they lack means to employ agents and detectives to get at the facts. The race must rally a mighty host to the support of their journals, and thus enable them to do much in the way of investigation.

Nothing is more definitely settled than he must act for himself. I have shown how he may employ the boycott, emigration and the press, and I feel that by a combination of all these agencies can be effectually stamped out lynch law, that last relic of barbarism and slavery. "The gods help those who help themselves."

5

Freedmen in the West

Reconstruction brought new opportunity to many former slaves, who built schools, farms, and community institutions and elected black senators and members of Congress. At various times during Reconstruction, blacks accounted for the majority of elected officials in South Carolina, Louisiana, and Mississippi. However, with little unclaimed land, the tiny Southern industrial economy, devastated by war and poor transportation networks, financiers were afraid to invest in a region where big questions of landownership, citizenship rights, and control of the military were still unresolved.

When President Rutherford B. Hayes removed the federal troops from the South in 1877, the balance permanently tilted back toward the plantation owners, who reclaimed title to their land and control over the government, often using violence and torture to deny freedmen their new rights. Driven by poverty and rumors of a restoration of slavery, ex-slaves known as "exodusters" migrated west to Kansas en masse. There they tried to set up utopian communities without masters or slaves.

Despite vigilante efforts by armed whites attempting to drive back the exodusters, more than fifty thousand made it to the Western states. Some prospered and stayed, but many arrived with few resources and little support from organized groups. Some of these refugees from slavery were forced farther west, and others returned to the South. The families shown in the first photograph are waiting for a ferry on their journey to Kansas.

*It is always tempting to identify African Americans with economic compulsion, po-
litical struggle, and racial tension, but blacks also were among the landless agricultural
workers known as cowboys, whose lifestyle provided much of the romance invested in
the old West. Young African Americans joined the world of rodeos, shooting, and wild
horseback competitions, and they took up the often dangerous and poorly paid work of
cattle herders. The second photograph features Nat Love, the most famous black cowboy,
who was known as Deadwood Dick for his shooting prowess. Born a slave, Love had
been freed by the Union Army at the age of fifteen and remade himself in the West as a
popular rodeo performer. In his later years, he became a Pullman porter and, like many
famous cowboys, wrote an autobiography.*

QUESTIONS TO CONSIDER

1. What do you think the photographer wanted to communicate in the
   photo of the Exodusters? What do you notice about the possessions
   of these migrants?
2. How do the photos of Nat Love and the Exodusters tell different stories about the role of African Americans in the peopling of the West?
3. How does the image of Nat Love correspond to your vision of a cowboy? How is it different?
4. Photos of "Deadwood Dick" were common in nineteenth-century
   America. Why do you think many Americans today would be surprised
   by the existence of African American cowboys?

Exodusters going west, late 1870s. *Library of Congress, Prints and Photographs
Division, LC-USZ62-26365.*

Nat Love, 1870s. *Granger, NYC—All rights reserved.*

6

CALEB G. FORSHEY AND
THE REVEREND JAMES SINCLAIR

White Southerners' Reactions to Reconstruction

Like their former slaves, white Southerners at the end of the Civil War exhibited a wide variety of attitudes. Granted generous surrender terms that protected them from charges of treason and allowed them to keep horses and mules "to put in a crop," returning

The Report of the Committees of the House of Representatives Made during the First Session, Thirty-Ninth Congress, 1865–1866, vol. 2 (Washington, DC: Government Printing Office, 1866), 129–32, 168–71.

Confederate soldiers at first were more resigned to the war's outcome than those who had stayed at home and had less direct experience of combat and loss. Although many in the South had initially been ready to accept peace on the conqueror's terms, Northern uncertainty as to what these terms should be made those Southerners waver and encouraged others who were already angry. The president called for one policy and Congress for another. Northerners elected a Republican Congress that demanded freedom, civil rights, and even the franchise for former slaves living in the South, and yet the same Northerners tolerated the denial of civil rights to African Americans living in the North. In the fall of 1865, three Republican states—Connecticut, Wisconsin, and Minnesota—voted down amendments to their constitutions that would have enfranchised blacks. This development fueled resistance to Republican demands among white Southerners.

Assembled to examine Southern representation in Congress, the Joint Committee of Fifteen was part of the Republican Congress's opposition to President Andrew Johnson's plan of Reconstruction. In 1866 the committee held hearings as part of its effort to develop the Fourteenth Amendment. Despite the president's veto, Congress had already enlarged the scope of the Freedmen's Bureau to care for displaced former slaves and to try by military commission those accused of depriving freedmen of their civil rights.

Of the two white Southerners whose interviews with the committee are included here, Caleb Forshey had supported secession, while James Sinclair, though a slaveholder, had opposed it. A Scottish-born minister who had moved to North Carolina in 1857, Sinclair expressed Unionist sentiments that led to the loss of his church and then to his arrest during the war. In 1865 he was working with the Freedmen's Bureau.

QUESTIONS TO CONSIDER

1. What did Caleb Forshey think of Union efforts to protect former slaves through military occupation and the Freedmen's Bureau?
2. What were Forshey's beliefs about African Americans?
3. What was the plight of former slaves and white Unionists, according to James Sinclair?

CALEB G. FORSHEY

Washington, D.C., March 28, 1866

Question: Where do you reside?
Answer: I reside in the State of Texas.
Question: How long have you been a resident of Texas?
Answer: I have resided in Texas and been a citizen of that State for nearly thirteen years.
Question: What opportunities have you had for ascertaining the temper and disposition of the people of Texas towards the government and authority of the United States?
Answer: For ten years I have been superintendent of the Texas Military Institute, as its founder and conductor. I have been in the confederate service

in various parts of the confederacy; but chiefly in the trans-Mississippi department, in Louisiana and Texas, as an officer of engineers. I have had occasion to see and know very extensively the condition of affairs in Texas, and also to a considerable extent in Louisiana. I think I am pretty well-informed, as well as anybody, perhaps, of the present state of affairs in Texas.

Question: What are the feelings and views of the people of Texas as to the late rebellion, and the future condition and circumstances of the State, and its relations to the federal government?

Answer: After our army had given up its arms and gone home, the surrender of all matters in controversy was complete, and as nearly universal, perhaps, as anything could be. Assuming the matters in controversy to have been the right to secede, and the right to hold slaves, I think they were given up tee-totally, to use a strong Americanism. When you speak of feeling, I should discriminate a little. The feeling was that of any party who had been cast in a suit he had staked all upon. They did not return from feeling, but from a sense of necessity, and from a judgment that it was the only and necessary thing to be done, to give up the contest. But when they gave it up, it was without reservation; with a view to look forward, and not back. That is my impression of the manner in which the thing was done. There was a public expectation that in some very limited time there would be a restoration to former relations. . . . It was the expectation of the people that, as soon as the State was organized as proposed by the President, they would be restored to their former relations, and things would go on as before.

Question: What is your opinion of a military force under the authority of the federal government to preserve order in Texas and to protect those who have been loyal, both white and black, from the aggressions of those who have been in the rebellion?

Answer: My judgment is well founded on that subject: that wherever such military force is and has been, it has excited the very feeling it was intended to prevent; that so far from being necessary it is very pernicious everywhere, and without exception. The local authorities and public sentiment are ample for protection. I think no occasion would occur, unless some individual case that our laws would not reach. We had an opportunity to test this after the surrender and before any authority was there. The military authorities, or the military officers, declared that we were without laws, and it was a long time before the governor appointed arrived there, and then it was sometime before we could effect anything in the way of organization. We were a people without law, order, or anything; and it was a time for violence if it would occur. I think it is a great credit to our civilization that, in that state of affairs, there was nowhere any instance of violence. I am proud of it, for I expected the contrary; I expected that our soldiers on coming home, many of them, would be dissolute, and that many of them would oppress the class of men you speak of; but it did not occur. But afterwards, wherever soldiers have been sent, there have been little troubles, none of them large; but personal collisions between soldiers and citizens.

Question: What is your opinion as to the necessity and advantages of the Freedmen's Bureau, or an agency of that kind, in Texas?

Answer: My opinion is that it is not needed; my opinion is stronger than that—that the effect of it is to irritate, if nothing else. While in New York City recently I had a conversation with some friends from Texas, from five distant points in the State. We met together and compared opinions; and the opinion of each was the same, that the negroes had generally gone to work since January; that except where the Freedmen's Bureau had interfered, or rather encouraged troubles, such as little complaints, especially between negro and negro, the negro's disposition was very good, and they had generally gone to work, a vast majority of them with their former masters. . . . The impression in Texas at present is that the negroes under the influence of the Freedmen's Bureau do worse than without it.

I want to state that I believe all our former owners of negroes are the friends of the negroes; and that the antagonism paraded in the papers of the north does not exist at all. I know the fact is the very converse of that; and good feeling always prevails between the masters and the slaves. But the negroes went off and left them in the lurch; my own family was an instance of it. But they came back after a time, saying they had been free enough and wanted a home.

Question: Do you think those who employ the negroes there are willing to make contracts with them, so that they shall have fair wages for their labor?

Answer: I think so; I think they are paid liberally, more than the white men in this country get; the average compensation to negroes there is greater than the average compensation of free laboring white men in this country. It seems to have regulated itself in a great measure by what each neighborhood was doing; the negroes saying, "I can get thus and so at such a place." Men have [been] hired from eight to fifteen dollars per month during the year, and women at about two dollars less a month; house-servants at a great deal more.

Question: Do the men who employ the negroes claim to exercise the right to enforce their contract by physical force?

Answer: Not at all; that is totally abandoned; not a single instance of it has occurred. I think they still chastise children, though. The negro parents often neglect that, and the children are still switched as we switch our own children. I know it is done in my own house; we have little house-servants that we switch just as I do our own little fellows.

Question: What is your opinion as to the respective advantages to the white and black races, of the present free system of labor and the institution of slavery?

Answer: I think freedom is very unfortunate for the negro; I think it is sad; his present helpless condition touches my heart more than anything else I ever contemplated, and I think that is the common sentiment of our slaveholders. I have seen it on the largest plantations, where the negro men had all left, and where only women and children remained, and the owners had to keep them and feed them. The beginning certainly presents a touching and sad spectacle. The poor negro is dying at a rate fearful to relate.

I have some ethnological theories that may perhaps warp my judgment; but my judgment is that the highest condition the black race has ever reached or can reach, is one where he is provided for by a master race. That is the result of a great deal of scientific investigation and observation of the negro character by me ever since I was a man. The labor question had become a most momentous one, and I was studying it. I undertook to investigate the condition of the negro from statistics under various circumstances, to treat it purely as a matter of statistics from the census tables of this country of ours. I found that the free blacks of the north decreased 8 per cent.; the free blacks of the south increased 7 or 8 per cent., while the slaves by their sides increased 34 per cent. I inferred from the doctrines of political economy that the race is in the best condition when it procreates the fastest; that, other things being equal, slavery is of vast advantage to the negro. I will mention one or two things in connexion with this as explanatory of that result. The negro will not take care of his offspring unless required to do it, as compared with the whites. The little children will die; they do die, and hence the necessity of very rigorous regulations on our plantations which we have adopted in our nursery system.

Another cause is that there is no continence among the negroes.[1] All the continence I have ever seen among the negroes has been enforced upon plantations, where it is generally assumed there is none. For the sake of procreation, if nothing else, we compel men to live with their wives. The discipline of the plantation was more rigorous, perhaps, in regard to men staying with their wives, than in regard to anything else; and I think the procreative results, as shown by the census tables, is due in a great measure to that discipline. . . .

Question: What is the prevailing inclination among the people of Texas in regard to giving the negroes civil or political rights and privileges?

Answer: I think they are all opposed to it. There are some men—I am not among them—who think that the basis of intelligence might be a good basis for the elective franchise. But a much larger class, perhaps nine-tenths of our people, believe that the distinctions between the races should not be broken down by any such community of interests in the management of the affairs of the State. I think there is a very common sentiment that the negro, even with education, has not a mind capable of appreciating the political institutions of the country to such an extent as would make him a good associate for the white man in the administration of the government. I think if the vote was taken on the question of admitting him to the right of suffrage there would be a very small vote in favor of it—scarcely respectable: that is my judgment.

---

1. **no continence among the negroes:** By this Forshey meant that they did not rein in their sexual impulses.

THE REVEREND JAMES SINCLAIR

Washington, D.C., January 29, 1866

Question: What is generally the state of feeling among the white people of North Carolina towards the government of the United States?

Answer: That is a difficult question to answer, but I will answer it as far as my own knowledge goes. In my opinion, there is generally among the white people not much love for the government. Though they are willing, and I believe determined, to acquiesce in what is inevitable, yet so far as love and affection for the government is concerned, I do not believe that they have any of it at all, outside of their personal respect and regard for President Johnson.

Question: How do they feel towards the mass of the northern people—that is, the people of what were known formerly as the free States?

Answer: They feel in this way: that they have been ruined by them. You can imagine the feelings of a person towards one whom he regards as having ruined him. They regard the northern people as having destroyed their property or taken it from them, and brought all the calamities of this war upon them.

Question: How do they feel in regard to what is called the right of secession?

Answer: They think that it was right . . . that there was no wrong in it. They are willing now to accept the decision of the question that has been made by the sword, but they are not by any means converted from their old opinion that they had a right to secede. It is true that there have always been Union men in our State, but not Union men without slavery, except perhaps among Quakers. Slavery was the central idea even of the Unionist. The only difference between them and the others upon that question was, that they desired to have that institution under the aegis of the Constitution, and protected by it. The secessionists wanted to get away from the north altogether. When the secessionists precipitated our State into rebellion, the Unionists and secessionists went together, because the great object with both was the preservation of slavery by the preservation of State sovereignty. There was another class of Unionists who did not care anything at all about slavery, but they were driven by the other whites into the rebellion for the purpose of preserving slavery. The poor whites are to-day very much opposed to conferring upon the negro the right of suffrage; as much so as the other classes of the whites. They believe it is the intention of government to give the negro rights at their expense. They cannot see it in any other light than that as the negro is elevated they must proportionately go down. While they are glad that slavery is done away with, they are bitterly opposed to conferring the right of suffrage on the negro as the most prominent secessionists; but it is for the reason I have stated, that they think rights conferred on the negro must necessarily be taken from them, particularly the ballot, which was the only bulwark guarding their superiority to the negro race.

Question: In your judgment, what proportion of the white people of North Carolina are really, and truly, and cordially attached to the government of the United States?

Answer: Very few, sir; very few. . . .

Question: Is the Freedmen's Bureau acceptable to the great mass of the white people in North Carolina?

Answer: No, sir; I do not think it is; I think that most of the whites wish the bureau to be taken away.

Question: Why do they wish that?

Answer: They think that they can manage the negro for themselves: that they understand him better than northern men do. They say, "Let us understand what you want us to do with [the] negro—what you desire of us; lay down your conditions for our readmission into the Union, and then we will know what we have to do, and if you will do that we will enact laws for the government of these negroes. They have lived among us, and they are all with us, and we can manage them better than you can." They think it is interfering with the rights of the State for a bureau, the agent and representative of the federal government, to [overrule] the State entirely, and interfere with the regulations and administration of justice before their courts.

Question: Is there generally a willingness on the part of the whites to allow the freedmen to enjoy the right of acquiring land and personal property?

Answer: I think they are very willing to let them do that, for this reason; to get rid of some portion of the taxes imposed upon their property by the government. For instance, a white man will agree to sell a negro some of his land on condition of his paying so much a year on it, promising to give him a deed of it when the whole payment is made, taking his note in the mean time. This relieves that much of the land from taxes to be paid by the white man. All I am afraid of is, that the negro is too eager to go into this thing; that he will ruin himself, get himself into debt to the white man, and be forever bound to him for the debt and never get the land. I have often warned them to be careful what they did about these things.

Question: There is no repugnance on the part of the whites to the negro owning land and personal property?

Answer: I think not.

Question: Have they any objection to the legal establishment of the domestic relations among the blacks, such as the relation of husband and wife, of parent and child, and the securing by law to the negro the rights of those relations?

Answer: That is a matter of ridicule with the whites. They do not believe the negroes will ever respect those relations more than the brutes. I suppose I have married more than two hundred couples of negroes since the war, but the whites laugh at the very idea of the thing. . . .

Question: What, in general, has been the treatment of the blacks by the whites since the close of hostilities?

Answer: It has not generally been of the kindest character, I must say that; I am compelled to say that.

Question: Are you aware of any instance of personal ill treatment towards the blacks by the whites?

Answer: Yes, sir.

Question: Give some instances that have occurred since the war.

Answer: [Sinclair describes the beating of a young woman across her buttocks in graphic detail.]

Question: What was the provocation, if any?

Answer: Something in regard to some work, which is generally the provocation.

Question: Was there no law in North Carolina at that time to punish such an outrage?

Answer: No, sir; only the regulations of the Freedmen's Bureau; we took cognizance of the case. In old times that was quite allowable; it is what was called "paddling."

Question: Did you deal with the master?

Answer: I immediately sent a letter to him to come to my office, but he did not come, and I have never seen him in regard to the matter since. I had no soldiers to enforce compliance, and I was obliged to let the matter drop.

Question: Have you any reason to suppose that such instances of cruelty are frequent in North Carolina at this time—instances of whipping and striking?

Answer: I think they are; it was only a few days before I left that a woman came there with her head all bandaged up, having been cut and bruised by her employer. They think nothing of striking them.

Question: And the negro has practically no redress?

Answer: Only what he can get from the Freedmen's Bureau.

Question: Can you say anything further in regard to the political condition of North Carolina—the feeling of the people towards the government of the United States?

Answer: I for one would not wish to be left there in the hands of those men; I could not live there just now. But perhaps my case is an isolated one from the position I was compelled to take in that State. I was persecuted, arrested, and they tried to get me into their service; they tried everything to accomplish their purpose, and of course I have rendered myself still more obnoxious by accepting an appointment under the Freedmen's Bureau. . . .

Question: Suppose the military pressure of the government of the United States should be withdrawn from North Carolina, would northern men and true Unionists be safe in that State?

Answer: A northern man going there would perhaps present nothing obnoxious to the people of the State. But men who were born there, who have been true to the Union, and who have fought against the rebellion, are worse off than northern men.

7

GRIMES FAMILY AND SWINDELL BROTHERS

Work under Sharecropper and Labor Contracts

The end of slavery and the impoverishment of the South in the aftermath of the Civil War seriously disrupted Southern agriculture. Five years after the war's end, Southern cotton production was still at only about half its level in the 1850s. The large plantations, no longer tended by gangs of slaves or hired freedmen, were broken up into smaller holdings, but the substantial capital required for profitable agriculture dictated that control of farming remained centralized in a limited elite of merchants and large landholders.

Various mechanisms arose to finance Southern agriculture. Tenants worked on leased land, and small landowners gave liens on their crops to get financing. But the most common method of financing agriculture was sharecropping. Agreements like the Grimes family's sharecrop contract determined the economic life of thousands of poor rural families in the South after the Civil War. Lacking capital for agriculture, families—both African American and white—were furnished seed, implements, and a line of credit for food and other necessities to sustain them through the growing season. Accounts were settled in the winter after the crops were in. Under these conditions, a small number of farmers managed to make money and eventually became landowners, but the larger part found themselves in ever deeper debt at the end of the year, with no choice but to contract again for the next year.

In another form of labor contract, employers such as the Swindell Brothers agreed to pay an immigrant's passage to America in exchange for that individual's promise to work for the employer for a fixed period of time. Under pressure from labor organizations, this type of contract, legalized during the Civil War, was banned in 1885.

QUESTIONS TO CONSIDER

1. What restrictions on the freedom of sharecroppers were built into the Grimes family's contract?
2. Which restrictions might have been the most significant in preventing sharecroppers from achieving independence? Why?
3. Why would labor organizations object to agreements like the Swindell contract?
4. What would motivate a worker to enter into such a contract?

Grimes Family Papers #3357, Southern Historical Collection, Wilson Library, University of North Carolina at Chapel Hill; Wayne Moquin, ed., *Makers of America*, vol. 4, *Seekers after Wealth* (Chicago: Encyclopaedia Britannica Educational, 1971).

GRIMES FAMILY PAPERS

To every one applying to rent land upon shares, the following conditions must be read, and *agreed to*.

To every 30 or 35 acres, I agree to furnish the team, plow, and farming implements, except cotton planters, and I *do not* agree to furnish a cart to every cropper. The croppers are to have half of the cotton, corn and fodder (and peas and pumpkins and potatoes if any are planted) if the following conditions are complied with, but—if not—they are to have only two fifths (2/5). Croppers are to have no part or interest in the cotton seed raised from the crop planted and worked by them. No vine crops of any description, that is, no watermelons, muskmelons, . . . squashes or anything of that kind, except peas and pumpkins, and potatoes, are to be planted in the cotton or corn. All must work under my direction. All plantation work to be done by the croppers. My part of the crop to be *housed* by them, and the fodder and oats to be hauled and put in the house. All the cotton must be topped about 1st August. If any cropper fails from any cause to save all the fodder from his crop, I am to have enough fodder to make it equal to one half of the whole if the whole amount of fodder had been saved.

For every mule or horse furnished by me there must be 1000 good sized rails . . . hauled, and the fence repaired as far as they will go, the fence to be torn down and put up from the bottom if I so direct. All croppers to haul rails and work on fence whenever I may order. Rails to be split when I may say. Each cropper to clean out every ditch in his crop, and where a ditch runs between two croppers, the cleaning out of that ditch is to be divided equally between them. Every ditch bank in the crop must be shrubbed down and cleaned off before the crop is planted and must be cut down every time the land is worked with his hoe and when the crop is "laid by," the ditch banks must be left clean of bushes, weeds, and seeds. The cleaning out of all ditches must be done by the first of October. The rails must be split and the fence repaired before corn is planted.

Each cropper must keep in good repair all bridges in his crop or over ditches that he has to clean out and when a bridge needs repairing that is outside of all their crops, then any one that I call on must repair it.

Fence jams to be done as ditch banks. If any cotton is planted on the land outside of the plantation fence, I am to have *three fourths* of all the cotton made in those patches, that is to say, no cotton must be planted by croppers in their home patches.

All croppers must clean out stables and fill them with straw, and haul straw in front of stables whenever I direct. All the cotton must be manured, and enough fertilizer must be brought to manure each crop highly, the croppers to pay for one half of all manure bought, the quantity to be purchased for each crop must be left to me.

No cropper to work off the plantation when there is any work to be done on the land he has rented, or when his work is needed by me or other croppers. Trees to be cut down on Orchard, House field & Evanson fences, leaving such as I may designate.

Road field to be planted from the *very edge of the ditch to the fence*, and all the land to be planted close up to the ditches and fences. *No stock of any kind* belonging to croppers to run in the plantation after crops are gathered.

If the fence should be blown down, or if trees should fall on the fence outside of the land planted by any of the croppers, any one or all that I may call upon must put it up and repair it. Every cropper must feed, or have fed, the team he works, Saturday nights, Sundays, and every morning before going to work, beginning to feed his team (morning, noon, and night *every day in the week*) on the day he rents and feeding it to and including the 31st day of December. If any cropper shall from any cause fail to repair his fence as far as 1000 rails will go, or shall fail to clean out any part of his ditches, or shall fail to leave his ditch banks, any part of them, well shrubbed and clean when his crop is laid by, or shall fail to clean out stables, fill them up and haul straw in front of them whenever he is told, he shall have only two-fifths (2/5) of the cotton, corn, fodder, peas and pumpkins made on the land he cultivates.

If any cropper shall fail to feed his team Saturday nights, all day Sunday and all the rest of the week, morning/noon, and night, for every time he so fails he must pay me five cents.

No corn nor cotton stalks must be burned, but must be cut down, cut up and plowed in. Nothing must be burned off the land except when it is *impossible* to plow it in.

Every cropper must be responsible for all gear and farming implements placed in his hands, and if not returned must be paid for unless it is worn out by use.

Croppers must sow & plow in oats and haul them to the crib, but *must have no part of them*. Nothing to be sold from their crops, nor fodder nor corn to be carried out of the fields until my rent is all paid, and all amounts they owe me and for which I am responsible are paid in full.

I am to gin & pack all the cotton and charge every cropper an eighteenth of his part, the cropper to furnish his part of the bagging, ties, & twine.

The sale of every cropper's part of the cotton to be made by me when and where I choose to sell, and after deducting all they owe me and all sums that I may be responsible for on their accounts, to pay them their half of the net proceeds. Work of every description, particularly the work on fences and ditches, to be done to my satisfaction, and must be done over until I am satisfied that it is done as it should be.

No wood to burn, nor light wood, nor poles, nor timber for boards, nor wood for any purpose whatever must be gotten above the house occupied by Henry Beasley—nor must any trees be cut down nor any wood used for any purpose, except for firewood, without my permission.

SWINDELL BROTHERS CONTRACT

Antwerp, Dec. 15, 1882

Agreement between the firm of Swindell Bros. of the first part, and John Schmidt, gatherer, and Carl Wagner, blower, of the second part.

The undersigned, of the second part, covenants and agrees with the party of the first part that they will for two consecutive years, beginning January 1, 1882, work and duly perform such duties as instructed by the party of the first part or his superintendents. The party of the first part covenants and agrees to pay the undersigned, who may duly perform their duties, the price generally paid by Baltimore manufacturers for the size of 16 by 24 inches, and all sheets shall be estimated at eight sheet of 36 by 54 inches for 100 square feet. The party of the first part covenants and agrees that the wages of each glassblower shall be an average of $80 per calendar month, on condition that he makes 180 boxes of 100 square feet per calendar month.

The gatherer shall receive 65 percent of the sum paid the blower for wages per calendar month for actual work performed during the fire. It is agreed that the party of the first part shall retain 10 percent of the wages of each and every workman until the expiration of this contract as a guarantee of the faithful performance of the provisions of this contract. The aforesaid 10 percent shall be forfeited by each and every workman who shall fail to comply with the provisions of this contract.

It is further agreed that the party of the first part shall advance the passage money for the parties of the second part.

It is further agreed that the party of the first part have the right to discharge any of the workmen for drunkenness or neglect of duty, or for disturbing the peace, or creating dissatisfaction among them, or for joining any association of American workmen.

The said Swindell Bros., their heirs, and assigns, shall be considered the parties of the first part, and they agree to pay each blower $12 per week and the gatherer $9.00 per week, on condition that each perform his work faithfully at every blowing. The parties of the first part agree to make monthly settlements for the parties of the second part, after the advances for the passage, etc., shall have been repaid. Provided you faithfully perform your work for the term of contract (two years), we will pay back the passage money from Europe to America.

Swindell Bros.
Yohonn Schmidt, Gatherer
Carl Wagener, Blower

8

ZITKALA-SA (GERTRUDE SIMMONS BONNIN)

School Days of an Indian Girl

From the mid-1880s to the 1930s, the thrust of American Indian policy was to as-similate Native Americans into the larger society. Boarding schools for Native American children became a common way to induct promising young Native Americans into white culture. Officials were particularly eager to educate girls, hoping through their influence to alter the domestic culture of the Indians.

In 1900 Zitkala-Sa, or Red Bird (1876–1938), a Sioux from the Yankton reserva-tion in South Dakota, described in a series of Atlantic Monthly *articles her experiences at a Quaker missionary school for Native Americans in Wabash, Indiana, which she at-tended from age eight to eleven. She returned to the school four years later to complete the course of study and then attended Earlham College in Richmond, Indiana. Zitkala-Sa somehow acquired the capacity to succeed in the white world without losing her Native American identity. After returning to the Sioux country, she married a Sioux and began a lifetime of work to improve the status and condition of indigenous peoples. In a long career that ended with her death in 1938, she played an influential role in the orga-nization of Native American communities, which led to major, though not thoroughly satisfying, federal reforms in the late 1920s and 1930s. In the excerpts from her nar-rative reprinted here, she offers glimpses of her efforts to integrate her Native American identity with the shifting realities and pressures of the world around her.*

QUESTIONS TO CONSIDER

1. What did Zitkala-Sa mean when she said she returned to the reser-vation "neither a wild Indian nor a tame one"? What did she reject about her education, and what did she accept?
2. Given the pain of her school experience, what reasons can you sug-gest for Zitkala-Sa's return to school?
3. What did Zitkala-Sa mean by her final comment about the Indian schools: "few there are who have paused to question whether real life or long-lasting death lies beneath this semblance of civilization"?

The first turning away from the easy, natural flow of my life occurred in an early spring. It was in my eighth year; in the month of March, I afterward

Zitkala-Sa (Gertrude Simmons Bonnin), "The School Days of an Indian Girl," *Atlantic Monthly*, January–March 1900, 45–47, 190, 192–94.

learned. At this age I knew but one language, and that was my mother's native tongue. . . .

"Mother, my friend Judéwin is going home with the missionaries. She is going to a more beautiful country than ours; the palefaces told her so!" I said wistfully, wishing in my heart that I too might go.

Mother sat in a chair, and I was hanging on her knee. Within the last two seasons my big brother Dawée had returned from a three years' education in the East, and his coming back influenced my mother to take a farther step from her native way of living. First it was a change from the buffalo skin to the white man's canvas that covered our wigwam. Now she had given up her wigwam of slender poles, to live, a foreigner, in a home of clumsy logs.

"Yes, my child, several others besides Judéwin are going away with the palefaces. Your brother said the missionaries had inquired about his little sister," she said, watching my face very closely.

My heart thumped so hard against my breast, I wondered if she could hear it.

"Did he tell them to take me, mother?" I asked, fearing lest Dawée had forbidden the palefaces to see me, and that my hope of going to the Wonderland would be entirely blighted.

With a sad, slow smile, she answered: "There! I knew you were wishing to go, because Judéwin has filled your ears with the white men's lies. Don't believe a word they say! Their words are sweet, but, my child, their deeds are bitter. You will cry for me, but they will not even soothe you. Stay with me, my little one! Your brother Dawée says that going East, away from your mother, is too hard an experience for his baby sister."

Thus my mother discouraged my curiosity about the lands beyond our eastern horizon; for it was not yet an ambition for Letters that was stirring me. But on the following day the missionaries did come to our very house. I spied them coming up the footpath leading to our cottage. A third man was with them, but he was not my brother Dawée. It was another, a young interpreter, a paleface who had a smattering of the Indian language. I was ready to run out to meet them, but I did not dare to displease my mother. With great glee, I jumped up and down on our ground floor. I begged my mother to open the door, that they would be sure to come to us. Alas! They came, they saw, and they conquered!

Judéwin had told me of the great tree where grew red, red apples; and how we could reach out our hands and pick all the red apples we could eat. I had never seen apple trees. I had never tasted more than a dozen red apples in my life; and when I heard of the orchards of the East, I was eager to roam among them. The missionaries smiled into my eyes, and patted my head. I wondered how mother could say such hard words against them.

"Mother, ask them if little girls may have all the red apples they want, when they go East," I whispered aloud in my excitement.

The interpreter heard me, and answered: "Yes, little girl, the nice red apples are for those who pick them; and you will have a ride on the iron horse if you go with these good people."

I had never seen a train, and he knew it.

"Mother, I'm going East! I like big red apples, and I want to ride on the iron horse! Mother, say yes!" I pleaded.

My mother said nothing. The missionaries waited in silence; and my eyes began to blur with tears, though I struggled to choke them back. The corners of my mouth twitched, and my mother saw me.

"I am not ready to give you any word," she said to them. "Tomorrow I shall send you my answer by my son." . . .

[The next day] my brother Dawée came for mother's decision. I dropped my play, and crept close to my aunt.

"Yes, Dawée, my daughter, though she does not understand what it all means, is anxious to go. She will need an education when she is grown, for then there will be fewer real Dakotas, and many more palefaces: This tearing her away, so young, from her mother is necessary, if I would have her an educated woman. The palefaces, who owe us a large debt for stolen lands, have begun to pay a tardy justice in offering some education to our children. But I know my daughter must suffer keenly in this experiment. For her sake, I dread to tell you my reply to the missionaries. Go, tell them that they may take my little daughter, and that the Great Spirit shall not fail to reward them according to their hearts." . . .

THE CUTTING OF MY LONG HAIR

The first day in the land of apples was a bitter-cold one; for the snow still covered the ground, and the trees were bare. A large bell rang for breakfast, its loud metallic voice crashing through the belfry overhead and into our sensitive ears. The annoying clatter of shoes on bare floors gave us no peace. The constant clash of harsh noises, with an undercurrent of many voices murmuring an unknown tongue, made a bedlam within which I was securely tied. And though my spirit tore itself in struggling for its lost freedom, all was useless.

A paleface woman, with white hair, came up after us. We were placed in a line of girls who were marching into the dining room. These were Indian girls, in stiff shoes and closely clinging dresses. The small girls wore sleeved aprons and shingled hair. As I walked noiselessly in my soft moccasins, I felt like sinking to the floor, for my blanket had been stripped from my shoulders. I looked hard at the Indian girls, who seemed not to care that they were even more immodestly dressed than I, in their tightly fitting clothes. While we marched in, the boys entered at an opposite door. I watched for the three young braves who came in our party. I spied them in the rear ranks, looking as uncomfortable as I felt.

A small bell was tapped, and each of the pupils drew a chair from under the table. Supposing this act meant they were to be seated, I pulled out mine and at once slipped into it from one side. But when I turned my head, I saw that I was the only one seated, and all the rest at our table remained standing. Just as I began to rise, looking shyly around to see how chairs were to be used, a second bell was sounded. All were seated at last, and I had to crawl back into my chair again. I heard a man's voice at one end of the hall, and I looked around to see him. But all the others hung their heads over their plates. As I glanced at the long chain of tables, I caught the eyes of a pale-face woman upon me. Immediately I dropped my eyes, wondering why I was so keenly watched by the strange woman. The man ceased his mutterings, and then a third bell was tapped. Every one picked up his knife and fork and began eating. I began crying instead, for by this time I was afraid to venture anything more.

But this eating by formula was not the hardest trial in that first day. Late in the morning, my friend Judéwin gave me a terrible warning. Judéwin knew a few words of English; and she had overheard the paleface woman talk about cutting our long, heavy hair. Our mothers had taught us that only unskilled warriors who were captured had their hair shingled by the enemy. Among our people, short hair was worn by mourners, and shingled hair by cowards!

We discussed our fate some moments, and when Judéwin said, "We have to submit, because they are strong," I rebelled.

"No, I will not submit! I will struggle first!" I answered.

I watched my chance, and when no one noticed I disappeared. I crept up the stairs as quietly as I could in my squeaking shoes,—my moccasins had been exchanged for shoes. Along the hall I passed, without knowing whither I was going. Turning aside to an open door, I found a large room with three white beds in it. The windows were covered with dark green curtains, which made the room very dim. Thankful that no one was there, I directed my steps toward the corner farthest from the door. On my hands and knees I crawled under the bed, and cuddled myself in the dark corner.

From my hiding place I peered out, shuddering with fear whenever I heard footsteps near by. Though in the hall loud voices were calling my name, and I knew that even Judéwin was searching for me, I did not open my mouth to answer. Then the steps were quickened and the voices became excited. The sounds came nearer and nearer. Women and girls entered the room. I held my breath and watched them open closet doors and peep behind large trunks. Some one threw up the curtains, and the room was filled with sudden light. What caused them to stoop and look under the bed I do not know. I remember being dragged out, though I resisted by kicking and scratching wildly. In spite of myself, I was carried downstairs and tied fast in a chair.

I cried aloud, shaking my head all the while until I felt the cold blades of the scissors against my neck, and heard them gnaw off one of my thick braids. Then I lost my spirit. Since the day I was taken from my mother I had suffered extreme indignities. People had stared at me. I had been tossed about in the air like a wooden puppet. And now my long hair was shingled like a coward's! In my anguish I moaned for my mother, but no one came to comfort me. Not a soul reasoned quietly with me, as my own mother used to do; for now I was only one of many little animals driven by a herder.

IRON ROUTINE

A loud-clamoring bell awakened us at half past six in the cold winter mornings. From happy dreams of Western rolling lands and unlassoed freedom we tumbled out upon chilly bare floors back again into a paleface day. We had short time to jump into our shoes and clothes, and wet our eyes with icy water, before a small hand bell was vigorously rung for roll call. . . .

A paleface woman, with a yellow-covered roll book open on her arm and a gnawed pencil in her hand, appeared at the door. Her small, tired face was coldly lighted with a pair of large gray eyes. . . .

Relentlessly her pencil black-marked our daily records if we were not present to respond to our names, and no chum of ours had done it successfully for us. No matter if a dull headache or the painful cough of slow consumption had delayed the absentee, there was only time enough to mark the tardiness. It was next to impossible to leave the iron routine after the civilizing machine had once begun its day's buzzing; and as it was inbred in me to suffer in silence rather than to appeal to the ears of one whose open eyes could not see my pain, I have many times trudged in the day's harness heavy-footed, like a dumb sick brute. . . .

I grew bitter, and censured the woman for cruel neglect of our physical ills. I despised the pencils that moved automatically, and the one teaspoon which dealt out, from a large bottle, healing to a row of variously ailing Indian children. I blamed the hard-working, well-meaning, ignorant woman who was inculcating in our hearts her superstitious ideas. Though I was sullen in all my little troubles, as soon as I felt better I was ready again to smile upon the cruel woman. Within a week I was again actively testing the chains which tightly bound my individuality like a mummy for burial. . . .

FOUR STRANGE SUMMERS

After my first three years of school, I roamed again in the Western country through four strange summers. During this time I seemed to hang in the heart of chaos, beyond the touch or voice of human aid. My brother, being almost ten years my senior, did not quite understand my feelings. My mother had never gone inside of a schoolhouse, and so she was not capable of comforting her daughter who could read and write. Even nature seemed to have no place for me. I was neither a wee girl nor a tall one; neither a wild Indian nor a tame one. This deplorable situation was the effect of my brief course in the East, and the unsatisfactory "teenth" in a girl's years.

INCURRING MY MOTHER'S DISPLEASURE

In the second journey to the East I had not come without some precautions. I had a secret interview with one of our best medicine men, and when I left his wigwam I carried securely in my sleeve a tiny bunch of magic roots. This possession assured me of friends wherever I should go. So absolutely did I believe in its charms that I wore it through all the school routine for more than a year. Then, before I lost my faith in the dead roots, I lost the little buckskin bag containing all my good luck.

At the close of this second term of three years I was the proud owner of my first diploma. The following autumn I ventured upon a college career against my mother's will.

I had written for her approval, but in her reply I found no encouragement. She called my notice to her neighbors' children, who had completed their education in three years. They had returned to their homes, and were then talking English with the frontier settlers. Her few words hinted that I had better give up my slow attempt to learn the white man's ways, and be content to roam over the prairies and find my living upon wild roots. I silenced her by deliberate disobedience.

Thus, homeless and heavy-hearted, I began anew my life among strangers.

As I hid myself in my little room in the college dormitory, away from the scornful and yet curious eyes of the students, I pined for sympathy. Often I wept in secret, wishing I had gone West, to be nourished by my mother's love, instead of remaining among a cold race whose hearts were frozen hard with prejudice.

During the fall and winter seasons I scarcely had a real friend, though by that time several of my classmates were courteous to me at a safe distance. . . .

. . . I appeared as the college representative in [an oratorical] contest. This time the competition was among orators from different colleges in our state. It was held at the state capital, in one of the largest opera houses.

Here again was a strong prejudice against my people. In the evening, as the great audience filled the house, the student bodies began warring among themselves. Fortunately, I was spared witnessing any of the noisy wrangling before the contest began. The slurs against the Indian that stained the lips of our opponents were already burning like a dry fever within my breast.

But after the orations were delivered a deeper burn awaited me. There, before that vast ocean of eyes, some college rowdies threw out a large white flag, with a drawing of a most forlorn Indian girl on it. Under this they had printed in bold black letters words that ridiculed the college which was represented by a "squaw." Such worse than barbarian rudeness embittered me. While we waited for the verdict of the judges, I gleamed fiercely upon the throngs of palefaces. My teeth were hard set, as I saw the white flag still floating insolently in the air.

Then anxiously we watched the man carry toward the stage the envelope containing the final decision.

There were two prizes given, that night, and one of them was mine!

The evil spirit laughed within me when the white flag dropped out of sight, and the hands which furled it hung limp in defeat.

Leaving the crowd as quickly as possible, I was soon in my room. The rest of the night I sat in an armchair and gazed into the crackling fire. I laughed no more in triumph when thus alone. The little taste of victory did not satisfy a hunger in my heart. In my mind I saw my mother far away on the Western plains, and she was holding a charge against me.

RETROSPECTION

. . . At this stage of my own evolution, I was ready to curse men of small capacity for being the dwarfs their God had made them. In the process of my education I had lost all consciousness of the nature world about me. Thus, when a hidden rage took me to the small white-walled prison which I then called my room, I unknowingly turned away from my one salvation.

Alone in my room, I sat like the petrified Indian woman of whom my mother used to tell me. I wished my heart's burdens would turn me to unfeeling stone. But alive, in my tomb, I was destitute!

For the white man's papers I had given up my faith in the Great Spirit. For these same papers I had forgotten the healing in trees and brooks. On account of my mother's simple view of life, and my lack of any, I gave her up, also. I made no friends among the race of people I loathed. Like a slender tree, I had been uprooted from my mother, nature, and God. I was shorn of my branches, which had waved in sympathy and love for home and friends. The natural coat of bark which had protected my oversensitive nature was scraped off to the very quick.

Now a cold bare pole I seemed to be planted in a strange earth. Still, I seemed to hope a day would come when my mute aching head, reared upward to the sky, would flash a zigzag lightning across the heavens. With this dream of vent for a long-pent consciousness, I walked again amid the crowds.

At last, one weary day in the schoolroom, a new idea presented itself to me. It was a new way of solving the problem of my inner self. I liked it. Thus I resigned my position as teacher; and now I am in an Eastern city, following the long course of study I have set for myself. Now, as I look back upon the recent past, I see it from a distance, as a whole. I remember how, from morning till evening, many specimens of civilized peoples visited the Indian school. The city folks with canes and eyeglasses, the countrymen with sunburnt cheeks and clumsy feet, forgot their relative social ranks in an ignorant curiosity. Both sorts of these Christian palefaces were alike astounded at seeing the children of savage warriors so docile and industrious.

As answers to their shallow inquiries they received the students' sample work to look upon. Examining the neatly figured pages, and gazing upon the Indian girls and boys bending over their books, the white visitors walked out of the schoolhouse well satisfied: they were educating the children of the red man! They were paying a liberal fee to the government employees in whose able hands lay the small forest of Indian timber.

In this fashion many have passed idly through the Indian schools during the last decade, afterward to boast of their charity to the North American Indian. But few there are who have paused to question whether real life or long-lasting death lies beneath this semblance of civilization.

9

The Homestead Act and the Peopling of the West

The phrase "manifest destiny" was first made popular by journalist John L. O'Sullivan in 1845, when he argued that it is "our manifest destiny to overspread and to possess the whole of the continent which Providence has given us for the development of the great experiment of liberty." Shortly thereafter, the United States took much of the Southwest from Mexico. However, the Civil War and struggles over slavery, freedom, and the future development of the West prevented the nation from doing much overspreading and possessing during the following two decades.

When the Civil War ended, the nation turned its full attention to the West, finally making good on the countless economic development schemes that had been promoted since the Louisiana Purchase of 1803. The transcontinental railroad and the Homestead Act defined this great shift westward. The Homestead Act of 1862 guaranteed 160 acres of public land to any family that had not taken up arms against the U.S. government during the Civil War, on the condition that they "improve" or farm the land. The news of this act spread throughout Europe and brought millions of immigrants from crowded cities, towns, and agricultural regions—with the poorest and most agricultural countries losing large percentages of their national populations.

Second only to Ireland in population lost to American immigration, Norway had whole regions stripped of people in the nineteenth century. The families pictured below exemplify the 800,000 Norwegians—a third of the population—who left Norway between 1825 and 1925, many to take up homesteads in America.

QUESTIONS TO CONSIDER

1. This photo was carefully posed. What do you notice about the choices that were made in the placement of people, clothing, and objects?
2. What story do you think the photographer was trying to tell about this family and its role in the peopling of the West?
3. Norwegians were some of the poorest migrants to come to the United States in the nineteenth century. What indicators of poverty do you see in this photo?

Norwegian immigrant family in the Dakota Territory, 1898. *Homestead site of Ole I. Gjevre, Osnabrock Township, Dakota Territory / Fred Hultstrand History in Pictures Collection, NDIRS-NDSU, Fargo (2028.58).*

PART TWO

The Gilded Age
Industrial Growth and Crisis

Before 1860, the United States' wealth had been chiefly based on producing food and raw materials for its own people and for consumers elsewhere in the Atlantic world. Agriculture continued to grow during the late nineteenth century, but it was the rapid expansion of industry that propelled the nation's economic rise. By the early twentieth century, the country had become the world's leading industrial power.

The industrialization of the United States changed not only the magnitude of American goods produced but also the very way in which Americans worked. As late as 1870, many city artisans were still self-employed, working as silversmiths, cabinetmakers, or other craftspeople. Cobblers made shoes by hand, and chandlers dipped tapers in hot wax one at a time. These craftspeople, like brass worker Joseph T. Finnerty, often took enormous pride in their work. By 1900, however, in a remarkable shift, about two-thirds of the labor force consisted of wage earners.

Factory workers typically labored under unsafe conditions, brought home paltry sums compared to their bosses, and enjoyed few modern-day benefits such as healthcare and holiday leave. Immigrant workers were subjected to racial and ethnic discrimination that sometimes, as in the case of the Chinese in the United States, resulted in the denial of basic civil rights. Aggrieved laborers formed unions to maximize their political power and organized strikes to wring concessions from bosses, as in the strike for an eight-hour workday at Chicago's McCormick Reaper Works factory that precipitated the bloody Haymarket riot in 1886. The Knights of Labor and the Industrial Workers of the World attracted thousands of members in a struggle to improve life for working men and women. Farmers, like industrial workers, also protested deteriorating economic conditions. In the Midwest and South, many sought relief from unsteady crop prices by backing the

People's Party, formed in 1892. The party's Omaha Platform called for federal reform of the economy, more liberal monetary policies, and tighter control over the transportation industry.

Rising militancy among laborers ignited national debates. In 1882, the Senate Committee on Education and Labor held hearings to probe the relationship between labor and capital. Members heard much about both the hardships and the opportunities of the new economy. In contrast to the convictions of many workers about their declining status, piano manufacturer William Steinway extolled the opportunities and higher standards of living created by vast manufacturing establishments. But it was not just workers who were threatened—and harmed—by the new economy. George Rice, who owned a small oil refinery in West Virginia, lost everything to the cutthroat business tactics of Standard Oil. Seeking relief from Standard's monopolistic practices, Rice was a plaintiff in a famous 1898 court case against John D. Rockefeller that spurred the passage of antitrust laws.

Change was slow in coming for working men and women. At the Triangle Shirtwaist Company in New York City, young immigrant women sewed garments for wealthy consumers in a dangerous high-rise factory with improper ventilation and lax fire control policies. The women's demands for better wages and a safer environment fell on deaf ears. In 1911 a fast-moving fire at the facility claimed 146 lives and raised the alarm, once again, about the perils of being a worker in the new industrial economy.

POINTS OF VIEW
The Rise of Labor Unions

10

THE KNIGHTS OF LABOR

Early Efforts at Labor Organizing

Secretly organized in 1869 by seven members of a local tailors' union in Philadelphia, the Knights of Labor initially functioned as a fraternal group. The organization changed

---

"Constitutions of the General Assembly, District Assemblies and Local Assemblies of the Order of the Knights of Labor," in *Record of Proceedings of the General Assembly of the [Knights of Labor] Held at Reading, Pennsylvania, January 1–4, 1878* (Reading, PA: The Assembly, 1878), 28–29, www.archive.org/stream/RecordOfProceedingsOfTheGeneralAssemblyOfTheKnights OfLabor/Knightslaborb#page/n15/mode/2up.

dramatically during the economic depression that began in 1873, when the unemployed and underemployed flocked to its doors. By 1880 the Knights numbered 28,000; six years later, membership was at 700,000. The group's rapid growth brought a rise in not only its political power but also organizational tensions. Infighting, mistrust among leaders, and charges of internal corruption cut short its life as an agent for workplace change. By 1890 membership had fallen to 100,000, and by the mid-twentieth century the group had disbanded.

During its heyday, the Knights of Labor offered a fresh vision of labor reform. Its most famous leader, Terence Powderly (1849–1924), led the charge for improved rights for all wage earners. He also called for the federal government to take on a new role as a vigorous protector of safety and fairness in the workplace. The following excerpt from a document adopted by the Knights in 1878 sets forth the organization's basic principles.

QUESTIONS TO CONSIDER

1. What vision of the country underlies the preamble to the Knights' constitution?
2. What historical relationship between business owners and workers is evoked by the preamble?
3. Which principles and calls for change would have been considered revolutionary at the time? Why?

PREAMBLE

The recent alarming development and aggression of aggregated wealth, which, unless checked, will inevitably lead to the pauperization and hope-less degradation of the toiling masses, render it imperative, if we desire to enjoy the blessings of life, that a check should be placed upon its power and upon unjust accumulation, and a system adopted which will secure to the laborer the fruits of his toil; much as this much-desired object can only be accomplished by the thorough unification of labor, and the united efforts of those who obey the divine injunction that "In the sweat of thy face shalt thou eat bread," we have formed the [Knights of Labor] with a view of secur-ing the organization and direction, by cooperative effort, of the power of the industrial classes; and we submit to the world the objects sought to be accomplished by our organization, calling upon all who believe in securing "the greatest good to the greatest numbers" to aid and assist us.

I. To bring within the folds of organization every department of pro-ductive industry, making knowledge a stand-point for action, and industrial, moral worth, not wealth, the true standard of individual and national greatness.

II. To secure to the toilers a proper share of the wealth they create; more of the leisure that rightfully belongs to them; more society ad-vantages; more of the benefits, privileges, and emoluments of the world; in a word, all those rights and privileges necessary to make them capable of enjoying, appreciating, defending, and perpetuating the blessings of good government.

III. To arrive at the true condition of the producing masses in their educational, moral, and financial condition, by demanding from the various governments the establishment of bureaus of labor statistics.

IV. The establishment of cooperative institutions, productive and distributive.

V. The reserving of the public lands — the heritage of the people — for the actual settler; — not another acre for railroads or speculators.

VI. The abrogation of all laws that do not bear equally upon capital and labor, and the removal of unjust technicalities, delays, and discriminations in the administration of justice, and the adoption of measures providing for the health and safety of those engaged in mining, manufacturing, and building pursuits.

VII. The enactment of laws to compel corporations to pay their employees weekly in full for labor performed during the preceding week, in the lawful money of the country.

VIII. The enactment of laws giving mechanics and laborers a first lien upon the product of their labor for their full wages.

IX. The abolishment of the contract system on national, State, and municipal work.

X. The substitution of arbitration for strikes, whenever and wherever employers and employees are willing to meet on equitable grounds.

XI. The prohibition of the employment of children in workshops, mines and factories before attaining their fourteenth year.

XII. To abolish the system of letting out by contract the labor of convicts in our prisons and reformatory institutions.[1]

XIII. To secure for both sexes equal pay for equal work.

XIV. The reduction of the hours of labor to eight per day, so that the laborers may have more time for social enjoyment and intellectual improvement, and be enabled to reap the advantages conferred by the labor-saving machinery which their brains have created.

XV. To prevail upon governments to establish a purely national circulating medium, based upon the faith and resources of the nation,

---

1. **letting out by contract . . . reformatory institutions:** The practice by which small factories or shops contracted with local prisons to have convicts perform jobs at wages far below those normally paid to everyday laborers.

and issued directly to the people, without the intervention of any system of banking corporations, which money shall be a legal tender in payment of all debts, public or private.

11

INDUSTRIAL WORKERS OF THE WORLD
Demanding a New Workplace

At the same time that the Knights of Labor declined in membership, a new labor union sprang up. Founded in Chicago in 1905 at a meeting of more than two hundred union radicals and socialists, the Industrial Workers of the World (IWW) focused on the speedy advancement of worker unity and power. Disheartened by a perceived failure on the part of other unions to secure lasting and meaningful workplace change, IWW spokespeople openly labeled "capitalists," or business and factory owners, as their enemies; embraced strikes as a legitimate form of protest; and called for every laborer, regardless of trade or skill level, to unite under the banner of radical reform. Unlike the Knights of Labor or any other union, the IWW opened its doors to women, blacks, and immigrants and regularly rotated its leaders. The IWW reached its height of popularity in the early 1920s, when membership surged to 100,000. Shortly thereafter, the organization fell apart when members split over the group's future direction.

At the time of its founding, the IWW garnered worldwide attention for its wide-sweeping calls for transformation in the relationships between not only workers and employers but also poor and rich citizens. It evidenced a profound distrust of the promises of American democracy and the ability of the government to adjudicate fairly between the competing claims of the haves and the have-nots on economic power. This excerpt from a report of New York State's Joint Legislative Committee Investigating Seditious Activities addresses the struggle between the working and employing classes.

QUESTIONS TO CONSIDER

1. According to the IWW's preamble, what were the main reasons for workers' lack of political power?
2. What does this excerpt say about the federal government's role in promoting a more balanced sharing of power between workers and employers?
3. Why was the IWW against the modern wage system?

Revolutionary Radicalism: Its History, Purpose and Tactics, with an Exposition and Discussion of the Steps Being Taken and Required to Curb It, Being the Report of the Joint Legislative Committee Investigating Seditious Activities, Filed April 24, 1920, in the Senate of the State of New York, vol. 2 (Albany, NY: J. B. Lyon, 1920), 1948–49.

PREAMBLE TO THE INDUSTRIAL WORKERS
OF THE WORLD (ADOPTED 1908)

The working class and the employing class have nothing in common. There can be no peace so long as hunger and want are found among millions of the working people and the few, who make up the employing class, have all the good things of life.

Between these two classes a struggle must go on until the workers of the world organize as a class, take possession of the means of production, abolish the wage system, and live in harmony with the Earth.

We find that the centering of the management of industries into fewer and fewer hands makes the trade unions unable to cope with the ever growing power of the employing class. The trade unions foster a state of affairs which allows one set of workers to be pitted against another set of workers in the same industry, thereby helping defeat one another in wage wars. Moreover, the trade unions aid the employing class to mislead the workers into the belief that the working class have interests in common with their employers.

These conditions can be changed and the interest of the working class upheld only by an organization formed in such a way that all its members in any one industry, or in all industries if necessary, cease work whenever a strike or lockout is on in any department thereof, thus making an injury to one an injury to all.

Instead of the conservative motto, "A fair day's wage for a fair day's work," we must inscribe on our banner the revolutionary watchword, "Abolition of the wage system."

It is the historic mission of the working class to do away with capitalism. The army of production must be organized, not only for everyday struggle with capitalists, but also to carry on production when capitalism shall have been overthrown. By organizing industrially we are forming the structure of the new society within the shell of the old.

FOR CRITICAL THINKING

1. How did the Knights of Labor and the Industrial Workers of the World differ in their key principles?
2. Why was the IWW more aggressive than the Knights in its calls for change?
3. Which union had a greater influence on the benefits enjoyed by working men and women today? Why?

12

The Industrial City

"The photographers of the American city during the nineteenth and early twentieth centuries," writes a historian of the photography of American urbanization, "were explorers in a cultural frontier. . . . They advertised and celebrated change—most fundamentally the transformation of America from a rural and agrarian nation to an urban and industrial one."

By the early twentieth century, the country's dramatic urbanization was inescapable. New York City housed over four million people, Chicago over two million, and Philadelphia over one and a half million. Their teeming populations made these cities among the world's largest at the time. Urban life was strange and uncomfortable, featuring vast crowds with foreign languages and manners, furious construction, monumental traffic jams, dense jungles of overhead wires, and the dilemmas of slums, disease, crime, vice, and corruption. At the same time, the cities swelled with promise and opportunity; they were places to escape age-old restrictions, gain new experience, achieve wealth, secure education, and discover new entertainments.

Photographers helped chart this new territory. Some captured the vitality of the urban scene, while others allied with journalists, urban planners, and social workers to bring the problems of the poor and the successes of reform movements into public view. Armed with important technological improvements—such as the more convenient dry plate photographic chemistry (which soon gave rise to the popular Kodak camera), crude forms of flash photography, and the halftone process that allowed the direct printing of photographs in books, newspapers, and magazines—these photographers documented their fascination with the changes overtaking the American scene.

Alvin Langdon Coburn (1882–1966) was part of a group of early-twentieth-century photographers who wished to establish photography as a serious art form. Working in a style of softened focus that emulated aspects of the Impressionist movement, which was then dominating the other visual arts, Coburn turned his camera away from traditional subjects to the new vistas of the urban landscape.

Unlike Coburn, who wanted to make art with his camera, journalist Jacob A. Riis (1849–1914) used photography to document the grimness of urban slums in a convincing way. Riis's images gave an emotional dimension to the statistics that he presented to his audiences in lectures, articles, and books about social problems and the need for reform. Most Americans did not understand the impoverished, overcrowded, disease-ridden world of the slum experienced by urban dwellers such as the men in the Ludlow Street cellar.

QUESTIONS TO CONSIDER

1. In what ways is Coburn's Manhattan skyscraper photo a critique of industrial America and in what ways is it a celebration?
2. Jacob Riis was a social reformer who believed poor people were not responsible for their own poverty, but that their problems were caused by social inequities. How do you see this argument communicated in the image of the Ludlow Street cellar?
3. What vision of cities and industry did Coburn and Riis likely share? In what ways did their visions differ? Which of the two images has the most impact today? Why?

Alvin Langdon Coburn, "Skyscrapers, Manhattan," from Alvin Langdon Coburn, *New York*, 1910. *Photo by SSPL/ Getty Images.*

Jacob A. Riis, "Shoemaker in Ludlow Street Cellar," ca. 1890. *The Museum of the City of New York/Art Resource.*

13

WILLIAM STEINWAY

Workers Prosper as Industry Grows

Labor disturbances formed a regular part of the post-Reconstruction landscape. Some— among them the railroad strike of 1877, the Homestead walkout of 1892, and the Pullman strike of 1894—made dramatic national headlines. Less remembered are the smaller strikes occurring each year by the hundreds, and then the thousands, in the last quarter of the nineteenth century.

Socially conscious Americans worried especially about the many working people in the great cities who lived in flimsy, overcrowded housing, with inadequate sanitation, that

Testimony of William Steinway, *Report of the Committee of the Senate upon the Relations between Labor and Capital*, vol. 2 (Washington, DC: Government Printing Office, 1885), 1085–95.

quickly degenerated into disease-ridden slums. People in such circumstances had no protection against dips in the economy, nor could they afford to educate their children, whose labor was needed for a family's survival. Contemporaries struggled to explain—or explain away—such problems. The Senate Committee on the Relations between Labor and Capital of 1883 heard many theories about the sources of labor discontent. The explanations offered by the piano manufacturer William Steinway (1835–1896), excerpted here, were characteristic of the beliefs of successful businessmen. Social mobility, Steinway argued, was not only still possible but also increasingly available with industrial growth. As proof, he pointed to his own experience of rising from apprentice to industrialist. Educational improvements and other practical reforms would render workers prosperous and content within the current economic system. Steinway especially urged apprenticeships and industrial schooling, as well as the movement of industry from downtown locations into suburbs, where workers could secure good housing at reasonable prices.

Yet much of Steinway's experience was atypical of U.S. industrial development, and the Steinway piano was an exotic bloom in nineteenth-century America. The nation had risen to industrial preeminence by supplying materials like steel and oil for industry and by creating inexpensive goods like Kodak cameras and cheap brass chandeliers for mass markets. It is hard to think of another nineteenth-century American product like the Steinway, a luxury item that competed with the finest European products. Nonetheless, nothing could have been more American than Steinway's testimony to the senators about his unaided rise to the apex of piano manufacturing, his faith in education, and his optimism that all social conflict could be resolved and that every worthy citizen could prosper.

QUESTIONS TO CONSIDER

1. What was William Steinway's opinion of labor unions?
2. What was his view of the condition of labor in the United States?
3. What did Steinway think was needed to improve the living conditions of U.S. workers?

New York, September 27, 1883

William Steinway examined.

By Mr. Call:

Question. Have you seen the resolution under which the committee is conducting this examination?—*Answer.* Yes, sir.

Mr. Call. The committee will be glad to hear from you any facts or opinions you may have to present on the several subjects mentioned in the resolution, first stating your residence and occupation and your connection with labor in this country and abroad.

The Witness. I was born in Brunswick, Germany, in 1836, and came to the city of New York in the spring of 1850, when fourteen years of age, with my father, mother, and the rest of our family. We worked for three years in the factories here, learning the language and the customs of the people, and in March, 1853, started the business of Steinway & Sons—my father, my two brothers, and myself—which has now become the most extensive establishment of its kind in existence. We have three distinct establishments, manufactories rather, our New York factory, at Fourth avenue and Fifty-second and Fifty-third streets; a large establishment at Astoria, N.Y., opposite One hundred and twentieth street, where we employ over 400 men, and where we have carried out our ideas of improving the condition of the workingmen by giving them light and air and good houses to live in, building them public baths, and laying out a public park, keeping up at our own expense in the public school a teacher who teaches German and music free of charge, and various other advantages. We employ about 1,000 workmen, a great majority of whom are skilled workmen. I will remark that in the first three years when I worked as an apprentice and journeyman, and in the first few years when our business was small, I had ample opportunities of studying the lot of the workingman by actual experience, also the way that workingmen worked, and I can say that skilled artisans to-day are far better off than they were a third of a century ago. At that time but very few people, even skilled laborers, were able to save money and put it in [the] bank. Today the skilled laborers, more especially in the piano-forte [piano] trade, and the woodworking establishments, have wages double what they were in those times; and from my experience also as director in savings banks, &c., I find that a great many skilled artisans, those blessed with health, have constituted a great portion of the depositors in banks. The wages in the piano-forte trade, that is to say, the skilled laborers, have averaged $20 per week (ranging from $15 to $30).

We ourselves have a branch establishment in Hamburg, and from my travels in Europe and my study of the condition of the workingmen in both hemispheres, especially in the piano-forte trade, I will say here that of my own personal knowledge the wages of skilled artisans in the piano-forte trade in the cities of New York, Boston, Baltimore, and Philadelphia, where they are most densely congregated, average precisely three times the amount that the skilled artisans of Europe do in the same trade.

The introduction of machinery in our business, and in the woodworking establishments, has been of great benefit by doing the hard work which formerly imperiled the health and lives of the skilled artisans. I will further state that of the about one hundred piano-forte manufacturers of the United States, which are chiefly concentrated in the four cities I have named, nearly all have been workingmen themselves.

Labor Ought to Organize

The relations between ourselves and our men have always been very good until lately disturbed by the entrance of the socialistic and the communistic element in the labor unions. I myself think that labor ought to organize, as it has organized. I am not opposed to labor unions, and any labor union that is carried on in a sensible way can do a great deal, not only toward bettering their own condition in the way of wages, but also in equalizing wages in the various cities, and in resisting in times of depression the great deterioration and fall of wages. We have gone through very hard strikes. We have been singled out. Our house being the strongest and largest, has been made the target of strikes. It is just about a year ago now that one of the most senseless strikes was inaugurated during my absence in Europe by the socialistic and communistic element inducing our men to strike against an honest, faithful bookkeeper, against whom they were unable to allege the slightest grievance, except that they did not want him, and that their union had so ordered. They were unsuccessful, however. . . . But, as I said . . . I am not opposed to labor unions; but on the contrary will here give it as my opinion that strikes are a necessity and should not be legislated against, and cannot be legislated against. . . .

Manufacturers Miscalled Capitalists

A great mistake is also made by the workingmen and the professional agitators, who foment strikes, by calling manufacturers capitalists.

Of about 100 piano-forte manufacturers in the United States known throughout the world to make the best pianos in existence, and conceded so by musical talent and authority in Europe, there are but four wealthy houses—about 20 to 25 people of moderate means—and the rest, that is, 60 or 70 manufacturers in the piano-forte trade, just manage to eke out a hand-to-mouth existence. These are hard words, but they are literally true.

The Horrors of the Tenement House System

. . . I consider [that] one of the greatest evils under which workingmen live, especially in the city of New York, is the horrors of the tenement houses— the terrible rents that they have to pay. The average workingman's family has one room in which they cook, wash, iron, and live, and one or two, or possibly three, bed rooms, of which generally one or two are dark rooms, without any windows, or without admitting God's pure air. This is a terrible evil, which is, however, chiefly caused by the insular position of the city of New York, where, in winter, in times of ice and fog, it is impossible that workingmen should come long distances and be in time for their work.

The horrors of the tenement houses are having a very baneful effect upon the morals and character of the coming generation; in fact, I may say a terrible effect. But I do not see what legislation can do. Capitalists consider tenement houses a poor investment, paying poor returns. The only thing that I can imagine is to do as *we* have done, remove the very large factories requiring much room and many men from out of the city of New York into the suburbs.

Want of an Apprentice Law

A second great evil under which we are suffering, and it seems to me it is an evil that has been increasing from year to year, is, that in no country of the wide world, as I have found during my experience and my extensive travels, are there so many young men growing up without learning a trade or any particular calling, as in the United States. We have no apprentice law. In our own business, as well as the wood-working business, everybody is unwilling to take an apprentice, for the simple reason that it is a well known fact that the first year or two when a boy is learning a trade he will produce nothing, and will spoil a great deal, and will take up the time of a skilled man to teach him, and yet the moment he has learned one little branch of the trade he leaves, shifts for himself. He has not learned the business properly, and the consequence is that he is dependent, and, in times of great depression, cannot find employment. Hence we have no supply of skilled artisans growing up, and have to draw for our extra skilled labor on Europe. When I came to this country, in 1850, the majority, indeed I might say seven-eighths, of the journeyman piano makers were Americans, skilled workmen. Through our apprentice law, or rather through the total want of one, the entire native element has been thrown out of the piano business, and to-day seven-eighths of the workingmen in the piano shops, and over one-half in the New England States, are Germans.

By the Chairman:

Q. Is that for lack of an apprentice law as much as it is from the fact that skilled labor already trained has found its way here from abroad and has entered into competition, and made the employment of apprentices by employers a thing undesirable on their part?—*A.* No, sir; I attribute it entirely, or chiefly, to the lack of a proper apprentice law.

Industrial Schools

The total want of industrial schools in this city is a very great evil. There ought to be industrial schools all over each city where boys can go and find for what business they have aptitude and talent. Then, under regular apprentice laws, under which a boy could be bound for, say, five years at rising wages, commencing at $3 a week for the first year, getting $3.50 the second year, $4 a week the third year, and so on, they would learn a trade well. During the last two or three years the employer could have the advantage, since during the first one or two years he lost. . . .

Compulsory Education

I would also advocate a law compelling every child between the ages of six and fourteen to go to school. I have found in my experience as an employer and executor, and as [a] worker in benevolent enterprises in which I have been engaged, that there is a great deal more ignorance in reading and writing among young men and women growing up in this city—mostly children of foreigners—than anybody has any idea of. During the war we raised a fund to assist the wives of men that went to the war, and I found that one-half of those who had grown up in this country, or had come here when they were little children, were unable to sign their names. I never would have believed it possible if I had not myself experienced it. Hence I think that a compulsory law compelling every child between the ages of six and fourteen years to be sent to school should be enacted, and that parents should be punished if they did not enforce it. . . .

Independence of Skilled Artisans

Having gone through the panics of 1861, 1867, and 1873, I know that skilled artisans are absolutely independent of bad times, for a skilled workman will always find employment. It is so in the piano-forte trade and in the kindred trade in wood. . . . I found that all the skilled piano-forte manufacturers and those in the wood-working trades readily retained and found employment at remunerative wages; whereas the half skilled men who knew only one little branch of a trade were thrown out of employment. Hence the necessity of educating our young men who wish to learn trades to make them thorough skilled workingmen. In other words, do away with the curse of the American mechanics—young men learning only one portion of a skilled trade, and being then absolutely dependent upon that because they do not know anything else. . . .

Legislative Measures; Child Labor; Industrial Schools, etc.

Q. Is there anything in the shape of public legislation or voluntary action that you would suggest that will improve that opportunity [for an individual to work his way up]?—A. I think that is one of the greatest problems, and I do not see that legislation can do much more than it has done now, with the exception of what I have indicated. There should be an apprentice law and a stringent law against child-labor, so as to give the children of the poor people a chance to perfect their education, and the industrial schools could be established and every effort made toward giving artisans and laboring people healthy, happy homes.

Q. With those things supplied, either by public law or voluntary action, would you consider the relations now existing under our institutions as favorable as they could be made?—A. As favorable as it is possible to make them, in my opinion. Anything further would simply help one class in opposition to another. In this country it must be left to individual talent and industry. I think in this country a young man has a better chance to work up in the world than anywhere else that I have seen. . . .

Removal of City Factories

By Mr. Pugh:

Q. I understood you to condemn the presence of those large manufacturing establishments in our cities, and to charge the discomfort of the operatives in them to the fact largely of the presence of such establishments in cities?—*A*. Yes; I think every effort ought to be directed to having the large establishments go out to the suburbs of the city, in order to give the workingmen a chance to live as human beings ought to live. . . .

Q. Your factory, I understand you to say, is removed from New York?—*A*. We still have a large factory, which we call our "finishing" factory, in New York. It is the case-making factory. The iron and steel works for making the hardware, &c., has been removed over to Astoria, and one department after another has been added thereto, and within a few years the entire establishment will be removed from New York to Astoria.

Q. Do your artisans there live in rented houses?—*A*. Some of our artisans have already acquired homes of their own, but others of them live in rented houses, and not more than two families in one house, where they have gas, water, free baths, free schools, and every advantage. We have upwards of four hundred men there.

Q. At Astoria?—*A*. At Astoria.

Q. And you have found them able to improve their condition there?—*A*. Oh, yes; very much so. There is no sickness or anything of that kind there, and they are all feeling comfortable and happy, and I think the large wealthy manufacturers should also remove their factories from the cities and establish them somewhere in the suburbs, and do something for their workingmen in that way.

Q. You think that that would be a solution of a great part of the trouble arising between labor and capital?—*A*. Certainly a solution of the tenement-house trouble.

Q. And that, you think, is a large part of the cause of distress and dissatisfaction among the people?—*A*. Yes; I think it is a great cause of dissatisfaction among the workingmen—the bad places that they have to live in, and the high rents they have to pay. Yet tenement houses are considered a very poor investment by capitalists.

14

GEORGE RICE

Losing Out to Standard Oil

Even the optimistic industrialist Andrew Carnegie noted in his lecture to young men that "as business gravitates more and more to immense concerns," opportunity might be

New York World, October 16, 1898, 25.

threatened. George Rice (1835–1905) did all that Carnegie would have suggested. Having entered the oil business early, Rice kept, as Carnegie advised, all his eggs in one basket and watched the basket closely. What he saw was the Standard Oil Company under John D. Rockefeller undercut his operation and eventually drive him out of business.

Rice's legal and intellectual counterattack on Standard Oil led the charge against "the trusts." He supplied information to two of the major reporters on that corporation, Henry Demarest Lloyd and Ida Tarbell, whose books and articles encouraged antitrust legislation. And he spent considerable time in legal pursuit of Standard Oil. His quest against the company never met with success during his lifetime but did inspire efforts that, over time, led to the breakup of the giant corporation in 1911.

After a dramatic personal encounter with Rockefeller in 1898 during depositions for one of Rice's many lawsuits against Standard Oil, Rice was interviewed by a reporter for the New York World. *Here is his explanation of how Standard Oil operated.*

QUESTIONS TO CONSIDER

1. How, according to George Rice, did Standard Oil undercut its competitors?
2. Do you agree with Rice that Standard's undercutting constituted unfair competition? Explain.
3. What was Rice's attitude toward large corporations?

"I have been twenty years fighting John D. Rockefeller and the Standard Oil Trust, and I am not through yet."

The man who said this was George Rice, of Marietta, O. He is the man who told John D. Rockefeller to his face last Wednesday in the New Netherland Hotel, where Mr. Rockefeller had been testifying before the State Commission sent from Ohio to get evidence in proceedings intended to prove him guilty of contempt of the Ohio Supreme Court, that his great wealth was built on wrecks of other men's business.

It was a dramatic scene. Mr. Rockefeller and Mr. Rice have known each other well for a generation. In a twenty-year fight men are apt to get well acquainted.

But when the great multi-millionaire walked across the parlor, and, extending his hand—which was not taken—said to George Rice in a suave tenor voice:

"HOW ARE YOU, GEORGE! WE ARE GETTING TO BE GRAY-HAIRED MEN NOW, AIN'T WE? DON'T YOU WISH YOU HAD TAKEN MY ADVICE YEARS AGO?" the group of onlookers were not prepared for what followed.

George Rice drew himself up to his full height, which is about 6 feet 2 inches, his bright gray eyes flashed fire, and his massive frame visibly vibrated with suppressed anger, as he looked the great oil magnate straight in the face and said:

"Perhaps it would have been better for me if I had. YOU HAVE CERTAINLY RUINED MY BUSINESS, AS YOU SAID YOU WOULD."

Mr. Rockefeller recoiled and his face showed a shade of pallor. The words of Rice had evidently stung him. Quickly recovering himself he turned from his accuser, saying, "Oh, pshaw, that isn't so, George!"

"But I say it is so," was the instant rejoinder of George Rice, and, raising his voice so that everybody in the room could hear him, he pointed his index finger at the Oil King, and added: "You know well that by the power of your great wealth you have ruined my business, and you cannot deny it."

MR. RICE TELLS HIS EXPERIENCE TO THE WORLD

This ended the episode in the hotel parlor. A few hours later, sitting in his private room, Mr. Rice gave to a *World* representative the full story of how he was ruined as an oil refiner by the machinations of the great Standard Oil Laocoon[1] in whose coils an uncounted multitude of competitors have been crushed to death.

"I am but one of many victims of Rockefeller's colossal combination," said Mr. Rice, "and my story is not essentially different from the rest. You ask me to tell you what I meant by telling Mr. Rockefeller, as I did publicly to-day, that he had ruined my business. The whole story, with all its inside details of intrigue and conspiracy, would require a volume to tell. I will tell you as much of it as you choose to ask me for. What particular phase of my experience do you care to have me relate?"

"Give me your personal story, Mr. Rice—just what happened to you in your own business."

"Well, I went into the oil-producing business in West Virginia in 1872, and in 1876 I went into the oil-refining business. Immediately I did that my fight with the Standard Oil people began. I established what was known as the Ohio Oil Works, which had a capacity of about 100,000 barrels of crude oil per annum. I found to my surprise at first, though I afterward understood it perfectly, that the Standard Oil Company was offering the same quality of oil at much lower prices than I could do—from one to three cents a gallon less than I could possibly sell it for.

"I sought for the reason and found that the railroads were in league with the Standard Oil concern at every point, giving it discriminating rates and privileges of all kinds as against myself and all outside competitors.

"For instance, I found that the railroads would not furnish tank-cars to any competitors, while the Standard combination was able by its immense wealth to buy its own cars. It owns from 8,000 to 10,000 tank-cars, and the railroads pay them sufficient mileage on the use of those Standard Oil cars to pay for the first cost of the cars inside of three years. A tank-car, when it comes back empty, cannot bring any goods. The transcontinental lines charge $105 to return an empty cylinder tank-car from the Pacific coast to the Missouri

---

1. **Laocoon:** Reference to El Greco's painting of the ancient Trojan priest Laocoon and his sons being crushed to death by serpents sent by the gods.

River, while they charge the trust nothing at all for the return of their own exclusive box tank-cars. This gives the trust an advantage of over $100 a car.

"Again, the independent competitor, like myself, was obliged to ship his oil in box-cars and pay 25 per cent more freight on the weight of the wooden barrels, while no charge at all was made to the Standard Oil Trust on the weight of the iron cylinders.

"Again, the railroads deduct 63 gallons (or over 400 pounds) from the filled capacity of each Standard Oil tank-car, which is the same as carrying 1 1/4 per cent of their rail products entirely free of cost. This went on up to March 15, 1890, and was one of the things that helped to wreck my business. Yet another thing helped to ruin me. The railroads allowed the trust to deliver its oils in less than carload quantities at the same rates as for full carloads. They allowed the trust to stop its cars, whether carrying oil in bulk or barrels, at different stations and take it off in small quantities without paying the higher rates which independent competitors were always charged for small quantities thus delivered. Of course, against such discriminations as these the independent competitor of moderate capital could not contend. He was driven to the wall every time, as I was."

MIGHT HAVE BEEN WORTH A MILLION

"My refinery," continued Mr. Rice, "has been shut down for two years. If I had had a fair and equal show with the railroads my refinery plant to-day would have been easily worth a million dollars and would have been growing all the time. As it is, I am out of the business, my plant is worthless and the men whom it would have employed are either idle or finding other work. These discriminations of which I have spoken are as bad to-day as they have ever been. The public needs to understand that the railroads and Standard Oil monopoly are really one and the same thing. The officers and directors of the Oil Trust are also the presidents and directors of one-fifth of the total railroad mileage of the United States. This is no mere statement of mine. It is proved by *Poor's Manual [of Railroads]*.

"The trust was formed in January, 1882, and from that time the lines were drawn tighter and tighter to oppress and strangle every competitor. It was the highwayman's policy of 'stand and deliver.' I had my choice offered me to either give up my business at a price far less than I knew it to be worth, or to be robbed of it under forms of law. I chose not to accept the price and my business was destroyed. The threat of the trust was made good, and I suppose that is what John D. Rockefeller must have meant when he asked me if I didn't wish I had been wiser and listened to him years ago."

"Well, do you now wish, Mr. Rice, that you had knuckled to the trust and saved your money?"

"Not a bit of it," replied the "ruined" but plucky oil refiner of Marietta. "I have made a fight for principle, and I am neither sorry for it nor ashamed of it. I have been before the courts many times; I have been before

Congressional committees; and I have appeared time and time again before the Interstate Commerce Commission, all the time trying to get relief from these gross discriminations. I confess I have made very little headway as yet. I shall go on with the fight as long as I live, and it may be that I shall never win. But, sooner or later, in my lifetime or afterward, the people of this country will surely take up this fight as their own and settle the question of whether they will rule the railroads and the trusts or be ruled by them."

LAWS NOT ENFORCED

"I have made a mistake, apparently, in supposing that the laws of our country could and would be enforced. I supposed the courts and the other authorities of the land would support me in my right to a free and equal chance in business with all my fellow-citizens, John D. Rockefeller included. But I have learned by long years of conflict and trial and tribulation, which have cost me untold worry and a lot of money, that this is not so; that I have no business rights which the railroads and this great trust can be made to respect.

"The Interstate Commerce Commission is all right in theory, but it does not have the courage of its powers; it suffers from the paralysis of political influences. The laws are neither feared nor respected by the men of many millions."

"Tell me just how the shoe was made to pinch you personally. How did the trust manage to close your refinery at Marietta?"

"Why, that's easy to tell. Every car of oil that I sent into any part of the United States the trust would jump on it and cut the life out of it. I mean to say that as soon as my oil arrived at the point to which it was shipped the trust would cut the price, so that the man who bought my oil lost money on the sale of it. They would not cut the prices to the whole town, but only to my one customer, and the whole town knew of this man's having lost money by trading with me. From that time forward, of course, I could get no orders in that town. . . .

"In 1872, the trunk lines of railroads made a contract with a corporation called 'The South Improvement Company,' which was only another name for the Standard Oil Company, under which the Standard Oil Company was allowed the most outrageous discriminating freight rates. It seems incredible that these contracts should have been made. They not only gave the Standard Oil Company heavy rebates on their own shipments of oil, but gave them rebates on the shipments of their competitors. At that time the Standard Oil Company only had 10 per cent of the petroleum industry of the country, while their competitors had 90 per cent. The rebates allowed to the Standard people were from 40 cents to $1.06 per barrel on crude petroleum, and from 50 cents to $1.32 per barrel on refined petroleum. Thus the Standard Oil Company received nine times as much for rebates on the shipments of its competitors than it did on its own.

"In 1874," continued Mr. Rice, "the railroads forced the independent pipe lines of the country to sell out their plants to the Standard Oil Company at the price of old junk, and gave to the latter, besides, still further discriminating rebates on freight. A circular was issued on Sept. 9, 1874, known as 'The Rutter Circular,' from the freight office of the New York Central and Hudson River Railroad Company, establishing new rates on refined and crude oil. Under this circular the Standard Oil Company was given an advantage of 20 cents a barrel in the freight charges on crude oil connected with its pipe-line system, which the independent refineries did not have. In that same year the Standard company secured the railroad terminal oil facilities of all the trunk lines centering in New York City. Many fortunes invested in the independent pipe lines were wrecked by that move, through no fault of their managers and no lack of business skill, but simply because the Standard Oil officials, acting in collusion with the railroad officials, had established these unfair discriminations in freight rates between the oil that came through the Standard pipes and that which came through other pipes.

"To show you how the rebate system worked in my own case, let me say that in 1885, I was charged 25 cents a barrel for carrying oil from Macksburg to Marietta, a distance of twenty-five miles, while the Standard Oil Company only paid 10 cents a barrel for the same distance. More than this, out of the 35 cents a barrel that I paid the trust actually received 25 cents. In other words, the trust received about two-thirds of all the money I paid for freight."

TRUST "GREATER" THAN THE COURTS OR THE COUNTRY

"You spoke of your having fought the trust for twenty years. Give me a general outline of your encounter with it."

"Well, about 1879 or 1880 I, with others, brought about a public investigation by the Legislature of Ohio as to the discriminations by the railroads of which I have spoken. Nothing came of that investigation except that we proved any number of facts on which further agitation and action was based. I have gone before the Interstate Commerce Commission in many cases trying to get these discriminations stopped. I brought an action through the Attorney-General of Ohio in 1887 to forfeit the charters of two railroads for gross discrimination, and I proved my case. The courts decided, clear up to the highest court, that these two railroads could not make those discriminating charges.

"I obtained at great cost a decree of the Court to that effect. Apparently it was a conclusive victory. In reality it was of no account. The discriminating rates went on as before, and they are still going on to-day. There is no use in trying to stop it. In March, 1892, the Ohio Supreme Court rendered a judgment against the Standard Oil Company, of Ohio, ordering it to discontinue all business relations with the trust.

"The company has pretended to comply with the decree. In fact the trust still exists and the Standard Oil Company, of Ohio, is still a part of it. The way they have got around it is this: On March 21, 1892, the trust resolved on paper to wind up its affairs, and trustees were appointed for that purpose. Then they issued another kind of trust certificate, called an 'Assignment of

Legal Title,' which they made marketable and allowed to be transferred from one holder to another on their trust transfer books, which makes this certificate just as negotiable and salable as the old original trust certificate."

$140,060,000 PROFITS IN SIX YEARS

"In this way the trust is still kept intact. In proof of this fact the trust is known to have declared and paid since March, 1892, up to September of this year, 26 regular quarterly dividends of 3 per cent, and 59 per cent besides in special dividends, or a total of 137 percent—dividends, which, based on their reported capitalization of $102,230,700, amounts to $140,060,000 paid in dividends since its pretended dissolution. No more proof is required that the trust has not been dissolved and that the decree of the Supreme Court of Ohio has been treated with contempt."

"But while you have been ruined, Mr. Rice, it is said, you know, that the mass of consumers have gained—that the price of oil is cheaper, because of the trust. What do you say to this suggestion that you, and others like you, have been crushed for the general good?"

"It is a trust lie," replied Mr. Rice warmly. "There is not the least truth in it. Refined oil for general consumption is as much higher in price as these gross rebates and discriminations amount to, because it is fair to assume, on general principles, that the railroads are making money on the transportation of Standard oil. It only costs three-eighths of a cent a gallon to refine oil. The Standard Oil Trust may possibly save one-eighth of a cent on that, but not more. How much does that amount to in the problem of the cost of oil to the retail consumer?

"Refined oil would certainly have been cheaper right along for the last twenty years but for the Standard combination. If the railroad rates had been honest, and the allowances for rebate had been fair and square to all oil producers and refiners, the mass of the people must and would have got the benefit of it. There is no question that the people have paid millions more for oil than they would have done if the laws against conspiracies and combinations in restriction of fair trade could have been enforced. The price of refined oil is notoriously high to-day compared with the low price of crude oil. There is a difference of from 100 to 300 per cent between crude and refined oil prices, when we all know that crude oil can be turned into refined oil and sold all within thirty days."

"Do you see no remedy ahead for the condition of things which ruined your business as a refiner?"

THE REMEDY—ENFORCE THE LAW

"No, I see no remedy, so long as the railroads are under their present management. I have myself tried every known avenue of relief, and my experience has satisfied me that Blackstone[2] did not foresee the conditions of law and justice now prevailing in this country when he wrote his famous maxim, "There is no wrong without a legal remedy." There is no relief for present conditions in this country except by the Government's acquiring ownership of the railroads. There is plenty of law existing now, but it cannot be enforced. It is a dead letter. The Interstate Commerce act has been law for ten years, and the penalty for the violation of it is a fine of $500 and two years in the State prison. It is violated every day, and it has been violated every day for ten years past, but I observe that no one has yet been sent to prison, and I do not believe that any violator of this law ever expects to be."

Speaking of Mr. Rockefeller, the man who said to him at the public hearing at the New Netherland Hotel, Thursday: "We are getting to be gray-haired men now, aren't we, George? Don't you wish you had taken my advice years ago?" Mr. Rice said: "There is no doubt whatever that Mr. Rockefeller, through the operations of the Standard Oil Trust, is the richest man in the world to-day. I know their business, because it is also mine, and I believe that the Rockefellers are now worth $200,000,000.

"John D. Rockefeller's personal income from the trust and other sources has for several years exceeded $12,000,000 per annum."

2. **Blackstone:** Sir William Blackstone was an eighteenth-century English jurist who wrote the four-volume *Commentaries on the Laws of England*.

15

JOSEPH T. FINNERTY

The Decline of the Independent Craftsman

By 1860, the United States was already among the richest of nations, its prosperity based on producing food and raw materials for its own people and for consumers elsewhere in the Atlantic world. In the half century that followed, it became the world's largest industrial power. While agriculture continued to grow, vast expansion of industry gave the era its particular character. In 1859, 140,000 establishments might have been called factories, most of them tiny undertakings with one owner and four or five workers. In 1914, the United States had 268,000 factories, many of them large firms with hundreds of workers.

Testimony of Joseph T. Finnerty, *Report of the Committee of the Senate upon the Relations between Labor and Capital*, vol. 1 (Washington, DC: Government Printing Office, 1885), pp. 740–46.

Americans who lived through the half century of growth did not need to see figures and graphs to understand what had taken place. Lying over the Lehigh Valley of eastern Pennsylvania, the Mahoning Valley of eastern Ohio, and the Ohio Valley at Pittsburgh, layers of smog covered steel and glass mills. Other than in the most rural and isolated areas, time was marked off by the rude blast of factory whistles summoning employees to work early in the morning and signaling an end to the day. New cities and towns sprang up everywhere to shelter people at the newly opened mines and factories.

Industrial workers experienced these changes in a poignant way. As late as 1870, few Americans worked for wages. Those who did usually labored side by side with their employers. Joseph T. Finnerty recalls here how labor and management worked closely together in the years after the Civil War. Many city artisans still produced their wares by hand and took enormous pride in their work. By 1900, however, about two-thirds of the labor force consisted of wage earners rather than self-employed people, and conditions between management and labor had deteriorated as firms grew larger. "The employer," one laborer observed, "has pretty much the same feeling toward the men that he has toward his machinery."

The rising number of industrial workers, increasingly frequent strikes occasioned by swings in the economy, and growing friction between labor and management became issues for national political debate. With economic statistics still primitive, arguments raged over whether workers were prospering or suffering in the new economy and whether their living and working conditions had deteriorated. In 1882, the United States Senate unanimously adopted a resolution directing its Committee on Education and Labor to conduct a broad investigation into "the relations between labor and capital, the wages and hours of labor, the condition of the laboring classes in the United States, and their relative condition and wages as compared with similar classes abroad, and to inquire into the division of labor and capital of their joint productions in the United States; also, the subject of labor strikes." In hearings held in various parts of the country the following year, the committee collected testimony from an unusually wide array of witnesses: industrialists, reformers, union leaders, workers, clergymen, and an assortment of unclassifiable crackpots. The senators on the panel did themselves great honor by their unfailing courtesy to witnesses, avoidance of partisan bickering, and welcoming stance to ordinary workers like Joseph T. Finnerty, giving the testimony permanent value in considering the impact of industrialism on working people.

QUESTIONS TO CONSIDER

1. To what extent do you think Joseph T. Finnerty's testimony should be read as that of a worker and to what extent as that of a representative of the Central Labor Union of New York?
2. What, according to Finnerty, were the main changes in the life of bronze workers over the previous fifteen years?
3. What effects did doing bronze work have on the workers? Why did they tend to drink heavily?

TESTIMONY INTRODUCED BY THE CENTRAL
LABOR UNION OF NEW YORK

New York, August 28, 1883

Joseph T. Finnerty sworn and examined.

By Mr. George:

Question. Please state your age and occupation.—*Answer.* I am thirty-two years old; I am a brass worker.

Q. How long have you been a brass worker?—*A.* Fourteen years.

Q. What were the wages that you received, say, fourteen years ago—I mean brass workers generally?

Decreased Wages

A. The wages paid in the trade fourteen years ago were from $18 to $21 a week.

Q. What are the wages now of the same class of workmen, with the same skill, and working the same number of hours—if they do work the same number of hours now?—*A.* From $12 to $18 a week; on an average $15 a week.

Q. Do you think $15 a week is a fair statement of the average now?—*A.* Yes, sir; it is rather above than below the average.

Division of Labor in the Trades

Q. Has there been any change in the last fourteen or fifteen years in the mode of working brass, as to the part that the brass worker performs in the business of production in that industry? If so, state what that change is?—*A.* There has been a change. Fourteen years ago the workman was supposed to finish all his own work right through, with a very small exception. To-day the trade is so broken up that it takes eight men to finish the same job.

Q. What do you call a "job"? Explain that?—*A.* Well, to make a water-cock or a chandelier, or a steam-valve, all such things as those are "jobs." The making of a water-cock is broken up now into twelve different parts.

Q. You say that fifteen years ago each man did one of these jobs complete?—*A.* Yes, sir; a man who was making a chandelier made it right through, a valve-maker made his work right through, and a cock-maker made his work right through.

Q. But now I understand you to say that in making a chandelier a man does but one-tenth of the work?—*A.* Yes; one-tenth or one-twelfth, and in making a brass cock or steam-valve he does only about one-fourth of it.

Q. How has that change been brought about?—*A.* Principally by the introduction of machinery for turning out the work faster and cheaper. A man now being employed on the machine gets no chance of learning the trade beyond the particular branch that he works at, and, being kept constantly at that one branch, he becomes very expert and turns that part of the work out quicker and cheaper than it could be done on the old plan.

Q. You say it takes twelve men now to make a brass cock; are there four different machines that are used in making a thing of that kind?—A. There are four different operations and machines; three lathes and a polishing machine. Fourteen years ago there was only one lathe used to do that job but now there are four besides the polishing machine.

Q. How is it in making a chandelier?—A. There are polishers, dippers, buffers, chasers, filers, and all of these have their own special branches and do nothing else.

Q. And each one of them, I suppose, does his part by the aid of a machine?—A. Yes, sir; with the exception of the dipper or bronzer, the man that gives the color. He puts it on by hand. All the others do their parts by machinery.

Q. The man's principal business, then, is to adjust the machine to the piece of brass, or the brass to the machine, and to keep it there till the work is done?—A. Yes, sir; but he has got to exercise a little skill, of course.

Q. Yes; of course, he must have sense enough to adjust it properly, but his principal duty is to keep the brass in the proper position with reference to the machine, and then the machine will do the work; is that correct?—A. That is correct as to one man, the dipper. The others have the machine running and it does the work. Formerly it was all done by hand.

Q. Then the result is that a man who works in brass now with this machinery never becomes a perfect workman—that is, he never learns to turn out a job complete?—A. No, sir.

Q. In other words he learns to do only one-tenth or one-fourth of a job, as the case may be. He does not learn the other parts of the trade?—A. No, sir; he does not.

Q. Of course, this subdivision of labor and this introduction of machinery has added very much to the production of brass work?—A. Yes, sir.

Production Increased—Quality Deteriorated

Q. Explain to the committee, in your own way, the difference in amount between the production of one man, say fifteen years ago, and what one man can now produce with the aid of machinery? Or, take a group of men, four, or five, or six, and explain to us how much value each man can impart to this work by the aid of machinery?—A. I think the best way I can explain that to the committee is to take some one article for an illustration? I will take a chandelier for instance. Fourteen years ago a man working one week at $21 a week would finish a chandelier and it could be sold for $300. Today, with all the machinery and all the branches of the business combined, eight or ten men can turn out thirty-six chandeliers, which can be sold at $150 apiece; making in the neighborhood of $4,000, for the week's work of the eight men.

Q. You say that formerly one man in a week would make a chandelier worth about $300?—A. Yes.

Q. And that now eight men working the one week and using machinery can make thirty-six chandeliers worth each $150?—A. Well, worth from $100 to $150.

Q. Would $125 be the average selling price of those chandeliers?—A. Yes, sir.

Q. So that one man fifteen years ago produced in a week a manufactured article worth $300?—A. Yes, sir.

Q. And now eight men working the same time produce articles worth about $4,350, which makes an average of about $540 for each man's work. Is that about correct?—A. Well, say $450. The other figure might be a little too high. I want to keep right down to the bottom facts.

Q. What was the value of the raw material put into a chandelier fifteen years ago?—A. The chandelier that was made fourteen or fifteen years ago was all solid bronze work—genuine work. The chandeliers that are made to-day are nothing but a mere hollow shell. There is considerable less bronze used in all bronze work now than there was fourteen years ago. Things were made solid and reliable at that time and intended to last, but now it is not so.

Q. About how much less material is used now in the manufacture of such an article?—A. I would say about one-quarter less; but that is only a guess.

Q. Do you mean one-quarter less or do you mean that there was four times as much bronze put into chandeliers fourteen years ago as there is now?—A. That is what I mean.

The Social Condition of the Men Getting Worse

Q. Tell us now, if you can, about the social condition of the bronze workers as compared with their condition fourteen or fifteen years ago, and whether it has grown better or worse.—A. Well, I remember that fourteen years ago the workmen and the foremen and the boss were all as one family; it was just as easy and as free to speak to the boss as any one else, but now the boss is superior, and the men all go to the superintendent or to the foreman; but we would not think of looking the foreman in the face now any more than we would the boss.

Q. Is that so when you are off duty as well as when you are on?—A. Off duty as well as on duty, we would not dream of speaking to him on the street, unless he was a personal acquaintance or some old reliable hand in the shop that might have grown up there. The average hand growing up in the shop now would not think of speaking to the boss, would not presume to recognize him, nor the boss would not recognize him either.

Q. By the "boss" I suppose you mean the owner of the factory?—A. Yes, sir.

Q. You have told us that the wages have been reduced. How is it as to the style of living of the workmen now compared with how they lived fourteen or fifteen years ago?—A. That appears to be about the same as far as house rent is concerned. There was a reduction of house rents some years ago, but they have reached up again.

Q. Are other things about equal?—A. About equal.

Q. Let me see if I understand you fully. You get less wages than you did fifteen years ago?—A. Yes.

Q. Now, do you mean to say that the wages which you receive at present will buy as much of the comforts of life as the wages which you received then would?—A. By no means. I say that the rents are the same as they were fourteen years ago, but the man who had apartments of four or five rooms at that time is confining himself to perhaps three rooms now.

Q. How are the social surroundings of the workingmen now, as to the character of the neighborhoods in which they live; for I have noticed that there are some very fine neighborhoods in this city and some others that are very poor.—A. The bronze workers as a rule live in tenement houses. They are surrounded by the poorest class, the cheapest class; the cheapest element of the laboring people, and they are no better than anybody else.

Q. Was that so fifteen years ago, or is there a difference since that time?—A. It was different then. A mechanic was considered somebody, and he felt that he was somebody; he was a skilled mechanic, and he was considered above the poor laborer on the street.

Q. How is it as to the neighborhoods where they live and the character of their dwellings at present as compared with fifteen years ago; are they better or worse than they were then?—A. If there is any change, it is for the worse; the tendency is to get worse.

Q. Are you a married man?—A. Yes.

Q. How long have you been married?—A. Six years.

Q. State now what opportunities you have of supporting your family comfortably and giving your children such social privileges and enjoyments as are necessary for their comfort and happiness.—A. I have not any other facilities beyond the average workingmen's opportunity to train up their children; that is, to send them to the public schools. We cannot go any further than that on our wages.

Q. Is that about the average condition of the bronze workers in this city?—A. The average is a little worse than my case; the average of the brass workers could not live as well as I do, because their average wages is only $15 a week, while my wages is $20 a week.

Impossibility of Saving from Present Wages

Q. Do the bronze workers who are married men lay up anything, as a general rule?—A. No, sir; they do not. If they happen to be able to make both ends meet at the end of the year they are doing wonders. Of course in every class of people there may be one or two in a hundred that would get rich, no matter what wages they received, but the bronze worker generally saves no money, and if he can keep his family in food and clothes and pay his rent he feels that he is doing wonders.

Q. Before the introduction of this machinery, by which the man has been reduced to being one-tenth or one-fourth of a complete tradesman, how much capital did it take to become a brass worker on one's own account?

Increased Difficulty of Starting in Business

A. At that time a man that had $300 or $400 could start a brass shop himself and make a living out of it, but to-day no man who understands the condition of the trade would start with less than $5,000. He would need that much to supply machinery and start his shop, and then he would have a hard road to travel.

Q. At that time, if a man had a room large enough to work in, and had his tools and a little money to buy the raw material, he could become an independent workman, you say, making his brass work himself and selling it to the public?—A. Yes, sir.

Q. But now the conditions have changed so much that it would take $5,000 even to start a shop and fit it up with the necessary machinery?—A. Yes, sir. There is one thing about brass shops that you had better understand, and that is that almost every brass shop has special patents and its own special line of business, and one does not compete with the others in their lines. In chandeliers, for instance, some make high-priced chandeliers, while others make a specialty of the cheap chandelier, and the regular brass shops each make a specialty of one department. John Mathews, for example, makes soda-water fountains; another shop makes a specialty of injectors, and another of pumps. So that, to a certain extent, each of these shops has got a monopoly of its own line of business. At the same time they may have the facilities for making anything that comes in their line, but their prices are so high for anything outside of their regular work, their specialty, that a man who wants any article will go to some shop that make a specialty of the kind of work he wants; a man who wants a pump will go to a pump factory, or a man who wants a soda-water fountain will go to a soda-fountain factory.

Q. Fourteen years ago, as I understand you, a brass worker might hope, by prudence and economy, to become an independent worker for himself?—A. Yes, sir; but now the trade is controlled by the larger companies. They have their drummers or agents in different parts of the country, and it takes capital to carry on the business in that way; and in order to establish an independent brass shop you have to have your connections made all through the country, something which a poor man cannot do.

Q. So you consider that it is about hopeless for a brass worker now to aspire to the condition of brass manufacturer?—A. Yes, sir; it is hopeless, and I think they will not try it any more.

Q. Has that change any effect on the habits of saving of the working men?—A. No, sir; I cannot say that it has any effect. They are living up to the way they are accustomed to live, and the minute you undertake to drive them down any lower than that there is a row.

Q. What I mean is this: Has the stimulus, the inducement to save by close living, and all that sort of thing been lessened in any degree by the fact that there is now no hope of a workman ever becoming a boss or having an independent establishment of his own?—A. All the brass worker cares about now is to hold his job, and he will put up with any kind of abuse as long as he is not discharged.

Q. But fourteen years ago you say it was different.—A. Yes, sir. He would not stand any abuse at all then, and no abuse would be offered to him then; he was treated as a skilled workman.

Q. Did many of the workers in brass fourteen years ago actually get into the position of independent brass manufacturers?—A. Oh, yes, sir. There are some of our leading firms to-day that started under the different condition that existed fourteen or fifteen years ago.

Q. Were these men more provident or economical or stingy at that time, as a rule, than the workmen are now, when they have no hope of becoming independent workers?—A. The men who are bosses now, and who were workmen at that time, were not saving or stingy, and while they were merely getting journeymen's wages they did not save anything; but when they got to be foremen, then they commenced to save, and when they became superintendents they made enough money to start for themselves.

The Brass Workers' Organization

Q. Is there a labor organization of the brass workers?—A. There is.

Q. Do you belong to it?—A. I do.

Q. Have they ever made a strike?—A. Only once—for eight hours—and they failed to get it. They have never struck for higher wages.

Q. Have you any rule in your organization limiting the number of apprentices that shall be taken into the shops?—A. No, sir. The organization does not attempt at all to interfere with the rights of the shop; we could not do it. In the first place the boss has entire power to hire whoever he pleases—boys or men; he can put in forty or fifty boys, and there is nobody going to object.

Brass Working Unhealthy

There is one thing that I want to say a word about, and that is the health of the men in the trade. Brass working is very injurious to the health. The polishers and the molders are all the time breathing the vapors or the particles that are floating around in the air, and the average life is only about thirty-five years among the molders, and out of every forty molders thirty are compelled to drink strong drink to drown this breathing of the vapors.

By the Chairman:

Q. Do you mean that they have to take it medicinally?—A. Yes, sir; either beer or whisky; in order to cure the effects of the fumes. Before they pour the metal they go out and take a drink; the fumes flow up and around slowly, and the men have to keep in the fumes until they have all their metals poured. Then they are perspiring, and they go out and have another drink; so that they are generally hard drinkers, and the trade makes them so.

Q. Your idea is that the alcohol in the drinks operates as a medicine to counteract the poisonous effects of the fumes that you speak of?—A. Yes, sir; they take it to drown the effects of the fumes. Polishers are always breathing the particles that float in the atmosphere. Polishing and molding are two branches of the trade that are very hard and laborious.

Q. How long have you worked at the business?—A. Fourteen years.

Q. What is your age?—A. Thirty-two years.

Q. How old is the oldest man in your employment that you are acquainted with who has pursued the business continually?—A. The oldest man I know is sixty years of age. There are only very few old men in the trade, which numbers about 4,000 men. I do not suppose you could raise a dozen old men in the trade. As soon as they get up to be a certain age they drop the trade or there is fault found with their work.

Q. Do you expect to follow the business for the remainder of your life?—A. No, sir; I expect to get out of it as soon as I can.

Q. Do you think you would live to be forty-five years old if you continued at your business?—A. I might.

Q. You are a pretty strong, healthy man naturally?—A. Yes, sir.

By Mr. George:

Q. Do your employers generally want apprentices, or are they required in the business?—A. There is no system of apprenticeship such as you mean known in a brass shop. If there are any boys wanted they advertise for them and take them and break them in on a lathe, and that is all there is about the boy business in a brass shop. In every shop, on an average, there is about one boy to four men.

16

ALBERT PARSONS
The Haymarket Riot

Following the Civil War, an explosion of investment in new industrial technologies and infrastructure transformed the United States. Huge industrial fortunes were amassed by "robber barons" like Andrew Carnegie and John D. Rockefeller—the latter estimated to be the richest man in history. Meanwhile, for the majority of factory workers who had created this unprecedented wealth, life was hard, pay was poor, food was scarce, and everybody in the family, including women and children, was forced into backbreaking toil in airless, sunless factories.

Some Americans justified these conditions as the price of progress. Others took to the streets and fought for better pay, better working conditions, and a better life for the mass of workers. What distinguished the Haymarket affair—a violent confrontation between police and protesting workers on May 4, 1886, in the center of Chicago—from the Gilded Age's many running battles between workers and industrialists was the publicity surrounding the arrest, conviction, and hanging of seven seemingly innocent men, whose primary crime had been to provide support to the movement for an eight-hour workday.

The riot at Haymarket Square had been preceded by several days of national protest and industrial action around the May 1, 1886, deadline set by the Federation of Organized Trades and Labor Unions for making eight hours of work the national standard. On May 3, just two days after hundreds of thousands of people across the country had marched for an eight-hour workday, striking workers at the McCormick Reaper Works factory tried to attack strikebreaking "scabs." Police fired into the crowd, killing several workers and inspiring anarchists who were supporting the movement to call for an evening of protest the next day in Haymarket Square.

A group of mostly German-speaking anarchists led the demonstration, which had been advertised as nonviolent and which drew a disappointingly small crowd on a rainy night. Around 10:30 P.M., as the last speaker was concluding, the police marched into the crowd, and somebody hurled a pipe bomb at them. Officer Mathias J. Degan was killed by the explosion, and the police opened fire. The barrage of gunshots wounded hundreds and killed four protesters as well as eight police officers, the latter probably the victims of "friendly fire."

The police never discovered who threw the bomb or why, but much of the world watched in horror as the organizers of the event and invited public speakers were put on trial, convicted, and executed for Officer Degan's murder. The trial appeared to be so patently unjust that seven years later, Illinois governor John Peter Altgeld pardoned several

---

Albert R. Parsons autobiography, 1886.

77

of the defendants. The idea of a May Day general strike, to be held on May 1 each year in honor of the eight-hour day and its martyrs, rapidly spread to the rest of the world.

Albert Parsons (1848–1887) was an Alabama-born writer, publisher, journalist, and socialist. Parsons served on the Confederate side in the Civil War but came to support the Republican Party as he saw former slaves denied rights and freedoms during Reconstruction. He met and married a former slave of mixed ancestry, Lucy Ella Gonzales, and together they moved to Chicago, where both became professional activists around a variety of social justice issues connected to the workers' movement.

A member of the Knights of Labor, Parsons was one of four men convicted on charges of criminal conspiracy and hanged for the violence at Haymarket. The following account is taken from his autobiography, written shortly before his execution on November 11, 1887. It reveals the simmering tensions between workers and business owners in the late nineteenth century and rising popular frustration with the state of the economy.

QUESTIONS TO CONSIDER

1. Do you trust this account of the Haymarket affair? What makes it reliable—or not?
2. What was at stake for Albert Parsons and his supporters in the effort to publicize this version of events? What public ideas about the labor movement is this account trying either to support or to counter?
3. What was the relationship between labor activity and violence?

The Trades & Labor Unions of the United States & Canada having set apart the first day of May 1886 to inaugurate the 8-hour system, I did all in my power to assist the movement. I feared conflict & trouble would arise between the authorities representing the employers of labor & the wage-workers who only represented themselves. I knew that defenseless men, women & children must finally succumb to the power of the discharge, black-list & lock-out & its consequent misery & hunger enforced by the militiaman's bayonet & the policeman's club. I did not advocate the use of force. But I denounced the capitalists for employing it to hold the laborers in subjection to them & declared that such treatment would of necessity drive the workingmen to employ the same means in self-defense.

The Labor organizations of Cincinnati Ohio decided to make a grand Eight-Hour demonstration & street parade & pic-nic on Sunday May 2nd in commemoration of the 8-hour work-day. On their invitation I went there to address them & left Chicago on Saturday, May 1st for that purpose. Returning on Monday night I reached Chicago on the morning of Tuesday May 4th, the day of the Haymarket meeting. On arriving home, Mrs. Parsons, who had theretofore attended & assisted in several large mass-meetings of the sewing girls of the city to organize them on the eight hour workday, suggested to me to call a meeting of the American Group of the International [Workingmen's Union] for that evening in order to make arrangements, i.e. appropriate money for hall rent, printing hand-bills, provide speakers, etc, to help organize the sewing women for 8-hours.

I left home about 11 a.m. and not being able to get a hall, finally published an announcement that the meeting would be held at 107 Fifth Ave, the office of the *Alarm* & *Arbeiter Zeitung*.[1] We had often held business meetings at the same place. Late in the afternoon I learned for the first time that a mass meeting had been called at the Haymarket for that evening, the object being to help on the 8-hour boom, & to protest against the Police atrocities upon 8-hour strikers at McCormicks factory the day before, where it was claimed six workmen had been shot down by the police & many others wounded. I did not fancy the idea of holding the meeting at that time, & said so, stating that I believed the manufacturers and corporations were so incensed at the 8-hour movement that they would defend the police in coming to the meeting to break it up and slaughtering the work people. I was invited to speak there, but declined on the ground that I had to attend another meeting that night.

About 8 o'clock p.m. accompanied by Mrs. Holmes, Mrs. Parsons & my two children (a boy 6 yrs old & a girl 4 years old) we walked from home to Halsted & Randolph Sts. There we observed knots of people standing about indicating that a mass-meeting was expected. Two newspaper reporters, one for the Tribune and the other for the Times, whom I recognized were strolling around picking up items & observing me, they inquired if I was to speak at the Haymarket meeting that night. I told them that I was not. That I had to attend another meeting & would not be there, & the ladies, the children & myself took a street-car for downtown.

Reaching the place of meeting of the American group of the International, it was at-once called to order & the objects of the meeting were stated to be how best to organize the sewing women of the city in the speediest manner. It was decided to print circulars, hire halls, & appoint organizers & speakers and money was appropriated for the purpose, when about 9 o'clock a committee entered the meeting & said that there was a large mass-meeting at the Haymarket but no speakers except Mr. Spies, & they were sent over to request Mr. Fielden & myself to come over at once & address the crowd.

We adjourned in a few moments afterwards & went over to the Haymarket in a body where I was introduced at once & spoke for about an hour to the 3,000 persons present urging them to support the 8-hour movement & stick to their unions. There was little said about the police brutalities of the previous day, other than to complain of the use of the military on every slight occasion. I said it was a shame that the moderate & just claims of the wage-workers should be met with police clubs, pistols & bayonets, or that the murmurs of discontented laborers should be drowned in their own blood.

1. **Alarm & Arbeiter Zeitung:** The *Alarm* was a radical anarchist newspaper edited by Parsons; the *Arbeiter-Zeitung* was the newspaper of the German Working-Men's Party.

When I had finished speaking & Mr. Fielden began, I got down from the wagon we were using as a speaker's stand & stepping over to another wagon near by on which sat the ladies (among them my wife & children) and it soon appearing as though it would rain & the crowd beginning to disperse and the speaker having announced that he would finish in a few moments, I assisted the ladies down from the wagon and accompanied them to Zepf's Hall[2] one block away where we intended to wait for the adjournment & the company of other friends on our walk home. I had been in this hall about 5 minutes & was looking towards the meeting expecting it to close every moment, & standing near by where the ladies sat, when there appeared a white sheet of light at the place of meeting, followed instantly by a load roar. This was at once followed by a fusillade of pistol shots (in full view of my sight) which appeared as though 50 or more men had emptied their self-acting revolvers as rapidly as possible. Several shots whizzed by & struck beside the door of the hall from which I was looking and soon men came rushing wildly into the building. I escorted the ladies to a place of safety in the rear where we remained about 20 minutes. Leaving the place to take the ladies home, we met a man named Brown, (who was well-known to us) at the corner of Milwaukee Ave. & Desplaines St., & asking him to loan me a dollar he replied that he didn't have the change whereupon I borrowed a five dollar gold piece from him. We then parted, he went his way & we started towards home. (This man Brown told of the circumstance the next day; that he had met & loaned me [$5]. He was at once arrested, and afterwards indicted for conspiracy & unlawful assembly, thrown into prison where he has lain ever since!)

The next day observing that many innocent people who were not even present at the meeting were being draggooned & imprisoned by the authorities, & not courting such indignities for myself, I left the city intending to return in a few days (and publishing a letter in the newspapers to that effect). I stopped at Elgin, 2 days at a boarding house when I went from there to Waukeshaw, Wisconsin, a place noted for its beautiful spring & health-giving waters, pure air, etc. At this summer resort I soon obtained employment first at carpentering & then as a painter, which occupations I pursued for seven weeks or until my return and voluntary surrender to the court for trial. I procured the Chicago newspapers every day & from them I learned that I with a great many others had been indicted for murder, conspiracy, and unlawful assembly at the Haymarket. From the editorials of the capitalist papers each day for two months during my seclusion I could see that the ruling class were wild with rage & fear against the labor organizations. Ample means were offered me to carry me safely to distant parts of the earth if I chose to go. I knew that the beastly howls against the Anarchists the demand for their bloody extermination made by the press and pulpit was merely a pretext of the ruling class to intimidate the growing power of organized labor in the United

2. **Zepf's Hall:** An anarchists' club.

States. And I knew that if we were sacrificed by the money maloch[3] it would be with the sole view to making examples of us from which workingmen could take warning by our fates. I also, perfectly understood the relentless hate & power of the ruling class. Nevertheless, knowing that I was innocent & that my comrades were innocent of the charge against them, I resolved to return, & share whatever persecution labor's enemies could impose upon them. Consequently on the night of June 20, I left Waukeshaw . . . & arrived in Chicago at 7:30 or 8 o'clock a.m.

I repaired to the house of Mrs. Ames at No. 14 S. Morgan St. I sent for my wife who came to me and a few moments later, I conveyed word to Capt. Black (our attorney) that I was prepared to surrender. After an affectionate parting with my noble, brave and loving wife and several devoted friends who were present—I at a little past 2 o'clock p.m. June 21st accompanied by Mrs. Ames & Mr. A. H. Simpson to the court house entrance was there joined by my attorney (Capt. Black) we walked up the broad stair-way, entered the court then in session, and standing before the bar of the court announced my presence and my voluntary surrender for trial and entering the plea "Not guilty." After this ceremony was over I approached the prisoner's dock where sat my arraigned comrades Fielden, Spies, Engel, Fischer, Lingg, Neebe & Schwab, & shaking hands with each of them I took a seat among them. After the adjournment of the Court I was conveyed with the others to a cell in the Cook Co. Bastile, and securely locked-up.

What of the Haymarket tragedy?

It is simple enough. A large number (over 3,000) of citizens (mostly workingmen) peaceably assemble to discuss their grievances viz: the 8-hour movement & the shooting, & clubbing of the McCormick lumber-yard strikers by the police the previous day.

Query? Was that meeting, thus assembled, a lawful and constitutional gathering of citizens? The Police, the grand jury, the verdict, and the monopolists all reply: "It was not."

After 10 o'clock when the meeting was adjourning, two (200) hundred armed police in menacing array, threatening wholesale slaughter of the people there peaceably (the Mayor of Chicago and others who were present testified so before the jury) assembled, commanded their instant dispersal under pains & penalties of Death.

Was that act of the police, lawful and constitutional? The Police, the grand jury, the verdict and the monopolists reply: "It was."

A person (unknown & unproven) threw a dynamite bomb among the police. It is claimed by some that the bomb was thrown in self-defense to prevent the slaughter of the people.

Was that a lawful, a Constitutional act? The ruling class shout in chorus: "It was not!"

---

3. **maloch:** Slang reference to a tyrannical power requiring great personal sacrifice.

My own belief, based on careful examination of all the conditions surrounding this Haymarket affair, is that the bomb was thrown by a man in the employ of certain monopolists who was sent from New York City to Chicago for that purpose, to break up the 8-hour movement, thrust the active men into prison, and scare and terrify the workingmen into submission. Such a course was advocated by all the leading mouth-pieces (newspapers) of monopoly in America just prior to May 1st. They carried out their programme & obtained the results they desired.

Is it lawful and Constitutional to put innocent men to death? Is it lawful & Constitutional to punish us for the deed of a man acting in furtherance of a conspiracy of the monopolists to crush-out the 8-hour movement? Every "law & order" tyrant from Chicago to St. Petersburg [Russia] cries, "Yes!"

Six of the condemned men were not present at the meeting, at the time of the tragedy two of them were not present at any time. One of the latter was addressing a mass-meeting of 2,000 workmen at Deering Harvester Works in Lakeview 5 miles away; the other one was at home abed & knew not of the affair till the next day. His verdict is 15 years in the Penitentiary. These facts stand unquestioned & undenied before the Court. There was no proof of our complicity with or knowledge of the person who threw the Bomb, nor is there any proof as to who did throw it.

The rapid growth of [the] whole labor movement had by May first given the monopolists of the country much cause for alarm. The organized power of labor was beginning to exhibit unexpected strength & boldness. This alarmed King Money-Bags[4] who saw in the Haymarket affair their golden opportunity to make a horrible example of the Anarchists, & by "the deep damnation of their taking off" give the discontented American workingmen a terrible warning.

Their verdict is the suppression of free speech, free press, & the assemblage of the people to discuss their grievances. More than that the verdict is the denial of the right of self-defense, it is a condemnation of the law of self-preservation in America.

4. **King Money-Bags:** Derogatory term for a capitalist or business owner.

17

Anti-Immigrant Sentiment in American Politics

By the 1870s, there were roughly seventy-five thousand Chinese in California, almost 10 percent of the state's population. With the end of the gold rush and the disappearance of the railroad jobs, the Chinese became the victims of probably the most well-orchestrated anti-immigrant campaign in American history. Politicians like Denis Kearney organized anti-Chinese political parties and violent anti-Chinese riots that killed many immigrants and diverted attention from the problems of rising inequality and unemployment in the Western states. Finally, in 1882 Congress passed the Chinese Exclusion Act, which took the remarkable step of barring people of Chinese descent from entering the United States even if they were citizens of countries other than China. The figure below suggests the open hostility that became acceptable in the Western states, where Chinese were typically not allowed to vote, to work in dozens of occupations, or to testify in court in their own defense.

QUESTIONS TO CONSIDER

1. Why do you think candidate O'Connell made a connection between the political bosses and the Chinese?
2. In what ways does his slogan, "The Best Coroner and will make the Best Mayor" suggest changes in the nature of mayors since the nineteenth century?
3. Find a current anti-immigration perspective on the Internet and describe the differences and similarities between how the issue of immigration reform was represented in the nineteenth century and how politicians present it now.

Anti-Chinese campaign ad, 1888. *Courtesy of the Bancroft Library, University of California Berkeley, call number x F850 W18 v. 21, 1888*

18

THE OMAHA PLATFORM
Agrarian Protests

Just as industrial laborers in the East organized unions to protest unfair wages and working conditions during the late nineteenth century, so farmers in the nation's agricultural centers bonded together to protect their livelihoods. Falling wheat and cotton prices and rising transportation costs sparked unprecedented levels of agrarian unrest, especially in Alabama, Mississippi, North Carolina, Texas, and the Plains states of Kansas and Nebraska. Farmers formed economic collectives and called for the overthrow of the gold standard of currency to lessen deflationary pressures on crop prices. They believed that bankers and social elites ran the major political parties with an iron fist and disregarded their needs and wants.

The most disgruntled citizens gathered in Omaha, Nebraska, in 1892 and founded the People's Party, or Populists. Advocating a blitz of social reforms designed to empower agricultural producers, the party ran James Weaver in the presidential election of that year. In a powerful showing, Weaver garnered more than a million votes and carried four states. Four years later, Populists threw their support behind Democratic presidential candidate William Jennings Bryan, who narrowly lost the election. The merger with the Democratic Party, however, led to the undoing of the People's Party. Conflicts over power sharing limited its ability to prosper, and it faded by the turn of the century.

The Populists officially announced their convictions at their first convention. In the 1892 Omaha Platform, the Populists articulated their hopes for a new America. They offered a series of proposals to empower workers and farmers and protect them from an uncertain economy—and from a government they saw as uncaring.

QUESTIONS TO CONSIDER

1. Why did the Omaha Platform open with a reminder to readers that in 1892 Americans were celebrating the 116th anniversary of the Declaration of Independence?
2. What grievances did the Omaha Platform lay out?
3. How were these grievances similar to those of union leaders at the time?
4. How did the Populists propose to improve the lives of working men and women?

From George Brown Tindall, ed., *A Populist Reader: Selections from the Works of American Populist Leaders* (New York: Harper & Row, 1966), 90–96.

Assembled upon the 116th anniversary of the Declaration of Independence, the People's Party of America, in their first national convention, invoking upon their action the blessing of Almighty God, put forth in the name and on behalf of the people of this country, the following preamble and declaration of principles:

PREAMBLE

The conditions which surround us best justify our cooperation; we meet in the midst of a nation brought to the verge of moral, political, and material ruin. Corruption dominates the ballot-box, the Legislatures, the Congress, and touches even the ermine of the [Supreme Court] bench.

The people are demoralized; most of the States have been compelled to isolate the voters at the polling places to prevent universal intimidation and bribery. The newspapers are largely subsidized or muzzled, public opinion silenced, business prostrated, homes covered with mortgages, labor impoverished, and the land concentrating in the hands of capitalists. The urban workmen are denied the right to organize for self-protection, imported pauperized labor beats down their wages, a hireling standing army, unrecognized by our laws, is established to shoot them down, and they are rapidly degenerating into European conditions. The fruits of the toil of millions are badly stolen to build up colossal fortunes for a few, unprecedented in the history of mankind; and the possessors of these, in turn, despise the Republic and endanger liberty. From the same prolific womb of governmental injustice we breed the two great classes—tramps and millionaires. The national power to create money is appropriated to enrich bond-holders; a vast public debt payable in legal-tender currency has been funded into gold-bearing bonds, thereby adding millions to the burdens of the people.

Silver, which has been accepted as coin since the dawn of history, has been demonetized to add to the purchasing power of gold by decreasing the value of all forms of property as well as human labor, and the supply of currency is purposely abridged to fatten usurers, bankrupt enterprise, and enslave industry. A vast conspiracy against mankind has been organized on two continents, and it is rapidly taking possession of the world. If not met and overthrown at once it forebodes terrible social convulsions, the destruction of civilization, or the establishment of an absolute despotism.

We have witnessed for more than a quarter of a century the struggles of the two great political parties for power and plunder, while grievous wrongs have been inflicted upon the suffering people. We charge that the controlling influences dominating both these parties have permitted the existing dreadful conditions to develop without serious effort to prevent or restrain them. Neither do they now promise us any substantial reform. They have agreed together to ignore, in the coming campaign, ever[y] issue but one. They propose to drown the outcries of a plundered people with the uproar of a sham battle over the tariff, so that capitalists, corporations, national banks, rings, trusts, watered stock, the demonetization of silver and the oppressions of the usurers may all be lost sight of. They propose to sacrifice our homes, lives, and children on the altar of mammon;[1] to destroy the multitude in order to secure corruption funds from the millionaires.

Assembled on the anniversary of the birthday of the nation, and filled with the spirit of the grand general and chief who established our independence, we seek to restore the government of the Republic to the hands of the "plain people," with which class it originated. We assert our purposes to be identical with the purposes of the National Constitution; to form a more perfect union and establish justice, insure domestic tranquility, provide for the common defense, promote the general welfare, and secure the blessings of liberty for ourselves and our posterity. . . .

Our country finds itself confronted by conditions for which there is not precedent in the history of the world; our annual agricultural productions amount to billions of dollars in value, which must, within a few weeks or months, be exchanged for billions of dollars' worth of commodities consumed in their production; the existing currency supply is wholly inadequate to make this exchange; the results are falling prices, the formation of combines and rings, the impoverishment of the producing class. We pledge ourselves that if given power we will labor to correct these evils by wise and reasonable legislation, in accordance with the terms of our platform. We believe that the power of government—in other words, of the people—should be expanded (as in the case of the postal service) as rapidly and as far as the good sense of an intelligent people and the teaching of experience shall justify, to the end that oppression, injustice, and poverty shall eventually cease in the land. . . .

PLATFORM

We declare, therefore—

First.—That the union of the labor forces of the United States this day consummated shall be permanent and perpetual; may its spirit enter into all hearts for the salvation of the republic and the uplifting of mankind.

Second.—Wealth belongs to him who creates it, and every dollar taken from industry without an equivalent is robbery. "If any will not work, neither shall he eat." The interests of rural and civil labor are the same; their enemies are identical.

Third.—We believe that the time has come when the railroad corporations will either own the people or the people must own the railroads; and should the government enter upon the work of owning and managing all railroads, we should favor an amendment to the constitution by which all persons engaged in the government service shall be placed under a civil-service

---

1. **mammon:** Greed.

regulation of the most rigid character, so as to prevent the increase of the power of the national administration by the use of such additional government employees.

FINANCE.—We demand a national currency, safe, sound, and flexible issued by the general government only, a full legal tender for all debts, public and private, and that without the use of banking corporations; a just, equitable, and efficient means of distribution direct to the people, at a tax not to exceed 2 per cent, per annum, to be provided as set forth in the subtreasury plan of the Farmers' Alliance, or a better system; also by payments in discharge of its obligations for public improvements.

> We demand free and unlimited coinage of silver and gold at the present legal ratio of 16 to 1.

> We demand that the amount of circulating medium be speedily increased to not less than $50 per capita.

> We demand a graduated income tax.

> We believe that the money of the country should be kept as much as possible in the hands of the people, and hence we demand that all State and national revenues shall be limited to the necessary expenses of the government, economically and honestly administered. We demand that postal savings banks be established by the government for the safe deposit of the earnings of the people and to facilitate exchange.

TRANSPORTATION.—Transportation being a means of exchange and a public necessity, the government should own and operate the railroads in the interest of the people. The telegraph and telephone, like the post-office system, being a necessity for the transmission of news, should be owned and operated by the government in the interest of the people.

LAND.—The land, including all the natural sources of wealth, is the heritage of the people, and should not be monopolized for speculative purposes, and alien ownership of land should be prohibited. All land now held by railroads and other corporations in excess of their actual needs, and all lands now owned by aliens should be reclaimed by the government and held for actual settlers only.

EXPRESSIONS OF SENTIMENTS

Your Committee on Platform and Resolutions beg leave unanimously to report the following: Whereas, Other questions have been presented for our consideration, we hereby submit the following, not as a part of the Platform of the People's Party, but as resolutions expressive of the sentiment of this Convention.

RESOLVED, That we demand a free ballot and a fair count in all elections and pledge ourselves to secure it to every legal voter without Federal Intervention, through the adoption by the States of the unperverted Australian or secret ballot system.

RESOLVED, That the revenue derived from a graduated income tax should be applied to the reduction of the burden of taxation now levied upon the domestic industries of this country.

RESOLVED, That we pledge our support to fair and liberal pensions to ex-Union soldiers and sailors.

RESOLVED, That we condemn the fallacy of protecting American labor under the present system, which opens our ports to the pauper and criminal classes of the world and crowds out our wage-earners; and we denounce the present ineffective laws against contract labor,[2] and demand the further restriction of undesirable emigration.

RESOLVED, That we cordially sympathize with the efforts of organized workingmen to shorten the hours of labor, and demand a rigid enforcement of the existing eight-hour law on Government work, and ask that a penalty clause be added to the said law.

RESOLVED, That we regard the maintenance of a large standing army of mercenaries, known as the Pinkerton system,[3] as a menace to our liberties, and we demand its abolition. . . .

RESOLVED, That we commend to the favorable consideration of the people and the reform press the legislative system known as the initiative and referendum.

RESOLVED, That we favor a constitutional provision limiting the office of President and Vice-President to one term, and providing for the election of Senators of the United States by a direct vote of the people.

RESOLVED, That we oppose any subsidy or national aid to any private corporation for any purpose.

RESOLVED, That this convention sympathizes with the Knights of Labor and their righteous contest with the tyrannical combine of clothing manufacturers of Rochester,[4] and declare it to be a duty of all who hate tyranny and oppression to refuse to purchase the goods made by the said manufacturers, or to patronize any merchants who sell such goods.

2. **contract labor:** The practice of hiring prisoners at low wages to perform tasks normally performed by citizens at higher wages.
3. **Pinkerton system:** Reference to the Pinkerton Detective Agency, frequently employed by business owners to spy on and assault labor radicals, strikers, and their supporters.
4. **tyrannical combine of clothing manufacturers of Rochester:** Reference to the refusal of textile makers in Rochester, New York, to negotiate with workers over wages and working conditions.

19

PAULINE NEWMAN ET AL.

Conditions at the Triangle Shirtwaist Company

"I think if you want to go into the . . . twelve-, fourteen- or fifteen-story buildings they call workshops," New York City's fire chief testified in 1910, "you will find it very interesting to see the number of people in one of these buildings with absolutely not one fire protection, without any means of escape in case of fire." At the time, more than half a million New Yorkers worked eight or more floors above ground level, beyond the eighty-five-foot reach of the firefighters' ladders. When the city's shirtwaist makers struck the year before, they demanded improved safety and sanitary conditions, as well as better wages. The strikers did not win most of their demands, and fire safety in particular did not improve.

On Saturday, March 25, 1911, the issues raised by the strike took on new significance when a fire broke out at the Triangle Shirtwaist Company on the eighth, ninth, and tenth floors of a modern, fireproof loft building in lower Manhattan. The number of exits was inadequate, doors were locked to prevent pilfering, other doors opened inward, and the stairwell had no exit to the roof. Hundreds of workers were trapped, and within half an hour, 146 of them, mostly young immigrant women, died. The owners of the company were later tried for manslaughter and found not guilty; they collected insurance to replace their factory.

The fire evoked a public cry for labor reform. More than 120,000 people attended a funeral for the unclaimed dead. The International Ladies' Garment Workers' Union and the Women's Trade Union League, both supporters of previous strikes and safety protests, were now joined by New York City's leading civic organizations in protest meetings and demands for factory safety laws, which were eventually passed by the state legislature.

In a speech to trade union women many years later, Pauline Newman, who became the first woman organizer for the International Ladies' Garment Workers' Union, recounted what it was like to work at the Triangle Shirtwaist Company. Kate Alterman, Anna Gullo, and Ida Nelson testified at the company owners' trial about their experiences during the fire. Rose Schneiderman's speech at the elite memorial meeting held at the Metropolitan Opera House on April 2, 1911, to commemorate the victims created a sensation and began the twenty-nine-year-old Schneiderman's career in labor reform.

Barbara Mayer Wertheimer, *We Were There: The Story of Working Women in America* (New York: Pantheon, 1977), 294–95; Leon Stein, *The Triangle Fire* (Philadelphia: Lippincott, 1962), 55–56, 59–60, 144–45, 191–92.

QUESTIONS TO CONSIDER

1. What were the main abuses that Pauline Newman recounted?
2. How did Kate Alterman, Anna Gullo, and Ida Nelson survive the fire?
3. Would a speech like Rose Schneiderman's help the cause of factory safety, or would it alienate potential supporters? Explain.

PAULINE NEWMAN

I'd like to tell you about the kind of world we lived in 75 years ago because all of you probably weren't even born then. . . .

That world 75 years ago was a world of incredible exploitation of men, women, and children. I went to work for the Triangle Shirtwaist Company in 1901. The corner of a shop would resemble a kindergarten because we were young, eight, nine, ten years old. It was a world of greed; the human being didn't mean anything. The hours were from 7:30 in the morning to 6:30 at night when it wasn't busy. When the season was on we worked until 9 o'clock. No overtime pay, not even supper money. There was a bakery in the garment center that produced little apple pies the size of this ashtray [*holding up ashtray for group to see*] and that was what we got for our overtime instead of money.

My wages as a youngster were $1.50 for a seven-day week. . . . If you worked there long enough and you were satisfactory you got 50 cents a week increase every year. So by the time I left the Triangle Waist Company in 1909, my wages went up to $5.50, and that was quite a wage in those days.

All shops were as bad as the Triangle Waist Company. When you were told Saturday afternoon, through a sign on the elevator, "If you don't come in on Sunday, you needn't come in on Monday," what choice did you have? You had no choice.

I worked on the 9th floor with a lot of youngsters like myself. Our work was not difficult. When the operators were through with sewing shirtwaists, there was a little thread left, and we youngsters would get a little scissors and trim the threads off.

And when the inspectors came around, do you know what happened? The supervisors made all the children climb into one of those crates that they ship material in, and they covered us over with finished shirtwaists until the inspector had left, because of course we were too young to be working in the factory legally.

The Triangle Waist Company was a family affair, all relatives of the owner running the place, watching to see that you did your work, watching when you went into the toilet. And if you were two or three minutes longer than foremen or foreladies thought you should be, it was deducted from your pay. If you came five minutes late in the morning because the freight elevator didn't come down to take you up in time, you were sent home for half a day without pay.

Rubber heels came into use around that time and our employers were the first to use them; you never knew when they would sneak up on you, spying, to be sure you did not talk to each other during working hours.

Most of the women rarely took more than $6.00 a week home, most less. The early sweatshops were usually so dark that gas jets (for light) burned day and night. There was no insulation in the winter, only a pot-bellied stove in the middle of the factory. If you were a finisher and could take your work with you (finishing is a hand operation) you could sit next to the stove in winter. But if you were an operator or a trimmer it was very cold indeed. Of course in the summer you suffocated with practically no ventilation.

There was no drinking water, maybe a tap in the hall, warm, dirty. What were you going to do? Drink this water or none at all. Well, in those days there were vendors who came in with bottles of pop for 2 cents, and much as you disliked to spend the two pennies you got the pop instead of the filthy water in the hall.

The condition was no better and no worse than the tenements where we lived. You got out of the workshop, dark and cold in winter, hot in summer, dirty unswept floors, no ventilation, and you would go home. What kind of home did you go to? You won't find the tenements *we* lived in. Some of the rooms didn't have any windows. I lived in a two-room tenement with my mother and two sisters and the bedroom had no windows, the facilities were down in the yard, but that's the way it was in the factories too. In the summer the sidewalk, fire escapes, and the roof of the tenements became bedrooms just to get a breath of air.

We wore cheap clothes, lived in cheap tenements, ate cheap food. There was nothing to look forward to, nothing to expect the next day to be better. . . .

KATE ALTERMAN

At the Fire

Then I went to the toilet room. Margaret [Schwartz] disappeared from me and I wanted to go up Greene Street side, but the whole door was in flames, so I went and hid myself in the toilet rooms and bent my face over the sink, and then I ran to the Washington side elevator, but there was a big crowd and I couldn't pass through there. Then I noticed someone, a whole crowd around the door and I saw Bernstein, the manager's brother, trying to open the door, and there was Margaret near him. Bernstein tried the door, he couldn't open it.

And then Margaret began to open the door. I take her on one side—I pushed her on the side and I said, "Wait, I will open that door." I tried, pulled the handle in and out, all ways and I couldn't open it. She pushed me on the other side, got hold of the handle and then she tried. And then I saw her bending down on her knees, and her hair was loose, and the trail of her dress was a little far from her, and then a big smoke came and I couldn't see.

I just know it was Margaret, and I said, "Margaret," and she didn't reply. I left Margaret, I turned my head on the side and I noticed the trail of her dress and the ends of her hair begin to burn. Then I ran in, in a small dressing room that was on the Washington side, there was a big crowd and I went out from there, stood in the center of the room, between the machines and between the examining tables.

I noticed afterwards on the other side, near the Washington side windows, Bernstein, the manager's brother throwing around like a wildcat at the window, and he was chasing his head out of the window, and pull[ed] himself back in — he wanted to jump, I suppose, but he was afraid. And then I saw the flames cover him. I noticed on the Greene Street side someone else fell down on the floor and the flames cover him.

And then I stood in the center of the room, and I just turned my coat on the left side with the fur to my face, the lining on the outside, got hold of a bunch of dresses that was lying on the examining table not burned yet, covered my head and tried to run through the flames on the Greene Street side. The whole door was a red curtain of fire, but a young lady came and she wouldn't let me in. I kicked her with my foot and I don't know what became of her.

I ran out through the Greene Street side door, right through the flames on to the roof.

ANNA GULLO

At the Fire

[T]he flames came up higher. I looked back into the shop and saw the flames were bubbling on the machines. I turned back to the window and made the sign of the cross. I went to jump out of the window. But I had no courage to do it. . . .

. . . I had on my fur coat and my hat with two feathers. I pulled my woolen skirt over my head. Somebody had hit me with water from a pail. I was soaked.

At the vestibule door there was a big barrel of oil. I went through the staircase door. As I was going down I heard a loud noise. Maybe the barrel of oil exploded. I remember when I passed the eighth floor all I could see was a mass of flames. The wind was blowing up the staircase.

When I got to the bottom I was cold and wet. I was crying for my sister. I remember a man came over to me. I was sitting on the curb. He lifted my head and looked into my face. It must have been all black from the smoke of the fire. He wiped my face with a handkerchief. He said, "I thought you were my sister." He gave me his coat.

I don't know who he was. I never again found my sister alive. I hope he found his.

IDA NELSON

At the Fire

I don't know what made me do it but I bent over and pushed my pay into the top of my stocking. Then I ran to the Greene Street side and tried to get into the staircase. . . .

[But where Anna Gullo had just exited, there was now a wall of fire.] I couldn't get through. The heat was too intense.

I ran back into the shop and found part of a roll of piece goods. I think it was lawn;[1] it was on the bookkeeper's desk. I wrapped it around and around me until only my face showed.

Then I ran right into the fire on the stairway and up toward the roof. I couldn't breathe. The lawn caught fire. As I ran, I tried to keep peeling off the burning lawn, twisting and turning as I ran. By the time I passed the tenth floor and got to the roof, I had left most of the lawn in ashes behind me. But I still had one end of it under my arm. That was the arm that got burned.

ROSE SCHNEIDERMAN

At the Memorial Meeting at the Metropolitan Opera House

I would be a traitor to those poor burned bodies if I were to come here to talk good fellowship. We have tried you good people of the public—and we have found you wanting.

The old Inquisition had its rack and its thumbscrews and its instruments of torture with iron teeth. We know what these things are today: the iron teeth are our necessities, the thumbscrews are the high-powered and swift machinery close to which we must work, and the rack is here in the firetrap structures that will destroy us the minute they catch fire.

This is not the first time girls have been burned alive in this city. Every week I must learn of the untimely death of one of my sister workers. Every year thousands of us are maimed. The life of men and women is so cheap and property is so sacred! There are so many of us for one job, it matters little if 140-odd are burned to death.

We have tried you, citizens! We are trying you now and you have a couple of dollars for the sorrowing mothers and brothers and sisters by way of a charity gift. But every time the workers come out in the only way they know to protest against conditions which are unbearable, the strong hand of the law is allowed to press down heavily upon us.

Public officials have only words of warning for us—warning that we must be intensely orderly and must be intensely peaceable, and they have the workhouse just back of all their warnings. The strong hand of the law beats us back when we rise—back into the conditions that make life unbearable.

I can't talk fellowship to you who are gathered here. Too much blood has been spilled. I know from experience it is up to the working people to save themselves. And the only way is through a strong working-class movement.

---

1. **lawn:** A thin cotton or linen fabric.

PART THREE

A Society in Flux

Preparing for an American Century

The quarter century before World War I was a period of growing nation-alism, industrialization, and empire. As the "Great Powers"—Britain, Germany, France, Japan, and Italy—consolidated their national economies and created modern notions of national citizenship, they also extended their reach across the seas and into the most distant corners of the world econ-omy. The world became a far smaller place as these global giants carved out huge blocs of the map for themselves.

For the United States, which was not far behind Britain, Germany, and France in its industrial prowess (and a couple of decades ahead of Japan), the consolidation and unification of a vast inland empire from the Atlantic to the Pacific proved successful beyond anybody's wildest dreams. But as the United States began to transform itself from a patchwork of economically linked com-munities to a nation with global reach, there were many domestic adjustments to be made, as well as unsettled social questions about the nation's identity. Americans did what they have always done: they fought publicly over morals, ethics, laws, norms, and standards of behavior.

Nowhere was the issue of national identity more clearly relevant than in the question of whether there would be an American empire to match those of the Great Powers. As the United States wrestled with whether to conquer places like the Philippines, Cuba, China, and Africa—or risk being left out of commerce there—Americans found themselves at odds in defining the appro-priate role for a nation that had itself been born out of an anticolonial war of independence. The Spanish-American War (1898) provided the first big chal-lenge to those on both sides of this battle, as the United States struggled with the postwar disposition of the territories it had won and its growing role in world affairs. Controversy over the publication of soldiers' letters home from service in the Philippines illuminates the bitterness of the national debate and the intense political conflicts over what America's next century would look like.

Domestically, the issues surrounding the questions of what the United States was and what its values, norms, and morals would be continued to be actively and sometimes violently contested. The arrival of nearly fifteen million immigrants from Europe, the Middle East, and Latin America raised the percentage of the population born abroad to about 15 percent, where it hovered until the 1920s. Many of these newcomers had little contact with native-born Americans, and the question of what it meant to make America their home loomed large. The "Bintel Brief" advice column of the *Jewish Daily Forward* suggests some of the challenges the recent transplants faced in adjusting to their new homeland.

During this age of uncertainty and social insecurity, reformers of every variety emerged. The movement for women's suffrage (the right to vote) thrived in this environment of reform and change. Women did not win universal suffrage at the federal level until 1920. But by the time Congress approved a constitutional amendment granting women's suffrage, many states and municipalities had already given women the right to vote, sometimes due to long-standing local sympathies for the cause and at other times due to the work of political activists like Alice Paul and Lucy Burns.

These struggles over what it meant to be an American often took on a more conservative tone. For example, the temperance movement burgeoned during this period. The growing anti-immigrant sentiment found expression in an English-language-only school movement that joined forces with temperance interests to target Europeans, particularly the German American majority in the Midwest that controlled the beer industry. Although German Americans fought the English-only school movement and hired lobbyists like Percy Andreae to combat this combined prohibitionist and anti-immigrant campaign, appeals to reason and tolerance often paled in comparison to pleas to save the family from alcohol. The direct actions of strange outsiders like Carrie Nation, who waged a reign of terror against saloon owners, also contributed to the passing of the Eighteenth Amendment, banning alcohol, in 1919. Fears of social change also contributed to Edwin W. Sims's support of the White Slave Traffic Act of 1910, which sought to protect women from being lured into prostitution but also served as a method by which all premarital and extramarital sexual relationships were criminalized.

World War I raised the stakes of all these national debates as young men from across the country left their communities to become a unified force to fight for the nation. The war exacerbated tensions between established Americans and immigrants and provoked new questions about who was an American, and who was loyal and who was not. Hundreds of socialists and anti-war activists, including Kate Richards O'Hare, were imprisoned for opposing the war.

Another major change wrought by the war was the movement of African Americans to Northern cities. As the letters assembled by Emmett J. Scott reveal, new opportunities in war industries, combined with the depredations of the boll weevil on cotton crops, stimulated a wave of black migration. This population shift would transform race relations and the nature of American cities for generations to come.

POINTS OF VIEW
Suppressing the "Dreadful Curse of Liquor" (1890–1919)

20

CARRIE NATION

Smashing the Evils of Alcohol

Carrie Nation (1846–1911), the United States' most notorious temperance advocate, was born Carrie Amelia Moore in Kentucky to a slave-owning family that was impoverished by emancipation. In 1867 Carrie, whose name is sometimes spelled Carry, married Dr. Charles Gloyd and later gave birth to a disabled daughter. The marriage soon fell apart because of Gloyd's severe alcoholism, which Carrie believed had caused their daughter's disabilities. After her divorce, she worked as a teacher, struggling with poverty and caring for her disabled daughter. In 1877 she married David Nation, an itinerant minister, lawyer, newspaper editor, and failed farmer, who moved them from place to place, finally settling in Medicine Lodge, Kansas. There Carrie became interested in politics and in 1894 helped organize a chapter of the Women's Christian Temperance Union (WCTU).

The WCTU was a women's social reform organization that had won several important legislative victories in Kansas during the late 1880s, including raising the age of sexual consent in Kansas from ten to eighteen, banning the sale of tobacco to children under age sixteen, and gaining women's suffrage in municipal elections. Nation soon became a recognized leader, preaching the evils of alcohol to schools across Kansas, writing a prohibitionist newspaper column, and organizing antidrinking conventions. In June 1900, Nation received what she said was a vision from God that called her to become a "smasher" of saloons.

Six feet tall and 175 pounds, the physically imposing Nation terrified drinkers in saloons with attacks that combined an element of surprise and the frightening spike-ended

---

Carry Amelia Nation, *The Use and Need of the Life of Carry A. Nation* (Topeka, KS: F. M. Steves & Sons, 1905), 126–46.

hatchet she wielded—which had replaced the rocks she used initially in her "smash-ings." A committed women's suffrage advocate, she defended herself in court by arguing that she had been forced into "hatchetations" by having no right to vote on prohibition. In the last years of her life, she published her own newspaper, the Hatchet; *sold souve-nir mini-hatchets from her home, Hatchet Hall; and appeared in vaudeville. She died in 1911, just a few years before the passage of the constitutional amendments that would ban alcohol and grant women the right to vote. The excerpt that follows describes how Nation began her ten-year campaign as America's most famous prohibitionist, vandal, and social reformer.*

QUESTIONS TO CONSIDER

1. Why did women often link alcohol prohibition with women's suffrage?
2. What effects, positive and/or negative, do you think Carrie Nation's gender had on her campaign's success?
3. What did Nation believe were the negative effects of alcohol?
4. Most historians have judged Prohibition a failure. How would Nation answer these critics?

At the time these dives were open, contrary to the statutes of our state, the of-ficers were really in league with this lawless element. I was heavily burdened and could see "the wicked walking on every side, and the vilest men exalted." I was ridiculed and my work was called "meddler" "crazy," was pointed at as a fanatic. I spent much time in tears, prayer and fasting. . . .

On the 6th of June [1900], before retiring, as I often did, I threw myself face downward at the foot of my bed and told the Lord to use me any way to suppress the dreadful curse of liquor; that He had ways to do it, that I had done all I knew, that the wicked had conspired to take from us the protection of homes in Kansas; to kill our children and break our hearts. I told Him I wished I had a thousand lives, that I would give Him all of them, and wanted Him to make it known to me, some way. The next morning, before I awoke, I heard these words very distinctly: "Go to Kiowa [in Kansas], and" (as in a vision and here my hands were lifted and cast down suddenly) "I'll stand by you." I did not hear these words as other words; there was no voice, but they seemed to be spoken in my heart. I sprang from my bed as if electrified, and knew this was directions given me, for I understood that it was God's will for me to go to Kiowa to break, or smash the saloons. I was so glad, that I hardly looked in the face of anyone that day, for fear they would read my thoughts, and do something to prevent me. I told no one of my plans, for I felt that no one would understand, if I should.

I got a box that would fit under my buggy seat, and every time I thought no one would see me, I went out in the yard and picked up some brick-bats, for rocks are scarce around Medicine Lodge, and I wrapped them up in news-papers to pack in the box under my buggy seat. . . .

I was doing my own work at the time God spoke to me; cooking, washing and ironing; was a plain home keeper. I cooked enough for my husband until next day, knowing that I would be gone all night. I told him I expected to stay all night with a friend, Mrs. Springer. I hitched my horse to the buggy, put the box of "smashers" in, and at half past three o'clock in the afternoon, the sixth of June, 1900, I started to Kiowa. Whenever I thought of the consequences of what I was going to do, and what my husband and friends would think, also what my enemies would do, I had a sensation of nervousness, almost like fright, but as soon as I would look up and pray, all that would leave me, and things would look bright. And I might say I prayed almost every step of the way. . . . I got there at 8:30 P.M. and stayed all night with a friend. Early next morning I had my horse put to the buggy and drove to the first place, kept by Mr. Dobson. I put the smashers on my right arm and went in. He and another man were standing behind the bar. These rocks and bottles being wrapped in paper looked like packages bought from a store. Be wise as devils and harmless as doves. I did not wish my enemies to know what I had.

I said: "Mr. Dobson, I told you last spring, when I held my county convention here, (I was W.C.T.U. president of Barber County,) to close this place, and you didn't do it. Now I have come with another remonstrance. Get out of the way. I don't want to strike you, but I am going to break this place up."

I began to throw at the mirror and the bottles below the mirror. Mr. Dobson and his companion jumped into a corner, seemed very much terrified. From that I went to another saloon, until I had destroyed three, breaking some of the windows in the front of the building. In the last place, kept by Lewis, there was quite a young man behind the bar. I said to him: "Young man, come from behind that bar, your mother did not raise you for such a place." I threw a brick at the mirror, which was a very heavy one, and it did not break, but the brick fell and broke everything in its way. I began to look around for something that would break it. I was standing by a billiard table on which there was one ball. I said: "Thank God," and picked it up, threw it, and it made a hole in the mirror. . . .

The other dive keepers closed up, stood in front of their places and would not let me come in. By this time, the streets were crowded with people; most of them seemed to look puzzled. There was one boy about fifteen years old who seemed perfectly wild with joy, and he jumped, skipped and yelled with delight. I have since thought of that as being a significant sign. For to smash saloons will save the boy.

I stood in the middle of the street and spoke in this way: "I have destroyed three of your places of business, and if I have broken a statute of Kansas, put me in jail; if I am not a law-breaker your mayor and councilmen are. You must arrest one of us, for if I am not a criminal, they are."

One of the councilmen, who was a butcher, said: "Don't you think we can attend to our business?"

"Yes," I said, "You can, but you won't. As Jail Evangelist of Medicine Lodge, I know you have manufactured many criminals and this county is burdened down with taxes to prosecute the results of these dives. Two murders have been committed in the last five years in this county, one in a dive I have just destroyed. You are a butcher of hogs and cattle, but they are butchering men, women and children, positively contrary to the laws of God and man, and the mayor and councilmen are more to blame than the jointist,[1] and now if I have done wrong in any particular, arrest me." When I was through with my speech I got in my buggy and said: "I'll go home."

The marshal held my horse and said: "Not yet; the mayor wishes to see you."

I drove up where he was, and the man who owned one of the dive-buildings I had smashed was standing by Dr. Korn, the mayor, and said: "I want you to pay for the front windows you broke of my building."

I said: "No, you are a partner of the dive-keeper and the statutes hold your building responsible. The man that rents the building for any business is no better than the man who carries on the business, and you are 'particepts criminus' or party to the crime." They ran back and forward to the city attorney several times. At last they came and told me I could go. As I drove through the streets the reins fell out of my hands and I, standing up in my buggy; lifted my hands twice, saying: "Peace on earth, good will to men." This action I know was done through the inspiration of the Holy Spirit. "Peace on earth, good will to men" being the result of the destruction of saloons and the motive for destroying them. . . .

This smashing aroused the people of the county to this outrage and these dive-keepers were arrested, although we did not ask the prosecuting attorney to get out a warrant, or sheriff to make an arrest. Neither did we take the case before any justice of the peace in Kiowa or Medicine Lodge, for they belong to the republican party and would prevent the prosecution. The cases were taken out in the country several miles from Kiowa before Moses E. Wright, a Free Methodist and a justice of the peace of Moore township.

The men were found guilty, and for the first time in the history of Barber County, all dives were closed. . . .

I will here speak of the attitude of some of the W.C.T.U. concerning the smashing. Most of this grand body of grand women endorsed me from the first. A few weeks after the Kiowa raid, I held a convention in Medicine Lodge. I got letters from various W.C.T.U. workers of the state that they would hold my convention for me. I said: "No, I will hold my own convention."

Up to this time, no one had ever offered to hold my convention, and I fully understood, although I did not say anything, that the W.C.T.U. did not want it to go out that they endorsed me in my work at Kiowa. The state president came to my home the first day of the convention. I believe this was done, thinking I would ask her to preside at the meeting, or convention. I was glad to see her and asked her to conduct a parliamentary drill. She came to me privately and asked me to state to the convention that the W.C.T.U. knew nothing about the smashing at Kiowa and was not responsible for this act

---

1. **jointist:** A seller of illegal alcohol.

of mine. I did so, saying the honor of smashing the saloons at Kiowa would have to be ascribed to myself alone, as the W.C.T.U. did not wish any of it. . . .

The Free Methodists, although few in number, and considered a church of but small influence, have been a great power in reform. They were the abolitionists of negro slavery to a man, and now they are the abolitionists of the liquor curse to a man. They were also my friends in this smashing. Father Wright and Bro. Atwood were at the convention I speak of. Father Wright, who has been an old soldier for the defence of Truth for many years said to me: "Never mind, Sister Nation, when they see the way the cat jumps, you will have plenty of friends." The ministers were also my friends and approved of the smashing. . . .

I never explained to the people that God told me to do this for some months, for I tried to shield myself from the almost universal opinion that I was partially insane. . . .

[Nation was then sued for slander of the prosecuting attorney, whom she had accused of taking bribes, and she was found guilty.]

The jury brought in a verdict of guilty; but the damages to the character of this republican county attorney was one dollar, and of course I sent him the dollar[;] but the cost which was, including all, about two hundred dollars was assessed to me and a judgement put on a piece of property, which I paid off, by the sale of my little hatchets, and lectures. Strange these trials never caused me to become discouraged, rather the reverse. I knew I was right, and God in his own time would come to my help. The more injustice I suffered, the more cause I had to resent the wrongs. I always felt that I was keeping others out of trouble, when I was in. I had resolved that at the first opportunity I would go to Wichita and break up some of the bold outlawed murder mills there. I thought perhaps it was God's will to make me a sacrifice as he did John Brown, and I knew this was a defiance of the national intrigue of both republican and democratic parties, when I destroyed this malicious property, which afforded them a means of enslaving the people, taxing them to gather a revenue they could squander, and giving them political jobs, thus creating a force to manage the interest and take care of the results of a business where the advantage was in the graft it gave to them and the brewers and distillers.

In two weeks from the close of this trial, on the 27th of December, 1900, I went to Wichita, almost seven months after the raid in Kiowa. . . .

I took a valise with me, and in that valise I put a rod of iron, perhaps a foot long, and as large around as my thumb. I also took a cane with me. I found out by smashing in Kiowa that I could use a rock but once, so I took the cane with me. I got down to Wichita about seven o'clock in the evening, that day, and went to the hotel near the Santa Fe depot and left my valise. I went up town to select the place I would begin at first. I went into about fourteen places, where men were drinking at bars, the same as they do in licensed places. The police standing with the others. This outrage of law and decency was in violation of the oaths taken by every city officer, including mayor and councilmen, and they were as much bound to destroy these joints as they would be to arrest a murderer, or break up a den of thieves, but many of these so-called officers encouraged the violation of the law and patronized these places. I have often explained that this was the scheme of politicians and brewers to make prohibition a failure, by encouraging in every way the violation of the constitution. I felt the outrage deeply, and would gladly have given my life to redress the wrongs of the people. As Esther said: "How can I see the desolation of my people? If I perish." As Patrick Henry said: "Give me liberty or give me death."

I finally came to the "Carey Hotel," next to which was called the Carey Annex or Bar. The first thing that struck me was the life-size picture of a naked woman, opposite the mirror. This was an oil painting with a glass over it, and was a very fine painting hired from the artist who painted it, to be put in that place for a vile purpose. I called to the bartender; told him he was insulting his own mother by having her form stripped naked and hung up in a place where it was not even decent for a woman to be in when she had her clothes on. I told him he was a law-breaker and that he should be behind prison bars, instead of saloon bars. He said nothing to me but walked to the back of his saloon. It is very significant that the picture[s] of naked women are in saloons. Women are stripped of everything by them. Her husband is torn from her, she is robbed of her sons, her home, her food and her virtue, and then they strip her clothes off and hang her up bare in these dens of robbery and murder. Well does a saloon make a woman bare of all things! The motive for doing this is to suggest vice, animating the animal in man and degrading the respect he should have for the sex to whom he owes his being, yes, his Savior also.

I decided to go to the Carey for several reasons. It was the most dangerous, being the finest. The low doggery will take the low and keep them low but these so-called respectable ones will take the respectable, make them low, then kick them out. A poor vagabond applied to a bar tender in one of these hells glittering with crystalized tears[2] and fine fixtures. The man behind the bar said, "You get out, you disgrace my place." The poor creature, who had been his mother's greatest treasure, shuffled out toward the door. Another customer came in, a nice looking young man with a good suit, a white collar, and looking as if he had plenty of money. The smiling bar tender mixed a drink and was handing it to him. The poor vagabond from the door called out, "Oh, don't begin on him. Five years ago, I came into your place, looking just like that young man. You have made me what you see me now. Give that drink to me and finish your work. Don't begin on him."

I went back to the hotel and bound the rod and cane together, then wrapped paper around the top of it. I slept but little that night, spending most of the night in prayer. I wore a large cape. I took the cane and walked down the back stairs the next morning, and out in the alley I picked up as many rocks as I could carry under my cape. I walked into the Carey Bar-room, and threw two rocks at the picture; then turned and smashed the mirror that covered almost the entire side of the large room. Some men drinking at the bar ran at

---

2. **crystalized tears:** A chandelier.

breakneck speed; the bartender was wiping a glass and he seemed transfixed to the spot and never moved. I took the cane and broke up the sideboard, which had on it all kinds of intoxicating drinks. Then I ran out across the street to destroy another one. I was arrested at 8:30 A.M., my rocks and cane taken from me, and I was taken to the police headquarters, where I was treated very nicely by the Chief of Police, Mr. Cubbin, who seemed to be amused at what I had done. This man was not very popular with the administration, and was soon put out. I was kept in the office until 6:30 P.M. Gov. Stanley was in town at that time, and I telephoned to several places for him. I saw that he was dodging me, so I called a messenger boy and sent a note to Gov. Stanley, telling him that I was unlawfully restrained of my liberty; that I wished him to call and see me, or try to relieve me in some way. The messenger told me, when he came back, that he caught him at his home, that he read the message over three times, then said: "I have nothing to say," and went in, and closed the door. This is the man who taught Sunday School in Wichita for twenty years, where they were letting these murder shops run in violation of the law. Strange that this man should pull wool over the eyes of the voters of Kansas. I never did have any confidence in him. . . .

Kansas has learned some dear lessons, and she will be wise indeed when she learns that only Prohibitionists will enforce prohibition laws. That republicans and democrats are traitors, and no one belonging to these parties should ever hold office, especially in Kansas.

21

PERCY ANDREAE

A Glimpse behind the Mask of Prohibition

The idea of an American society without alcohol has been popular since the seventeenth century, when the General Court of Massachusetts first made spirits illegal. During the mid-nineteenth century, Protestant moral reformers combined with an emerging women's movement to advocate for temperance. While this first temperance movement organized its own political party and won some victories, such as a brief ban on alcohol in Maine in the 1850s and the Kansas prohibition of 1881, the movement never gained enough popularity or political power to impose its beliefs on the country as a whole.

By the late nineteenth century, however, the prohibition movement drew strength from growing anti-immigrant sentiment. Nativists looked on disapprovingly as European immigrants, particularly Germans, built community sociality around public drinking

Percy Andreae, *The Prohibition Movement in Its Broader Bearings upon Our Social, Commercial, and Religious Liberties* (Chicago: Felix Mendelsohn, 1915), 9–19.

spaces such as saloons, beer gardens, and pubs. In addition, Progressive Era activists and the growing social work profession identified alcohol consumption as a key factor in the vice, social disorganization, and poverty that was plaguing big industrial cities. This confluence of concerns about drinking gave the temperance movement the political power it needed to enter the national stage and influence elections across the country.

Prohibition was not taken up by either presidential candidate in the 1916 election, since there were "wet" (pro-alcohol) and "dry" (anti-alcohol) factions in both parties. However, the idea of legally barring the manufacture and sale of alcoholic beverages was widely debated. Drugs such as heroin and cocaine, once a part of everyday American life, had been made illegal under the Harrison Act of 1915. Furthermore, hints of the United States' entry into World War I on the side of the British had led to a bipartisan desire to reduce the power and visibility of German Americans, who were probably a majority in the Midwestern states and whose tradition of bringing their families to beer gardens after church made them among the strongest anti-prohibitionists.

Percy Andreae (b. 1858 died ?) made a career out of anti-prohibitionist political action. In the early twentieth century, Andreae, who received financial support from the largely German-owned beer industry in Ohio, organized and led a lobbying group called the National Association of Commerce and Labor, which fought against prohibition. The following passage is taken from his 1915 book, a collection of his writings, letters, and speeches on a variety of topics, including the cultural, economic, and social importance of beer and the beer industry.

QUESTIONS TO CONSIDER

1. Identify three key arguments that Percy Andreae used against prohibition. Would they be convincing today? Explain.
2. What did Andreae mean by "government by emotion"?
3. What audience do you think Andreae was trying to reach with this polemic?

Somewhere in the Bible it is said: "If thy right hand offend thee, cut it off." I used to think the remedy somewhat radical. But to-day, being imbued with the wisdom of the prohibitionist, I have to acknowledge that, if the Bible in general, and that passage in it in particular, has a fault, it lies in its ultra-conservativeness. What? Merely cut off my own right hand if it offend me? What business have my neighbors to keep their right hands if I am not able to make mine behave itself? Off with the lot of them! Let there be no right hands; then I am certain that mine won't land me in trouble.

I have met many active prohibitionists, both in this and in other countries, all of them thoroughly in earnest. In some instances I have found that their allegiance to the cause of prohibition took its origin in the fact that some near relative or friend had succumbed to over-indulgence in liquor. In one or two cases the man himself had been a victim of this weakness, and had come to the conclusion, firstly that every one else was constituted as he was, and, therefore, liable to the same danger; and secondly, that unless every one were prevented from drinking, he would not be secure from the temptation to do so himself.

This is one class of prohibitionists. The other, and by far the larger class, is made up of religious zealots, to whom prohibition is a word having at bottom a far wider application than that which is generally attributed to it. The liquor question, if there really is such a question per se, is merely put forth by them as a means to an end, an incidental factor in a fight which has for its object the supremacy of a certain form of religious faith. The belief of many of these people is that the Creator frowns upon enjoyment of any and every kind, and that he has merely endowed us with certain desires and capacities for pleasure in order to give us an opportunity to please Him by resisting them. They are, of course, perfectly entitled to this belief, though some of us may consider it eccentric and somewhat in the nature of a libel on the Almighty. But are they privileged to force that belief on all their fellow beings? That, in substance, is the question that is involved in the present-day prohibition movement.

For it is all nonsense to suppose that because, perhaps, one in a hundred or so of human beings is too weak to resist the temptation of over-indulging in drink—or of over-indulging in anything else, for the matter of that—therefore all mankind is going to forego the right to indulge in that enjoyment in moderation. The leaders of the so-called prohibition movement know as well as you and I do that you can no more prevent an individual from taking a drink if he be so inclined than [you] can prevent him from scratching himself if he itches. They object to the existence of the saloon, not, bear in mind, to that of the badly conducted saloon, but to that of the well-regulated, decent saloon, and wherever they succeed in destroying the latter, their object, which is the manifestation of their political power, is attained. That for every decent, well-ordered saloon they destroy, there springs up a dive, or speakeasy, or blind tiger, or whatever other name it may be known by, and the dispensing of drink continues as merrily as before, doesn't disturb them at all. They make the sale of liquor a crime, but steadily refuse to make its purchase and consumption an offense. Time and again the industries affected by this apparently senseless crusade have endeavored to have laws passed making dry territories really dry by providing for the punishment of the man who buys drink as well as the man who sells it. But every such attempt has been fiercely opposed by the prohibition leaders. And why? Because they know only too well that the first attempt to really prohibit drinking would put an end to their power forever. They know that 80 per cent of those who, partly by coercion, partly from sentiment, vote dry, are perfectly willing to restrict the right of the remaining 20 per cent to obtain drink, but that they are not willing to sacrifice that right for themselves.

And so the farce called prohibition goes on, and will continue to go on as long as it brings grist to the mill of the managers who are producing it. But the farce conceals something far more serious than that which is apparent to the public on the face of it. Prohibition is merely the title of the movement.

Its real purpose is of a religious, sectarian character, and this applies not only to the movement in America, but to the same movement in England, a fact which, strangely enough, has rarely, if at all, been recognized by those who have dealt with the question in the public press.

If there is any one who doubts the truth of this statement, let me put this to him: How many Roman Catholics are prohibitionists? How many Jews, the most temperate race on earth, are to be found in the ranks of prohibition? Or Lutherans? Or German Protestants generally? What is the proportion of Episcopalians to that of Methodists, Baptists and Presbyterians, and the like, in the active prohibition army? The answer to these questions will, I venture to say, prove conclusively the assertion that the fight for prohibition is synonymous with the fight of a certain religious sect, or group of religious sects, for the supremacy of its ideas. In England it is the Nonconformists, which is in that country the generic name for the same sects, who are fighting the fight, and the suppression of liquor there is no more the ultimate end they have in view than it is here in America. It is the fads and restrictions that are part and parcel of their lugubrious notion of Godworship which they eventually hope to impose upon the rest of humanity; a Sunday without a smile, no games, no recreation, no pleasures, no music, card-playing tabooed, dancing anathematized, the beauties of art decried as impure—in short, this world reduced to a barren, forbidding wilderness in which we, its inhabitants, are to pass our time contemplating the joys of the next. Rather problematical joys, by the way, if we are to suppose we shall worship God in the next world in the same somber way as we are called upon by these worthies to do in this.

To my mind, and that of many others, the hearty, happy laugh of a human being on a sunny Sunday is music sweeter to the ears of that being's Creator than all the groaning and moanings, and *misericordias* [pities] that rise to heaven from the lips of those who would deprive us altogether of the faculty and the privilege of mirth. That some overdo hilarity and become coarse and offensive, goes without saying. There are people without the sense of proportion or propriety in all matters. Yet none of us think of abolishing pleasures because a few do not know how to enjoy them in moderation and with decency, and become an offense to their neighbors.

The drink evil has existed from time immemorial, just as sexual excess has, and all other vices to which mankind is and always will be more or less prone, though less in proportion as education progresses and the benefits of civilization increase. Sexual excess, curiously enough, has never interested our hyper-religious friends, the prohibitionists, in anything like the degree that the vice of excessive drinking does. Perhaps this is because the best of us have our pet aversions and our pet weaknesses. Yet this particular vice has produced more evil results to the human race than all other vices combined, and, in spite of it, mankind, thanks not to prohibitive laws and restrictive legislation, but to the forward strides of knowledge and to patient and intelligent education, is to-day ten times sounder in body and healthier in mind than it ever was in the world's history.

Now, if the habit of drinking to excess were a growing one, as our prohibitionist friends claim that it is, we should to-day, instead of discussing this question with more or less intelligence, not be here at all to argue it; for the evil, such as it is, has existed for so many ages that, if it were as general and as contagious as is claimed, and its results as far-reaching as they are painted, the human race would have been destroyed by it long ago. Of course, the contrary is the case. The world has progressed in this as in all other respects. Compare, for instance, the drinking to-day with the drinking of a thousand years ago, nay, of only a hundred odd years ago, when a man, if he wanted to ape his so-called betters, did so by contriving to be carried to bed every night "drunk as a lord." Has that condition of affairs been altered by legislative measures restricting the right of the individual to control himself? No. It has been altered by that far greater power, the moral force of education and the good example which teaches mankind the very thing that prohibition would take from it: the virtue of self-control and moderation in all things.

And here we come to the vital distinction between the advocacy of temperance and the advocacy of prohibition. Temperance and self-control are convertible terms. Prohibition, or that which it implies, is the direct negation of the term self-control. In order to save the small percentage of men who are too weak to resist their animal desires, it aims to put chains on every man, the weak and the strong alike. And if this is proper in one respect, why not in all respects? Yet, what would one think of a proposition to keep all men locked up because a certain number have a propensity to steal? Theoretically, perhaps, all crime or vice could be stopped by chaining us all up as we chain up a wild animal, and only allowing us to take exercise under proper supervision and control. But while such a measure would check crime, it would not eliminate the criminal. It is true, some people are only kept from vice and crime by the fear of punishment. Is not, indeed, the basis of some men's religiousness nothing else but the fear of Divine punishment? The doctrines of certain religious denominations not entirely unknown in the prohibition camp make self-respect, which is the foundation of self-control and of all morality, a sin. They decry rather than advocate it. They love to call themselves miserable, helpless sinners, cringing before the flaming sword, and it is the flaming sword, not the exercise of their own enlightened will, that keeps them within decent bounds. Yet has this fear of eternal punishment contributed one iota toward the intrinsic betterment of the human being? If it had, would so many of our Christian creeds have discarded it, admitting that it is the precepts of religion, not its dark and dire threats, that make men truly better and stronger within themselves to resist that which our self-respect teaches us is bad and harmful? The growth of self-respect in man, with its outward manifestation, self-control, is the growth of civilization. If we are to be allowed to exercise it no longer, it must die in us from want of nutrition, and men must become savages once more, fretting now at their chains, which they will break as inevitably as the sun will rise to-morrow and herald a new day.

I consider the danger which threatens civilized society from the growing power of a sect whose views on prohibition are merely an exemplification of their general low estimate of man's ability to rise to higher things by his own volition to be of infinitely greater consequence than the danger that, in putting their narrow theories to the test, a few billions of invested property will be destroyed, a number of great wealth-producing industries wiped out, the rate of individual taxation largely increased, and a million or so of struggling wage earners doomed to face starvation. These latter considerations, of course, must appeal to every thinking man but what are they compared with the greater questions involved? Already the government of our State, and indeed of a good many other States, has passed practically into the hands of a few preacher-politicians of a certain creed. With the machine they have built up, by appealing to the emotional weaknesses of the more or less unintelligent masses, they have lifted themselves on to a pedestal of power that has enabled them to dictate legislation or defeat it at their will, to usurp the functions of the governing head of the State and actually induce him to delegate to them the appointive powers vested in him by the Constitution. When a Governor elected by the popular vote admits, as was recently the case, that he can not appoint a man to one of the most important offices of the State without the indorsement of the irresponsible leader of a certain semi-religious movement, and when he submits to this same personage for correction and amendment his recommendation to the legislative body, there can scarcely be any doubt left in any reasonable mind as to the extent of the power wielded by this leader, or as to the uses he and those behind him intend putting it to.

And what does it all mean? It means that government by emotion is to be substituted for government by reason, and government by emotion, of which history affords many examples, is, according to the testimony of all ages, the most dangerous and pernicious of all forms of government. It has already crept into the legislative assemblies of most of the States of the Union, and is being craftily fostered by those who know how easily it can be made available for their purposes—purposes to the furtherance of which cool reason would never lend itself. Prohibition is but one of its fruits, and the hand that is plucking this fruit is the same hand of intolerance that drove forth certain of our forefathers from the land of their birth to seek the sheltering freedom of these shores.

What a strange reversal of conditions! The intolerants of a few hundred years ago are the upholders of liberty to-day, while those they once persecuted, having multiplied by grace of the very liberty that has so long sheltered them here, are now planning to impose the tyranny of their narrow creed upon the descendants of their persecutors of yore.

Let the greater public, which is, after all, the arbiter of the country's destinies, pause and ponder these things before they are allowed to progress too far. Prohibition, though it must cause, and is already causing, incalculable damage, may never succeed in this country; but that which is behind it, as the catapults and the cannon were behind the battering rams in the battles of olden days, is certain to succeed unless timely measures of prevention are resorted to; and if it does succeed, we shall witness the enthronement of a monarch in this land of liberty compared with whose autocracy the autocracy of the Russian Czar is a mere trifle.

The name of this monarch is Religious Intolerance.

FOR CRITICAL THINKING

1. Based on what you have read, how do you think Carrie Nation would have responded to Percy Andreae's key arguments about ethnic exclusion and the economy?
2. If Nation and Andreae had debated each other in public, with which part of the documentary selections would they probably have begun their presentations? Why?
3. From the perspective of the present, which of these two writers seems to have been right? Explain.

22

LETTERS FROM THE BATTLEFRONT AND THE HOME FRONT

Debating War in the Philippines

Although the Spanish-American War (1898) lasted for only ten weeks before Spain sued for peace, the conflict, which was fought across the Caribbean and the Pacific, provoked bitter debates over the United States' role in world affairs that continue to this day. Not since the Mexican-American War of 1846–1848 had a military entanglement with a foreign power so divided the nation. Even after the war's end, controversies raged between pro- and anti-imperialist political camps. Populist William Jennings Bryan and writer Mark Twain were at the forefront of the anti-imperialists. President William McKinley, the Hearst newspapers, and ex–New York City police commissioner Theodore Roosevelt led the pro-imperialist charge.

With respect to the tiny island colonies of Puerto Rico and Guam, postwar annexation was relatively swift and posed comparatively few immediate problems for the United States. In the cases of Cuba and the Philippines, however, the peace was complex and difficult. Of the two, the Philippines proved the more confusing and painful. For pro-imperialists like Senator Albert Beveridge, the Philippine Islands were the key to a future

Philip S. Foner and Richard C. Winchester, *The Anti-Imperialist Reader: A Documentary History of Anti-Imperialism in the United States,* vol. 1, *From the Mexican War to the Election of 1900* (New York: Holmes & Maier, 1984), 316–27.

global empire. Beveridge argued that "the power that rules the Pacific . . . is the power that rules the world. And, with the Philippines, that power is and will forever be the American Republic." The problem was how to establish control over the diverse archipelago.

The collapse of Spanish power had led independence fighters to form a Philippine republic that was not ready to be a "dividend-paying fleet," as Beveridge described the islands, for U.S. power in the Pacific. Led by its president, Emilio Aguinaldo, and supported by a growing educated middle class that had come together in the fight with Spain, the Philippine republic declared war on the invaders in 1899. Thus began the Philippine-American War, which would continue until 1902. By the time the U.S. military fully subdued the Philippines in 1913, more than four thousand U.S. soldiers had died, two Philippine presidents had been hanged by the U.S. Army, and conservative estimates suggest that at least fifty thousand Filipinos—the majority of them civilians—had been killed.

The McKinley administration engaged in an aggressive campaign of press censorship but failed to stop letters sent home by soldiers in the field. The letters were collected by sympathizers of the American Anti-Imperialist League, of which Mark Twain was a prominent member. In 1899 the anti-imperialists published them in a pamphlet that became a political flash point for angry debates over the United States' increasingly interventionist role in international affairs. Following are some examples of these letters and two responses to them. The documents capture some of the pressing questions that emerged concerning the Philippine-American War.

QUESTIONS TO CONSIDER

1. What were the soldiers' primary arguments for why the United States should not have been in the Philippines?
2. In what ways do these soldiers' accounts suggest respect for the Filipinos, and in what ways do they show disrespect?
3. What was Catherine Meredith's primary argument against considering the validity of the letters?

SOLDIERS' LETTERS BEING MATERIALS FOR THE HISTORY OF A WAR OF CRIMINAL AGGRESSION

Private Fred B. Hinchman, Company A, United States Engineers, writes from Manila, February 22d:

"At 1:30 o'clock the general gave me a memorandum with regard to sending out a Tennessee battalion to the line. He tersely put it that 'they were looking for a fight.' At the Puente Colgante (suspension bridge) I met one of our company, who told me that the Fourteenth and Washingtons were driving all before them, and taking no prisoners. This is now our rule of procedure for cause. After delivering my message I had not walked a block when I heard shots down the street. Hurrying forward, I found a group of our men taking pot-shots across the river, into a bamboo thicket, at about 1,200 yards. I longed to join them, but had my reply to take back, and that, of course, was the first thing to attend to. I reached the office at 3 P.M., just in time to see a platoon of the Washingtons, with about fifty prisoners, who had been taken before they learned how not to take them."

Arthur H. Vickers, Sergeant in the First Nebraska Regiment:
"I am not afraid, and am always ready to do my duty, but I would like some one to tell me what we are fighting for."

Guy Williams of the Iowa Regiment:
"The soldiers made short work of the whole thing. They looted every house, and found almost everything, from a pair of wooden shoes up to a piano, and they carried everything off or destroyed it. Talk of the natives plundering the towns: I don't think they are in it with the Fiftieth Iowa."

General Reeve, lately Colonel of the Thirteenth Minnesota Regiment:
"I deprecate this war, this slaughter of our own boys and of the Filipinos, because it seems to me that we are doing something that is contrary to our principles in the past. Certainly we are doing something that we should have shrunk from not so very long ago." . . .

Charles Bremer, of Minneapolis, Kansas, describing the fight at Caloocan:
"Company I had taken a few prisoners, and stopped. The colonel ordered them up in to line time after time, and finally sent Captain Bishop back to start them. There occurred the hardest sight I ever saw. They had four prisoners, and didn't know what to do with them. They asked Captain Bishop what to do, and he said: 'You know the orders,' and four natives fell dead." . . .

Martin P. Olson, of the Fourteenth Regulars:
"We can lick them, but it will take us a long time, because there are about 150,000 of the dagos back in the hills, and as soon as one of them gets killed or wounded there is a man to take his place at once; and we have but a few men in the first place, but we are expecting about 8,000 more soldiers every day, and I hope they will soon get here, or we will all be tired out and sick. . . . This is an awful bad climate and there have been from two to four funerals every day. The boys have chronic diarrhea and dysentery, and it just knocks the poor boys out. You musn't feel uneasy about me, because I don't think there is a Spanish bullet made to kill me; it is disease that I am most afraid of." . . .

Ellis G. Davis, Company A, 20th Kansas:
"They will never surrender until their whole race is exterminated. They are fighting for a good cause, and the Americans should be the last of all nations to transgress upon such rights. Their independence is dearer to them than life, as ours was in years gone by, and is today. They should have their independence, and would have had it if those who make the laws in America had not been so slow in deciding the Philippine question. Of course, we

have to fight now to protect the honor of our country but there is not a man who enlisted to fight these people, and should the United States annex these islands, none but the most bloodthirsty will claim himself a hero. This is not a lack of patriotism, but my honest belief." . . .

Tom Crandall, of the Nebraska Regiment:
"The boys are getting sick of fighting these heathens, and all say we volunteered to fight Spain, not heathens. Their patriotism is wearing off. We all want to come home very bad. If I ever get out of this army I will never get into another. They will be fighting four hundred years, and then never whip these people, for there are not enough of us to follow them up. . . . The people of the United States ought to raise a howl and have us sent home."

Captain Elliott, of the Kansas Regiment, February 27th:
"Talk about war being 'hell,' this war beats the hottest estimate ever made of that locality. Caloocan was supposed to contain seventeen thousand in-habitants. The Twentieth Kansas swept through it, and now Caloocan con-tains not one living native. Of the buildings, the battered walls of the great church and dismal prison alone remain. The village of Maypaja, where our first fight occurred on the night of the fourth, had five thousand people in it at that day,—now not one stone remains upon top of another. You can only faintly imagine this terrible scene of desolation. War is worse than hell."

Leonard F. Adams, of Ozark, in the Washington Regiment:
"I don't know how many men, women, and children the Tennessee boys did kill. They would not take any prisoners. One company of the Tennessee boys was sent into headquarters with thirty prisoners, and got there with about a hundred chickens and no prisoners." . . .

Theodore Conley, of a Kansas Regiment:
"Talk about dead indians! Why, they are lying everywhere. The trenches are full of them. . . . More harrowing still: think of the brave men from this country, men who were willing to sacrifice their lives for the freedom of Cuba, dying in battle and from disease, in a war waged for the purpose of conquer-ing a people who are fighting as the Cubans fought against Spanish tyranny and misrule. There is not a feature of the whole miserable business that a patriotic American citizen, one who loves to read of the brave deeds of the American colonists in the splendid struggle for American independence, can look upon with complacency, much less with pride. This war is reversing his-tory. It places the American people and the government of the United States in the position occupied by Great Britain in 1776. It is an utterly causeless and defenceless war, and it should be abandoned by this government without de-lay. The longer it is continued, the greater crime it becomes—a crime against human liberty as well as against Christianity and civilization. . . . Those not killed in the trenches were killed when they tried to come out. . . . No wonder

they can't shoot, with that light thrown on them; shells bursting and infantry pouring in lead all the time. Honest to God, I feel sorry for them."

F. A. Blake, of California, in charge of the Red Cross:
"I never saw such execution in my life, and hope never to see such sights as met me on all sides as our little corps passed over the field, dressing wounded. Legs and arms nearly demolished; total decapitation; horrible wounds in chests and abdomens, showing the determination of our soldiers to kill every native in sight. The Filipinos did stand their ground heroically, contesting every inch, but proved themselves unable to stand the deadly fire of our well-trained and eager boys in blue. I counted seventy-nine dead natives in one small field, and learn that on the other side of the river their bodies were stacked up for breastworks." . . .

Anthony Michea, of the Third Artillery:
"We bombarded a place called Malabon, and then we went in and killed every native we met, men, women, and children. It was a dreadful sight, the killing of the poor creatures. The natives captured some of the Americans and literally hacked them to pieces, so we got orders to spare no one."

Lieut. Henry Page, of the Regular Army:
"After a stay of about eight months among these people, during which time no opportunity has been lost to study their qualities, I find myself still unable to express a decided opinion about the matter, but I can unreservedly affirm that the more evidence collected the greater my respect for the native and his capacities. . . . The recent battle of February 5th was somewhat of a revelation to Americans. They expected the motley horde to run at the firing of the first gun. It was my good fortune to be placed—about ten hours afterward—near the spot where this first gun was fired. I found the Americans still held in check. Our artillery then began to assail the enemy's position, and it was only by the stoutest kind of fighting that the Tennessee and Nebraska Regiments were able to drive them out. The Filipinos' retreat, however, was more creditable than their stand. Perfect order prevailed. One of their companies would hold our advance until the company in their rear could retire and reload, when in turn this company would stand until the former had retired and reloaded. A frequent exclamation along our lines was: 'Haven't these little fellows got grit?' They had more than grit—they had organization. . . . In each town a church, a convent or priest's home, a 'tribunal,' which is courthouse, jail, and record office all in one, and a school, constitute the public buildings. The schools were neat, substantial buildings, which testified that the Spanish made an honest effort to educate the masses. The Filipino is very anxious to learn, and the new government of Aguinaldo used every effort to start afresh these schools. The number of natives who speak Spanish as well as their native tongue, and who also know how to read and write, is remarkable. No school teacher has been appointed in San Jose, and the school buildings

are held by the American officers. In spite of this discouragement there is a private school flourishing in a native hut."

Charles R. Wyland, Company C, Washington Volunteers, March 27:
"This war is something terrible. You see sights you could hardly believe, and a life is hardly worth a thought. I have seen a shell from our artillery strike a bunch of Filipinos, and then they would go scattering through the air, legs, arms, heads, all disconnected. And such sights actually make our boys laugh and yell, 'That shot was a peach.' A white man seems to forget that he is human. . . . Hasty intrenchments were thrown up to protect our troops from this fire, the bodies of many slain Filipinos being used as a foundation for this purpose, intrenching tools being scarce. Other bodies were thrown into the deep cuts across the road, and with a little top dressing of dirt made a good road again for the Hotchkiss gun serving with the left wing to advance to a position commanding the bridge, where the regiment was to force a crossing in the morning. Many other bodies were thrown into the trenches and covered with dirt, while others, scattered about in the woods and fields over which the battle-line swept, still remain unburied."

Albert Brockway, Company M, Twentieth Kansas:
"We must all bear our portion of the shame and disgrace which this great political war has forced upon us. Unless speedily remedied it will be, or at least should be, the death-knell of the administration. To those who intend to make the army their profession, and have more regard for personal interests and glory (?) than for the country's welfare it is a grand opportunity. I wonder how reports are given in the United States of matters here! The press censorship will not allow our papers to publish accounts of deaths, etc., hence we, on one end of the line, scarcely know how the others are getting along." . . .

A. A. Barnes, Battery G, Third United States Artillery:
"The town of Titatia was surrendered to us a few days ago, and two companies occupy the same. Last night one of our boys was found shot and his stomach cut open. Immediately orders were received from General Wheaton to burn the town and kill every native in sight, which was done to a finish. About one thousand men, women, and children were reported killed. I am probably growing hard-hearted, for I am in my glory when I can sight my gun on some dark-skin and pull the trigger. Let me advise you a little, and should a call for volunteers be made for this place, do not be so patriotic as to come here. Tell all my inquiring friends that I am doing everything I can for Old Glory and for America I love so well." . . .

Rev. C. F. Dole writes:
"I have a letter from a father in another State whose son is a soldier at Manila:
" 'The longer I stay here, and the more I see and think of the matter, the more fully convinced I am that the American nation was and is making a

blunder. I do not believe the United States is equal to the task of conquering this people, or even governing them afterwards. . . . I don't think I would miss the truth if I said more noncombatants have been killed than actual native soldiers. I don't believe the people in the United States understand the question or the condition of things here or the inhuman warfare now being carried on. Talk about Spanish cruelty: they are not in with the Yank. Even the Spanish are shocked. Of course I don't expect to have war without death and destruction, but I do expect that when an enemy gets down on his knees and begs for his life that he won't be shot in cold blood. But it is a fact that the order was not to take a prisoner, and I have seen enough to almost make me ashamed to call myself an American.'"

Raymond Ellis, late corporal in the Seventeenth United States Infantry, makes some unusual charges in a letter to his father. He was in the Santiago campaign, and after returning to the States was sent to the hospital at the Columbus (O.) barracks. He had hardly recovered from his illness, and had but three months to serve of his enlistment, when the regiment was ordered to Manila. Corporal Ellis asked permission to remain, as his time was almost up. This was refused, and he arrived at Manila just before his time expired. On the date of expiration he says he asked for a discharge and transportation home. The commanding officer wanted him to re-enlist, and on his failure to do so, refused transportation home, and he had to work his way on a transport which has recently arrived in San Francisco. . . .

Harvey Stark, of the Hospital Corps:
    "I am a pronounced anti-expansionist, and the boys are all anxious to come home. Out of twenty-five thousand troops on the island, I do not think that a regiment of them would care to re-enlist, providing their time was out." . . .

TO THE EDITOR OF *CITY AND STATE*

Your correspondent, Catherine K. Meredith, who, I fear, is as ready to believe idle tales in favor of the Administration as she thinks you are to believe tales against it, will do well to write to the Secretary of the Anti-Imperialist League, 44 Kilby Street, Boston, for the pamphlet, "Soldiers' Letters," if she is a seeker after truth.
    This contains more than fifty extracts from officers' and privates' letters, written at the seat of war, most of them bearing their writers' names, and containing most definite and circumstantial statements of "massacres" and the murder of prisoners by order of officers.

. . .

    These letters carry with them every evidence of authenticity, and the painful proof that they were in many cases written by men whose sense of duty and loyalty to the country does not blind them to the vileness of the work in which they are involved, and of which they would gladly be rid.

In the light which they throw upon the brutalities which our criminal aggression necessarily carries with it, Secretary Long's[1] late assurance that the Government is deeply concerned in carrying "the blessings of our civilization" and a "generous happy life" to the Filipinos, reads like trenchant irony.

W. HENRY WINSLOW.
City and State, June 8, 1899

TO THE EDITOR OF *CITY AND STATE*

Being, as I hope, "a seeker after truth," I have followed the advice of Mr. W. Henry Winslow, in your journal of June 8th, sent to Boston for the pamphlet published by the Anti-Imperialist League, and carefully read "Soldiers' Letters." The "more than fifty extracts from officers' and privates' letters" mentioned by Mr. Winslow dwindle to forty-three by actual count, and of these only fifteen allude to the so-called "massacres." The majority of the letters are written by homesick and discontented soldiers, from whom the best army is never absolutely free.

Harvey Stark writes: "I am a pronounced anti-expansionist, and the boys are all anxious to come home." Colonel Stotzenberg: "I am tired of fighting, and I am tired of seeing my men killed." And more letters to the same effect.

So far from these letters carrying with them every evidence of authenticity, as claimed by Mr. Winslow, just the reverse effect is produced, it seems to me, and for these reasons: The names of the "reputable newspapers" from whom the letters have been obtained are not given; the writers are unidentified and their statements unsupported; they are at variance with other letters from officers of the regular army in the Philippines, some of which I have read.

I still hold, Mr. Winslow to the contrary notwithstanding, that these "idle tales" are not worthy of belief when contradicted by the definite statements of Secretary Long (who, it would seem, ought to be believed in Boston, even by anti-expansionists) and by the members of the United States Philippine Commission.

But, granting all the letters to be genuine and worthy of credit, what does their united testimony amount to? Forty-three letters in all, many of them of mere childish discontent, from an army of 75,000 men! Just about the proportion at home between the anti-expansionists and the expansionists. . . .

CATHERINE K. MEREDITH
City and State, June 29, 1899

---

1. **Secretary Long:** John Davis Long, Secretary of the Navy (1897–1902).

23

ABRAHAM CAHAN

A Bintel Brief

Years before Ann Landers, Dear Abby, Ask Amy, and other contemporary advice columns, there was "A Bintel Brief." In 1906 the Jewish Daily Forward, *a Yiddish-language newspaper addressing the more than half a million Jewish immigrants in New York City, began running an advice column under a title that translates as "a bundle of letters." The column spoke to Jews from Russia, Hungary, Poland, Romania, and the Middle East, all with different traditions and dialects as well as various skills and opportunities, struggling with one another as well as with their new circumstances in overcrowded urban neighborhoods. These immigrants and their neighborhoods were among the subjects favored by reform journalist Jacob Riis, whose images of poverty so influenced Americans' vision of U.S. cities. (See the "The Industrial City" on page 53.)*

The editor of the Jewish Daily Forward *was Abraham Cahan (1860–1951), who also wrote several novels about immigrant life. Cahan contributed some of the letters for the column as well as the responses. "A Bintel Brief" gave advice on all kinds of personal problems. These excerpts from the column's early years offer fascinating glimpses into Jewish immigrant life at the turn of the century and speak of issues central to the experiences of most immigrants.*

QUESTIONS TO CONSIDER

1. What were the major tensions of immigrant life as revealed in the letters?
2. What conflicts do you detect between different types of immigrant Jews, and what conflicts do you see between Jews and the host society? How do these conflicts differ?
3. How does Abraham Cahan's advice compare to that given today in similar newspaper columns and daytime talk shows?

Worthy Editor,

We are a small family who recently came to the "Golden Land." My husband, my boy and I are together, and our daughter lives in another city.

Isaac Metzker, *A Bintel Brief: Sixty Years of Letters from the Lower East Side to the* Jewish Daily Forward (New York: Doubleday, 1971), 42–44, 49–51, 54–55, 58–59, 63–64, 68–70, 109–10, 117–18.

I had opened a grocery store here, but soon lost all my money. In Europe we were in business; we had people working for us and paid them well. In short, there we made a good living but here we are badly off.

My husband became a peddler. The "pleasure" of knocking on doors and ringing bells cannot be known by anyone but a peddler. If anybody does buy anything "on time," a lot of the money is lost, because there are some people who never intend to pay. In addition, my husband has trouble because he has a beard, and because of the beard he gets beaten up by the hoodlums.

Also we have problems with our boy, who throws money around. He works every day till late at night in a grocery for three dollars a week. I watch over him and give him the best because I'm sorry that he has to work so hard. But he costs me plenty and he borrows money from everybody. He has many friends and owes them all money. I get more and more worried as he takes here and borrows there. All my talking doesn't help. I am afraid to chase him away from home because he might get worse among strangers. I want to point out that he is well versed in Russian and Hebrew and he is not a child any more, but his behavior is not that of an intelligent adult.

I don't know what to do. My husband argues that he doesn't want to continue peddling. He doesn't want to shave off his beard, and it's not fitting for such a man to do so. The boy wants to go to his sister, but that's a twenty-five dollar fare. What can I do? I beg you for a suggestion.

Your Constant reader,
F.L.

Answer:

Since her husband doesn't earn a living anyway, it would be advisable for all three of them to move to the city where the daughter is living. As for the beard, we feel that if the man is religious and the beard is dear to him because the Jewish law does not allow him to shave it off, it's up to him to decide. But if he is not religious, and the beard interferes with his earnings, it should be sacrificed.

Dear Editor,

For a long time I worked in a shop with a Gentile girl, and we began to go out together and fell in love. We agreed that I would remain a Jew and she a Christian. But after we had been married for a year, I realized that it would not work.

I began to notice that whenever one of my Jewish friends comes to the house, she is displeased. Worse yet, when she sees me reading a Jewish newspaper her face changes color. She says nothing, but I can see that she has changed. I feel that she is very unhappy with me, though I know she loves me. She will soon become a mother, and she is more dependent on me than ever.

She used to be quite liberal, but lately she is being drawn back to the Christian religion. She gets up early Sunday mornings, runs to church and comes home with eyes swollen from crying. When we pass a church now and then, she trembles.

Dear Editor, advise me what to do now. I could never convert, and there's no hope for me to keep her from going to church. What can we do now?

Thankfully,
A Reader

Answer:

Unfortunately, we often hear of such tragedies, which stem from marriages between people of different worlds. It's possible that if this couple were to move to a Jewish neighborhood, the young man might have more influence on his wife.

Dear Editor,

I am a girl from Galicia and in the shop where I work I sit near a Russian Jew with whom I was always on good terms. Why should one worker resent another?

But once, in a short debate, he stated that all Galicians were no good. When I asked him to repeat it, he answered that he wouldn't retract a word, and that he wished all Galician Jews dead.

I was naturally not silent in the face of such a nasty expression. He maintained that only Russian Jews are fine and intelligent. According to him, the *Galitzianer* are inhuman savages, and he had the right to speak of them so badly.

Dear Editor, does he really have a right to say this? Have the Galician Jews not sent enough money for the unfortunate sufferers of the pogroms in Russia? When a Gentile speaks badly of Jews, it's immediately printed in the newspapers and discussed hotly everywhere. But that a Jew should express himself so about his own brothers is nothing? Does he have a right? Are Galicians really so bad? And does he, the Russian, remain fine and intelligent in spite of such expressions?

As a reader of your worthy newspaper, I hope you will print my letter and give your opinion.

With thanks in advance,
B.M.

Answer:

The Galician Jews are just as good and bad as people from other lands. If the Galicians must be ashamed of the foolish and evil ones among them, then the Russians, too, must hide their heads in shame because among them there is such an idiot as the acquaintance of our letter writer.

Worthy Editor,

I am eighteen years old and a machinist by trade. During the past year I suffered a great deal, just because I am a Jew.

It is common knowledge that my trade is run mainly by the Gentiles and, working among the Gentiles, I have seen things that cast a dark shadow on the American labor scene. Just listen:

I worked in a shop in a small town in New Jersey, with twenty Gentiles. There was one other Jew besides me, and both of us endured the greatest hardships. That we were insulted goes without saying. At times we were even beaten up. We work in an area where there are many factories, and once, when we were leaving the shop, a group of workers fell on us like hoodlums and beat us. To top it off, we and one of our attackers were arrested. The hoodlum was let out on bail, but we, beaten and bleeding, had to stay in jail. At the trial, they fined the hoodlum eight dollars and let him go free.

After that I went to work on a job in Brooklyn. As soon as they found out that I was a Jew they began to torment me so that I had to leave the place. I have already worked at many places, and I either have to leave, voluntarily, or they fire me because I am a Jew.

Till now, I was alone and didn't care. At this trade you can make good wages, and I had enough. But now I've brought my parents over, and of course I have to support them.

Lately I've been working on one job for three months and I would be satisfied, but the worm of anti-Semitism is beginning to eat at my bones again. I go to work in the morning as to Gehenna,[1] and I run away at night as from a fire. It's impossible to talk to them because they are common boors, so-called "American sports." I have already tried in various ways, but the only way to deal with them is with a strong fist. But I am too weak and there are too many.

Perhaps you can help me in this matter. I know it is not an easy problem.

Your reader,
E.H.

Answer:

In the answer, the Jewish machinist is advised to appeal to the United Hebrew Trades and ask them to intercede for him and bring up charges before the Machinists Union about this persecution. His attention is also drawn to the fact that there are Gentile factories where Jews and Gentiles work together and get along well with each other.

Finally it is noted that people will have to work long and hard before this senseless racial hatred can be completely uprooted.

1. **Gehenna:** Hell.

Worthy Editor,

I was born in America and my parents gave me a good education. I studied
Yiddish and Hebrew, finished high school, completed a course in bookkeep-
ing and got a good job. I have many friends, and several boys have already
proposed to me.

Recently I went to visit my parents' home in Russian Poland. My mother's
family in Europe had invited my parents to a wedding, but instead of going
themselves, they sent me. I stayed at my grandmother's with an aunt and
uncle and had a good time. Our European family, like my parents, are quite
well off and they treated me well. They indulged me in everything and I stayed
with them six months.

It was lively in the town. There were many organizations and clubs and
they all accepted me warmly, looked up to me—after all, I was a citizen of
the free land, America. Among the social leaders of the community was an
intelligent young man, a friend of my uncle's, who took me to various gath-
erings and affairs.

He was very attentive, and after a short while he declared his love for me
in a long letter. I had noticed that he was not indifferent to me, and I liked
him as well. I looked up to him and respected him, as did all the townsfolk.
My family became aware of it, and when they spoke to me about him, I could
see they thought it was a good match.

He was handsome, clever, educated, a good talker and charmed me, but I
didn't give him a definite answer. As my love for him grew, however, I wrote
to my parents about him, and then we became officially engaged.

A few months later we both went to my parents in the States and they
received him like their own son. My bridegroom immediately began to learn
English and tried to adjust to the new life. Yet when I introduced him to my
friends they looked at him with disappointment. "This 'greenhorn'² is your
fiancé?" they asked. I told them what a big role he played in his town, how
everyone respected him, but they looked at me as if I were crazy and scoffed
at my words.

At first I thought, Let them laugh, when they get better acquainted with
him they'll talk differently. In time, though, I was affected by their talk and
began to think, like them, that he really was a "greenhorn" and acted like one.

In short, my love for him is cooling off gradually. I'm suffering terribly
because my feelings for him are changing. In Europe, where everyone admired
him and all the girls envied me, he looked different. But, here, I see before me
another person.

I haven't the courage to tell him, and I can't even talk about it to my parents. He still loves me with all his heart, and I don't know what to do. I choke

2. **greenhorn:** A new arrival (such as a recent immigrant) who is inexperienced with local
   ways of life.

it all up inside myself, and I beg you to help me with advice in my desperate situation.

Respectfully,
A Worried Reader

Answer:

The writer would make a grave mistake if she were to separate from her bridegroom now. She must not lose her common sense and be influenced by the foolish opinions of her friends who divided the world into "greenhorns" and real Americans.

We can assure the writer that her bridegroom will learn English quickly. He will know American history and literature as well as her friends do, and be a better American than they. She should be proud of his love and laugh at those who call him "greenhorn."

Dear Editor,

Since I do not want my conscience to bother me, I ask you to decide whether a married woman has the right to go to school two evenings a week. My husband thinks I have no right to do this.

I admit that I cannot be satisfied to be just a wife and mother. I am still young and I want to learn and enjoy life. My children and my house are not neglected, but I go to evening high school twice a week. My husband is not pleased and when I come home at night and ring the bell, he lets me stand outside a long time intentionally, and doesn't hurry to open the door.

Now he has announced a new decision. Because I send out the laundry to be done, it seems to him that I have too much time for myself, even enough to go to school. So from now on he will count out every penny for anything I have to buy for the house, so I will not be able to send out the laundry any more. And when I have to do the work myself there won't be any time left for such "foolishness" as going to school. I told him that I'm willing to do my own washing but that I would still be able to find time for study.

When I am alone with my thoughts, I feel I may not be right. Perhaps I should not go to school. I want to say that my husband is an intelligent man and he wanted to marry a woman who was educated. The fact that he is intelligent makes me more annoyed with him. He is in favor of the emancipation of women, yet in real life he acts contrary to his beliefs.

Awaiting your opinion on this, I remain,

Your reader,
The Discontented Wife

Answer:

Since this man is intelligent and an adherent of the women's emancipation movement, he is scolded severely in the answer for wanting to keep his wife so enslaved. Also the opinion is expressed that the wife absolutely has the right to go to school two evenings a week.

Dear Editor,

I plead with you to open your illustrious newspaper and take in my "Bintel Brief" in which I write about my great suffering.

A long gloomy year, three hundred and sixty-five days, have gone by since I left my home and am alone on the lonely road of life. Oh, my poor dear parents, how saddened they were at my leaving. The leave-taking, their seeing me on my way, was like a silent funeral.

There was no shaking of the alms box, there was no grave digging and no sawing of boards, but I, myself, put on the white shirt that was wet with my mother's tears, took my pillow, and climbed into the wagon. Accompanying me was a quiet choked wail from my parents and friends.

The wheels of the wagon rolled farther and farther away. My mother and father wept for their son, then turned with heavy hearts to the empty house. They did not sit shive[3] even though they had lost a child.

I came to America and became a painter. My great love for Hebrew, for Russian, all of my other knowledge was smeared with paint. During the year that I have been here I have had some good periods, but I am not happy, because I have no interest in anything. My homesickness and loneliness darken my life.

Ah, home, my beloved home. My heart is heavy for my parents whom I left behind. I want to run back, but I am powerless. I am a coward, because I know that I have to serve under "Fonie"[4] for three years. I am lonely in my homesickness and I beg you to be my counsel as to how to act.

Respectfully,
V.A.

Answer:

The answer states that almost all immigrants yearn deeply for dear ones and home at first. They are compared with plants that are transplanted to new ground. At first it seems that they are withering, but in time most of them revive and take root in the new earth.

The advice to this young man is that he must not consider going home, but try to take root here. He should try to overcome all these emotions and strive to make something of himself so that in time he will be able to bring his parents here.

3. **shive:** Period of mourning.
4. **"Fonie":** The Russian czar.

24

Immigrant Labor at the Turn of the Twentieth Century

The West, like all economically developing regions, needed far more labor than could be provided domestically. The exclusion of the Chinese forced employers in the West to reach out to other countries across the Pacific for workers. Japanese migrants filled part of the gap created by Chinese exclusion, but this migration eventually slowed because of expanding economic opportunities in Japan. The Japanese who stayed in California often imported brides, started families, and established their own farms.

The Indian subcontinent, then a British colony, also filled some of the labor demand in the Western states. Sikhs in particular came in the late nineteenth and early twentieth centuries and were employed in agriculture and other jobs requiring heavy manual labor as shown below. As was the case with many migrant laborers in the nineteenth century, nearly all Sikhs who came to the United States were male, and most expected to return to their native land. However, many ended up staying, building their own temples and either importing wives from South Asia or marrying into the large Mexican community.

QUESTIONS TO CONSIDER

1. What are the traditional notions of how the West was peopled, and how does this photo of Sikh railway workers challenge those notions?
2. The photo of the Sikh migrants was taken with twentieth-century photographic equipment that required less staging and posing than nineteenth-century apparatus, but choices were still made. List some of these choices and discuss their implications for the story being told.
3. What impact do you think the absence of female migrants among Sikhs had on their integration into American life?

Sikh railroad workers, 1908. *Plumas County Museum, Quincy, California*

25

EMMETT J. SCOTT ET AL.

Letters from the Great Migration

These letters to the Chicago Defender, *collected by the distinguished African American educator and editor Emmett J. Scott (1873–1957), document one of the most important events of American social history, the Great Migration of about half a million African Americans, largely from the rural South, to Northern cities early in the twentieth century. World War I both stimulated business and cut off immigration from Europe, which created opportunities that had never existed before for African Americans. The widespread circulation of Chicago newspapers throughout the South, particularly the* Defender, *gave blacks there a picture of the thriving economies and available jobs in Chicago and other Northern cities.*

There were numerous reasons why African Americans sought to escape the South: Jim Crow, political disenfranchisement, lynching and other forms of mob violence, and, more immediately, injury to the rural economy from floods and boll weevil infestations. The migration northward was a great, leaderless folk movement—the individual decisions of

Emmett J. Scott, "Letters of Negro Migrants of 1916–1918," *Journal of Negro History* (July 1919): 177–80.

hundreds of thousands to flee the South by whatever means possible in search of better schools, greater personal safety and dignity, and the chance for economic improvement.

The migration had enormous long-term effects. In the next half century, six million African Americans left the South, most moving to cities. The migration brought political power and cultural authority to black America and moved many blacks into the middle class. It also pushed questions of racial inequality and conflict between African and non-African-descended Americans out of the rural South and into the cities of the North, placing the issue front and center on the national political stage.

QUESTIONS TO CONSIDER

1. What were the main purposes of the letters to the *Chicago Defender*?
2. What were the hopes of the letter writers?
3. To what extent were these hopes realistic?

Sherman, Ga., Nov. 28, 1916

Dear Sir:

This letter comes to ask for all infirmations concerning employment in your connection in the warmest climate. Now I am in a family of (11) eleven more or less boys and girls (men and women) mixed sizes who want to go north as soon as arrangements can be made and employment given places for shelter and so on (etc) now this are farming people they were raised on the farm and are good farm hands I of course have some experience and qualefication as a coman school teacher and hotel waiter and along few other lines.

I wish you would write me at your first chance and tell me if you can give us employment at what time and about what wages will you pay and what kind of arrangement can be made for our shelter. Tell me when can you best use us now or later.

Will you send us tickets if so on what terms and at what price what is the cost per head and by what route should we come. We are Negroes and try to show ourselves worthy of all we may get from any friendly source we endeavor to be true to all good causes, if you can we thank you to help us to come north as soon as you can.

Anniston, Ala., April 23, 1917

Dear Sir:

Please gave me some infamation about coming north i can do any kind of work from a truck gardin[1] to farming i would like to leave here and i cant make no money to leave I ust make enough to live one please let me here from you at once i want to get where i can put my children in school.

---

1. **truck gardin:** "Truck garden"—a garden given over to producing vegetables for the market.

Brookhaven, Miss., April 24, 1917

Gents:

The cane growers of Louisiana have stopped the exodus from New Orleans, claiming shortage of labor which will result in a sugar famine.

Now these laborers thus employed receive only 85 cents a day and the high cost of living makes it a serious question to live.

There is a great many race people around here who desires to come north but have waited rather late to avoid car fare, which they have not got. isnt there some way to get the concerns who wants labor, to send passes here or elsewhere so they can come even if they have to pay out of the first months wages? Please done publish this letter but do what you can towards helping them to get away. If the R. R. Co. would run a low rate excursion they could leave that way. Please ans.

Savannah, Ga., April 24, 1917

Sir:

I saw an advertisement in the Chicago Ledger where you would send tickets to any one desireing to come up there. I am a married man with a wife only, and I am 38 years of age, and both of us have so far splendid health, and would like very much to come out there provided we could get good employment regarding the advertisement.

Fullerton, La., April 28, 1917

Dear Sir:

I was reading about you was neading labor ninety miles of Chicago what is the name of the place and what R R extends ther i wants to come north and i wants a stedy employment ther what doe you pay per day i dont no anything about molding works but have been working around machinery for 10 years. Let me no what doe you pay for such work and can you give me a job of that kind or a job at common labor and let me no your prices and how many hours for a day.

Atlanta, Ga., April 30, 1917

Dear Sir:

In reading the Chicago Defender I find that there are many jobs open for workmen, I wish that you would or can secure me a position in some of the northern cities; as a workman and not as a loafer. One who is willing to do any kind of hard in side or public work, have had broad experience in machinery and other work of the kind. A some what alround man can also cook, well trained devuloped man; have travel extensively through the western and southern states; A good strong *morial religious* man no habits. I will accept transportation on advance and deducted from my wages later. It does not matter where, that is; as to city, country, town or state since you secure the positions. I am quite sure you will be delighted in securing a position for a man of this description. I'll assure you will not regret of so doing. Hoping to hear from you soon.

Houston, Tx., April 30, 1917

Dear Sir:

wanted to leave the South and Go any Place where a man will be any thing Except a Ker [cur] I thought would write you for Advise as where would be a Good Place for a Comporedly young man That want to Better his Standing who has a very Promising young Family.

I am 30 years old and have Good Experience in Freight Handler and Can fill Position from Truck to Agt [agent].

would like Chicago or Philadelphia But I dont Care where so long as I Go where a man is a man.

Beaumont, Texas, May 7, 1917

Dear Sir:

I see in one of your recent issue of collored men woanted in the North I wish you would help me to get a position in the North I have no trade I have been working for one company eight years and there is no advancement here for me and I would like to come where I can better my condition I woant work and not affraid to work all I wish is a chance to make good. I believe I would like machinist helper or Molder helper. If you can help me in any way it will be highly appreciate hoping to hear from you soon.

26

LUCY BURNS AND ALICE PAUL

Prison Notes

Although the American Revolution led to a great expansion of suffrage, it was not until the 1840s that property qualifications were removed from the voting rights of white male citizens. Strangely, as the right to vote became more widespread and tied to citizenship rather than property ownership, the circumstances in which a woman, as the inheritor of property, might vote were reduced and finally eliminated. By the time of the 1848 Seneca

---

Doris Stevens, *Jailed for Freedom* (New York: Liveright Publishing, 1920), 200–2, 214–17, 220–25.

Falls Woman's Rights Convention, there were no longer any places in the United States where a woman might vote. The extension of this right was one of the key platforms adopted by the women who met at Seneca Falls, New York.

In 1869, a year before African American men achieved the right to vote, the Wyoming Territory granted women's suffrage. Over the next half century, nearly every Western state granted full suffrage to women, and many Midwestern states allowed women to vote in certain types of elections, such as those for school boards and the presidency. However, most of the eastern seaboard states continued to refuse women voting rights. At the federal level, there was still no universal mandate at the end of World War I, by which time much of Europe had granted women the vote.

For the young, ambitious, and largely university-educated white women who made up most of the American women's suffrage movement, the idea that their fathers, brothers, and husbands could vote but they could not seemed absurd and unjust. The large role that women played in Europe during World War I intensified this contradiction and led thousands of women—and many men—to take to the streets to demand universal suffrage for women.

Lucy Burns and Alice Paul were among the most famous and militant of these suffragists. They met while studying at university in England before the war and came under the influence of Emmeline Pankhurst, the leader of the women's suffrage movement there. When they returned home to the United States, Burns and Paul joined the National American Woman Suffrage Association and helped found the National Woman's Party.

The leaders of a controversial demonstration in support of women's suffrage that disrupted Woodrow Wilson's inauguration in 1913, and later of a picket line in front of the White House during the winter of 1917, these two women faced frequent violence, death threats, public abuse, and imprisonment in their quest for the right to vote. The first few passages that follow come from notes Burns secretly wrote—using stolen pencils and tiny scraps of paper—while in prison for picketing the White House. Sympathetic women maintenance workers smuggled her writings out so that she could report on conditions inside prison and continue to provide leadership to the suffrage movement beyond the prison walls.

QUESTIONS TO CONSIDER

1. Why do you think the imprisoned women decided to go on a hunger strike?
2. Why was their hunger strike so successful?
3. In what ways do you think they made effective strategic use of the fact that they were women to the benefit of their cause?

Here are some of the scraps of Miss Burn[s]'s day-by-day log, smuggled out of the workhouse. Miss Burns is so gifted a writer that I feel apologetic for using these scraps in their raw form, but I know she will forgive me.

Wednesday, November 14. Demanded to see Superintendent Whittaker. Request refused. Mrs. Herndon, the matron, said we would have to wait up all night. One of the men guards said he would "put us in sardine box and put mustard on us." Superintendent Whittaker came at 9 P.M. He refused to hear our demand for political rights. Seized by guards from behind, flung off my feet, and shot out of the room. All of us were seized by men guards and dragged to cells in men's part. Dorothy Day was roughly used—back twisted. Mrs. Mary A. Nolan (73-year-old picket from Jacksonville, Florida) flung into cell. Mrs. Lawrence Lewis shot past my cell. I slept with Dorothy Day in a single bed. I was handcuffed all night and manacled to the bars part of the time for asking the others how they were, and was threatened with a straitjacket and a buckle gag.

Thursday, November 16. . . . Asked for Whittaker, who came. He seized Julia Emory by the back of her neck and threw her into the room very brutally. She is a little girl. I asked for counsel to learn the status of the case. I was told to "shut up," and was again threatened with a straitjacket and a buckle gag. Later I was taken to put on prison clothes, refused and resisted strenuously. I was then put in a room where delirium tremens patients are kept.

On the seventh day, when Miss Lucy Burns and Mrs. Lawrence Lewis were so weak that Mr. Whittaker feared their death, they were forcibly fed and taken immediately to the jail in Washington. . . .

Of this experience, Miss Burns wrote on tiny scraps of paper:

Wednesday, 12 m. Yesterday afternoon at about four or five, Mrs. Lewis and I were asked to go to the operating room. Went there and found our clothes. Told we were to go to Washington. No reason as usual. When we were dressed, Dr. Gannon appeared, and said he wished to examine us. Both refused. Were dragged through halls by force, our clothing partly removed by force, and we were examined, heart tested, blood pressure and pulse taken. Of course such data was of no value after such a struggle. Dr. Gannon told me then I must be fed. Was stretched on bed, two doctors, matron, four colored prisoners present, Whittaker in hall. I was held down by five people at legs, arms, and head. I refused to open mouth. Gannon pushed tube up left nostril. I turned and twisted my head all I could, but he managed to push it up. It hurts nose and throat very much and makes nose bleed freely. Tube drawn out covered with blood. Operation leaves one very sick. Food dumped directly into stomach feels like a ball of lead. Left nostril, throat and muscles of neck very sore all night. After this I was brought into the hospital in an ambulance. Mrs. Lewis and I placed in same room. Slept hardly at all. This morning Dr. Ladd appeared with his tube. Mrs. Lewis and I said we would not be forcibly fed. Said he would call in men guards and force us to submit. Went away and we were not fed at all this morning. We hear them outside now cracking eggs. . . .

I am going to let Alice Paul tell her own story, as she related it to me one day after her release:

It was late afternoon when we arrived at the jail. There we found the suffragists who had preceded us, locked in cells.

The first thing I remember was the distress of the prisoners about the lack of fresh air. Evening was approaching, every window was closed tight. The air in which we would be obliged to sleep was foul. There were about eighty negro and white prisoners crowded together, tier upon tier, frequently two in a cell. I went to a window and tried to open it. Instantly a group of men, prison guards, appeared; picked me up bodily, threw me into a cell and locked the door. Rose Winslow and the others were treated in the same way.

Determined to preserve our health and that of the other prisoners, we began a concerted fight for fresh air. The windows were about twenty feet distant from the cells, and two sets of iron bars intervened between us and the windows, but we instituted an attack upon them as best we could. Our tin drinking cups, the electric light bulbs, every available article of the meagre supply in each cell, including my treasured copy of Browning's poems which I had secretly taken in with me, was thrown through the windows. By this simultaneous attack from every cell, we succeeded in breaking one window before our supply of tiny weapons was exhausted. The fresh October air came in like an exhilarating gale. The broken window remained untouched throughout the entire stay of this group and all later groups of suffragists. Thus was won what the "regulars" in jail called the first breath of air in their time.

The next day we organized ourselves into a little group for the purpose of rebellion. We determined to make it impossible to keep us in jail. We determined, moreover, that as long as we were there we would keep up an unremitting fight for the rights of political prisoners. . . .

There is absolutely no privacy allowed a prisoner in a cell. You are suddenly peered at by curious strangers, who look in at you all hours of the day and night, by officials, by attendants, by interested philanthropic visitors, and by prison reformers, until one's sense of privacy is so outraged that one rises in rebellion. We set out to secure privacy, but we did not succeed, for, to allow privacy in prison, is against all institutional thought and habit. Our only available weapon was our blanket, which was no sooner put in front of our bars than it was forcibly taken down by Warden Zinkhan.

Our meals had consisted of a little almost raw salt pork, some sort of liquid—I am not sure whether it was coffee or soup—bread and occasionally molasses. How we cherished the bread and molasses! We saved it from meal to meal so as to try to distribute the nourishment over a longer period, as almost every one was unable to eat the raw pork. Lucy Branham, who was more valiant than the rest of us, called out from her cell, one day, "Shut your eyes tight, close your mouth over the pork and swallow it without chewing it. Then you can do it." This heroic practice kept Miss Branham in fairly good health, but to the rest it seemed impossible, even with our eyes closed, to crunch our teeth into the raw pork. . . .

At the end of two weeks of solitary confinement, without any exercise, without going outside of our cells, some of the prisoners were released, having finished their terms, but five of us were left serving seven months' sentences, and two, one month sentences. With our number thus diminished to seven, the authorities felt able to cope with us. The doors were unlocked and we were permitted to take exercise. Rose Winslow fainted as soon as she got into the yard, and was carried back to her cell. I was too weak to move from my bed. Rose and I were taken on stretchers that night to the hospital.

For one brief night we occupied beds in the same ward in the hospital. Here we decided upon the hunger strike, as the ultimate form of protest left us—the strongest weapon left with which to continue within the prison our battle against the Administration. . . .

From the moment we undertook the hunger strike, a policy of unremitting intimidation began. One authority after another, high and low, in and out of prison, came to attempt to force me to break the hunger strike.

"You will be taken to a very unpleasant place if you don't stop this," was a favorite threat of the prison officials, as they would hint vaguely of the psychopathic ward, and St. Elizabeth's, the Government insane asylum. They alternately bullied and hinted. Another threat was "You will be forcibly fed immediately if you don't stop"—this from Dr. Gannon. There was nothing to do in the midst of these continuous threats, with always the "very unpleasant place" hanging over me, and so I lay perfectly silent on my bed.

After about three days of the hunger strike a man entered my room in the hospital and announced himself as Dr. White, the head of St. Elizabeth's. He said that he had been asked by District Commissioner Gardner to make an investigation. I later learned that he was Dr. William A. White, the eminent alienist.

Coming close to my bedside and addressing the attendant, who stood at a few respectful paces from him, Dr. White said: "Does this case talk?"

"Why wouldn't I talk?" I answered quickly.

"Oh, these cases frequently will not talk, you know," he continued in explanation.

"Indeed I'll talk," I said gaily, not having the faintest idea that this was an investigation of my sanity.

"Talking is our business," I continued, "we talk to any one on earth who is willing to listen to our suffrage speeches."

"Please talk," said Dr. White. "Tell me about suffrage; why you have opposed the President; the whole history of your campaign, why you picket, what you hope to accomplish by it. Just talk freely."

I drew myself together, sat upright in bed, propped myself up for a discourse of some length, and began to talk. The stenographer whom Dr. White brought with him took down in shorthand everything that was said.

I may say it was one of the best speeches I ever made. I recited the long history and struggle of the suffrage movement from its early beginning and narrated the political theory of our activities up to the present moment, outlining the status of the suffrage amendment in Congress at that time. In short, I told him everything. He listened attentively, interrupting only occasionally to say, "But, has not President Wilson treated you women very badly?" Whereupon, I, still unaware that I was being examined, launched forth into an explanation of Mr. Wilson's political situation and the difficulties he had confronting him. I continued to explain why we felt our relief lay with him; I cited his extraordinary power, his influence over his party, his undisputed leadership in the country, always painstakingly explaining that we opposed President Wilson merely because he happened to be President, not because he was President Wilson. Again came an interruption from Dr. White, "But isn't

President Wilson directly responsible for the abuses and indignities which have been heaped upon you? You are suffering now as a result of his brutality, are you not?" Again I explained that it was impossible for us to know whether President Wilson was personally acquainted in any detail with the facts of our present condition, even though we knew that he had concurred in the early decision to arrest our women.

Presently Dr. White took out a small light and held it up to my eyes. Suddenly it dawned upon me that he was examining me personally; that his interest in the suffrage agitation and the jail conditions did not exist, and that he was merely interested in my reactions to the agitation and to jail. Even then I was reluctant to believe that I was the subject of mental investigation and I continued to talk.

But he continued in what I realized with a sudden shock, was an attempt to discover in me symptoms of the persecution mania. How simple he had apparently thought it would be, to prove that I had an obsession on the subject of President Wilson!

The day following he came again, this time bringing with him the District Commissioner, Mr. Gardner, to whom he asked me to repeat everything that had been said the day before. For the second time we went through the history of the suffrage movement, and again his inquiry suggested his persecution mania clue. When the narrative touched upon the President and his responsibility for the obstruction of the suffrage amendment, Dr. White would turn to his associate with the remark: "Note the reaction."

Then came another alienist, Dr. Hickling, attached to the psychopathic ward in the District Jail, with more threats and suggestions, if the hunger strike continued. Finally they departed, and I was left to wonder what would happen next. Doubtless my sense of humor helped me, but I confess I was not without fear of this mysterious place which they continued to threaten.

It appeared clear that it was their intention either to discredit me, as the leader of the agitation, by casting doubt upon my sanity, or else to intimidate us into retreating from the hunger strike.

After the examination by the alienists, Commissioner Gardner, with whom I had previously discussed our demand for treatment as political prisoners, made another visit. "All these things you say about the prison conditions may be true," said Mr. Gardner, "I am a new Commissioner, and I do not know. You give an account of a very serious situation in the jail. The jail authorities give exactly the opposite. Now I promise you we will start an investigation at once to see who is right, you or they. If it is found you are right, we shall correct the conditions at once. If you will give up the hunger strike, we will start the investigation at once."

"Will you consent to treat the suffragists as political prisoners, in accordance with the demands laid before you?" I replied.

Commissioner Gardner refused, and I told him that the hunger strike would not be abandoned. But they had by no means exhausted every possible facility for breaking down our resistance. I overheard the Commissioner say to Dr. Gannon on leaving, "Go ahead, take her and feed her."

I was thereupon put upon a stretcher and carried into the psychopathic ward.

There were two windows in the room. Dr. Gannon immediately ordered one window nailed from top to bottom. He then ordered the door leading into the hallway taken down and an iron-barred cell door put in its place. He departed with the command to a nurse to "observe her."

Following this direction, all through the day once every hour, the nurse came to "observe" me. All through the night, once every hour she came in, turned on an electric light sharp in my face, and "observed" me. This ordeal was the most terrible torture, as it prevented my sleeping for more than a few minutes at a time. And if I did finally get to sleep it was only to be shocked immediately into wide-awakeness with the pitiless light.

Dr. Hickling, the jail alienist, also came often to "observe" me. Commissioner Gardner and others—doubtless officials—came to peer through my barred door.

One day a young interne came to take a blood test. I protested mildly, saying that it was unnecessary and that I objected. "Oh, well," said the young doctor with a sneer and a supercilious shrug, "you know you're not mentally competent to decide such things." And the test was taken over my protest.

It is scarcely possible to convey to you one's reaction to such an atmosphere. Here I was surrounded by people on their way to the insane asylum. Some were waiting for their commitment papers. Others had just gotten them. And all the while everything possible was done to attempt to make me feel that I too was a "mental patient."

At this time forcible feeding began in the District Jail. Miss Paul and Miss Winslow, the first two suffragists to undertake the hunger strike, went through the operation of forcible feeding this day and three times a day on each succeeding day until their release from prison three weeks later. The hunger strike spread immediately to other suffrage prisoners in the jail and to the workhouse as recorded [earlier].

One morning [Miss Paul's story continues] the friendly face of a kindly old man standing on top of a ladder suddenly appeared at my window. He began to nail heavy boards across the window from the outside. He smiled and spoke a few kind words and told me to be of good cheer. He confided to me in a sweet and gentle way that he was in prison for drinking, that he had been in many times, but that he believed he had never seen anything so inhuman as boarding up this window and depriving a prisoner of light and air. There was only time for a few hurried moments of conversation, as I lay upon my bed watching the boards go up until his figure was completely hidden and I heard him descending the ladder.

After this window had been boarded up no light came into the room except through the top half of the other window, and almost no air. The authorities seemed determined to deprive me of air and light.

Meanwhile in those gray, long days, the mental patients in the psychopathic ward came and peered through my barred door. At night, in the early morning, all through the day there were cries and shrieks and moans from the patients. It was terrifying. . . .

The nurses could not have been more beautiful in their spirit and offered every kindness. But imagine being greeted in the morning by a kindly nurse, a new one who had just come on duty, with, "I know you are not insane." The nurses explained the procedure of sending a person to the insane asylum. Two alienists examine a patient in the psychopathic ward, sign an order committing the patient to St. Elizabeth's Asylum, and there the patient is sent at the end of one week. No trial, no counsel, no protest from the outside world! This was the customary procedure.

I began to think as the week wore on that this was probably their plan for me. I could not see my family or friends; counsel was denied me; I saw no other prisoners and heard nothing of them; I could see no papers; I was entirely in the hands of alienists, prison officials and hospital staff.

I believe I have never in my life before feared anything or any human being. But I confess I was afraid of Dr. Gannon, the jail physician. I dreaded the hour of his visit.

"I will show you who rules this place. You think you do. But I will show you that you are wrong." Some such friendly greeting as this was frequent from Dr. Gannon on his daily round. "Anything you desire, you shall not have. I will show you who is on top in this institution," was his attitude.

After nearly a week had passed, Dudley Field Malone finally succeeded in forcing an entrance by an appeal to court officials and made a vigorous protest against confining me in the psychopathic ward. He demanded also that the boards covering the window be taken down. This was promptly done and again the friendly face of the old man became visible, as the first board disappeared.

"I thought when I put this up America would not stand for this long," he said, and began to assure me that nothing dreadful would happen. I cherish the memory of that sweet old man.

The day after Mr. Malone's threat of court proceedings, the seventh day of my stay in the psychopathic ward, the attendants suddenly appeared with a stretcher. I did not know whither I was being taken, to the insane asylum, as threatened, or back to the hospital—one never knows in prison where one is being taken, no reason is ever given for anything. It turned out to be the hospital.

After another week spent by Miss Paul on hunger strike in the hospital, the Administration was forced to capitulate. The doors of the jail were suddenly opened, and all suffrage prisoners were released.

27

EDWIN W. SIMS

War on the White Slave Trade

The two decades before World War I are often called "the Progressive Era" for the way in which social reformers increasingly used government regulation to improve social life. Reformers fought for and won popular antitrust laws, consumer protection laws like the Pure Food and Drug Act, and laws protecting children from labor exploitation in factories and other worksites. However, many Progressive Era laws were divisive, unpopular, and often not very progressive. Among the most contentious were the laws regulating personal behaviors that are often called "victimless crimes."

During this period state and local governments across America passed many such laws. There were alcohol-prohibition laws that targeted immigrant sociality (see Document 21 (on page 103), Percy Andreae, "A Glimpse behind the Mask of Prohibition") and anti-narcotics laws that targeted "negro cocaine" and "Chinese opium," driving drug use underground and effectively segregating Chinese Americans and African Americans from whites. In addition there was the White Slave Traffic Act of 1910, which made it a felony to transport or assist in transporting "any woman or girl for the purpose of prostitution or debauchery [excessive indulgence in sensual pleasure], or for any other immoral purpose."

More commonly known as the Mann Act, it addressed widespread fears of globalization, new immigrants, and new freedoms deriving from female employment outside the home. As with contemporary laws against human sex trafficking, the White Slave Traffic Act and the social movement it was built on coincided with a sustained period of increased immigration and a globalizing economy. Between 1890 and 1910, over 14 percent of people living in the United States were foreign-born—the highest percentage since the United States started collecting records on nativity. While concerns about white slavery focused on fears of unaccountable lawless foreigners, the intentionally ambiguous language ultimately criminalized all premarital or extramarital sexual relationships involving interstate travel. This left law enforcement with a nearly limitless choice of targets for arrest and prosecution. Not surprisingly interracial and interethnic couples, as well as public figures committing adultery, were often the most vulnerable.

Hon. Edwin W. Sims (1870–1948) was the United States district attorney for Chicago between 1906 and 1911, where he built a national profile leading the movement against white slavery. Claiming to have evidence of an organized national white slavery ring that was kidnapping, buying, and selling innocent young girls, Sims helped organize churches, synagogues, Progressive Era women's organizations, social hygiene

Edwin W. Sims, "Introduction" and "Menace of the White Slave Trade" in Ernest A. Bell, *Fighting the Traffic in Young Girls, or War on the White Slave Trade* (Chicago: G. S. Ball, 1910), 13–14, 68–72.

activists, law enforcement and justice officials, and politicians to create legislation to eradicate what he called "this ghastly traffic." While he never produced evidence of this network of traffickers, he became the most important face of anti-trafficking and marketed himself as "the man most feared by all white slave traders." After World War I he helped found and was elected president of the Chicago Crime Commission, an organization of lawyers and small businessmen advocating against organized crime. While some of their work was indeed directed toward violent street crime, much of it entailed politically motivated attacks on organized labor. The following passage is from Sims's contribution to a wide-ranging compendium on white slavery published by Ernest A. Bell in 1910 and written while Sims was helping to draft the Mann Act.

QUESTIONS TO CONSIDER

1. Who do you think was the target audience for Sims's essay? What evidence from the document leads you to that conclusion?
2. In what ways do you think that laws like the Mann Act may have helped protect and rescue young girls? In what ways do you think they might have hindered such efforts?
3. Imagine you are a teenage girl who has won a college scholarship to study in a city in 1910 and your parents made you read the passage by Sims. How would you react to this piece?

I am firmly convinced that when the people of this nation understand and fully appreciate the unspeakable villainy of "The White Slave Traffic" they will rise in their might and put a stop to it. The growth of this "trade in white women," as it has been officially designated by the Paris Conference, was so insidious that it reached the proportions of an international problem almost before the people of the civilized nations of the world learned of its existence.

The traffic increased rapidly, owing largely to the fact that it was tremendously profitable to those depraved mortals who indulged in it, and because the people generally, until very recently, were ignorant of the fact that it was becoming so extensive. And even at this time, when a great deal has been said by the pulpit and the press about the horrors of the traffic, the public idea of just what is meant by the "white slave traffic" is confused and indefinite. . . .

. . . The term "white slave" includes only those women and girls who are actually slaves—those women who are owned and held as property and chattels—whose lives are lives of involuntary servitude. The white slave trade may be said to be the business of securing white women and of selling them or exploiting them for immoral purposes. It includes those women and girls who, if given a fair chance, would, in all probability, have been good wives and mothers and useful citizens. . . .

I cannot escape the conclusion that the country girl is in greater danger from the "white slavers" than the city girl. The perusal of the testimony of many "white slaves" enforces this conclusion. That is because they are less sophisticated, more trusting and more open to the allurements of those who are waiting to prey upon them.

It is a fact which parents of girls in the country should remember that the "white slavers" are busy on the trains coming into the city and make it a point to "cut out" an attractive girl whenever they can. This "cutting out" process (I use the technical term) consists of making the girl's acquaintance, gaining her confidence and, on one pretext or another, inducing her to leave the train before the main depot is reached. This is done because the various protective and law and order organizations have watchers at the main railroad stations who are trained to the work of "spotting," and quickly detect a girl in the hands of one of these human beasts of prey. Generally these watchers are women and wear the badges of their organizations.

But suppose that the girl from the country does not chance to fall in with the "white slaver" on the train, that she reaches the city in safety, becomes located in a position—or perhaps in the stenographic school or business college which she has come to attend—and secures a room in a boarding house. No human being, it seems to me, is quite so lonely as the young girl from the country when she first comes to the city and starts in the struggle of life there without acquaintances. All her instincts are social, and she is, for the time being, almost desolately alone in a wilderness of strange human beings. She must have some one to talk to—it is the law of youth as well as the law of her sex to crave constant companionship. And the consequences? She is sentimentally in a condition to prepare her for the slaughter, to make her an easy prey to the wiles of the "white slave" wolf. . . .

In view of what I have learned in the course of the recent investigation and prosecution of the "white slave" traffic, I can say, in all sincerity, that if I lived in the country and had a young daughter I would go any length of hardship and privation myself rather than allow her to go into the city to work or to study—unless that studying were to be done in the very best type of an educational institution where the girl students were always under the closest protection. The best and the surest way for parents of girls in the country to protect them from the clutches of the "white slaver" is to keep them in the country. But if circumstances should seem to compel a change from the country to the city, then the only safe way is to go with them into the city; but even this last has its disadvantages from the fact that, in that case the parents would themselves be unfamiliar with the usages and pitfalls of metropolitan life, and would not be able to protect their daughters as carefully as if they had spent their own lives in the city.

One thing should be made very clear to the girl who comes up to the city, and that is that the ordinary ice cream parlor is very likely to be a spider's web for her entanglement. This is perhaps especially true of those ice cream saloons and fruit stores kept by foreigners. Scores of cases are on record where young girls have taken their first step towards "white slavery" in places of this character. And it is hardly too much to say that a week does not pass in Chicago without the publication in some daily paper of the details of a police court case in which the ice cream parlor of this type is the scene of a regrettable tragedy. The only safe rule is to keep away from places of this kind, whether in a big city like Chicago or in a large country town. I believe that there are good grounds for the suspicion that the ice cream parlor, kept by the foreigner in the large country town, is often a recruiting station, and a feeder for the "white slave" traffic. It is certain that this is the case in the big city, and many evidences point to the conclusion that there is a kind of free-masonry among these foreign proprietors of refreshment parlors which would make it entirely natural and convenient for the proprietor of a city establishment of this kind, who is entangled in the "white slave" trade, to establish relations with a man in the same business and of the same nationality in the country town. I do not mean to intimate by this that all the ice cream and fruit "saloons" having foreign-born proprietors are connected with the "white slave" traffic—but some of them are, and this fact is sufficient to cause all careful and thoughtful parents of young girls to see that they do not frequent these places.

28

KATE RICHARDS O'HARE ET AL.

The Trial of Kate Richards O'Hare

In 1917 and 1918, respectively, Woodrow Wilson signed the Espionage Act and the Sedition Act, providing up to twenty years in prison for anyone who would "willfully obstruct the recruiting or enlistment service of the United States" or use seditious language about the form of government. Enacted during World War I, these laws were directed primarily at the Socialist Party of America, which in recent years had become a third national party, garnering almost a million votes in the 1912 presidential election. In 1917 the party's membership voted to oppose the war, declaring it of benefit to capitalists, not workers—a stand that led to the imprisonment of hundreds of party members.

Kate Richards O'Hare (1877–1948), known as "Red Kate," was a fiery leader of the Socialist Party whose evangelical rhetoric had converted poor farmers across the Plains states to socialism. Committed to ending what she believed to be an immoral war, O'Hare had already given dozens of speeches in small towns throughout the United States by the time the Espionage Act was passed. Not until July 17, 1917, when she spoke at Bowman, North Dakota, however, did the law catch up with her. At that time, North Dakota was a center of socialism and populism. In 1915 the Nonpartisan League,

"The Trial of Kate Richards O'Hare for Disloyalty, Bismarck, North Dakota, 1917, Hon. Martin J. Wade, Judge," in Robert Marcus and Anthony Marcus, eds., *On Trial: American History through Court Proceedings and Hearings*, vol. 2 (St. James, NY: Brandywine Press, 1998), 96–98, 100–4.

a broad farmers' movement that included many socialists, had swept into power in the state. Though not explicitly antiwar, the Nonpartisan League had gained popularity partially through its intense criticism of war profiteering. The league's major political enemies, the Democrats, seeking to identify the league with O'Hare's "unpatriotic" opposition to the war, made an issue of her speech, and her arrest for obstructing recruitment and enlistment of men for the armed forces soon followed.

At her trial, the proceedings of which are excerpted here, O'Hare faced a judge who had made public statements against both socialism and women who were active in public life. Her jury, selected from a county populated by impoverished farmers, was composed of twelve conservative businessmen. She was found guilty and sentenced to five years in prison. A higher court rejected her appeal, and she served fourteen months in prison before her sentence was commuted by the U.S. Department of Justice in accordance with a nationwide amnesty.

Upon her release, O'Hare helped lead the 1920 presidential campaign of fellow Espionage Act prisoner Eugene V. Debs, who garnered more than 900,000 votes for the Socialist Party ticket from his prison cell. O'Hare's incarceration also made her an ardent advocate of prison reform, a cause she championed until her death in 1948.

QUESTIONS TO CONSIDER

1. Why did Kate Richards O'Hare oppose U.S. involvement in World War I?
2. What was O'Hare's defense at her trial?
3. Did O'Hare believe that she was serving her country? Explain.
4. Did O'Hare receive a fair trial? Why or why not?

Mr. Hildreth.[1] Gentlemen of the jury: The Congress of the United States declared war on Germany on the 6th day of April, 1917. The purposes of that war are known to all men. It is to settle the great question as to whether democracy shall rule the world or autocracy. Our soldiers are now crossing the seas. Back of the men who go into the line of entrenchments to do or die must rest the great reserve forces of the Nation.

Our government has called to the colors under the draft act young men between the ages of 21 and 31 years. The man power of the Nation not only is involved, the resources of the Nation are not only involved, but greater than all of these elements of national strength is the spirit of our people. Whatever tends to destroy the spirit of the people, the patriotism of the people, to lessen it here at home while our troops are fighting the battles of the Nation in Europe, lessens our strength as a Nation, minimizes the patriotism of our people, and contributes in no small degree to strengthening the armies of the Central Powers.

---

1. **Mr. Hildreth:** Melvin Hildreth, the prosecuting attorney.

One of the methods that have been used in the past in the wars of the Republic to injure the patriotism of the people has been the abuse of free speech. In every war we have been engaged in we have been confronted with the propagandist, the agitator, and the corruptionist. These forces have made it difficult for us to win battles, have prolonged wars, injured the unity of the Nation and been destructive of complete success on the battlefield. It was true of the Revolutionary War, the War of 1812, the Mexican War, and the great Rebellion; and it is true today that in this country, where we have a written Constitution, trial by jury, freedom of the press, and liberty of speech, we are met with a hostility on our own shores far more dangerous than the guns of our European foes.

This great evil was known to all men. Therefore Congress, on the 15th day of June, 1917, passed this Espionage act, and the defendant is charged in this indictment with having violated that act.

She went to Bowman and before an audience of from 100 to 150 people made a speech which, in some respects, has no parallel in the English language. She said: "Any person who enlists in the army of the United States of America will be used for fertilizer, and that is all that he is good for; and the women of the United States are nothing more or less than brood sows to raise children to get into the army and be made into fertilizer." Search the annals of history and you will find no parallel in any country in the world. It was a direct blow at the spirit of the people, at the patriotism of the people. It was made intentionally and for the purpose charged. It was made to willfully obstruct the enlistment service of the United States, to the injury of the service of the United States, and to obstruct the recruiting service of the United States. . . .

This lecture, this speech, stirred this Commonwealth as no other speech. Why? Because this woman had gone upon the rostrum and, before the people of a great country, had instilled in their hearts and minds that this was [the financier J. P.] Morgan's war and not the war of the United States; that this was a war to protect the investments of financiers and not the democracy of the world; that this was a war that was brought about by moneyed interests; that this was a war not intended to break down the autocracy of Europe, but to build up the moneyed interests of the country; that this war was unjust and was being waged for that purpose and that alone, when she knew that the United States had suffered injury after injury at the hands of the German Government, when she knew that its ships that had a right to sail upon the seas had been sunk and the bodies of thousands of men, women, and children consigned to a watery grave under circumstances of the greatest atrocity and in violation of every principle of the laws of nations and of humanity. And yet she was telling the people that this was a war not in the defense of the American people on the sea and on the land, but that it was a war for the benefit of the moneyed interests of the country. False and pernicious doctrine! A doctrine that, if instilled in the minds of the people of this country, would prevent us from raising armies and navies and would be more potential in behalf of the Central Powers than the soldiers that are across the seas to fight the battles of the Republic. . . .

Gentlemen of the jury, we are not concerned with the politics of this defendant. We are indifferent as to whether she is a Socialist, a Democrat, or a Republican. But we are not indifferent to her violation of this statute which forbade her efforts upon the rostrum to carry out the evil intentions which this statute was aimed to prevent. . . .

Gentlemen of the jury, this case is one of the most important that has ever been tried in the United States. The defendant made her speech on the 17th of July, 1917. She has repeated that speech in many places throughout this Commonwealth. Here in this State, . . . she would instill in the minds of the young, not the patriotism of the fathers of this Republic but the zeal of those who would destroy this Government, destroy its institutions, and drag this flag in the dust of Socialism. . . .

THE VERDICT AND SENTENCE

The *Jury* retired, and after a short time, returned to the court room. The fore-man handed the following written verdict to the clerk: "We, the jury, find the defendant *guilty* as charged in the indictment. —A. L. Peart, Foreman."

JUDGE WADE. Is there anything to be said now why sentence should not be imposed upon this defendant?

Mrs. O'Hare. Yes, your Honor: I was taught in high school that law was pure logic. Abstract law may be pure logic but the application of the law of testimony in this case seems to have gone far afield from logic. As your Honor knows, I am a professional woman, following the profession of delivering lectures whereby I hope to induce my hearers to study the philosophy of socialism. In the regular course of my profession and work I delivered during this year lectures all over the United States. . . . The men who were in the employ of the United States in the Department of Justice were present at my meetings. These men were trained, highly efficient, and highly paid, detectors of crime and criminals. In all these months, when my lecture was under the scrutiny of this kind of men, there was no suggestion at any time that there was anything in it that was objectionable, treasonable or seditious. . . .

And then in the course of the trip I landed at Bowman—a little, sordid, wind-blown, sun-blistered, frost-scarred town on the plains of Western Dakota. There was nothing unusual in my visit to Bowman, except the fact that it was unusual to make a town of this size. The reason I did was because there was one man whose loyalty and faithfulness and unselfish service to the cause to which I had given my life wanted me to come, and I felt he had a right to demand my services. I delivered my lecture there just as I had delivered it many, many times before. There was nothing in the audience that was unusual except the fact that it was a small audience—a solid, substantial, stolid type of farmer crowd. There was not the great enthusiasm that had prevailed at many of my meetings. There was nothing to stir me or arouse me or cause me to make a more impassioned appeal than usual. There was nothing at all in that little sordid, wind-blown town, that commonplace audience, that should have for a moment overbalanced my reason and judgment and common sense and have caused me to have been suddenly smitten with hydrophobia of sedition. But I found there were peculiar conditions existing at Bowman, and they are common to the whole state of North Dakota. In this State in the last year and a half the greatest and most revolutionary social phenomena that has occurred since the foundation of this Government, has taken place. The story is one that is so well known that I need spend little time on it. Here to these wind-blown, frost-scarred plains came men hard of face and feature and muscle who subdued this desert and made it bloom and produce the bread to feed the world; and these men, toiling in their desperate struggle with adverse conditions and with nature, gradually had it forced on their minds that in some way they were not receiving a just return for the labor expended; that after their wheat was raised and garnered in the processes of marketing, men who toiled not and suffered none of the hardships of production were robbing them of the product of their labor. . . .

And your Honor, it seems to me one of those strange grotesque things that can only be the outgrowth of this hysteria that is sweeping over the world today that a judge on the bench and a jury in the box and a prosecuting attorney should attempt to usurp the prerogatives of God Almighty and look down into the heart of a human being and decide what motives slumber there. There is no charge that if my intent or my motive was criminal that that intent or motive ever was put into action—only the charge that in my heart there was an intent, and on that strange charge of an intent so securely buried in a human heart that no result and no effect came from it, I went to trial. . . .

Your Honor, there are 100,000 people in the United States who know me personally. They have listened to my voice, looked in my face and have worked side by side with me in every great reform movement of the last twenty years. My life has been an open book to them. . . . And, your Honor, no judge on earth and no ten thousand judges or ten thousand juries can ever convince these hundred thousand people who know me and have worked with me, and these millions who have read my writings, that I am a criminal, or that I have ever given anything to my country except my most unselfish devotion and service. You cannot convince the people who know me that I am dangerous to the United States Government. They are willing to admit I am dangerous to some things in the United States, and I thank God that I am. I am dangerous to the invisible government of the United States; to the special privileges of the United States; to the white-slaver and the saloonkeepers, and I thank God that at this hour I am dangerous to the war profiteers of this country who rob the people on the one hand and rob and debase the Government on the other, and then with their pockets and wallets stuffed with the blood-stained profits of war, wrap the sacred folds of the Stars and Stripes about them and shout their blatant hypocrisy to the world. You can convince the people that I am dangerous to these men; but no jury and no judge can convince them that I am a dangerous woman to the best interests of the United States. . . .

JUDGE WADE. It is never a pleasant duty for me to sentence any one to prison, and it certainly is not a pleasant duty to send a woman to prison; in the course of a trial, in all the years I have been on the bench in the State and Federal courts, I have made it a rule to try to find out who I am sending to prison, because we all make mistakes in this world at times. On the spur of the moment and under excitement, sometimes people are misled and commit offenses, and I have a hard time to reconcile my view of things with heavy sentences in those cases. Therefore, when this case was closed, I made up my mind that I would find out before imposing sentence in this case what were the activities of this defendant.

She testified here to her loyalty, and her support of the President, and I was hoping in my heart that somewhere I would find out that after all, she was such a woman as she has here pictured herself today, and that thus a small penalty for this offense might be adequate, because I realize this is a serious business. The Nation is at war. Every sane man and woman knows that there is only one way that this war can be won, and that is by having men and money and spirit. Those three things are necessary—spirit in the men, in the service, and spirit in the men and women behind the men. And it was because of these absolute essentials that Congress enacted the Espionage law, to reach out and take hold of those who are trying to kill the spirit of the American people, in whole or in part; trying to put in their hearts hate toward this Government and towards the officials of this Government conducting the war. And realizing that this was such a grave matter, I investigated it as far as possible to find out really what character of woman this defendant is, and had been, in her work. I heard the evidence in this case. I had nothing to do with the question of whether she was guilty or innocent. The jury settled that question, and in my judgment, settled it right.

I received information from another town in North Dakota, and this information was given in the presence of counsel for the defendant that at Garrison, in her lecture there, she made the statement that mothers who reared sons to go into the army, were no better than animals on a North Dakota farm; that this war was in behalf of the capitalists, and that if we had loaned our money to Germany instead of to the allies, we would be now fighting with Germany instead of with the allies. That she had boys, but that they are not old enough to go to war, but that if they were, they would not go. That the way to stop the war was to strike, and if the laboring men of this nation would strike, the war would soon be ended. Of course that was an *ex parte* matter. I have heard enough of testimony in my life, and I have seen enough of human nature to know that sometimes these things are stretched because of the feeling on one side or another of the question. So I thought I would go back and see what she had been doing. I wired the Postoffice Department at Washington, and I received a telegram which states:

Party is on editorial staff of publication, *Social Revolution*, Saint Louis, Missouri, which has been barred from the mails for gross violations of Espionage Act, and is successor to *Ripsaw*.[2] The party appears to be of the extreme type who have attempted to handicap the Government in every way in the conduct of the present war.

That was only a statement of an opinion. I tried to get copies of the *Social Revolution*, and have not succeeded in getting either the number for June or July. At some period during that time the Postmaster General barred this from the mails. I have the April and May numbers. In April they published from Eugene Debs this statement:

> As we have said, the bankers are for bullets—for the fool patriots that enlist at paupers' wages to stop the bullets, while the bankers clip coupons, boost food prices, increase dividends, and pile up millions and billions for themselves. Say, Mr. Workingman, suppose you have sense enough to be as patriotic as the banker, but not a bit more so. When you see the bankers on the firing line with guns in their hands ready to stop bullets as well as start them, then it is time enough for you to be seized with the patriotic itch and have yourself shot into a crazy-quilt for their profit and glory. Don't you take a fit and rush to the front until you see them there. They own the country and if they don't set the example of fighting for it, why should you?

This was in April, before the war was declared. Up to that time I realize that every person in this country had the right to discuss the war, express their opinions against the war, give any reasons they might have against the war. But you will find here in this statement the note which rings out from the statement of the defendant here in court this afternoon and which forms the foundation of the entire gospel of hate which she and her associates are preaching to the American people: That the Nation is helpless, prostrate, down-trodden by a few capitalists, and that the average man has not a chance on earth; that this war is a war of capitalism; that it was brought about by capital and in the interest of capital; that 100, 200, or 300 millionaires and billionaires if you please, in these United States dominate the souls and consciences of the other 99,000,000 American people.

---

2. **Ripsaw:** A St. Louis–based Socialist Party newspaper.

PART FOUR

A New Society
Between the Wars

World War I and its social, political, and technological effects helped to transform the economic organization of the United States and move the country into a "consumer age." A rapidly expanding advertising industry encouraged Americans to embrace new consumer goods. People with the means to do so rushed to purchase cars, radios, and other household items. Yet many Americans developed doubts about whether the political and cultural values that had worked for a previous generation would work as well for them. Although these doubts fueled creativity in literature, the arts, and social movements, they also provoked defensive reassertions of nineteenth-century values.

These social tensions were displayed in many arenas. The Scopes trial pitted William Jennings Bryan, the hero of rural America, against the renowned defense lawyer Clarence Darrow and other champions of modernism. The trial highlighted the chasm, in terms of their religious and social values, that separated fundamentalists and modernists. The Harlem Renaissance, which brought poet Langston Hughes to New York City, revealed new possibilities in race relations that exhilarated some Americans but frightened many others. Notably, the Ku Klux Klan enjoyed a resurgence in popularity and power by pandering to racial and social fears. And Margaret Sanger's crusade for birth control challenged traditional attitudes in the sensitive areas of family planning and sexuality.

The assumption that modern American life meant unending growth, expansion, and prosperity came into question during the Great Depression of the 1930s. Although citizens everywhere encountered the same overwhelming set of events, the degree to which individuals were affected by the Depression varied. Some ruminated over fortunes lost on the stock market; others joined radical organizations; still others, like Morey Skaret, took to the road, drifting from place to place. Newcomers to America, including many Mexicans, struggled to navigate not only new customs but also the economic crisis and rising xenophobia. In the face of the era's hardships, the labor movement evolved a new weapon, the sit-down strike, which created powerful industry-wide unions. With this development, a national political base for labor was formed that raised wages and involved millions of workers and community supporters, among them Genora Dollinger.

POINTS OF VIEW
The Great Depression

29

ANONYMOUS

Down and Out in the Great Depression

President Franklin D. Roosevelt (1882–1945), in his famous "fireside chats," was the first president to use radio to communicate directly and effectively to the nation. And Eleanor Roosevelt (1884–1962) was different from all previous first ladies in her public championing of the underdog. Victims of the Great Depression of the 1930s sometimes wrote to the president, to Mrs. Roosevelt, or to various agencies and administrators responsible for carrying out government-sponsored plans for relief. This was largely a new phenomenon in American life. President Hoover employed one secretary to answer mail from the public; the Roosevelt White House needed fifty.

The archives of the New Deal era contain tens of millions of letters from ordinary people expressing their concerns and frequently asking for help. This trove of information about the forgotten men and women of the 1930s reveals attitudes about government, wealth and poverty, opportunity, and patriotism. Unlike many secondary sources for understanding the ways events affected everyday people, these letters are not articles filtered through the perception of an interviewer or memoirs written long after the events.

Robert S. McElvaine, *Down and Out in the Great Depression: Letters from the "Forgotten Man"* (Chapel Hill: University of North Carolina Press, 1983).

Robert S. McElvaine, who edited these letters for publication in Down and Out in the Great Depression *(1983), uses them to understand the real experience of unemployment and destitution in the 1930s.*

QUESTIONS TO CONSIDER

1. What attitudes toward the government were held by the people writing to the Roosevelts? What attitudes about social class do you find in the letters?
2. Can you identify the prejudices these people had? What groups were they prejudiced against, and for what reasons?
3. What can you infer about the successes and failures of the New Deal?

[Oil City, Penn.
December 15, 1930]

Col Arthur Woods
Director, Presidents Committee
Dear Sir:

. . . I have none of these things [that the rich have], what do they care how much we suffer, how much the health of our children is menaced. Now I happen to know there is something can be done about it and Oil City needs to be awakened up to that fact and compelled to act.

Now that our income is but $15.60 a week (their are five of us My husband Three little children and myself). My husband who is a world war Veteran and saw active service in the trenches, became desperate and applied for Compensation or a pension from the Government and was turned down and that started me thinking. . . . [There should be] enough to pay all world war veterans a pension, dysabeled or not dysabeled and there by relieve a lot of suffering, and banish resentment that causes Rebellions and Bolshevism. Oh why is it that it is always a bunch of overley rich, selfish, dumb, ignorant money hogs that persist in being Senitors, legislatures, representitives? Where would they and their possessions be if it were not for the Common Soldier, the common laborer that is compelled to work for a starvation wage. for I tell you again the hog of a Landlord gets his there is not enough left for the necessaries if a man has three or more children. Not so many years ago in Russia all the sufferings of poverty (and you can never feel them you are on the other side of the fence but try to understand) conceived a child, that child was brought forth in agony, and its name was Bolshevism. I am on the other side of the fence from you, you are not in a position to see, but I, I can see and feel and understand. I have lived and suffered too. I know, and right now our good old U.S.A. is sitting on a Seething Volcano. In the Public Schools our little children stand at salute and recite a "rig ma role" in which is mentioned "Justice to all." What a lie, what a naked lie, when honest, law abiding citizens, decendents of Revilutionary heros, Civil War heros, and World war heros are denied the priviledge of owning their own homes, that foundation of good citizenship, good morals, and the very foundation of good government the world over. Is all that our Soldiers of all wars fought bled and died for to be sacrificed to a God awful hideious Rebellion? in which all our Citizens will be involved, because of the dumb bungling of rich politicians? Oh for a few Statesmen, oh for but one statesman, as fearless as Abraham Lincoln, the amancipator who died for us. and who said, you can fool some of the people some of the time, But you can't fool all of the people all of the time. Heres hoping you have read this to the end and think it over. I wish you a Mery Christmas and a Happy New Year.

Very Truly Yours
Mrs. M. E. B

Phila., Pa.
November 26, 1934

Honorable Franklin D. Roosevelt
Washington, D.C.
Dear Mr. President:

I am forced to write to you because we find ourselves in *a very serious condition.* For the last three or four years we have had depression and *suffered* with my *family* and little children *severely.* Now Since the Home Owners Loan Corporation opened up, I have been going there in order to save my home, because there has been unemployment in my house for more than three years. You can imagine that I and my family have suffered from lack of water supply in my house for more than two years. Last winter I did not have coal and the pipes burst in my house and therefore could not make heat in the house. Now winter is here again and we are suffering of cold, no water in the house, and we are facing to be forced out of the house, because I have no money to move or pay so much money as they want when after making settlement I am mother of little children, am sick and losing my health, and we are eight people in the family, and where can I go when I don't have money because no one is working in my house. The Home Loan Corporation wants $42. a month rent or else we will have to be on the street. I am living in this house for about ten years and when times were good we would put our last cent in the house and now I have *no money, no home* and *no wheres to go.* I beg of you to please help me and my family and little children for the sake of a sick mother and suffering family to give this your immediate attention so we will not be forced to move or put out in the street.

Waiting and Hoping that you will act quickly.
Thanking you very much I remain

Mrs. E. L.

Lincoln Nebraska
May 19/ 34

Mrs Franklin D. Roosevelt
Washington, D.C.
Dear Mrs Roosevelt:

Will you be kind enough to read the following as it deals with a very important subject which you are very much interested in as well as my self.

In the Presidents inaugral adress delivered from the capitol steps the afternoon of his inaugration he made mention of The Forgotten Man, and I with thousands of others am wondering if the folk who was borned here in America some 60 or 70 years a go are this Forgotten Man, the President had in mind, if we are this Forgotten Man then we are still Forgotten.

We who have tried to be diligent in our support of this most wonderful nation of ours boath social and other wise, we in our younger days tried to do our duty without complaining.

We have helped to pay pensions to veterans of some thre wars, we have raised the present young generation and have tried to train them to honor and support this our home country.

And now a great calamity has come upon us and seamingly no cause of our own it has swept away what little savings we had accumulated and we are left in a condition that is imposible for us to correct, for two very prominent reasons if no more.

First we have grown to what is termed Old Age, this befalls every man.

Second as we put fourth every effort in our various business lines trying to rectify and reestablish our selves we are confronted on every hand with the young generation, taking our places, this of corse is what we have looked forward to in training our children. But with the extra ordinary crisese which left us helpless and placed us in the position that our fathers did not have to contend with.

Seamingly every body has been assisted but we the Forgotten Man, and since we for 60 years or more have tried to carry the loan without complaining, we have paid others pensions we have educated and trained the youth, now as we are Old and down and out of no reason of our own, would it be asking to much of our Government and the young generation to do by us as we have tried our best to do by them even without complaint.

We have been honorable citizens all along our journey, calamity and old age has forced its self upon us please donot send us to the Poor Farm but instead allow us the small pension of $40.00 per month and we will do as we have done in the past (not complain).

I personly Know of Widows who are no older than I am who own their own homes and draw $45.00 per month pension, these ladies were born this side of the civil war the same as I, therefore they never experianced war trouble.

Please donot think of us who are asking this assitsnce as Old Broken down dishonorable cotizens, but we are of those borned in this country and have done our bit in making this country, we are folk in all walks of life and businesse.

For example I am an architect and builder I am not and old broken down illiterate dishonorable man although I am 69 years old, but as I put forth every effort to regain my prestage in business I am confronted on every side by the young generation taking my place, yes this is also the case even in the effort of the government with its recovery plan, even though I am qualifyed to suprentend any class of construction but the young man has captured this place also.

What are we to do since the calamity has swept our all away,? We are just asking to be remembered with a small part as we have done to others[;] $40.00 a month is all we are asking.

Mrs. Roosevelt I am asking a personal favor of you as it seems to be the only means through which I may be able to reach the President, some evening very soon, as you and Mr. Roosevelt are having dinner together privately will you ask him to read this. And we American citizens will ever remember your kindness.

Yours very truly.
R. A. [male]

[February, 1936]

Mr. and Mrs. Roosevelt.
Wash. D.C.
Dear Mr. President:

I'm a boy of 12 years. I want to tell you about my family. My father hasn't worked for 5 months. He went plenty times to relief, he filled out application. They won't give us anything. I don't know why. Please you do something. We haven't paid 4 months rent, Everyday the landlord rings the door bell, we don't open the door for him. We are afraid that we will be put out, been put out before, and don't want to happen again. We haven't paid the gas bill, and the electric bill, haven't paid grocery bill for 3 months. My brother goes to Lane Tech. High School. he's eighteen years old, hasn't gone to school for 2 weeks because he got no carfare. I have a sister she's twenty years, she can't find work. My father he staying home. All the time he's crying because he can't find work. I told him why are you crying daddy, and daddy said why shouldn't I cry when there is nothing in the house. I feel sorry for him. That night I couldn't sleep. The next morning I wrote this letter to you. in my room. Were American citizens and were born in Chicago, Ill. and I don't know why they don't help us Please answer right away because we need it. will starve Thank you.

God bless you.

[Anonymous]
Chicago, Ill.

Dec. 14—1937
Columbus, Ind.

Mrs. F. D. Roosevelt,
Washington, D.C.

Mrs. Roosevelt: I suppose from your point of view the work relief, old age pensions, slum clearance and all the rest seems like a perfect remedy for all the ills of this country, but I would like for you to see the results, as the other half see them.

We have always had a shiftless, never-do-well class of people whose one and only aim in life is to live without work. I have been rubbing elbows with this class for nearly sixty years and have tried to help some of the most promising and have seen others try to help them, but it can't be done. We cannot help those who will not try to help themselves and if they do try a square deal is all they need, and by the way that is all this country needs or ever has needed: a square deal for all and then, let each one paddle their own canoe, or sink.

There has never been any necessity for any one who is able to work, being on relief in this locality, but there have been many eating the bread of charity and they have lived better than ever before. I have had taxpayers tell me that their children came from school and asked why they couldn't have nice lunches like the children on relief.

The women and children around here have had to work at the fields to help save the crops and several women fainted while at work and at the same time we couldn't go up or down the road without stumbling over some of the reliefers, moping around carrying dirt from one side of the road to the other and back again, or else asleep. I live alone on a farm and have not raised any crops for the last two years as there was no help to be had. I am feeding the stock and have been cutting the wood to keep my home fires burning. There are several reliefers around here now who have been kicked off relief, but they refuse to work unless they can get relief hours and wages, but they are so worthless no one can afford to hire them.

As for the clearance of the real slums, it can't be done as long as their inhabitants are allowed to reproduce their kind. I would like for you to see what a family of that class can do to a decent house in a short time. Such a family moved into an almost new, neat, four-room house near here last winter. They even cut down some of the shade trees for fuel, after they had burned everything they could pry loose. There were two big idle boys in the family and they could get all the fuel they wanted, just for the cutting, but the shade trees were closer and it was taking a great amount of fuel, for they had broken out several windows and they had but very little bedding. There were two women there all the time and three part of the time and there was enough good clothing tramped in the mud around the yard to have made all the bedclothes they needed. It was clothing that had been given them and they had worn it until it was too filthy to wear any longer without washing, so they threw it out and begged more. I will not try to describe their filth for you would not believe me. They paid no rent while there and left between two suns owing everyone from whom they could get a nickels worth of anything. They are just a fair sample of the class of people on whom so much of our hard earned tax-money is being squandered and on whom so much sympathy is being wasted.

As for the old people on beggars' allowances: the taxpayers have provided homes for all the old people who never liked to work, where they will be neither cold nor hungry: much better homes than most of them have ever tried to provide for themselves. They have lived many years through the most prosperous times of our country and had an opportunity to prepare for old age, but they spent their lives in idleness or worse and now they expect those who have worked like slaves, to provide a living for them and all their worthless descendants. Some of them are asking for from thirty to sixty dollars a month when I have known them to live on a dollar a week rather than go to work. There is many a little child doing without butter on its bread, so that some old sot can have his booze and tobacco: some old sot who spent his working years loafing around pool rooms and saloons, boasting that the world owed him a living.

Even the child welfare has become a racket. The parents of large families are getting divorces, so that the mothers and children can qualify for aid. The children to join the ranks of the "unemployed" as they grow up, for no child that has been raised on charity in this community has ever amounted to anything.

You people who have plenty of this worlds goods and whose money comes easy, have no idea of the heart-breaking toil and self-denial which is the lot of the working people who are trying to make an honest living, and then to have to shoulder all these unjust burdens seems like the last straw. During the worst of the depression many of the farmers had to deny their families butter, eggs, meat etc. and sell it to pay their taxes and then had to stand by and see the deadbeats carry it home to their families by the arm load, and they knew their tax money was helping pay for it. One woman saw a man carry out eight pounds of butter at one time. The crookedness, selfishness, greed and graft of the crooked politicians is making one gigantic racket out of the new deal and it is making this a nation of dead-beats and beggars and if it continues the people who will work will soon be nothing but slaves for the pampered poverty rats and I am afraid these human parasites are going to become a menace to the country unless they are disfranchised. No one should have the right to vote theirself a living at the expense of the tax payers. They learned their strength at the last election and also learned that they can get just about what they want by "voting right." They have had a taste of their coveted life of idleness, and at the rate they are increasing, they will soon control the country. The twentieth child arrived in the home of one chronic reliefer near here some time ago.

Is it any wonder the taxpayers are discouraged by all this penalizing of thrift and industry to reward shiftlessness, or that the whole country is on the brink of chaos?

M. A. H. [female]
Columbus, Ind.

[no address]
Jan. 18, 1937

[Dear Mrs. Roosevelt:]

I . . . was simply astounded to think that anyone could be nitwit enough to wish to be included in the so called social security act if they could possibly avoid it. Call it by any name you wish it, in my opinion, (and that of many people I know) is nothing but downright stealing. . . .

Personally, I had my savings so invested that I would have had a satisfactory provision for old age. Now thanks to his [FDR's] desire to "get" the utilities I cannot be sure of anything, being a stockholder, as after business has survived his merciless attacks (*if* it does) insurance will probably be no good either.

[She goes on to complain about the lack of profits.]

Then the president tells them they should hire more men and work shorter hours so that the laborers, who are getting everything now raises etc. can have a "more abundant life." That simply means taking it from the rest of us in the form of taxes or otherwise. . . .

Believe me, the only thing we want from the president, unless or if you except Communists and the newly trained chiselers, is for him to balance the budget and reduce taxes. That, by the way, is a "mandate from the people" that isn't getting much attention.

I am not an "economic royalist," just an ordinary white collar worker at $1600 per. Please show this to the president and ask him to remember the wishes of the forgotten man, that is, the one who dared to vote against him. We expect to be tramped on but we do wish the stepping would be a little less hard.

Security at the price of freedom is never desired by intelligent people.

M. A. [female]

[Mr. Harry Hopkins
Washington, D.C.]
[Dear Mr. Hopkins:]

Will you please investigate the various relief agencies in many cities of the United States. The cities where there are a large foreign and jewish population. No wonder the cities are now on the verge of bankruptcy because we are feeding a lot of ignorant foreigners by giving them relief. And, they are turning against us every day. I would suggest to deport all foreigners and jews who are not citizens over the United States back to any land where they choose to go and who will admit them. As America is now over crowded with too much immigration and it can not feed even its own citizens without feeding the citizens of other foreign nations. I have found out after careful investigation that we are feeding many foreigners who send out their wives to work and who have money in the bank. While the men drink wine and play cards in saloons and cafes. I have spoken to one Italian whom I met. And I ask him what he was doing for a living. He said me drinka da dago red wine and play cards and send the wife out to work. Isn't a very good thing for us to support them. No wonder the taxpayers are grumbling about taxes. Most of them are a race of black hands murders boot leggers bomb throwers. While most of the sheeney jews as they are called are a race of dishonest people who get rich by swindling, faking and cheating the poor people. Besides the jews are responsible by ruining others in business by the great amount of chisling done. And selling even below the cost prices, in order to get all the others business. The foreigners and jews spend as little as they can to help this country. And, they live as cheap as they can. And, work as cheap as they can, and save all the money they can. And when they have enough they go back to their country. Why don't we deport them under the section of the United States Immigration Laws which relates to paupers and those who become a public charge. The Communist Party is composed mostly by foreigners and jews. The jews are the leaders of the movement and urge the downfall of this government. . . .

A Taxpayer

30

MOREY SKARET

On the Road during the Great Depression

The Great Depression of the 1930s was devastating to many American families. As people lost their jobs and depleted their savings, millions of families were forced to abandon their homes, some living on the streets or, if they were lucky, doubling and tripling up with relatives and friends. While such compromises made sense economically, they often led to tensions and explosive outbreaks between individuals used to having their own space. Domestic violence and depression were all too common, and many families were unable to survive the stress. Everywhere, it seemed, men who had been breadwinners took to the road. Some had been thrown out by women unable to cope with the men's inability to secure work. Others had stolen away in the middle of the night, the shame of not taking care of their families too much to bear. Perhaps they believed they were doing their families a favor by reducing the number of mouths to feed while increasing their prospects for finding work.

Morey Skaret, "Morey Skaret: Riding the Rails in the 1930s," ed. Cassandra Tate, June 15, 2001, Essay 3369, HistoryLink.org, http://www.historylink.org/index.cfm?DisplayPage =output.cfm&file_id=3369.

So many men left home for the open road that a subculture developed around this lifestyle that came to be called hobo. *A hobo was a homeless man living on the cheap, illegally hopping freight trains and sleeping where he could, and all the while looking for work. Hoboes were believed to share the camaraderie of nights beneath the stars and the romance of the road, evolving their own vocabulary and ethical codes, which they used to distinguish themselves from more traditional tramps, who also "rambled," but without an interest in employment. Hoboes were featured in movies, comics, books, songs, and radio dramas.*

Despite serious housing shortages after World War II, the robust postwar economy and record low unemployment largely put an end to the hobo lifestyle. However, a new generation of postwar artists and writers, who had grown up in a more comfortable and predictable economic environment, would celebrate hobo ways in songs, poetry, and fiction.

The following account is by Norwegian-born Morest L. "Morey" Skaret (b. 1913), who at age ten moved to Seattle with his family. After completing a fifth year of high school, thanks to a special program offered by the Seattle school district in response to high unemployment levels, Skaret took to the road. He eventually became a police officer and wrote his autobiography.

QUESTIONS TO CONSIDER

1. During the Great Depression, high schoolers like Morey Skaret often stayed in school after graduation. Why might so many people have responded to the economic crisis by continuing their education?
2. Although there were female hoboes, among them "Boxcar" Bertha Thompson, most of those who lived the hobo life during the Depression were men. Why do you think this was the case?
3. What dangers and hardships did Skaret and Charlie Shellfisher face?
4. How do the representations of hoboes in this account compare with the ways homeless people are regarded today?

ON THE BUM

By the time I got to high school, the whole town was well into the Great Depression. It was tough times. I got my diploma but I couldn't afford to go to university so I took advantage of the extra year of high school that the district offered. After that, I did what a lot of young men from large families did then to relieve the load on the home place: I went on the bum. Charlie Shellfisher, my good friend all through school, and I went together. Although Native American not Norwegian, his family was similar to mine — hard-working and hard-pressed. We left Seattle in the spring and returned before winter.

Charlie and I usually rode freight trains. When a gondola car was empty of grain or coal, we could get shelter from the wind inside. A boxcar was even better because it would also keep us dry. If we couldn't get inside a freight car, we rode the rods under it. Two thick rods about five feet apart span between the front and rear wheels of a freight car to give it strength. To "ride the rods," you would lie on a plank wired across those two rods. You could usually count on finding a plank and some wire in the rail yard. The wire is essential because, if your plank falls off when the train's going 40 miles an hour or so, you're dead. Charlie and I always tried to put our planks together so we could get some warmth from each other.

If no freight train was coming, we would catch a passenger train and "ride the blinds." Similar to our articulated buses now, the accordion-like folds of a train's blinds are what enabled it to "bend" around curves. The blinds of one passenger car would butt up to the blinds of the car in front of it to make an articulated compartment. At the time, trains were powered by coal. Where the coal car met the first passenger car, you had just a single, open blind. Charlie and I would jump in there and cuddle in the corner away from the wind. The railroads didn't like you riding their passenger trains and we would do it only as a last resort. If you didn't get off before the train reached the yard, the bulls [railway security officers] would come after you with those big sticks they had.

One day Charlie and I scrambled out from under a car to face a yard bull in Cheyenne, Wyoming. "How much money do you have, boys?" he demanded.

"We don't have any," I responded.

"Well, this town has an ordinance that says, if you don't have at least 35 cents, you're a vagrant and under arrest," he said. "Come on."

We figured out later that, when someone in town needed workers, the yard bull would provide them! We happened along when the town needed to move its library from one side of the street to the other. For four days, Charlie and I carried books. We spent three nights in jail, where our meals arrived in a bucket! When we were finished, the sheriff drove us in an old Dodge panel truck out to the edge of town.

"That's the way to Laramie," he said, pointing down a gray ribbon of highway. "Don't you ever come back to Cheyenne."

"No sir, we won't!" I said. We thumbed our way to the next town and sought out the hobo jungle near the railroad tracks where we could find out when to catch a train going north.

To sustain ourselves, Charlie and I would first ask for work in exchange for a meal, then if we couldn't get work, we would ask for a meal. Because most of the places we asked were on the regular routes that bums traveled, feeding them got to be too much for many of those dear, kind people.

We were in one jungle when Charlie got sick and was shaking with cold. I found a long cardboard box, the kind that a hot-water tank might have come in, and put it under a bridge out of the rain. Charlie crawled inside and I stuffed newspapers all around him for warmth. I went into the town and asked the baker for work in order to get my sick friend something to eat. He said he was asked all the time and usually said no but he had garbage cans out back that needed cleaning and I could have that job.

Never clean a baker's garbage cans! The stuff on the sides was as hard as concrete. I pretty much had to chisel them clean! When I got finished, the baker's wife saw that I had worked hard and she put a full piece of beef steak inside each of two sandwiches. When I got back to Charlie with this food, an old Negro man had come in with a few other hobos and started a fire. They took a square five-gallon tin can and cut one end out to feed in the wood and a hole in the other end to get the draft going and it made a darn good stove. The old man got the beef steak all heated and cut up for Charlie. He began to feel better and soon we were back on our way to Seattle.

One story from that time I know to be true but I'm not sure who did it. It could have been Charlie; I know it wasn't me because such a deception wasn't in my nature.

We were hungry one day when we came across a little boy playing near an irrigation ditch. Charlie thought a minute and then all of a sudden he grabbed the kid by the neck of his shirt and dunked him under the water. Charlie carried the dripping kid to the mother and said, "Your little boy fell in the irrigation ditch!"

"Oh my goodness," she said. "I'm so glad you were there! Johnny, I told you not to go near that irrigation ditch. Now you thank the nice man." Well, of course, the kid's eyes got big and he backed away and started to cry. He didn't want to have anything to do with Charlie! We got a good meal out of it but it was a dirty trick.

On the bum, you're always moving. At first you're searching, anxious to get to the next town or farming area because that may be where you find a job. After you realize that nothing's out there, you're hurrying home. We got as far as Cheyenne before we decided we'd better turn around.

Oldtimers had warned us against riding through a long tunnel—that we could suffocate from the fumes. We took a chance, though, and made it through one long tunnel north of Everett and another just before Union Station in Seattle. As we came out of the second tunnel, we hung on the side of the car and paced with one foot to tell if the train had slowed enough for us to jump. When I jumped, I landed right in the cinders. Charlie was more nimble and made it fine.

We brushed ourselves off and walked down to Skid Road with just 10 cents between us. We got a bowl of soup and dry bread for 5 cents each at the Klondike Café, then walked home. Mother was glad to see me. I had turned 20 on the bum.

FOR CRITICAL THINKING

1. Morey Skaret wrote his memoirs over sixty years after the events he describes happened, but the letters to the Roosevelts were written as the events were taking place. How do you think the distance of time might have changed the way these two sources present the Great Depression?

2. Historians have learned much about how ordinary people experienced the Great Depression from thousands of letters to the president and his wife, but millions of suffering people never wrote. How might the perspectives of the people who didn't write to the president change our understanding of life in the Great Depression?
3. How might a person's age or point in the life cycle have affected the way he or she responded to the Great Depression?
4. How do you think Morey Skaret would have responded to the letters to the Roosevelts?

31

Food Relief

Economists argue about why there are economic downturns roughly every five to seven years, why some downturns turn into global crises roughly every fifty to seventy years, and whether there is anything that can be done to avoid these boom–bust cycles. Nearly all economists agree, however, that government policy can have an impact on the length, depth, and destructiveness of a crisis. The world economic crisis of the 1930s triggered by the U.S. stock market collapse of October 1929 was widely experienced as the longest, deepest, and most destructive economic crisis in U.S. history. Called "the Great Depression," this crisis is still the standard against which all other crises are measured.

Policymakers and pundits viewed the start of the Great Depression as just another ordinary downturn in the business cycle. However, as more and more ordinary Americans found themselves without employment, shelter, and basic necessities, it become difficult to dismiss the millions suffering as intemperate poor people being punished for their laziness and personal disorder—as was popular to do in the early twentieth century. Not surprisingly, feeding the hungry became a focal point of government aid. With a majority of the population that was, for the first time, urban, most Americans simply did not have the option of growing their own food and borrowing from local merchants against land and future harvests. For the nearly 60 percent of Americans who lived in cities, unemployment raised the fear of malnourishment, stunted growth of children, and, possibly, starvation. To make matters worse, as world markets collapsed and less money circulated, a deflationary spiral took hold that drove down the price of basic foodstuffs, often making it more expensive to bring crops to market than to use them for fuel.

As the crisis continued into the early 1930s and the suffering deepened, outgoing president Herbert Hoover created the Emergency Relief Administration, subsequently renamed the Federal Emergency Relief Administration (FERA) in 1933 by the new presi-

dent Franklin D. Roosevelt. This was the beginning of what is often called the "alphabet agencies" of Roosevelt's New Deal. In one of Roosevelt's early attempts to address the problem of deflation, the Agricultural Adjustment Administration planned and implemented the destruction of millions of tons of food in 1933, in the hopes that it would bring up prices and once again make it worth growing, transporting, and marketing food. Prices did not go up, people in cities continued to lack basic food, and the public outcry was immense, leading Roosevelt and his planners to develop a new approach that involved the unprecedented step of government food redistribution to schools, local relief agencies, and other community organizations that committed to getting it to the needy.

These Depression-era experiments formed the prehistory of many contemporary policies, including U.S. Department of Agriculture Food Stamps, school lunches and breakfasts, agricultural subsidies, and varied other relief and social welfare policies that are now commonplace. The photo reprinted here depicts food relief that was probably distributed by a local community agency, using food that had been diverted from the billions of kilocalories of foodstuffs rotting and unsold in agricultural areas.

QUESTIONS TO CONSIDER

1. What do you see in this picture that suggests that such food relief is a new Roosevelt-era program?
2. What story is told in this photo, and how would you imagine the backstory?
3. Roosevelt was accused of being a socialist for implementing programs like food redistribution. Food relief is now commonplace in the form of the Supplemental Nutrition Assistance Program, or SNAP (formerly known as Food Stamps). What current debates about government assistance echo the nutrition assistance controversy?

Children wait for their father to collect potato rations in Cleveland, Ohio.
Universal History Archive / UIG / Bridgeman Images.

32

WILLIAM JENNINGS BRYAN AND CLARENCE DARROW

In Defense of the Bible

In July 1925, John T. Scopes was tried for teaching the theory of evolution in the Dayton, Tennessee, high school. The first trial in U.S. history to be broadcast nationally over radio, the proceedings were "monkey business" to some and "the trial of the century" to others.

The Tennessee legislature had passed the Butler Act in March 1925, making it a crime for anyone in any state-supported school (including universities) to teach "any theory that denies the story of the Divine Creation of man as taught in the Bible, and

---

Sheldon Norman Grebstein, *Monkey Trial: The State of Tennessee vs. John Thomas Scopes* (Boston: Houghton Mifflin, 1960), 150–63.

to teach instead that man has descended from a lower order of animals." A few Daytonians decided to test the law and persuaded Scopes, a young high school biology teacher, to become the defendant.

Larger forces, however, were at work. The Protestant churches were sharply dividing between fundamentalists who believed in the literal truth of the Bible and liberals who accepted the findings of science. The split corresponded to a division between rural and urban values, a division that was also sharply reflected in national, and especially Democratic Party, politics. The South was a stronghold of fundamentalism, and laws like the Butler Act had much support throughout the region.

A famous orator led each legal team in the Scopes proceedings. William Jennings Bryan (1860–1925), long identified with the values of the countryside, had been the Democratic Party candidate for president in 1896, 1900, and 1908 and had served as Woodrow Wilson's first secretary of state. Clarence Darrow (1857–1938) was a nationally known trial lawyer and lecturer on evolution and various reforms. When the presiding judge, John T. Raulston, banned the use of expert witnesses on the theory of evolution, Darrow called Bryan himself to the stand as an authority on the Bible. Bryan agreed to testify, and the judge permitted his testimony to proceed—but without the jury, which the judge had ruled was not to decide matters of the truth of either evolution or the Bible but only whether Scopes had taught evolution to his high school class. Yet as the following excerpts show, Darrow made it seem as if Bryan, fundamentalism, and perhaps even the Bible were on trial and revealed Bryan's spotty knowledge of scientific matters. The following day, the judge changed his mind, expunged all of Bryan's testimony, and sent the case to the jury for the inevitable finding of Scopes's admitted guilt.

QUESTIONS TO CONSIDER

1. Why might William Jennings Bryan have agreed to testify?
2. How could Bryan have made his arguments stronger? What values was he defending?
3. Evaluate Clarence Darrow's performance. Was he, as some have said, putting the Bible on trial? In what ways do you think Darrow's use of science strengthened his argument? In what ways do you think it weakened it?

EXAMINATION OF W. J. BRYAN BY CLARENCE DARROW, COUNSEL FOR THE DEFENSE

The Court: The question is whether or not Mr. Scopes taught man descended from the lower order of animals.

Q: You have given considerable study to the Bible, haven't you, Mr. Bryan?

A: Yes, sir, I have tried to.

Q: Well, we all know you have; we are not going to dispute that at all. But you have written and published articles almost weekly, and sometimes have made interpretations of various things.

A: I would not say interpretations, Mr. Darrow, but comments on the lesson.

Q: If you comment to any extent, these comments have been interpretations?

A: I presume that any discussion might be to some extent interpretations, but they have not been primarily intended as interpretations.

Q: Then you have made a general study of it?

A: Yes, I have; I have studied the Bible for about fifty years, or some time more than that, but, of course, I have studied it more as I have become older than when I was but a boy.

Q: Do you claim that everything in the Bible should be literally interpreted?

A: I believe everything in the Bible should be accepted as it is given there; some of the Bible is given illustratively. For instance: "Ye are the salt of the earth." I would not insist that man was actually salt, or that he had flesh of salt, but it is used in the sense of salt as saving God's people.

Q: You believe the story of the flood to be a literal interpretation?

A: Yes, sir.

Q: When was that flood?

A: I would not attempt to fix the date. The date is fixed, as suggested this morning.

Q: About 4004 B.C.?

A: That has been the estimate of a man that is accepted today. I would not say it is accurate.

Q: That estimate is printed in the Bible?

A: Everybody knows, at least, I think most of the people know, that was the estimate given.

Q: But what do you think that the Bible, itself, says? Don't you know how it was arrived at?

A: I never made a calculation.

Q: What do you think?

A: I do not think about things I don't think about.

Q: Do you think about things you do think about?

A: Well, sometimes.

The Bailiff: Let us have order.

Mr. Darrow: Mr. Bryan, you have read these dates over and over again?

A: Not very accurately; I turn back sometimes to see what the time was.

Q: You want to say now you have no idea how these dates were computed?

A: No, I don't say, but I have told you what my idea was. I say I don't know how accurate it was.

Q: You say from the generation of man —

Gen. Stewart:[1] I am objecting to his cross-examining his own witness.

Mr. Darrow: He is a hostile witness.

The Court: I am going to let Mr. Bryan control —

The Witness: I want him to have all the latitude he wants, for I am going to have some latitude when he gets through.

---

1. **Gen. Stewart:** Arthur Thomas Stewart, attorney general of Tennessee and chief prosecutor in the Scopes trail.

Mr. Darrow: You can have latitude and longitude.

The Court: Order.

Gen. Stewart: The witness is entitled to be examined as to the legal evidence of it. We were supposed to go into the argument today, and we have nearly lost the day, your Honor.

Mr. McKenzie:[2] I object to it.

Gen. Stewart: Your Honor, he is perfectly able to take care of this, but we are attaining no evidence. This is not competent evidence.

The Witness: These gentlemen have not had much chance—they did not come here to try this case. They came here to try revealed religion. I am here to defend it, and they can ask me any question they please.

The Court: All right.

Mr. Darrow: Great applause from the bleachers.

The Witness: From those whom you call "yokels."

Mr. Darrow: I have never called them yokels.

The Witness: That is the ignorance of Tennessee, the bigotry.

Mr. Darrow: You mean who are applauding you?

The Witness: Those are the people whom you insult.

Mr. Darrow: You insult every man of science and learning in the world because he does not believe in your fool religion.

The Court: I will not stand for that.

Mr. Darrow: For what he is doing?

The Court: I am talking to both of you.

Gen. Stewart: This has gone beyond the pale of a lawsuit, your Honor. I have a public duty to perform under my oath, and I ask the Court to stop it. Mr. Darrow is making an effort to insult the gentleman on the witness stand and I ask that it be stopped, for it has gone beyond the pale of a lawsuit.

The Court: To stop it now would not be just to Mr. Bryan. He wants to ask the other gentlemen questions along the same line.

Gen. Stewart: It will all be incompetent.

The Witness: The jury is not here.

The Court: I do not want to be strictly technical.

Mr. Darrow: Then your Honor rules, and I accept.

Gen. Stewart: The jury is not here.

Mr. Darrow: How long ago was the flood, Mr. Bryan?

A: Let me see Ussher's calculation[3] about it?

Mr. Darrow: Surely.

A: I think this does not give it.

Q: It gives an account of Noah. Where is the one in evidence? I am quite certain it is there.

The Witness: Oh, I would put the estimate where it is, because I have no reason to vary it. But I would have to look at it to give you the exact date.

Q: I would, too. Do you remember what book the account is in?

2. **Mr. McKenzie:** Benjamin McKenzie, part of the prosecution team.
3. **Ussher's calculation:** In his book *The Annals of the Old Testament,* the seventeenth-century Irish bishop James Ussher had calculated Earth's age to be about four thousand years.

A: Genesis.

Mr. Hays:[4] Is that the one in evidence?

Mr. Neal:[5] That will have it; that is the King James Version.

Mr. Darrow: The one in evidence has it.

The Witness: It is given here, as 2,348 years B.C.

Q: Well, 2,348 years B.C. You believe that all the living things that were not contained in the ark were destroyed.

A: I think the fish may have lived.

Q: Outside of the fish?

A: I cannot say.

Q: You cannot say?

A: No, I accept that just as it is; I have no proof to the contrary.

Q: I am asking you whether you believe?

A: I do.

Q: That all living things outside of the fish were destroyed?

A: What I say about the fish is merely a matter of humor.

Q: I understand.

The Witness: Due to the fact a man wrote up here the other day to ask whether all the fish were destroyed, and the gentleman who received the letter told him the fish may have lived.

Q: I am referring to the fish, too.

A: I accept that as the Bible gives it and I have never found any reason for denying, disputing, or rejecting it.

Q: Let us make it definite, 2,348 years?

A: I didn't say that. That is the time given there [*indicating the Bible*] but I don't pretend to say that is exact.

Q: You never figured it out, these generations, yourself?

A: No, sir; not myself.

Q: But the Bible you have offered in evidence says 2,340 something, so that 4,200 years ago there was not a living thing on the earth, excepting the people on the ark and the animals on the ark and the fishes?

A: There have been living things before that.

Q: I mean at that time.

A: After that.

Q: Don't you know there are any number of civilizations that are traced back to more than 5,000 years?

A: I know we have people who trace things back according to the number of ciphers they have. But I am not satisfied they are accurate.

Q: You are not satisfied there is any civilization that can be traced back 5,000 years?

A: I would not want to say there is because I have no evidence of it that is satisfactory.

4. **Mr. Hays:** Arthur Garfield Hays, general counsel for the American Civil Liberties Union and a member of the defense team.
5. **Mr. Neal:** John R. Neal, professor of law at the University of Tennessee and official chief defense attorney.

Q: Would you say there is not?

A: Well, so far as I know, but when the scientists differ from 24,000,000 to 306,000,000 in their opinion as to how long ago life came here, I want them to be nearer, to come nearer together, before they demand of me to give up my belief in the Bible.

Q: Do you say that you do not believe that there were any civilizations on this earth that reach back beyond 5,000 years?

A: I am not satisfied by any evidence that I have seen.

Q: I didn't ask you what you are satisfied with. I asked you if you believe it?

The Witness: Will you let me answer it?

The Court: Go right on.

The Witness: I am satisfied by no evidence that I have found that would justify me in accepting the opinions of these men against what I believe to be the inspired Word of God.

Q: And you believe every nation, every organization of men, every animal, in the world outside of the fishes—

The Witness: The fish, I want you to understand, is merely a matter of humor.

Q: You believe that all the various human races on the earth have come into being in the last 4,000 years or 4,200 years, whatever it is?

A: No, it would be more than that.

[Here Bryan and Darrow engaged in some calculations as to when man was created, according to the chronology Bryan was defending.]

Q: That makes 4,262 years. If it is not correct, we can correct it.

A: According to the Bible there was a civilization before that, destroyed by the flood.

Q: Let me make this definite. You believe that every civilization on the earth and every living thing, except possibly the fishes, that came out of the ark were wiped out by the flood?

A: At that time.

Q: At that time. And then whatever human beings, including all the tribes, that inhabited the world, and have inhabited the world, and who run their pedigree straight back, and all the animals, have come onto the earth since the flood?

A: Yes.

Q: Within 4,200 years. Do you know a scientific man on the face of the earth that believes any such thing?

A: I cannot say, but I know some scientific men who dispute entirely the antiquity of man as testified to by other scientific men.

Q: Oh, that does not answer the question. Do you know of a single scientific man on the face of the earth that believes any such thing as you stated, about the antiquity of man?

A: I don't think I have ever asked one the direct question.

Q: Quite important, isn't it?

A: Well, I don't know as it is.

Q: It might not be?

A: If I had nothing else to do except speculate on what our remote ancestors were and what our remote descendants have been, but I have been more interested in Christians going on right now to make it much more important than speculation on either the past or the future.

Q: You have never had any interest in the age of the various races and people and civilizations and animals that exist upon the earth today, is that right?

A: I have never felt a great deal of interest in the effort that has been made to dispute the Bible by the speculations of men, or the investigations of men.

Q: Are you the only human being on earth who knows what the Bible means?

Gen. Stewart: I object.

The Court: Sustained.

Mr. Darrow: You do know that there are thousands of people who profess to be Christians who believe the earth is much more ancient and that the human race is much more ancient?

A: I think there may be.

Q: And you never have investigated to find out how long man has been on the earth?

A: I have never found it necessary—

Q: For any reason, whatever it is?

A: To examine every speculation; but if I had done it I never would have done anything else.

Q: I ask for a direct answer.

A: I do not expect to find out all those things, and I do not expect to find out about races.

Q: I didn't ask you that. Now, I ask you if you know if it was interesting enough or important enough for you to try to find out about how old these ancient civilizations were?

A: No; I have not made a study of it.

Q: Don't you know that the ancient civilizations of China are 6,000 or 7,000 years old, at the very least?

A: No; but they would not run back beyond the creation, according to the Bible, 6,000 years.

Q: You don't know how old they are, is that right?

A: I don't know how old they are, but probably you do. [*Laughter in the courtroom.*] I think you would give preference to anybody who opposed the Bible, and I give the preference to the Bible.

Q: I see. Well, you are welcome to your opinion. Have you any idea how old the Egyptian civilization is?

A: No.

Q: Do you know of any record in the world, outside of the story of the Bible, which conforms to any statement that it is 4,200 years ago or thereabouts that all life was wiped off the face of the earth?

A: I think they have found records.

Q: Do you know of any?

A: Records reciting the flood, but I am not an authority on the subject.

Q: Now, Mr. Bryan, will you say if you know of any record, or have ever heard of any records, that describe that a flood existed 4,200 years ago, or about that time, which wiped all life off the earth?

A: The recollection of what I have read on that subject is not distinct enough to say whether the records attempted to fix a time, but I have seen in the discoveries of archaeologists where they have found records that described the flood.

Q: Mr. Bryan, don't you know that there are many old religions that describe the flood?

A: No, I don't know.

Q: You know there are others besides the Jewish?

A: I don't know whether these are the record of any other religion or refer to this flood.

Q: Don't you ever examine religion so far to know that?

A: Outside of the Bible?

Q: Yes.

A: No; I have not examined to know that, generally.

Q: You have never examined any other religions?

A: Yes, sir.

Q: Have you ever read anything about the origins of religions?

A: Not a great deal.

Q: You have never examined any other religion?

A: Yes, sir.

Q: And you don't know whether any other religion ever gave a similar account of the destruction of the earth by the flood?

A: The Christian religion has satisfied me, and I have never felt it necessary to look up some competing religions.

Q: Do you consider that every religion on earth competes with the Christian religion?

A: I think everybody who does not believe in the Christian religion believes so —

Q: I am asking what you think?

A: I do not regard them as competitive because I do not think they have the same sources as we have.

Q: You are wrong in saying "competitive"?

A: I would not say competitive, but the religious unbelievers.

Q: Unbelievers of what?

A: In the Christian religion.

Q: What about the religion of Buddha?

A: I can tell you something about that, if you want to know.

Q: What about the religion of Confucius or Buddha?

A: Well, I can tell you something about that, if you would like to know.

Q: Did you ever investigate them?

A: Somewhat.

Q: Do you regard them as competitive?

A: No, I think they are very inferior. Would you like for me to tell you what I know about it?

Q: No.

A: Well, I shall insist on giving it to you.

Q: You won't talk about free silver,[6] will you?

A: Not at all.

---

6. **free silver:** A reference to backing the U.S. dollar with silver in addition to gold, a position Bryan advocated during his 1896 presidential campaign against William McKinley.

33

LANGSTON HUGHES

The Harlem Renaissance

"I went up the steps and out into the bright September sunlight," recalled poet Langston Hughes (1902–1967) in his autobiography. "Harlem! I stood there, dropped my bags, took a deep breath, and felt happy again." What was there, in this Upper East Side subway stop of 1921, to excite a young black Midwesterner?

Although Harlem was a poor district with little in the way of a prosperous middle class, what gave excitement to the place was its reputation as a "race capital"—a center of social and cultural independence. For Harlem residents, being a visible part of the great metropolis, tough and streetwise rather than deferential and under the surveillance of suspicious white neighbors and hostile Southern police, was liberating. The main black civil rights organizations and journals were anchored in Harlem. Black American troops had been honored with a parade in New York City for their service during World War I. And the speakeasies and jazz cabarets, as well as the rent parties that turned shabby apartments into informal nightclubs, blared with the new, exciting sound that would soon make both whites and blacks talk glowingly of "the Jazz Age."

In 1921 Harlem was in the first stages of an artistic and literary flowering richer than anything African Americans had yet achieved. Over the next several years, popular musicians like Duke Ellington and Bessie Smith, writers like Langston Hughes (whose memories of this period are excerpted here), artists, and intellectuals would create a distinctive cultural energy charged with the rhythms and themes of the African American experience. The so-called Harlem Renaissance and the jazz explosion soon attracted worldwide interest.

Langston Hughes, *The Big Sea* (New York: Hill & Wang, 1963), 223–28, 235–40, 243–47.

QUESTIONS TO CONSIDER

1. What was Langston Hughes's attitude toward the era "when the Negro was in vogue"? What did he like about it? What did he dislike?
2. According to Hughes, what was it like to be a writer during the Harlem Renaissance?
3. What was A'Lelia Walker's role in the Harlem Renaissance? Why did Hughes devote so many paragraphs to her? Why was her funeral so important to him?
4. In what ways is the contemporary relationship between "mainstream" and African American entertainment, culture, and the arts similar to that relationship during the Harlem Renaissance? In what ways is it different?

EXCERPT FROM "WHEN THE NEGRO WAS IN VOGUE"

The 1920's were the years of Manhattan's black Renaissance. . . . [C]ertainly it was the musical revue, *Shuffle Along*, that gave a scintillating send-off to that Negro vogue in Manhattan, which reached its peak just before the crash of 1929, the crash that sent Negroes, white folks, and all rolling down the hill toward the Works Progress Administration.

Shuffle Along was a honey of a show. Swift, bright, funny, rollicking, and gay, with a dozen danceable, singable tunes. Besides, look who were in it: The now famous choir director, Hall Johnson, and the composer, William Grant Still, were part of the orchestra. Eubie Blake and Noble Sissle wrote the music and played and acted in the show. Miller and Lyles were the comics. Florence Mills skyrocketed to fame in the second act. Trixie Smith sang "He May Be Your Man But He Comes to See Me Sometimes." And Caterina Jarboro, now a European prima donna, and the internationally celebrated Josephine Baker were merely in the chorus. Everybody was in the audience—including me. People came back to see it innumerable times. It was always packed.

To see *Shuffle Along* was the main reason I wanted to go to Columbia. When I saw it, I was thrilled and delighted. From then on I was in the gallery of the Cort Theatre every time I got a chance. . . . [*Shuffle Along*] gave just the proper push—a pre-Charleston kick—to that Negro vogue of the '20's, that spread to books, African sculpture, music, and dancing.

Put down the 1920's for the rise of Roland Hayes,[1] who packed Carnegie Hall, the rise of Paul Robeson in New York and London, of Florence Mills over two continents, of Rose McClendon in Broadway parts that never measured up to her, the booming voice of Bessie Smith and the low moan of Clara on thousands of records, and the rise of that grand comedienne of song, Ethel Waters, singing: "Charlie's elected now! He's in right for sure!" Put down the 1920's for Louis Armstrong and Gladys Bentley and Josephine Baker.

1. **Roland Hayes:** Probably the first internationally famous African American male classical singer.

White people began to come to Harlem in droves. For several years they packed the expensive Cotton Club on Lenox Avenue. But I was never there, because the Cotton Club was a Jim Crow club for gangsters and monied whites. They were not cordial to Negro patronage, unless you were a celebrity like Bojangles. So Harlem Negroes did not like the Cotton Club and never appreciated its Jim Crow policy in the very heart of their dark community. Nor did ordinary Negroes like the growing influx of whites toward Harlem after sundown, flooding the little cabarets and bars where formerly only colored people laughed and sang, and where now the strangers were given the best ringside tables to sit and stare at the Negro customers—like amusing animals in a zoo.

The Negroes said: "We can't go downtown and sit and stare at you in your clubs. You won't even let us in your clubs." But they didn't say it out loud—for Negroes are practically never rude to white people. So thousands of whites came to Harlem night after night, thinking the Negroes loved to have them there, and firmly believing that all Harlemites left their houses at sundown to sing and dance in cabarets, because most of the whites saw nothing but the cabarets, not the houses.

Some of the owners of Harlem clubs, delighted at the flood of white patronage, made the grievous error of barring their own race, after the manner of the famous Cotton Club. But most of these quickly lost business and folded up, because they failed to realize that a large part of the Harlem attraction for downtown New Yorkers lay in simply watching the colored customers amuse themselves. And the smaller clubs, of course, had no big floor shows or a name band like the Cotton Club, where Duke Ellington usually held forth, so, without black patronage, they were not amusing at all.

Some of the small clubs, however, had people like Gladys Bentley, who was something worth discovering in those days, before she got famous, acquired an accompanist, specially written material, and conscious vulgarity. But for two or three amazing years, Miss Bentley sat, and played a big piano all night long, literally all night, without stopping—singing songs like "The St. James Infirmary," from ten in the evening until dawn, with scarcely a break between the notes, sliding from one song to another, with a powerful and continuous underbeat of jungle rhythm. Miss Bentley was an amazing exhibition of musical energy—a large, dark, masculine lady, whose feet pounded the floor while her fingers pounded the keyboard—a perfect piece of African sculpture, animated by her own rhythm.

But when the place where she played became too well known, she began to sing with an accompanist, became a star, moved to a larger place, then downtown, and is now in Hollywood. The old magic of the woman and the piano and the night and the rhythm being one is gone. But everything goes, one way or another. The '20's are gone and lots of fine things in Harlem night life have disappeared like snow in the sun—since it became utterly commercial, planned for the downtown tourist trade, and therefore dull.

The lindy-hoppers at the Savoy even began to practise acrobatic routines, and to do absurd things for the entertainment of the whites, that probably never would have entered their heads to attempt merely for their own effortless amusement. Some of the lindy-hoppers had cards printed with their names on them and became dance professors teaching the tourists. Then Harlem nights became show nights for the Nordics.

Some critics say that that is what happened to certain Negro writers, too—that they ceased to write to amuse themselves and began to write to amuse and entertain white people, and in so doing distorted and over-colored their material, and left out a great many things they thought would offend their American brothers of a lighter complexion. Maybe—since Negroes have writer-racketeers, as has any other race. But I have known almost all of them, and most of the good ones have tried to be honest, write honestly, and express their world as they saw it.

All of us know that the gay and sparkling life of the so-called Negro Renaissance of the '20's was not so gay and sparkling beneath the surface as it looked. Carl Van Vechten, in the character of Byron in *Nigger Heaven*, captured some of the bitterness and frustration of literary Harlem that Wallace Thurman later so effectively poured into his *Infants of the Spring*—the only novel by a Negro about that fantastic period when Harlem was in vogue.

It was a period when, at almost every Harlem upper-crust dance or party, one would be introduced to various distinguished white celebrities there as guests. It was a period when almost any Harlem Negro of any social importance at all would be likely to say casually: "As I was remarking the other day to Heywood—," meaning Heywood Broun.[2] Or: "As I said to George—," referring to George Gershwin. It was a period when local and visiting royalty were not at all uncommon in Harlem. And when the parties of A'Lelia Walker, the Negro heiress, were filled with guests whose names would turn any Nordic social climber green with envy. It was a period when Harold Jackman, a handsome young Harlem school teacher of modest means, calmly announced one day that he was sailing for the Riviera for a fortnight, to attend Princess Murat's yachting party. It was a period when Charleston preachers opened up shouting churches as sideshows for white tourists. It was a period when at least one charming colored chorus girl, amber enough to pass for a Latin American, was living in a pent house, with all her bills paid by a gentleman whose name was banker's magic on Wall Street. It was a period when every season there was at least one hit play on Broadway acted by a Negro cast. And when books by Negro authors were being published with much greater frequency and much more publicity than ever before or since in history. It was a period when white writers wrote about Negroes more successfully (commercially speaking) than Negroes did about themselves. It was the period (God help us!) when Ethel Barrymore[3] appeared in blackface in *Scarlet Sister Mary*! It was the period when the Negro was in vogue.

I was there. I had a swell time while it lasted. But I thought it wouldn't last long. (I remember the vogue for things Russian, the season the Chauve-Souris[4] first came to town.) For how could a large and enthusiastic number of

2. **Heywood Broun:** A left-wing New York City journalist who later ran for Congress as a Socialist Party candidate.
3. **Ethel Barrymore:** Probably the most famous stage actress of the 1920s.
4. **Chauve-Souris:** A popular Russian dance troupe.

people be crazy about Negroes forever? But some Harlemites thought the millennium had come. They thought the race problem had at last been solved through Art plus Gladys Bentley. They were sure the New Negro would lead a new life from then on in green pastures of tolerance created by Countee Cullen, Ethel Waters, Claude McKay, Duke Ellington, Bojangles, and Alain Locke.[5]

I don't know what made any Negroes think that—except that they were mostly intellectuals doing the thinking. The ordinary Negroes hadn't heard of the Negro Renaissance. And if they had, it hadn't raised their wages any. As for all those white folks in the speakeasies and night clubs of Harlem—well, maybe a colored man could find *some* place to have a drink that the tourists hadn't yet discovered.

EXCERPT FROM "HARLEM LITERATI"

During the summer of 1926, Wallace Thurman, Zora Neale Hurston, Aaron Douglas, John P. Davis, Bruce Nugent, Gwendolyn Bennett, and I decided to publish "a Negro quarterly of the arts" to be called *Fire*—the idea being that it would burn up a lot of the old, dead conventional Negro-white ideas of the past, *épater le bourgeois*[6] into a realization of the existence of the younger Negro writers and artists, and provide us with an outlet for publication not available in the limited pages of the small Negro magazines then existing, the *Crisis*, *Opportunity*, and the *Messenger*—the first two being house organs of inter-racial organizations, and the latter being God knows what.

Sweltering summer evenings we met to plan *Fire*. Each of the seven of us agreed to give fifty dollars to finance the first issue. Thurman was to edit it, John P. Davis to handle the business end, and Bruce Nugent to take charge of distribution. The rest of us were to serve as an editorial board to collect material, contribute our own work, and act in any useful way that we could. For artists and writers, we got along fine and there were no quarrels. But October came before we were ready to go to press. I had to return to Lincoln, John Davis to Law School at Harvard, Zora Hurston to her studies at Barnard. . . .

Only three of the seven had contributed their fifty dollars, but the others faithfully promised to send theirs out of tuition checks, wages, or begging. Thurman went on with the work of preparing the magazine. He got a printer. He planned the layout. It had to be on good paper, he said, worthy of the drawings of Aaron Douglas. It had to have beautiful type, worthy of the first Negro art quarterly. It had to be what we seven young Negroes dreamed our magazine would be—so in the end it cost almost a thousand dollars, and nobody could pay the bills.

---

5. Important figures in the Harlem Renaissance. Countee Cullen was a poet; Ethel Waters, a singer; Claude McKay, another prominent poet; Duke Ellington, a musician and bandleader; Bojangles, a popular performer; and Alain Locke, a well-known philosopher and educator.
6. **épater le bourgeois**: "Shock the middle class."

I don't know how Thurman persuaded the printer to let us have all the copies to distribute, but he did. I think Alain Locke, among others, signed notes guaranteeing payments. But since Thurman was the only one of the seven of us with a regular job, for the next three or four years his checks were constantly being attached and his income seized to pay for *Fire.* And whenever I sold a poem, mine went there, too—to *Fire.*

None of the older Negro intellectuals would have anything to do with *Fire.* Dr. Du Bois[7] in the *Crisis* roasted it. The Negro press called it all sorts of bad names, largely because of a green and purple story[8] by Bruce Nugent, in the Oscar Wilde tradition, which we had included. Rean Graves, the critic for the *Baltimore Afro-American,* began his review by saying: "I have just tossed the first issue of *Fire* into the fire." . . .

So *Fire* had plenty of cold water thrown on it by the colored critics. The white critics (except for an excellent editorial in the *Bookman* for November, 1926) scarcely noticed it at all. We had no way of getting it distributed to bookstands or news stands. Bruce Nugent took it around New York on foot and some of the Greenwich Village bookshops put it on display, and sold it for us. But then Bruce, who had no job, would collect the money and, on account of salary, eat it up before he got back to Harlem.

Finally, irony of ironies, several hundred copies of *Fire* were stored in the basement of an apartment where an actual fire occurred and the bulk of the whole issue was burned up. Even after that Thurman had to go on paying the printer.

Now *Fire* is a collector's item, and very difficult to get, being mostly ashes.

That taught me a lesson about little magazines. But since white folks had them, we Negroes thought we could have one, too. But we didn't have the money. . . .

About the future of Negro literature Thurman was very pessimistic. He thought the Negro vogue had made us all too conscious of ourselves, had flattered and spoiled us, and had provided too many easy opportunities for some of us to drink gin and more gin, on which he thought we would always be drunk. With his bitter sense of humor, he called the Harlem literati, the "niggerati."

Of this "niggerati," Zora Neale Hurston was certainly the most amusing. Only to reach a wider audience, need she ever write books—because she is a perfect book of entertainment in herself. In her youth she was always getting scholarships and things from wealthy white people, some of whom simply paid her just to sit around and represent the Negro race for them, she did it in such a racy fashion. She was full of side-splitting anecdotes, humorous tales, and tragicomic stories, remembered out of her life in the South as a daughter of a travelling minister of God. She could make you laugh one minute and cry the next. To many of her white friends, no doubt, she was

---

7. **Dr. Du Bois:** W. E. B. Du Bois (1868–1963), American educator, sociologist, and a founder of the National Association for the Advancement of Colored People.
8. **green and purple story:** An exaggerated story.

a perfect "darkie," in the nice meaning they give the term—that is a naïve, childlike, sweet, humorous, and highly colored Negro.

But Miss Hurston was clever, too—a student who didn't let college give her a broad *a* and who had great scorn for all pretensions, academic or otherwise. That is why she was such a fine folk-lore collector, able to go among the people and never act as if she had been to school at all. . . .

When Miss Hurston graduated from Barnard she took an apartment in West 66th Street near the park, in that row of Negro houses there. She moved in with no furniture at all and no money, but in a few days friends had given her everything, from decorative silver birds, perched atop the linen cabinet, down to a footstool. And on Saturday night, to christen the place, she had a *hand*-chicken dinner, since she had forgotten to say she needed forks.

She seemed to know almost everybody in New York. She had been a secretary to Fannie Hurst,[9] and had met dozens of celebrities whose friendships she retained. Yet she was always having terrific ups-and-downs about money. She tells this story on herself, about needing a nickel to go downtown one day and wondering where on earth she would get it. As she approached the subway, she was stopped by a blind beggar holding out his cup.

"Please help the blind! Help the blind! A nickel for the blind!"

"I need money worse than you today," said Miss Hurston, taking five cents out of his cup. "Lend me this! Next time, I'll give it back." And she went on downtown.

Harlem was like a great magnet for the Negro intellectual, pulling him from everywhere. Or perhaps the magnet was New York—but once in New York, he had to live in Harlem, for rooms were hardly to be found elsewhere unless one could pass for white or Mexican or Eurasian and perhaps live in the Village—which always seemed to me a very arty locale, in spite of the many real artists and writers who lived there. Only a few of the New Negroes lived in the Village, Harlem being their real stamping ground.

EXCERPT FROM "PARTIES"

In those days of the late 1920's, there were a great many parties, in Harlem and out, to which various members of the New Negro group were invited. . . .

A'Lelia Walker was the then great Harlem party giver, although Mrs. Bernia Austin fell but little behind. And at the Seventh Avenue apartment of Jessie Fauset, literary soirées with much poetry and but little to drink were the order of the day. The same was true of Lillian Alexander's, where the older intellectuals gathered.

A'Lelia Walker, however, big-hearted, night-dark, hair-straightening heiress, made no pretense at being intellectual or exclusive. At her "at homes" Negro poets and Negro number bankers mingled with downtown poets and seat-on-the-stock-exchange racketeers. Countee Cullen would be there and

---

9. **Fannie Hurst:** A famous Jewish American novelist and former apartment mate of Hurston's.

Witter Bynner, Muriel Draper and Nora Holt, Andy Razaf and Taylor Gordon. And a good time was had by all.

A'Lelia Walker had an apartment that held perhaps a hundred people. She would usually issue several hundred invitations to each party. Unless you went early there was no possible way of getting in. Her parties were as crowded as the New York subway at the rush hour—entrance, lobby, steps, hallway, and apartment a milling crush of guests, with everybody seeming to enjoy the crowding. Once, some royal personage arrived, a Scandinavian prince, I believe, but his equerry saw no way of getting him through the crowded entrance hall and into the party, so word was sent in to A'Lelia Walker that His Highness, the Prince, was waiting without. A'Lelia sent word back that she saw no way of getting His Highness in, either, nor could she herself get out through the crowd to greet him. But she offered to send refreshments downstairs to the Prince's car.

A'Lelia Walker was a gorgeous dark Amazon, in a silver turban. She had a town house in New York (also an apartment where she preferred to live) and a country mansion at Irvington-on-the-Hudson, with pipe organ programs each morning to awaken her guests gently. Her mother made a great fortune from the Madame Walker Hair Straightening Process, which had worked wonders on unruly Negro hair in the early nineteen hundreds—and which continues to work wonders today. The daughter used much of that money for fun. A'Lelia Walker was the joy-goddess of Harlem's 1920's. . . .

When A'Lelia Walker died in 1931, she had a grand funeral. It was by invitation only. But, just as for her parties, a great many more invitations had been issued than the small but exclusive Seventh Avenue funeral parlor could provide for. Hours before the funeral, the street in front of the undertaker's chapel was crowded. The doors were not opened until the cortège arrived—and the cortège was late. When it came, there were almost enough family mourners, attendants, and honorary pallbearers in the procession to fill the room; as well as the representatives of the various Walker beauty parlors throughout the country. And there were still hundreds of friends outside, waving their white, engraved invitations aloft in the vain hope of entering.

Once the last honorary pallbearers had marched in, there was a great crush at the doors. . . .

Soft music played and it was very solemn. When we were seated and the chapel became dead silent, De Lawd[10] said: "The Four Bon Bons will now sing."

A night club quartette that had often performed at A'Lelia's parties arose and sang for her. They sang Noel Coward's "I'll See You Again," and they swung it slightly, as she might have liked it. It was a grand funeral and very much like a party. Mrs. Mary McLeod Bethune[11] spoke in that great deep voice of hers, as only she can speak. . . .

---

10. **De Lawd:** Hughes's description of the presiding minister, who looked like the character of God in Marc Connelly's play *The Green Pastures*, which had an all-black cast.
11. **Mary McLeod Bethune** (1875–1955): African American educator, civil rights leader, and adviser to President Franklin D. Roosevelt.

Then a poem of mine was read by Edward Perry, "To A'Lelia." And after that the girls from the various Walker beauty shops throughout America brought their flowers and laid them on the bier.

That was really the end of the gay times of the New Negro era in Harlem, the period that had begun to reach its end when the crash came in 1929 and the white people had much less money to spend on themselves, and practically none to spend on Negroes, for the depression brought everybody down a peg or two. And the Negroes had but few pegs to fall.

34

MARGARET SANGER
My Fight for Birth Control

Margaret Sanger (1879–1966) was not the first champion of the right to use contraception, but she was an important organizer of the twentieth-century movement to make "birth control"—an expression she coined in 1914—legal and widely available. Sanger's account of the life and death of Sadie Sacks, excerpted here from her autobiography, was discussed in countless speeches throughout her career. While the incident did not initiate her concern for birth control access or for the plight of poor women, it did fix her decision to focus her work on this issue, as she did for the rest of her life.

In 1873 Congress passed the Comstock Act, which imposed fines and imprisonment for providing information to another person "for the prevention of conception or procuring of abortion." The state of New York had a similar statute. Therefore, virtually all of Sanger's activities to further her cause were illegal. Opening a birth control clinic in 1916 was an act of civil disobedience—much like the acts practiced by the civil rights movement half a century later. Sanger, by violating the law, forced changes in it.

While contraception was to remain illegal in some states into the 1960s, this determined reformer brought about a major change. When she began her crusade, middle-class women had informal access to birth control information and devices, but poor women generally did not. By 1921, when Sanger formed the American Birth Control League—which in 1942 would become Planned Parenthood—courts had already begun to allow doctors to disseminate birth control information and devices to married women, and prosecutions under the Comstock Act virtually ceased.

QUESTIONS TO CONSIDER

1. Is it, as Margaret Sanger wrote at the beginning of this selection, "futile and useless to relieve . . . misery" if you do not get at its roots? Explain.

Margaret Sanger, *My Fight for Birth Control* (New York: Farrar-Rinehart, 1931), 46–56, 152–60.

2. When she had her revelation after Sadie Sacks's death, Sanger wrote, "I could now see clearly the various social strata of our life; all its mass problems seemed to be centered around uncontrolled breeding." Do you agree with this observation? What are the merits and the dangers of such an argument?

3. In Sanger's view, what made Brooklyn a good location for her birth control clinic?

[1912]

Early in the year 1912 I came to a sudden realization that my work as a nurse and my activities in social service were entirely palliative and consequently futile and useless to relieve the misery I saw all about me. . . .

Were it possible for me to depict the revolting conditions existing in the homes of some of the women I attended in that one year, one would find it hard to believe. There was at that time, and doubtless is still today, a substratum of men and women whose lives are absolutely untouched by social agencies.

The way they live is almost beyond belief. They hate and fear any prying into their homes or into their lives. They resent being talked to. The women slink in and out of their homes on their way to market like rats from their holes. The men beat their wives sometimes black and blue, but no one interferes. The children are cuffed, kicked and chased about, but woe to the child who dares to tell tales out of the home! Crime or drink is often the source of this secret aloofness, usually there is something to hide, a skeleton in the closet somewhere. The men are sullen, unskilled workers, picking up odd jobs now and then, unemployed usually, sauntering in and out of the house at all hours of the day and night.

The women keep apart from other women in the neighborhood. Often they are suspected of picking a pocket or "lifting" an article when occasion arises. Pregnancy is an almost chronic condition amongst them. I knew one woman who had given birth to eight children with no professional care whatever. The last one was born in the kitchen, witnessed by a son of ten years who, under his mother's direction, cleaned the bed, wrapped the placenta and soiled articles in paper, and threw them out of the window into the court below. . . .

In this atmosphere abortions and birth become the main theme of conversation. On Saturday nights I have seen groups of fifty to one hundred women going into questionable offices well known in the community for cheap abortions. I asked several women what took place there, and they all gave the same reply: a quick examination, a probe inserted into the uterus and turned a few times to disturb the fertilized ovum, and then the woman was sent home. Usually the flow began the next day and often continued four or five weeks. Sometimes an ambulance carried the victim to the hospital for a curetage,[1] and if she returned home at all she was looked upon as a lucky woman.

---

1. **curetage:** Curettage—the surgical removal from a woman's womb of dead tissue resulting from an abortion or miscarriage.

This state of things became a nightmare with me. There seemed no sense to it all, no reason for such waste of mother life, no right to exhaust women's vitality and to throw them on the scrap-heap before the age of thirty-five.

Everywhere I looked, misery and fear stalked—men fearful of losing their jobs, women fearful that even worse conditions might come upon them. The menace of another pregnancy hung like a sword over the head of every poor woman I came in contact with that year. The question which met me was always the same: What can I do to keep from it? or, What can I do to get out of this? Sometimes they talked among themselves bitterly.

"It's the rich that know the tricks," they'd say, "while we have all the kids." Then, if the women were Roman Catholics, they talked about "Yankee tricks," and asked me if I knew what the Protestants did to keep their families down. When I said that I didn't believe that the rich knew much more than they did I was laughed at and suspected of holding back information for money. They would nudge each other and say something about paying me before I left the case if I would reveal the "secret." . . .

Finally the thing began to shape itself, to become accumulative during the three weeks I spent in the home of a desperately sick woman living on Grand Street, a lower section of New York's East Side.

Mrs. Sacks was only twenty-eight years old; her husband, an unskilled worker, thirty-two. Three children, aged five, three and one, were none too strong nor sturdy, and it took all the earnings of the father and the ingenuity of the mother to keep them clean, provide them with air and proper food, and give them a chance to grow into decent manhood and womanhood.

Both parents were devoted to these children and to each other. The woman had become pregnant and had taken various drugs and purgatives, as advised by her neighbors. Then, in desperation, she had used some instrument lent to her by a friend. She was found prostrate on the floor amidst the crying children when her husband returned from work. Neighbors advised against the ambulance, and a friendly doctor was called. The husband would not hear of her going to a hospital, and as a little money had been saved in the bank a nurse was called and the battle for that precious life began.

It was in the middle of July. The three-room apartment was turned into a hospital for the dying patient. Never had I worked so fast, never so concentratedly as I did to keep alive that little mother. Neighbor women came and went during the day doing the odds and ends necessary for our comfort. The children were sent to friends and relatives and the doctor and I settled ourselves to outdo the force and power of an outraged nature.

Never had I known such conditions could exist. July's sultry days and nights were melted into a torpid inferno. Day after day, night after night, I slept only in brief snatches, ever too anxious about the condition of that feeble heart bravely carrying on, to stay long from the bedside of the patient. . . .

At the end of two weeks recovery was in sight, and at the end of three weeks I was preparing to leave the fragile patient to take up the ordinary duties of her life, including those of wifehood and motherhood. Everyone was congratulating her on her recovery. All the kindness of sympathetic and understanding neighbors poured in upon her in the shape of convalescent dishes, soups, custards, and drinks. Still she appeared to be despondent and worried. She seemed to sit apart in her thoughts as if she had no part in these congratulatory messages and endearing welcomes. I thought at first that she still retained some of her unconscious memories and dwelt upon them in her silences.

But as the hour for my departure came nearer, her anxiety increased, and finally with trembling voice she said: "Another baby will finish me, I suppose."

"It's too early to talk about that," I said, and resolved that I would turn the question over to the doctor for his advice. When he came I said: "Mrs. Sacks is worried about having another baby."

"She well might be," replied the doctor, and then he stood before her and said: "Any more such capers, young woman, and there will be no need to call me."

"Yes, yes—I know, Doctor," said the patient with trembling voice, "but," and she hesitated as if it took all of her courage to say it, "*what* can I do to prevent getting that way again?"

"Oh ho!" laughed the doctor good naturedly. "You want your cake while you eat it too, do you? Well, it can't be done." Then, familiarly slapping her on the back and picking up his hat and bag to depart, he said: "I'll tell you the only sure thing to do. Tell Jake to sleep on the roof!"

With those words he closed the door and went down the stairs, leaving us both petrified and stunned.

Tears sprang to my eyes, and a lump came in my throat as I looked at that face before me. It was stamped with sheer horror. I thought for a moment she might have gone insane, but she conquered her feelings, whatever they may have been, and turning to me in desperation said: "He can't understand, can he?—he's a man after all—but you do, don't you? You're a woman and you'll tell me the secret and I'll never tell it to a soul."

She clasped her hands as if in prayer, she leaned over and looked straight into my eyes and beseechingly implored me to tell her something—something *I really did not know*. It was like being on a rack and tortured for a crime one had not committed. To plead guilty would stop the agony; otherwise the rack kept turning.

I had to turn away from that imploring face. I could not answer her then. I quieted her as best I could. She saw that I was moved by the tears in my eyes. I promised that I would come back in a few days and tell her what she wanted to know. The few simple means of limiting the family like *coitus interruptus* or the condom were laughed at by the neighboring women when told these were the means used by men in the well-to-do families. That was not believed, and I knew such an answer would be swept aside as useless were I to tell her this at such a time.

A little later when she slept I left the house, and made up my mind that I'd keep away from those cases in the future. I felt helpless to do anything at all. I seemed chained hand and foot, and longed for an earthquake or a volcano to shake the world out of its lethargy into facing these monstrous atrocities.

The intelligent reasoning of the young mother—how to *prevent* getting that way again—how sensible, how just she had been—yes, I promised myself I'd go back and have a long talk with her and tell her more, and perhaps she would not laugh but would believe that those methods were all that were really known.

But time flew past, and weeks rolled into months. That wistful, appealing face haunted me day and night. I could not banish from my mind memories of that trembling voice begging so humbly for knowledge she had a right to have. I was about to retire one night three months later when the telephone rang and an agitated man's voice begged me to come at once to help his wife who was sick again. It was the husband of Mrs. Sacks, and I intuitively knew before I left the telephone that it was almost useless to go.

I dreaded to face that woman. I was tempted to send someone else in my place. I longed for an accident on the subway, or on the street—anything to prevent my going into that home. But on I went just the same. I arrived a few minutes after the doctor, the same one who had given her such noble advice. The woman was dying. She was unconscious. She died within ten minutes after my arrival. It was the same result, the same story told a thousand times before—death from abortion. She had become pregnant, had used drugs, had then consulted a five-dollar professional abortionist, and death followed.

After I left that desolate house I walked and walked and walked; for hours and hours I kept on, bag in hand, thinking, regretting, dreading to stop; fearful of my conscience, dreading to face my own accusing soul. At three in the morning I arrived home still clutching a heavy load the weight of which I was quite unconscious.

I entered the house quietly, as was my custom, and looked out of the window down upon the dimly lighted, sleeping city. . . .

. . . For hours I stood, motionless and tense, expecting something to happen. I watched the lights go out, I saw the darkness gradually give way to the first shimmer of dawn, and then a colorful sky heralded the rise of the sun. I knew a new day had come for me and a new world as well.

It was like an illumination. I could now see clearly the various social strata of our life; all its mass problems seemed to be centered around uncontrolled breeding. There was only one thing to be done: call out, start the alarm, set the heather on fire! Awaken the womanhood of America to free the motherhood of the world! I released from my almost paralyzed hand the nursing bag which unconsciously I had clutched, threw it across the room, tore the uniform from my body, flung it into a corner, and renounced all palliative work forever.

I would never go back again to nurse women's ailing bodies while their miseries were as vast as the stars. I was now finished with superficial cures, with doctors and nurses and social workers who were brought face to face with this overwhelming truth of women's needs and yet turned to pass on the other side. They must be made to see these facts. I resolved that women should have knowledge of contraception. They have every right to know about their own bodies. I would strike out—I would scream from the housetops. I would tell the world what was going on in the lives of these poor women. I *would* be heard. No matter what it should cost. *I would be heard.*

[1916]

The selection of a place for the first birth control clinic was of the greatest importance. No one could actually tell how it would be received in any neighborhood. I thought of all the possible difficulties: The indifference of women's organizations, the ignorance of the workers themselves, the resentment of social agencies, the opposition of the medical profession. Then there was the law—the law of New York State.

Section 1142 was definite. It stated that *no one* could give information to prevent conception to *anyone* for any reason. There was, however, Section 1145, which distinctly stated that physicians (*only*) could give advice to prevent conception for the cure or prevention of disease. I inquired about the section, and was told by two attorneys and several physicians that this clause was an exception to 1142 referring only to venereal disease. But anyway, as I was not a physician, it could not protect me. Dared I risk it?

I began to think of the doctors I knew. Several who had previously promised now refused. I wrote, telephoned, asked friends to ask other friends to help me find a woman doctor to help me demonstrate the need of a birth control clinic in New York. None could be found. No one wanted to go to jail. No one cared to test out the law. Perhaps it would have to be done without a doctor. But it had to be done; that I knew.

Fania Mindell, an enthusiastic young worker in the cause, had come on from Chicago to help me. Together we tramped the streets on that dreary day in early October, through a driving rainstorm, to find the best location at the cheapest terms possible. . . .

Finally at 46 Amboy Street, in the Brownsville section of Brooklyn, we found a friendly landlord with a good place vacant at fifty dollars a month rental; and Brownsville was settled on. It was one of the most thickly populated sections. It had a large population of working-class Jews, always interested in health measures, always tolerant of new ideas, willing to listen and to accept advice whenever the health of mother or children was involved. I knew that here there would at least be no breaking of windows, no hurling of insults into our teeth; but I was scarcely prepared for the popular support, the sympathy and friendly help given us in that neighborhood from that day to this.

With a small bundle of handbills and a large amount of zeal, we fared forth each morning in a house-to-house canvass of the district in which the clinic was located. Every family in that great district received a "dodger" printed in English, Yiddish and Italian. . . .

It was on October 16, 1916, that the three of us—Fania Mindell, Ethel Byrne and myself—opened the doors of the first birth control clinic in America. I believed then and do today, that the opening of those doors to the mothers of Brownsville was an event of social significance in the lives of American womanhood.

News of our work spread like wildfire. Within a few days there was not a darkened tenement, hovel or flat but was brightened by the knowledge that motherhood could be voluntary; that children need not be born into the world unless they are wanted and have a place provided for them. For the first time, women talked openly of this terror of unwanted pregnancy which had haunted their lives since time immemorial. The newspapers, in glaring headlines, used the words "birth control," and carried the message that somewhere in Brooklyn there was a place where contraceptive information could be obtained by all overburdened mothers who wanted it.

Ethel Byrne, who is my sister and a trained nurse, assisted me in advising, explaining, and demonstrating to the women how to prevent conception. As all of our 488 records were confiscated by the detectives who later arrested us for violation of the New York State law, it is difficult to tell exactly how many more women came in those few days to seek advice; but we estimate that it was far more than five hundred. As in any new enterprise, false reports were maliciously spread about the clinic; weird stories without the slightest foundation of truth. We talked plain talk and gave plain facts to the women who came there. We kept a record of every applicant. All were mothers; most of them had large families.

It was whispered about that the police were to raid the place for abortions. We had no fear of that accusation. We were trying to spare mothers the necessity of that ordeal by giving them proper contraceptive information. It was well that so many of the women in the neighborhood knew the truth of our doings. Hundreds of them who had witnessed the facts came to the courtroom afterward, eager to testify in our behalf.

One day a woman by the name of Margaret Whitehurst came to us. She said that she was the mother of two children and that she had not money to support more. Her story was a pitiful one—all lies, of course, but the government acts that way. She asked for our literature and preventives, and received both. Then she triumphantly went to the District Attorney's office and secured a warrant for the arrest of my sister, Mrs. Ethel Byrne, our interpreter, Miss Fania Mindell, and myself.

I refused to close down the clinic, hoping that a court decision would allow us to continue such necessary work. I was to be disappointed. Pressure was brought upon the landlord, and we were dispossessed by the law as a "public nuisance." In Holland the clinics were called "public utilities."

When the policewoman entered the clinic with her squad of plain clothes men and announced the arrest of Miss Mindell and myself (Mrs. Byrne was not present at the time and her arrest followed later), the room was crowded to suffocation with women waiting in the outer room. The police began bullying these mothers, asking them questions, writing down their names in order to subpoena them to testify against us at the trial. These women, always afraid of trouble which the very presence of a policeman signifies, screamed and cried aloud. The children on their laps screamed, too. It was like a panic for a few minutes until I walked into the room where they were stampeding and begged them to be quiet and not to get excited. I assured them that nothing could happen to them, that I was under arrest but they would be allowed to return home in a few minutes. That quieted them. The men were blocking the door to prevent anyone from leaving, but I finally persuaded them to allow these women to return to their homes, unmolested though terribly frightened by it all.

Crowds began to gather outside. A long line of women with baby carriages and children had been waiting to get into the clinic. Now the streets were filled, and police had to see that traffic was not blocked. The patrol wagon came rattling through the streets to our door, and at length Miss Mindell and I took our seats within and were taken to the police station.

35

UNKNOWN PHOTOGRAPHER

Capitalizing on New Fears: The Ku Klux Klan in the 1920s

The Ku Klux Klan (KKK) enjoyed a powerful surge in membership during the 1920s. All but defunct at the turn of the century, this hate group broadened its appeal by capitalizing on rising social fears and tensions brought on by modernization. KKK leaders pitched their message of "100 percent Americanism" to anyone who would listen—and multitudes did listen. Tens of thousands of recruits poured in from former Confederate states and Northern and Midwestern states alike. What united this generation of members was their uneasiness over the swelling number of immigrants, the relocation of tens of thousands of black Americans outside the South during the Great Migration, and the steady rise in the number of Catholics. The KKK's call to protect white families, white women, and white Protestantism from the ravages of a changing America struck a popular chord with many citizens of Anglo-Saxon heritage.

Massive marches of Klansmen took place around the country. None was arguably more important symbolically than the parade in Washington, D.C., in 1925—an event that served as a powerful sign of the group's rising power and visibility.

QUESTIONS TO CONSIDER

1. In anticipation of the KKK parade, newspapers across the country debated whether the Klansmen should be allowed to march. The debate was over whether it was safer to keep them in the light of day or deny them the public credibility by banning them. What do you think should have been done?
2. Why do you think that photos of this march on Washington, D.C., were such potent recruiting tools for the KKK in the 1920s?

Ku Klux Klan members march in Washington, D.C., on August 8, 1925.
Associated Press / AP Images.

36

LUIS TENORIO ET AL.

Mexican Migrants and the Promise of America

The nearly 2,000-mile frontier between the United States and Mexico is the most crossed border in the world, with about 250 million people traversing it annually. While there is much discussion about the roughly 500,000 people who enter the United States illegally each year, these individuals represent a tiny percentage of the masses who make their way across this border every day. Individuals from both sides cross to work, study, visit friends and relatives, get their cars fixed, go to the dentist, see ball games, worship, and shop. It is, in fact, a commuter border, and despite more restrictions on crossing and more

The Mexican Immigrant: His Life Story, Autobiographic Documents Collected by Manuel Gamio (Chicago: University of Chicago Press, 1969), 4–6, 134–39, 253–59.

border patrol agents than at any time in history, it continues to be a largely invisible line that does as much to weld these two countries together as it does to separate them.

For more than two centuries, Anglo families have lived in Mexico, Mexican families have resided in the United States, and countless thousands have lived on both sides of the border with ambiguous identities. Until the 1980s, there was effectively free movement back and forth, with no paperwork involved. Especially during the 1920s, many Mexicans came north to live and work, particularly in the cities of the Midwest.

The Mexican Revolution (1910–1920) and an ensuing decade of political unrest left almost a million people dead and drove as many into exile, most of them to the United States. In 1924 the United States passed the Johnson-Reed Act, which severely restricted immigration from overseas, leaving the booming postwar economy with labor shortages and creating a strong pull for Mexicans, who were suddenly in high demand. While many stayed, particularly in Chicago, Los Angeles, and Texas, there was a big return migration in the 1930s, as the Great Depression caused jobs to disappear and intensified the often violent xenophobia of nativist groups.

Manuel Gamio (1883–1960), the Mexican anthropologist who compiled the following first-person life-narratives from Mexicans living in the United States, also wrote several books on the indigenous peoples of Mexico. In 1925 he spent five years in the United States, where he interviewed Mexicans living in this country. The excerpts reprinted here from Gamio's The Mexican Immigrant: His Life Story paint a richly hued canvas of the experiences of four such individuals in both their native country and their new land, and illuminate the powerful emotional ties that continued to bind them to Mexican traditions even as they established themselves in the U.S. communities.

QUESTIONS TO CONSIDER

1. What evidence can you find in these excerpts indicating that crossing the border into the United States was easier in the past than it is today?
2. How did the ease of crossing affect Mexicans' experience of life in the United States?
3. What seem to be the major difficulties that these Mexicans faced in adapting to life in the United States?

LUIS TENORIO

Tenorio is white, a native of Jalisco. He has lived in the United States since 1915.

"My mother was poor and worked as a servant on an estate near Ocampo, Guanajuato, but she inherited some wealth from an uncle and then we had enough with which to live in some comfort. She was the friend of a lady who was left a widow but in possession of much land and money. This lady had a son named Clemente. We were brought up together, we went to school together and we loved each other like brothers. When we grew up we both went into farming. I worked his land on shares and we kept on being good friends. He told me all his secrets and I told him mine. About this time the revolution began. It kept on growing and growing until 1915, when Clemente joined it, with a group of countrymen who followed him. He sent me letters several times by certain persons telling me to come and join him. But I didn't care to go around with these mobs and besides I didn't want to leave my mother alone. . . . In 1914, I was married in the town of Ocampo, Guanajuato, of which my wife is also a native. I was very happy in that town with my wife when one afternoon Clemente's troops arrived and peacefully took possession of the plaza. After these troops had been there about three days, Clemente came to my house with ten men, all well armed. . . . He told me all about his adventures and his ideas and kept urging me to join him. Then he said that he was hungry and I told my wife to get up and get us something to eat. He stayed with three of his men and sent the others to the barracks. While we were waiting to eat he took out two bottles of *tequila*, good *tequila* which he had with him, and we began to drink and drink. Finally when we had eaten and I felt my spirit quickened by the drinks, for then one is made to feel capable of anything, I told him that I would go with him and that he should come for me the next day. He said good-bye for the night and came for me with three horses and asked me to choose the one I wanted. By this time I had thought it over and didn't want to go, but as I had already given my word I had to keep it. So I said good-bye to my wife and to my mother and went with Clemente. I wasn't given any military rank and didn't go as a soldier but as a companion to my friend. I kept with him through the forests and over the roads for about a week until we came to a small town. When we had taken possession of it peacefully and Clemente and I and his escort were going down the street we saw a man standing on the corner. Clemente told us to go and order him to accompany us and to take him to a place where he had established his barracks and that he would wait for us there. We went there and I got an idea when I saw that Clemente had gone. I told the man to come with us and then I told the soldiers to go ahead with him. They did so and then I fled down a road and kept on going until I managed to catch the train to Ciudad Juarez. I let the horse go and went to Ciudad Juarez. That was in 1915. I went over to American territory and signed up for work on the railroad in Arizona, and I began to work very hard there. Later I came to Los Angeles and got a job in cement work, that is in the paving of the streets, a very hard job in which I have almost used up my strength. When I had been here about two years and had saved a little money I wrote to my wife to come. I went to Ciudad Juarez for her and I brought her to Los Angeles. We only had one child then. We had another one here, this time a girl."

TOMÁS MARES

Sr. Tomás Mares, *mestizo*, has lived in the United States during the last seven years. . . .

"By working hard but always hopefully I have been able to get ahead here and come to have what I now have, my garage, in which I have four automobiles of my own and my repair shop for batteries and automobile parts which is in front of the Cathedral of St. Francis in this city. I also work as a pressman on a newspaper. . . . I work as though I was the head, for no one gives me orders. They pay me $1.00 an hour and they have to give me the forms of the paper at one-thirty in the afternoon. If they give them to me later then they have to pay me time and a half extra. . . .

"I am going to tell you the truth as to why I came to this country. My father and my brother edited a daily newspaper in Guaymas which came out for about ten years. I ran the press. I left my father's press and went to Nuevo Leon. There I worked as a mechanic. I was the first to drive the first automobiles which came to Sonora. I think that was in about 1904. When a steam automobile came and then gasoline cars I learned to drive them and make repairs. At that time there in Arizona they didn't even know automobiles. After being in Nuevo Leon for a while I came to Tucson and from here I went again to Sonora. I was a long time in Madero's revolution.[1] I went again to Guaymas to see my family. When I was there I told my father that it was better that he shouldn't get into politics with his newspaper, and that he shouldn't favor either one side or the other and thus he would get along better. My father had already been in jail due to the corruption of Sonora or rather of the politics of the state. . . . I was in Hermosillo, Altar, and in other parts of Sonora until finally I decided to come to Arizona and since then I have been settled here. First I worked as a watchmaker with my brother, for I also have a brother who has lived here for a long time. I also worked repairing automobiles in private garages until I had enough to begin to establish myself, enough at least to get credit and in that way I started my garage. The work on the newspaper I have had since I came. . . . When things get settled I will go to Guaymas where I have thought of establishing a repair shop for automobiles. This would give me a lot more money than here, for that business isn't very well established there or rather they don't know very much about it. I could cover the territory from Guaymas to close to Hermosillo and from there perhaps to the River Mayo, quite a large territory. The trouble is that one can't work satisfactorily there because the soldiers come and ask for so many gallons of gasolines to be charged to the garrison and then they don't pay one anything. If one has automobiles and trucks they also take those away because they say that they need to send troops to such and such a place. The fact is that they don't let one do anything or live in peace. I would like to go there to educate my children more than anything else. I have three sons already quite large who are going to the American school but I want them to go to a Mexican school so that they will be educated in their own country and learn to love and respect it. I don't have anything for which to complain about here. I have always been treated well, as all the Mexicans are. There is no race prejudice as there is in Texas and in California. I have heard by the papers that there they treat the Mexicans like dogs, but here they don't and why should one say what isn't true. In business and sometimes legally some differences are made, the Americans are always preferred in everything. Here in my work in

---

1. **Madero's revolution:** The Mexican Revolution.

my automobile repair shop I have many Americans who prefer that I do their work and I charge the same as the American shops. On the other hand there are a great many Mexicans who instead of helping one out by giving one their work, give it to the American shops, even though they don't do it well. I also ought to tell you that of the Americans who have brought me work none has ever done me out of a cent but the Mexicans on the other hand have robbed me of a lot, for many times they haven't paid me for what I have done for them.

"Just now, even if I wanted to, I couldn't go back to Mexico because they have me on a list in Nogales as being among the enemies of the Government and they wouldn't let me pass. . . . As the Mexican Consulate here, as it is everywhere, is only a nest of spies, they put me on the list of the enemies of the Government for no reason. . . .

"I always keep up with everything that happens in Mexico because I read the Mexican newspapers. I read *La Prensa* of San Antonio, Texas, and I read *El Heraldo de Mexico* and once in a while I buy *El Universal* and *Excelsior* so that they can't tell me anything. I know about everything that happens over there.

"I haven't lost my rights as a Mexican citizen nor those of my children, for I have registered in the Consulate here and I have registered them also. These Consulates don't do anything but serve as centers of espionage. When a Mexican goes to ask for help they ask him if he has his Mexican citizenship papers and if through ignorance or carelessness or some other cause he doesn't have them they say that he isn't a Mexican citizen and tell him to go and don't pay any attention to him. That happens in all the Consulates of our country and everyone knows it. It would be better not to have Consulates if they are going to do that. The so-called *Pochos*[2] here don't like us. They think that because one comes from Mexico one is going to take the country away from them. But our worst enemies are the Mexicans who have lived here for a great many years and have gotten settled and have become American citizens. They don't like us and they try to do us all the harm possible. But if one doesn't mix with them they can't do anything.

"I am a member of mutual aid societies in this city. I have always liked to be united with my fellow-countrymen and work for our mutual protection. We always celebrate the national holidays on the 16th of September and the 5th of May and we always have to put together the American and Mexican flags."

SRA. ANTONIA VILLAMIL DE ARTHUR

This woman is a native of a little town near Zamora, Michoacan. She has lived in Arizona for more than thirteen years. She is married to an American.

---

2. **Pochos:** A Mexican word for Chicanos or Mexican-descended people from the United States.

". . . My mother had several pieces of property in Zamora, which my father had left her, but we did not remain there but went about to different parts of the state until we settled permanently in Morelia. I finished growing up there and went to school there. I had some aunts there and some other relatives. I was left an orphan there, for my mother died when I was about fifteen. She left me some money with which I established a little store and this enabled me to live comfortably without worrying or working very much. Shortly after reaching the age of fifteen I was married. After six or seven years of married life I was left a widow with one child. My husband when he died left me several properties, among which were two little houses which I still retain and which shall some day be my son's. He is already quite grown up and is in Los Angeles now. It has been about fifteen years since I have seen him. I lived in Morelia until 1910. When the revolution began I went to Monterrey, Nuevo Leon. There I lived with a family who were friends of mine. This family afterwards came to Texas, first to San Antonio and afterwards to other places, until we got to El Paso. We were only sight-seeing and I had left my son in the care of a sister of mine. In El Paso I became acquainted with Arthur who is now my husband. At that time I returned to Morelia. Arthur went there too, and we were married. Then we came right back to Phoenix. Here he continued for a time his work on the railroad, but later he became a cook in a restaurant. He knows how to cook very well. Then he left this work and we established a fruit and drink stand. We remained a number of years with this business for we made money at it. Then we started a grocery store and engaged in some other business but just lately we bought this hotel. [They have bought the furnishings, the business rights, etc., but not the building.] The two of us take care of it. . . . Sometimes we go to the movies at night. I go mostly because my husband doesn't like the movies and the films hurt his eyes. When I don't have anything to do I read some Spanish novels because often months and months go by when I don't speak the language. Only Americans come to the hotel and they all speak English. It is true that my husband speaks Spanish. If he hadn't spoken it I wouldn't have married him but he no longer likes to talk it and it seems as though he was forgetting it. I hardly ever read any Mexican newspapers. We only get the morning daily in English. Once in a while some fellow countryman comes here to the hotel, as you have, and then I take real pleasure in speaking the language. We have a phonograph with several Mexican pieces, 'La Golondrina,' 'Entrada a los Toros,' 'Perjura' and others which are very pretty so that even the Americans like to hear them a lot. Since I have been in this country so long I have learned to speak English a little, to read it and to understand it. I understand it better than I can speak it but I have to speak it anyway in order to wait on those who come to the hotel. . . . My husband doesn't know that I have two pieces of property in Zamora because I haven't told him. As he is a foreigner one can't help but be a little suspicious of him. Anyway, as my first husband left me that property I am going to leave it to my son because they really belong to him. . . . It has been many years, about fourteen, since I have seen my son because I haven't seen him since I was married. He grew up gradually and I know that he learned the mechanic's or carpenter's trade in some way. He came with some friends to the United States. It seems to me that he has been in Chicago and other large cities of this country but now he is in Los Angeles, for he has written me from there. I have hopes of seeing him soon for he has said that he is coming to see me. I wish that he would come with all my heart. I have no reason to complain of my husband, only he is blunt once in a while and very serious, as all Americans are. . . . I live very happily with him, although at times we have our misunderstandings, for the truth is one can't ever make one's self understood as one can with a Mexican. I like everything that there is in this country, the ease with which one can go around alone, can go to the movies, and so on. I think that it would be hard for me to go back to the customs of Mexico. Some six or seven years ago I went to visit in Morelia. My uncle found me very much changed. . . ."

DOMINGO RAMÍREZ

He is white, twenty-one years of age, a native of Cananea, Sonora.

"My parents brought me here at the age of seven and I am now twenty-one. I have been educated in the American schools, but my father has taught me to read Spanish and he also taught me the geography and history of Mexico. He also told my brothers and me that before everything else we ought to love Mexico, because that is our country. That is true, for we are Mexicans. We are dark and speak Spanish and it is no use to try to make ourselves American. My father was governor of Cananea but came to this country on account of the revolution, I think. My father has several properties over there in Sonora. He was first a teacher and then he went into politics. He also had some cattle and a store. My oldest brother has just finished inventing a way of making ice-cream sticks (*paletas*). It is a special formula so that the sticks don't go to pieces even in twenty-four hours. These sticks are called 'Alaska,' and the Americans, the Mexicans and the Indians buy them here. They like them a lot. For fifteen years we have had an ice-cream shop in this city, and in other places. My brother has been for several years in the Capital of Mexico and there he also had ice-cream stores. He sold the 'Alaska' sticks. He has now sent a plant there so that the 'Alaska' sticks can be made. He has sold concessions to several Americans so that they can develop the business in El Paso and San Antonio, in Phoenix, Arizona, and in other important cities.

"I learned English in school and went as far as high school but I didn't want to go on. I found it better to help the company by taking charge of the sale of the *paletas* here. I think that the Americans know a lot more about business than the Mexicans, for they advertise all their merchandise well. They take whole pages in the papers but the Mexicans don't. They carry on their business according to the old ideas and they don't advertise or anything. That is why they hardly ever get very far.

"My father wants us always to talk Spanish at home and to follow the Mexican customs, and we do that. Mother does also. At home food is prepared in true Mexican style, for the American style isn't any good. The food has no flavor. The only thing that I like that the Americans have are the salads. They know how to prepare those very well.

"Just to go out with, I like the American girls better. They aren't as particular as the Mexicans. The Americans go out with one and give one kisses that get one all excited, while the Mexicans don't even want to allow themselves to be kissed. But if I were to marry I would marry a Mexican girl because they are obedient and are grateful for everything. They know how to work in the house and they have a different way about them. The American girls do everything they want to and they don't pay any attention to their husbands. The trouble with the Mexican girls is that they are affected and make a lot of fuss about doing this and that. That is why I don't like to go around with them very much.

"I would like to go to Mexico, but perhaps I wouldn't go there to live because now I am used to this city. I can almost say that I am a native. What I don't like about Mexico is that they are fighting all the time, revolutions and revolutions. All want to be in power to rob and that is why the country doesn't progress and there is almost no business. My father says that he has hopes of returning when everything is peaceful but as long as it is at war he likes it better here."

37

GENORA DOLLINGER

Taking a Stand: The Sit-Down Strikes of the 1930s

The New Deal's reform efforts began to wane after a flurry of legislation in 1935 known as the Second Hundred Days. Subsequently, in 1936 and 1937, organized labor's drive toward national organization wielded a powerful tool that simultaneously gave the New Deal an institutional base and solidified opposition to it. Labor's new weapon was the sit-down strike.

The story begins early in 1936, when the Firestone Tire and Rubber Company of Akron, Ohio, fired several unionists for organizing against a proposed wage cut. In defense of their sacked union brothers, workers remained after their work shifts to occupy the factory. Within just two days, Firestone gave in. When a similar situation occurred across town at Goodyear, the police deputized 150 strikebreakers to help clear the

Genora (Johnson) Dollinger, *Striking Flint: Remembering the 1936–37 General Motors Sit-Down Strike*, told to Susan Rosenthal, PDF e-book, pp. 9–12, 17, ColdType.net, http://susan rosenthal.com/pamphlets/striking-flint; printed version, Haymarket Books, http://haymarket books.org.

factory. There they were met by thousands of angry workers from all over Akron. Good-year, too, surrendered, and the new strategy spread across the nation. More than five hundred sit-downs occurred during 1936 and 1937, achieving more success for union-ization in a year than labor had accomplished in decades.

What explains the effectiveness of this tactic? The sit-down strike worked because of business owners' fears of having their equipment dashed along with their hopes of industrial recovery. Moreover, the new strategy prevented management from hiring nonunion "scab" workers to replace strikers. And both federal and state governments no longer expected public support for the use of force—the traditional response to labor militancy. So industry after industry yielded to the workers' new aggressiveness. The effect on union numbers was staggering: in 1936, before the sit-downs began, scarcely four million workers had belonged to unions, but by the end of 1937, the figure was over seven million. The nation entered World War II with more than eleven million workers organized.

The most famous sit-down strike occurred in December 1936 at General Motors' Fisher Body plant in Flint, Michigan, in response to the firing of two union members. The following excerpt is from an account by Genora Dollinger, as told to Susan Rosen-thal, an oral history interviewer from the United Automobile Workers (UAW), in 1995. Dollinger, twenty-three at the time of the strike, realized early on that police would find it difficult to attack women physically. She organized the Women's Auxiliary and the Women's Emergency Brigade of the UAW, providing food and support for the striking workers.

QUESTIONS TO CONSIDER

1. What were the advantages for workers of a sit-down strike over a conventional picket line? What were the disadvantages of this strategy?
2. How did a sit-down strike depend on different types of external support?
3. Why were sit-down strikes so effective in the 1930s? Would they be as effective today? Why or why not?

Conditions in Flint before the strike were very, very depressing for working people. We had a large influx of workers come into the city from the deep South. They came north to find jobs, because there was no work back home. They came with their furniture strapped on old jalopies and they'd move into the cheapest housing that they could find. Usually these were just little one or two-room structures with no inside plumbing and no inside heating arrangements. They just had kerosene heaters to heat their wash water, their bath water, and their homes. You could smell kerosene all over their clothing. They were very poor. . . .

Before the strike, the women didn't have the opportunity to participate in any activities. The small neighborhood churches were the only places they had to go to. They knew some of their neighbors and they would go to some of these little churches, but that's all. The men frequented the beer gardens and talked to other men about shop problems or whatever. They got to be shop buddies.

When you worked in the factory in those days, no one cared what your name was. You became "Whitey" if you happened to be blonde. Or you might be "Blacky" if you had black hair. If you asked, "Well, who is he?" you'd get, "I don't know, he works in department so-and-so, Plant 4, on the line half way down." It was just "Blacky" or "Shorty" or some nickname. They were wage slaves with a complete loss of identity and rights inside the plant.

At first, when these workers were approached to join the union, they were afraid they might lose this job that was so very valuable to them. At that time, men working in the auto plants were getting around forty-five cents an hour. The younger girls that worked in the A.C. Sparkplug division of General Motors, were being paid twelve-and-a-half cents an hour to make minor car instruments. That was the only plant that employed women.

I'll tell you about the conditions of these young women. After the strike, a Senate investigating committee found that in one department of A.C. alone, the girls had all been forced to go to the county hospital and be treated for venereal disease traced to one foreman. Those were the conditions that young women had to accept in order to support their families. Sometimes they earned just enough to provide food for the family and they couldn't lose their jobs because nobody else in the family had a job.

Flint was a General Motors town—lock, stock and barrel! If you drove past one of the huge GM plants in Flint, you could see workers sitting on the front lawns along the side of the plant just waiting for a foreman to come to the door and call them in. And maybe they'd work them for an hour or maybe for a day, and that was it. But workers were so desperate that they would come and sit every day on that lawn in the hopes of being called in and possibly getting a permanent job. That's how poor these General Motors workers really were, at least the ones in hopes of getting a job at GM. . . .

Conditions were terrible inside the plants, which were notorious for their speed-up systems. They had men with stop watches timing the workers to see if they could squeeze one or two more operations in. You saw Charlie Chaplin in the movie, *Modern Times*? Well, this is exactly what happened. They did everything but tie a broom to their tail. It was so oppressive that there were several cases of men just cracking up completely and taking a wrench and striking their foreman. When that happened, the worker was sentenced to what was then called an insane asylum in Pontiac, Michigan.

The speed-up was the biggest issue. The men just couldn't take it. They would come home at night, and they couldn't hold their forks in their swollen fingers. They would just lie down on the floor. Many of them wound up in beer gardens to try to forget their problems and their aches and pains. . . .

They used to say, "Once you pass the gates of General Motors, forget about the United States Constitution." Workers had no rights when they entered that plant. If a foreman didn't like the way you parted your hair— or whatever he didn't like about you—you may have looked at him the wrong way, or said something that rubbed him the wrong way—he could fire you. No recourse, no nothing. And practically all foremen expected workers to bring them turkeys on Thanksgiving and gifts for Christmas and repair their motor cars and even paint their houses. The workers were kept intimidated because if they didn't comply with what the foreman told them to do, they would lose their jobs and their families would starve. You can see what a feeling of slavery and domination workers felt inside the GM plants.

Not only that, but when workers started talking about organizing, management hired lip-readers to watch the men talk to each other, even when they were right close to each other, so they could tell if they were talking union. One of our friends who was a member of the Socialist Party wore the first UAW button into the Chevrolet plant. He was fired immediately. He didn't even get to his job. They spotted the button and that was it. If you went into a beer garden or other place like that and began to talk about unions, very often you didn't get home without getting an awful beating by GM-hired thugs.

That was the condition inside the plants. Combined with the bad conditions on the outside: poor living conditions, lack of proper food, lack of proper medical attention and everything else, the auto workers came to the conclusion that there was no way they could ever escape any of this injustice without joining a union. But they didn't all decide at one time. . . .

The first sit-down was on December 30 in the small Fisher Body Plant 2 over a particularly big grievance that had occurred. The workers were at the point where they had just had enough, and under a militant leadership, they sat down. When the UAW leaders in the big Fisher Body Plant 1 heard about the sit-down in Fisher 2, they sat down, also. That took real guts, and it took political leadership. The leaders of the political parties knew what they had to do because they'd studied labor history and the ruthlessness of the corporations.

Picket lines were established and also a big kitchen in the south end of Flint, across from the large Fisher 1 plant. Every day, gallons and gallons of food were prepared, and anybody who was on the picket lines would get a ticket with notification that they had served on the line so they'd be able to get a good hot meal.

The strike kitchen was primarily organized by the Communist Party women. They brought a restaurant man from Detroit to help organize this huge kitchen. They were the ones who made all of those good meals.

We also had what we called scavengers, groups of people who would go to the local farmers and ask for donations of food for the strikers. Many people in these small towns surrounding Flint were factory workers who would also raise potatoes, cabbages, tomatoes, corn or whatever. So great quantities of food were sent down to be made into dishes for the strikers. People were very generous. . . .

After the first sit-down started, I went down to see what I could do to help. I was either on the picket lines or up at the Pengelly Building all the time, but some of the strike leaders didn't know who I was and didn't know that I had been teaching classes in unionism and so on. So they said, "Go to the kitchen. We need a lot of help out there." They didn't know what else to tell a woman to do. I said, "You've got a lot of little, skinny men around here who can't stand to be out on the cold picket lines for very long. They can peel potatoes as well as women can." I turned down the idea of kitchen duty.

Instead, I organized a children's picket line. I got Bristol board and paints, and I was painting signs for this children's picket line. One of my socialist comrades came up and said, "Hey, Genora, what are you doing here?" I said, "I'm doing your job." Since he was a professional sign painter, I turned the sign-painting project over to him and that was the beginning of the sign-painting department.

We could only do the children's picket line once because it was too dangerous, but we got an awful lot of favorable publicity from it, much of it international. The picture of my two-year-old son, Jarvis, holding a picket sign saying, "My daddy strikes for us little tykes," went all over the nation, and people sent me articles from French newspapers and from Germany and from other European countries. I thought it was remarkable that the news traveled so far.

PART FIVE

"The American Century"
War, Affluence, and Uncertainty

World War II affected virtually every part of American life. Problems of economic depression vanished with the growth of productivity in war industries and—to the surprise of most economists—did not return after the war. The federal government expanded during the war and never returned to its prewar size. Family life changed dramatically: fathers were absent, mothers worked outside the home, families moved to crowded centers of war industry, consumer goods were rationed or unavailable, and divorce rates soared. Science was transformed by both the scale of its activities and its subjection to military security regulations. Loyalties and antipathies shifted in extraordinary ways. The communist Soviet Union became one of the United States' most important allies against Germany, Italy, and Japan and bore the brunt of the war's casualties. German Americans and Italian Americans became suspect, and many Japanese Americans were locked up in internment camps.

Part Five's readings sample the drama of World War II and its aftermath. J. Robert Oppenheimer, who directed scientific work at the Los Alamos National Laboratory, one of the top sites for the development of the first atomic bomb, recounts the controversy surrounding the bomb's creation. Paul Tibbets, pilot of the *Enola Gay*, recollects dropping the bomb on Hiroshima, and George Weller describes the aftereffects of using the bomb on Nagasaki. Fanny Christina Hill was one of the many women—collectively dubbed "Rosie the Riveter" in the newspapers—who found new opportunities in the war industries. Ben Yorita and Philip Hayasaka describe the internment camps that they and their families were forced to endure throughout much of the war.

Victory in the war planted seeds of both hope and fear. Uncertainties about the United States' future were accompanied by ideological quarrels with the Soviet Union. The cold war between the superpowers was tested on the Korean peninsula, where Otto Apel and other Americans fought for the containment of communism. The anxious transition to a peacetime economy and then back to the quasi-war footing of the cold war provoked the Red Scare, the fear of communist espionage that Oscar-winner Ring Lardner Jr. struggled with during the 1950s. The USSR's launch of *Sputnik 1*, the first man-made object in space, combined with cold war propaganda to heighten this fear, giving men like Charles Douglas Jackson an important place in an emerging national security apparatus that had penetrated the government, media, and daily life. However, *Sputnik's* advent also led to a vast expansion of the public education system that brought less affluent Americans into higher education and subsequently into technical and professional careers. As Americans embarked on what would prove to be an era of unprecedented prosperity, social commentators became concerned that the nation was growing soft and complacent, even conformist, as evidenced by the perfectly planned, uniform suburbs of Levittown and their imitators. Of course, many Americans, particularly women and minorities, were left out of the postwar economic boom. Fanny Christina Hill, for instance, found that after the war, it was difficult to make a living wage. For her and countless others, it was a period of struggle, envy, and disappointment.

POINTS OF VIEW
Building and Using an Atomic Bomb (1942–1945)

38

J. ROBERT OPPENHEIMER

To Build an Atomic Bomb

In the early 1930s, with the rise of Hitler, Mussolini, and Stalin, politics began noticeably intruding on sciences even as remote as theoretical physics. Less noticeably, scientific theories and discoveries began ever so slowly to intrude on politics. By 1938, when scientists in Germany at last figured out that neutrons could "split" certain atoms and release great quantities of energy, the fate of people and nations suddenly hung in the balance.

Scientists in Great Britain and the United States could only speculate on what progress Hitler's scientists might be making in harnessing nuclear fission. In June 1942, American and British scientists developed plans for a uranium-based atomic bomb. Full-scale efforts to construct such a bomb, code-named the Manhattan Project, thus began in the shadow of Germany's possible head start. Only later was Germany's lack of progress discovered.

The Manhattan Project was overseen by the Army Corps of Engineers. Under the direction of General Leslie R. Groves, massive facilities in Los Alamos, New Mexico; Oak Ridge, Tennessee; and Hanford, Washington, were built, involving about 125,000 workers and costing $2 billion. Los Alamos—a site chosen by the brilliant physicist J. Robert Oppenheimer (1904–1967), who was selected to lead the project—was the scientific capital of the endeavor.

"My two great loves," Oppenheimer often told friends, "are physics and New Mexico. It's a pity they can't be combined." Two decades later his wish came true when the nation's need for secrecy and his own longtime affection for the area made it the appropriate site of a great adventure for many physicists and their families.

At Los Alamos, scientists who were accustomed to open communications lived under the rule of secrecy and military security. They could not tell relatives where they were going or what they were doing; even their spouses might not have known about the laboratory's mission. Often the scientists were unaware of what the other units in the laboratory were working on, and few knew the project's ultimate objective. Oppenheimer recruited scientists worldwide and directed their work on the tightest of deadlines toward their ultimate goal: beating the Germans to the bomb. Their success, and the ironies of that success, are the subjects of Oppenheimer's autobiographical sketch and November 1945 speech excerpted here.

QUESTIONS TO CONSIDER

1. What changed J. Robert Oppenheimer from an unworldly scientist to a man who could direct a large and important enterprise?
2. What responsibilities did he envision for scientists after the war?
3. After he opposed the development of the hydrogen bomb, Oppenheimer lost his security clearance to engage in or advise on government research on nuclear weapons. What foreshadowings of his doubts about nuclear weapons do you see in his November 1945 speech?

Michael B. Stoff, Jonathan F. Fanton, and R. Hal Williams, eds., *The Manhattan Project: A Documentary Introduction to the Atomic Age* (New York: McGraw-Hill, 1991), 29–32; J. Robert Oppenheimer, "Speech to the Association of Los Alamos Scientists," in Alice Kimball Smith and Charles Weiner, eds., *Robert Oppenheimer: Letters and Recollections* (Cambridge, MA: Harvard University Press, 1980), 315–20, 324–25.

AUTOBIOGRAPHICAL SKETCH (1954)

I was born in New York in 1904. My father had come to this country at the age of 17 from Germany. He was a successful businessman and quite active in community affairs. My mother was born in Baltimore and before her marriage was an artist and teacher of art. I attended Ethical Culture School and Harvard College, which I entered in 1922. I completed the work for my degree in the spring of 1925. I then left Harvard to study at Cambridge University and in Goettingen, where in the spring of 1927 I took my doctor's degree. . . . I had learned a great deal in my student days about the new physics; I wanted to pursue this myself, to explain it and to foster its cultivation. I had had many invitations to university positions, 1 or 2 in Europe, and perhaps 10 in the United States. I accepted concurrent appointments as assistant professor at the California Institute of Technology in Pasadena and at the University of California in Berkeley. For the coming 12 years, I was to devote my time to these 2 faculties. . . .

My friends, both in Pasadena and in Berkeley, were mostly faculty people, scientists, classicists, and artists. I studied and read Sanskrit with Arthur Rider. I read very widely, mostly classics, novels, plays, and poetry; and I read something of other parts of science. I was not interested in and did not read about economics or politics. I was almost wholly divorced from the contemporary scene in this country. I never read a newspaper or a current magazine like *Time* or *Harper's*; I had no radio, no telephone; I learned of the stock-market crash in the fall of 1929 only long after the event; the first time I ever voted was in the presidential election of 1936. To many of my friends, my indifference to contemporary affairs seemed bizarre, and they often chided me with being too much of a highbrow. I was interested in man and his experience; I was deeply interested in my science; but I had no understanding of the relations of man to his society.

Beginning in late 1936, my interests began to change. . . . I can discern in retrospect more than one reason for these changes. I had had a continuing, smoldering fury about the treatment of Jews in Germany. I had relatives there, and was later to help in extricating them and bringing them to this country. I saw what the depression was doing to my students. Often they could get no jobs, or jobs which were wholly inadequate. And through them, I began to understand how deeply political and economic events could affect men's lives. I began to feel the need to participate more fully in the life of the community. But I had no framework of political conviction or experience to give me perspective in these matters. . . .

Ever since the discovery of nuclear fission, the possibility of powerful explosives based on it had been very much in my mind, as it had in that of many other physicists. We had some understanding of what this might do for us in the war, and how much it might change the course of history. In the autumn of 1941, a special committee was set up by the National Academy of Sciences under the chairmanship of Arthur Compton to review the prospects and feasibility of the different uses of atomic energy for military purposes. I attended a meeting of this committee; this was my first official connection with the atomic energy program.

After the academy meeting, I spent some time in preliminary calculations about the consumption and performance of atomic bombs, and became increasingly excited at the prospects. . . . I also began to consult, more or less regularly, with the staff of the Radiation Laboratory in Berkeley on their program for the electromagnetic separation of uranium isotopes. . . . I attended the conference in Chicago at which the Metallurgical Laboratory (to produce plutonium) was established and its initial program projected.

In the spring of 1942, Compton called me to Chicago to discuss the state of work on the bomb itself. During this meeting Compton asked me to take the responsibility for this work, which at that time consisted of numerous scattered experimental projects. Although I had no administrative experience and was not an experimental physicist, I felt sufficiently informed and challenged by the problem to be glad to accept. At this time I became an employee of the Metallurgical Laboratory.

After this conference I called together a theoretical study group in Berkeley, in which Hans Bethe, Emil Konopinski, Robert Serber, Edward Teller, John H. Van Vleck, and I participated. We had an adventurous time. We spent much of the summer of 1942 in Berkeley in a joint study that for the first time really came to grips with the physical problems of atomic bombs, atomic explosions, and the possibility of using fission explosions to initiate thermonuclear reactions. I called this possibility to the attention of Dr. Vannevar Bush during the late summer; the technical views on this subject were to develop and change from then until the present day.

After these studies there was little doubt that a potentially world-shattering undertaking lay ahead. We began to see the great explosion at Alamogordo[1] and the greater explosions at Eniwetok[2] with a surer foreknowledge. We also began to see how rough, difficult, challenging, and unpredictable this job might turn out to be. . . .

In later summer, after a review of the experimental work, I became convinced, as did others, that a major change was called for in the work on the bomb itself. We needed a central laboratory devoted wholly to this purpose, where people could talk freely with each other, where theoretical ideas and experimental findings could affect each other, where the waste and frustration and error of the many compartmentalized experimental studies could be eliminated, where we could begin to come to grips with chemical, metallurgical, engineering, and ordnance problems that had so far received no consideration. We therefore sought to establish this laboratory for a direct attack on all the problems inherent in the most rapid possible development and production of atomic bombs.

---

1. **Alamogordo:** New Mexico site of the first detonation of an atomic device.
2. **Eniwetok:** Pacific island used as an atomic test site.

In the autumn of 1942 General Leslie R. Groves assumed charge of the Manhattan Engineer District. I discussed with him the need for an atomic bomb laboratory. . . .

In early 1943, I received a letter signed by General Groves and Dr. James B. Conant, appointing me director of the laboratory, and outlining their conception of how it was to be organized and administered. The necessary construction and assembling of the needed facilities were begun. All of us worked in close collaboration with the engineers of the Manhattan District.

The site of Los Alamos was selected in part at least because it enabled those responsible to balance the obvious need for security with the equally important need of free communication among those engaged in the work. Security, it was hoped, would be achieved by removing the laboratory to a remote area, fenced and patrolled, where communication with the outside was extremely limited. Telephone calls were monitored, mail was censored, and personnel who left the area—something permitted only for the clearest of causes—knew that their movements might be under surveillance. On the other hand, for those within the community, fullest exposition and discussion among those competent to use the information was encouraged. . . .

The program of recruitment was massive. Even though we then underestimated the ultimate size of the laboratory, which was to have almost 4,000 members by the spring of 1945, and even though we did not at that time see clearly some of the difficulties which were to bedevil and threaten the enterprise, we knew that it was a big, complex and diverse job. Even the initial plan of the laboratory called for a start with more than 100 highly qualified and trained scientists, to say nothing of the technicians, staff, and mechanics who would be required for their support, and of the equipment that we would have to beg and borrow since there would be no time to build it from scratch. We had to recruit at a time when the country was fully engaged in war and almost every competent scientist was already involved in the military effort.

The primary burden of this fell on me. To recruit staff I traveled all over the country talking with people who had been working on one or another aspect of the atomic-energy enterprise, and people in radar work, for example, and underwater sound, telling them about the job, the place that we were going to, and enlisting their enthusiasm.

In order to bring responsible scientists to Los Alamos, I had to rely on their sense of the interest, urgency, and feasibility of the Los Alamos mission. I had to tell them enough of what the job was, and give strong enough assurance that it might be successfully accomplished in time to affect the outcome of the war, to make it clear that they were justified in their leaving other work to come to this job.

The prospect of coming to Los Alamos aroused great misgivings. It was to be a military post; men were asked to sign up more or less for the duration; restrictions on travel and on the freedom of families to move about [were] to be severe; and no one could be sure of the extent to which the necessary technical freedom of action could actually be maintained by the laboratory.

The notion of disappearing into the New Mexico desert for an indeterminate period and under quasi-military auspices disturbed a good many scientists, and the families of many more. But there was another side to it. Almost everyone realized that this was a great undertaking. Almost everyone knew that if it were completed successfully and rapidly enough, it might determine the outcome of the war. Almost everyone knew that it was an unparalleled opportunity to bring to bear the basic knowledge and art of science for the benefit of his country. Almost everyone knew that this job, if it were achieved, would be a part of history. This sense of excitement, of devotion and of patriotism in the end prevailed. Most of those with whom I talked came to Los Alamos. Once they came, confidence in the enterprise grew as men learned more of the technical status of the work; and though the laboratory was to double and redouble its size many times before the end, once it had started it was on the road to success.

We had information in those days of German activity in the field of nuclear fission. We were aware of what it might mean if they beat us to the draw in the development of atomic bombs. The consensus of all our opinions, and every directive that I had, stressed the extreme urgency of our work, as well as the need for guarding all knowledge of it from our enemies. . . .

. . . Time and again we had in the technical work almost paralyzing crises. Time and again the laboratory drew itself together and faced the new problems and got on with the work. We worked by night and by day; and in the end the many jobs were done. . . .

SPEECH TO THE ASSOCIATION OF LOS ALAMOS SCIENTISTS

Los Alamos, November 2, 1945

. . . I should like to talk tonight—if some of you have long memories perhaps you will regard it as justified—as a fellow scientist, and at least as a fellow worrier about the fix we are in. . . . I think there are issues which are quite simple and quite deep, and which involve us as a group of scientists—involve us more, perhaps than any other group in the world. I think that it can only help to look a little at what our situation is—at what has happened to us—and that this must give us some honesty, some insight, which will be a source of strength in what may be the not-too-easy days ahead. . . .

I think that it hardly needs to be said why the impact [of the atomic bomb and atomic weapons] is so strong. There are three reasons: one is the extraordinary speed with which things which were right on the frontier of science were translated into terms where they affected many living people, and potentially all people. Another is the fact, quite accidental in many ways, and connected with the speed, that scientists themselves played such a large part, not merely in providing the foundation for atomic weapons, but in actually making them. In this we are certainly closer to it than any other group. The third is that the thing we made—partly because of the technical nature of the problem, partly because we worked hard, partly because we had good breaks—really arrived in the world with such a shattering reality and suddenness that there was no opportunity for the edges to be worn off.

But when you come right down to it the reason that we did this job is because it was an organic necessity. If you are a scientist you cannot stop such a thing. If you are a scientist you believe that it is good to find out how the world works; that it is good to find out what the realities are; that it is good to turn over to mankind at large the greatest possible power to control the world and to deal with it according to its rights and its values.

There are many people who try to wiggle out of this. They say the real importance of atomic energy does not lie in the weapons that have been made; the real importance lies in all the great benefits which atomic energy, which the various radiations, will bring to mankind. There may be some truth in this. I am sure that there is truth in it, because there has never in the past been a new field opened up where the real fruits of it have not been invisible at the beginning. I have a very high confidence that the fruits—the so-called peacetime applications—of atomic energy will have in them all that we think, and more. There are others who try to escape the immediacy of this situation by saying that, after all, war has always been very terrible; after all, weapons have always gotten worse and worse; that this is just another weapon and it doesn't create a great change; that they are not so bad; bombings have been bad in this war and this is not a change in that—it just adds a little to the effectiveness of bombing; that some sort of protection will be found. I think that these efforts to diffuse and weaken the nature of the crisis make it only more dangerous. I think it is for us to accept it as a very grave crisis, to realize that these atomic weapons which we have started to make are very terrible, that they involve a change, that they are not just a slight modification: to accept this, and to accept with it the necessity for those transformations in the world which will make it possible to integrate these developments into human life.

. . . It is a new field, in which the position of vested interests in various parts of the world is very much less serious than in others. It is serious in this country, and that is one of our problems. It is a new field, in which the role of science has been so great that it is to my mind hardly thinkable that the international traditions of science, and the fraternity of scientists, should not play a constructive part. It is a new field, in which just the novelty and the special characteristics of the technical operations should enable one to establish a community of interest which might almost be regarded as a pilot plant for a new type of international collaboration. I speak of it as a pilot plant because it is quite clear that the control of atomic weapons cannot be in itself the unique end of such an operation. The only unique end can be a world that is united, and a world in which war will not occur. But those things don't happen overnight, and in this field it would seem that one could get started, and get started without meeting those insuperable obstacles which history has so often placed in the way of any effort of cooperation. Now, this is not an easy thing, and the point I want to make, the one point I want to hammer home, is what an enormous change in spirit is involved. There are things which we hold very dear, and I think rightly hold very dear; I would say that the word democracy perhaps stood for some of them as well as any other word. There are many parts of the world in which there is no democracy. There are other things which we hold dear, and which we rightly should. And when I speak of a new spirit in international affairs I mean that even to these deepest of things which we cherish, and for which Americans have been willing to die—and certainly most of us would be willing to die—even in these deepest things, we realize that there is something more profound than that; namely, the common bond with other men everywhere. It is only if you do that that this makes sense; because if you approach the problem and say, "We know what is right and we would like to use the atomic bomb to persuade you to agree with us," then you are in a very weak position and you will not succeed, because under those conditions you will not succeed in delegating responsibility for the survival of men. It is a purely unilateral statement; you will find yourselves attempting by force of arms to prevent a disaster.

I don't have very much more to say. There are a few things which scientists perhaps should remember, that I don't think I need to remind us of; but I will, anyway. One is that they are very often called upon to give technical information in one way or another, and I think one cannot be too careful to be honest. And it is very difficult, not because one tells lies, but because so often questions are put in a form which makes it very hard to give an answer which is not misleading. I think we will be in a very weak position unless we maintain at its highest the scrupulousness which is traditional for us in sticking to the truth, and in distinguishing between what we know to be true from what we hope may be true.

The second thing I think it right to speak of is this: it is everywhere felt that the fraternity between us and scientists in other countries may be one of the most helpful things for the future; yet it is apparent that even in this country not all of us who are scientists are in agreement. There is no harm in that; such disagreement is healthy. But we must not lose the sense of fraternity because of it; we must not lose our fundamental confidence in our fellow scientists.

I think that we have no hope at all if we yield in our belief in the value of science, in the good that it can be to the world to know about reality, about nature, to attain a gradually greater and greater control of nature, to learn, to teach, to understand. I think that if we lose our faith in this we stop being scientists, we sell out our heritage, we lose what we have most of value for this time of crisis.

But there is another thing: we are not only scientists; we are men, too. We cannot forget our dependence on our fellow men. I mean not only our material dependence, without which no science would be possible, and without which we could not work; I mean also our deep moral dependence, in that the value of science must lie in the world of men, that all our roots lie there. These are the strongest bonds in the world, stronger than those even that bind us to one another, these are the deepest bonds—that bind us to our fellow men.

39

PAUL TIBBETS AND GEORGE WELLER

To Use an Atomic Bomb

It was far from an easy decision to drop atomic bombs on the Japanese cities of Hiro-shima and Nagasaki on August 6 and 9, 1945. Nazi Germany had surrendered on May 8, 1945, and been carved up into occupation zones by the increasingly rivalrous British, French, U.S., and Soviet armies. Alone, Japan was hopelessly overmatched and faced inevitable defeat. The June capture of Okinawa, considered by most Japanese to be part of their nation, provided the United States and its allies with an important strategic base close to the main Japanese island. All that remained was to decide the terms under which Japan would cease fighting.

U.S. leaders had determined that they needed nothing short of unconditional sur-render, but many Japanese generals found such terms unacceptable. While the leaders of Japan searched for a formula that would allow them to end the war, the Allies prepared for an invasion of the main Japanese island. Adding to the complexity was the fact that Roosevelt and Stalin had agreed at Yalta in February that the Soviet Union would declare war in the Pacific and invade Japan within three months of Germany's capitula-tion. Casualties on both sides were expected to be enormous, since it was assumed that the Japanese would fight to the death.

These were the challenges President Harry Truman and his advisers faced in decid-ing whether to use the new and incredibly powerful secret weapon that J. Robert Op-penheimer discusses in Document 38. On August 6, 1945, the United States dropped an atomic bomb on Hiroshima, followed by another three days later on Nagasaki. That was enough. Emperor Hirohito broadcast to the Japanese people his acceptance of sur-render, and Japan came under U.S. occupation.

Hiroshima and Nagasaki brought just what the U.S. government wanted: its troops were spared the enormous bloodshed sure to accompany an invasion. But the question of the morality of the bombings has haunted the world ever since. Did the United States and its allies have to demand total surrender, when a few concessions, such as allowing Japa-nese war crimes to be tried in Japanese courts, might have avoided both invasion and the horror of the two atomic bombs? Were there fewer civilian casualties from the two bombs than the millions who might have died had the U.S. military invaded Japan, as defend-ers of Truman's decision have argued? Was the desire to avoid the type of power sharing between the United States and the Soviet Union that had occurred in Europe after the Nazi surrender part of Truman's calculation? Finally, what is the future of a world where such devices may be built and used by one nation, forcing others to develop similar technologies?

Paul Tibbets, interview by Studs Terkel, *Guardian*, August 6, 2002; George Weller, published with the permission of Anthony Weller, Gloucester, Massachusetts, through Dunow & Carl-son Literary Agency, New York, via Tuttle-Mori Agency, Inc., Tokyo.

In the first excerpt here, the pilot of the Enola Gay, *Paul Tibbets (1915–2007), talks with journalist Studs Terkel about dropping the bomb over Hiroshima. In the second reading, Pulitzer Prize–winning journalist George Weller (1907–2002), the first American reporter to enter Nagasaki after the second bomb was dropped, describes the devastation there. The head of the U.S. occupation forces in Japan, General Douglas MacArthur, suppressed Weller's eyewitness accounts, and they were not released to the public until June 2005.*

QUESTIONS TO CONSIDER

1. How did Paul Tibbets feel about his role in dropping the bomb? Explain any reservations he might have had, along with his justifications for his actions.
2. Why do you think General MacArthur censored George Weller's stories?

PAUL TIBBETS

An Interview with the Pilot of the Enola Gay

Studs Terkel: You got the go-ahead on August 5.

Paul Tibbets: Yeah. We were in Tinian[1] at the time we got the OK. They had sent this Norwegian to the weather station out on Guam[2] and I had a copy of his report. We said that, based on his forecast, the sixth day of August would be the best day that we could get over Honshu.[3] So we did everything that had to be done to get the crews ready to go: airplane loaded, crews briefed, all of the things checked that you have to check before you can fly over enemy territory.

General Groves had a brigadier-general who was connected back to Washington, D.C., by a special teletype machine. He stayed close to that thing all the time, notifying people back there, all by code, that we were preparing these airplanes to go any time after midnight on the sixth. And that's the way it worked out. We were ready to go at about four o'clock in the afternoon on the fifth and we got word from the president that we were free to go: "Use 'em as you wish." They give you a time you're supposed to drop your bomb on target and that was 9:15 in the morning, but that was Tinian time, one hour later than Japanese time. I told Dutch, "You figure it out what time we have to start after midnight to be over the target at 9 A.M."

Studs Terkel: That'd be Sunday morning.

Paul Tibbets: Well, we got going down the runway at right about 2:15 A.M. and we took off, we met our rendezvous guys, we made our flight up to what we call the initial point, that would be a geographic position that you could

1. **Tinian:** The U.S. island base in the Pacific.
2. **Guam:** The United States' westernmost territory.
3. **Honshu:** The island on which Hiroshima is located.

not mistake. Well, of course we had the best one in the world with the rivers and bridges and that big shrine. There was no mistaking what it was.

Studs Terkel: So you had to have the right navigator to get it on the button.

Paul Tibbets: The airplane has a bombsight connected to the autopilot and the bombardier puts figures in there for where he wants to be when he drops the weapon, and that's transmitted to the airplane. We always took into account what would happen if we had a failure and the bomb bay doors didn't open: we had a manual release put in each airplane so it was right down by the bombardier and he could pull on that. And the guys in the airplanes that followed us to drop the instruments needed to know when it was going to go. We were told not to use the radio, but, hell, I had to. I told them I would say, "One minute out," "Thirty seconds out," "Twenty seconds" and "Ten" and then I'd count, "Nine, eight, seven, six, five, four seconds," which would give them a time to drop their cargo. They knew what was going on because they knew where we were. And that's exactly the way it worked, it was absolutely perfect.

After we got the airplanes in formation I crawled into the tunnel and went back to tell the men. I said, "You know what we're doing today?" They said, "Well, yeah, we're going on a bombing mission." I said, "Yeah, we're going on a bombing mission, but it's a little bit special." My tailgunner, Bob Caron, was pretty alert. He said, "Colonel, we wouldn't be playing with atoms today, would we?" I said, "Bob, you've got it just exactly right." So I went back up in the front end and I told the navigator, bombardier, flight engineer, in turn. I said, "OK, this is an atom bomb we're dropping." They listened intently but I didn't see any change in their faces or anything else. Those guys were no idiots. We'd been fiddling round with the most peculiar-shaped things we'd ever seen.

So we're coming down. We get to that point where I say "one second" and by the time I'd got that second out of my mouth the airplane had lurched, because 10,000 lbs had come out of the front. I'm in this turn now, tight as I can get it, that helps me hold my altitude and helps me hold my airspeed and everything else all the way round. When I level out, the nose is a little bit high and as I look up there the whole sky is lit up in the prettiest blues and pinks I've ever seen in my life. It was just great. . . .

Studs Terkel: Did you hear an explosion?

Paul Tibbets: Oh yeah. The shockwave was coming up at us after we turned. And the tailgunner said, "Here it comes." About the time he said that, we got this kick in the ass. I had accelerometers installed in all airplanes to record the magnitude of the bomb. It hit us with two and a half G.[4] Next day, when we got figures from the scientists on what they had learned from all the things, they said, "When that bomb exploded, your airplane was 10 and half miles away from it."

Studs Terkel: Did you see that mushroom cloud?

4. **G:** G-force; 1 G is equal to the force of Earth's gravity.

Paul Tibbets: You see all kinds of mushroom clouds, but they were made with different types of bombs. The Hiroshima bomb did not make a mushroom. It was what I call a stringer. It just came up. It was black as hell, and it had light and colours and white in it and grey colour in it and the top was like a folded-up Christmas tree.

Studs Terkel: Do you have any idea what happened down below?

Paul Tibbets: Pandemonium! I think it's best stated by one of the historians, who said: "In one micro-second, the city of Hiroshima didn't exist."

Studs Terkel: You came back, and you visited President Truman.

Paul Tibbets: We're talking 1948 now. I'm back in the Pentagon and I get notice from the chief of staff, Carl Spaatz, the first chief of staff of the air force. When we got to General Spaatz's office, General Doolittle was there, and a colonel named Dave Shillen. Spaatz said, "Gentlemen, I just got word from the president he wants us to go over to his office immediately." On the way over, Doolittle and Spaatz were doing some talking; I wasn't saying very much. When we got out of the car we were escorted right quick to the Oval Office. There was a black man there who always took care of Truman's needs and he said, "General Spaatz, will you please be facing the desk?" And now, facing the desk, Spaatz is on the right, Doolittle and Shillen. Of course, militarily speaking, that's the correct order: because Spaatz is senior, Doolittle has to sit to his left.

Then I was taken by this man and put in the chair that was right beside the president's desk, beside his left hand. Anyway, we got a cup of coffee and we got most of it consumed when Truman walked in and everybody stood on their feet. He said, "Sit down, please," and he had a big smile on his face and he said, "General Spaatz, I want to congratulate you on being first chief of the air force," because it was no longer the air corps. Spaatz said, "Thank you, sir, it's a great honour and I appreciate it." And he said to Doolittle: "That was a magnificent thing you pulled flying off of that carrier," and Doolittle said, "All in a day's work, Mr. President." And he looked at Dave Shillen and said, "Colonel Shillen, I want to congratulate you on having the foresight to recognize the potential in aerial refueling. We're gonna need it bad some day." And he said thank you very much.

Then he looked at me for 10 seconds and he didn't say anything. And when he finally did, he said, "What do you think?" I said, "Mr. President, I think I did what I was told." He slapped his hand on the table and said: "You're damn right you did, and I'm the guy who sent you. If anybody gives you a hard time about it, refer them to me."

Studs Terkel: Anybody ever give you a hard time?

Paul Tibbets: Nobody gave me a hard time.

Studs Terkel: Do you ever have any second thoughts about the bomb?

Paul Tibbets: Second thoughts? No. Studs, look. Number one, I got into the air corps to defend the United States to the best of my ability. That's what I believe in and that's what I work for. Number two, I'd had so much experience with airplanes . . . I'd had jobs where there was no particular direction about how you do it and then of course I put this thing together with my own thoughts on how it should be because when I got the directive I was to be self-supporting at all times.

On the way to the target I was thinking: I can't think of any mistakes I've made. Maybe I did make a mistake: maybe I was too damned assured. At 29 years of age I was so shot in the ass with confidence I didn't think there was anything I couldn't do. Of course, that applied to airplanes and people. So, no, I had no problem with it. I knew we did the right thing because when I knew we'd be doing that I thought, yes, we're going to kill a lot of people, but by God we're going to save a lot of lives. We won't have to invade [Japan].

GEORGE WELLER

The First American Report on the Bombing of Nagasaki

NAGASAKI, Sept. 8—The following conclusions were made by the writer— as the first visitor to inspect the ruins—after an exhaustive, though still in-complete study of this wasteland of war.

Nagasaki is an island roughly resembling Manhattan in size and shape, running north and south in direction with ocean inlets on both sides. What would be the New Jersey and Manhattan sides of the Hudson River are lined with huge war plants owned by the Mitsubishi and Kawasaki families. . . .

It is about two miles from the scene of the bomb's 1,500 feet high explo-sion where the harbor has narrowed to the 250 feet wide Urakame [Urakami] River that the atomic bomb's force begins to be discernible.

The area is north of downtown Nagasaki, whose buildings suffered some freakish destruction, but are generally still sound.

The railroad station, destroyed except for the platforms[,] is already op-erating. Normally it is sort of a gate to the destroyed part of the Urakame valley. . . . For two miles stretches a line of congested steel and some concrete factories with the residential district "across the tracks." The atomic bomb landed between and totally destroyed both with half [illegible] living per-sons in them. The known dead number 20,000[;] police tell me they estimate about 4,000 remain to be found.[5]

The reason the deaths were so high—the wounded being about twice as many according to Japanese official figures—was twofold:

1. Mitsubishi air raid shelters were totally inadequate and the civil-ian shelters remote and limited.
2. That the Japanese air warning system was a total failure.

I inspected half a dozen crude short tunnels in the rock wall valley which the Mitsubishi Co., considered shelters. I also picked my way through the

---

5. The actual number of deaths was approximately seventy-five thousand, with many thousands more to die in the years to come due to radiation poisoning.

tangled iron girders and curling roofs of the main factories to see concrete shelters four inches thick but totally inadequate in number. Only a grey concrete building topped by a siren, where the clerical staff had worked had reasonable cellar shelters, but nothing resembling the previous had been made.

A general alert had been sounded at seven in the morning, four hours before two B-29's appeared, but it was ignored by the workmen and most of the population. The police insist that the air raid warning was sounded two minutes before the bomb fell, but most people say they heard none. . . .

All around the Mitsubishi plant are ruins which one would gladly have spared. The writer spent nearly an hour in 15 deserted buildings in the Nagasaki Medical Institute hospital. . . . Nothing but rats live in the debris choked halls. On the opposite side of the valley and the Urakame river is a three story concrete American mission college called Chin Jei, nearly totally destroyed.

Japanese authorities point out that the home area flattened by American bombs was traditionally the place of Catholic and Christian Japanese.

But sparing these and sparing the allied prison camp, which the Japanese placed next to an armor plate factory[,] would have meant sparing Mitsubishi's ship parts plant with 1,016 employees who were mostly Allied. It would have spared a Mounting factory connecting with 1,750 employees. It would have spared three steel foundries on both sides of the Urakame, using ordinarily 3,400 workers but that day 2,500. And besides sparing many subcontracting plants now flattened it would have meant leaving untouched the Mitsubishi torpedo and ammunition plant employing 7,500 which was nearest where the bomb [detonated].

All these latter plants today are hammered flat. But no saboteur creeping among the war plants of death could have placed the atomic bomb by hand more scrupulously given Japan's inertia about common defense.

NAGASAKI, Saturday, Sept. 8—In swaybacked or flattened skeletons of the Mitsubishi arms plants is revealed what the atomic bomb can do to steel and stone, but what the riven atom can do against human flesh and bone lies hidden in two hospitals of downtown Nagasaki. Look at the pushed-in facade of the American consulate, three miles from the blast's center, or the face of the Catholic cathedral, one mile in the other direction, torn down like gingerbread, and you can tell that the liberated atom spares nothing in the way. . . .

Showing them to you, as the first American outsider to reach Nagasaki since the surrender, your propaganda-conscious official guide looks meaningfully in your face and wants to know: "What do you think?" What this question means is: do you intend saying that America did something inhuman in loosing this weapon against Japan? That is what we want you to write about.

Several children, some burned and others unburned but with patches of hair falling out, are sitting with their mothers. Yesterday Japanese photographers took many pictures with them. About one in five is heavily bandaged, but none are showing signs of pain.

Some adults are in pain as they lie on mats. They moan softly. One woman caring for her husband, shows eyes dim with tears. It is a piteous scene and your official guide studies your face covertly to see if you are moved.

Visiting many litters, talking lengthily with two general physicians and one X-ray specialist, gains you a large amount of information and opinion on the victims. . . .

Most of the patients who were gravely burned have now passed away and those on hand are rapidly curing. Those not curing are people whose unhappy lot provides the mystery aura around the atomic bomb's effects. They are victims of what Lt. Jakob Vink, Dutch medical officer and now allied commandant of prison camp 14 at the mouth of Nagasaki Harbor, calls "disease." Vink himself was in the allied prison kitchen abutting the Mitsubishi armor plate department when the ceiling fell in but he escaped this mysterious "disease X" which some allied prisoners and many Japanese civilians got.

Vink points out a woman on a yellow mat in the hospital, who according to hospital doctors Hikodero Koga and Uraji Hayashida have [sic] just been brought in. She fled the atomic area but returned to live. She was well for three weeks except a small burn on her heel. Now she lies moaning with a blackish mouth stiff as though with lockjaw and unable to utter clear words. Her exposed legs and arms are speckled with tiny red spots in patches.

Near her lies a 15-year-old fattish girl who has the same blotchy red pinpoints and nose clotted with blood. A little farther on is a widow lying down with four children, from one to about 8, around her. The two smallest children have lost some hair. Though none of these people has either a burn or a broken limb, they are presumed victims of the atomic bomb.

Dr. Uraji Hayashida shakes his head somberly and says that he believes there must be something to the American radio report about the ground around the Mitsubishi plant being poisoned. But his next statement knocks out the props from under this theory because it develops that the widow's family has been absent from the wrecked area ever since the blast yet shows symptoms common with those who returned.

According to Japanese doctors, patients with these late developing symptoms are dying now a month after the bomb's fall, at the rate of about 10 daily. The three doctors calmly stated that the disease has them nonplussed and that they are giving no treatment whatever but rest. . . .

NAGASAKI, Sept. 9 — The atomic bomb's peculiar "disease," uncured because it is untreated and untreated because it is not diagnosed, is still snatching away lives here.

Men, women, and children with no outward marks of injury are dying daily in hospitals, some after having walked around three or four weeks thinking they have escaped. . . .

Kyushu's leading X-ray specialist, who arrived today from the island's chief city Fukuoka, elderly Dr. Yosisada Nakashima, told the writer that he is convinced that these people are simply suffering from the atomic bomb's beta Gamma, or the neutron ray is taking effect.

"All the symptoms are similar," said the Japanese doctor. "You have a reduction in white corpuscles, constriction in the throat, vomiting, diarrhea and small hemorrhages just below the skin. All of these things happen when an overdose of Roentgen rays is given. Bombed children's hair falls out. That is natural because these rays are used often to make hair fall artificially and sometimes takes several days before the hair becomes loose." . . .

At emergency hospital No. 2, commanding officer young Lt. Col. Yoshitaka Sasaki, with three rows of campaign ribbons on his breast, stated that 200 patients died of 343 admitted and that he expects about 50 more deaths.

Most severe ordinary burns resulted in the patients' deaths within a week after the bomb fell. But this hospital began taking patients only from one to two weeks afterward. It is therefore almost exclusively "disease" cases and the deaths are mostly therefrom.

Nakashima divides the deaths outside simple burns and fractures into two classes on the basis of symptoms observed in the post mortem autopsies. The first class accounts for roughly 60 percent of the deaths, the second for 40 percent. Among exterior symptoms in the first class are falling hair from the head, armpits, and pubic zones, spotty local skin hemorrhages looking like measles all over the body, lip sores, diarrhea but without blood discharge, swelling in the throat . . . and a descent in numbers of red and white corpuscles. Red corpuscles fall from a normal 5,000,000 to one-half, or one-third while the whites almost disappear, dropping from 7,000 or 8,000 to 300 to 500. Fever rises to 104 and stays there without fluctuating. . . .

Nakashima considers that it is possible that the atomic bomb's rare rays may cause deaths in the first class, as with delayed X-ray burns. But the second class [deaths] has him totally baffled. These patients begin with slight burns which make normal progress for two weeks. They differ from simple burns, however, in that the patient has a high fever. Unfevered patients with as much as one-third of the skin area burned have been known to recover. But where fever is present after two weeks, healing of burns suddenly halts and they get worse. . . .

Up to five days from the turn to the worse, they die. Their bloodstream has not thinned as in the first class and their organs after death are found in a normal condition of health. But they are dead—dead of the atomic bomb—and nobody knows why.

Twenty-five Americans are due to arrive Sept. 11 to study the Nagasaki bombsite. The Japanese hope that they will bring a solution to Disease X.

FOR CRITICAL THINKING

1. Compare and contrast J. Robert Oppenheimer's views of the atomic bomb with Paul Tibbets's and George Weller's views. What stance, if any, did each of these men take toward the bomb, and how did their writing reflect it? Note particular differences or similarities in their reactions to the bomb's power.

2. Joseph Rothblat, a Polish scientist recruited to work at Los Alamos, insisted on leaving the project at the end of 1944 when it became apparent that there was no danger of any other nation's building a nuclear weapon before the United States. Based on your reading of these selections, what do you think of his decision? Should other scientists have followed his lead? Why or why not?

3. At Hiroshima and Nagasaki in August 1945, and at the World Trade Center in New York City on September 11, 2001, civilians were targeted for the sake of larger objectives: in the first case, for military victory; in the second, as a statement in the name of Islam. In modern warfare, distinguishing between fighting an enemy military and attacking an enemy population may be impossible. If this is the case, how does one distinguish between just and unjust warfare? Will such distinctions be obvious in future wars? Explain.

40

FANNY CHRISTINA HILL

Rosie the Riveter

World War II generated a massive need for a larger labor force. Millions of men were under arms, yet the United States, billing itself as the "arsenal of democracy" for the Allied forces, strove for giant increases in the production of planes, ships, trucks, tanks, armaments, food, clothing, and all the other supplies that fuel a war. In 1940, 11.5 million women were employed outside the home, principally single women, widows, and wives from poor families. African American women like Fanny Christina Hill expected to work in whatever jobs were available to them—most commonly domestic service.

On Columbus Day 1942, however, President Franklin D. Roosevelt called for a new attitude in the workplace: "In some communities employers dislike to hire women. In others they are reluctant to hire Negroes. We can no longer afford to indulge such prejudices." Soon, as described in this excerpt, women like Hill shifted from "women's jobs" to defense work, prompting other women who had previously not worked to adopt these new roles as well.

War production peaked in 1944. By the middle of that year, pressure grew to persuade women to return to their homes even before the war reached its conclusion. Defense plant newspapers replaced features on women production workers with "cheesecake"

Sherna Berger Gluck, *Rosie the Riveter Revisited* (Boston: Twayne, 1987), 28–33, 35–38, 40–45, 48–49.

contests. Tales of neglected children became a theme of popular journalism. Even so, 75 percent of women surveyed in 1944 and 1945 expressed the desire to continue working after the war. A cultural battle had begun that would outlast the war itself.

QUESTIONS TO CONSIDER

1. How was Fanny Christina Hill's life affected by her wartime work?
2. Why did Hill continue to work after the war? Was she influenced by the pressure to cease working?
3. What examples of prejudice affecting her life do you find? How did she deal with these situations?

I went to a little small town—Tyler, Texas. . . . And the only thing I could do there for a living was domestic work and it didn't pay very much. So I definitely didn't like it.

But I left Tyler. I was saying, "I don't like it here because you can't make any money." I discovered I didn't have any trade. I had nothing I could do other than just that, and that wasn't what I wanted. So I decided I'd better get out of this town. I didn't like Dallas because that was too rough. Then someone told me, "Well, why don't you try California?" So then I got Los Angeles in my mind. I was twenty and I saved my money till I was twenty-one. In August 1940, I came here.

When I first came, when my aunt met me down at the station, I had less than ten dollars. I went on to her house and stayed. In less than ten days I had found a job living on the place doing domestic work. I stayed there from some time in August until Christmas. I was making thirty-five dollars a month. That was so much better than what I was making at home, which was twelve dollars a month. I saved my money and I bought everybody a Christmas present and sent it. Oh, I was the happiest thing in the world! . . .

I liked to go on outings a lot. So when I first came to California, when I'd have my day off, I'd go to the parks and to the beach and museum. Just go sightseeing; walking and look in the windows. Sometimes my aunt would go along with me or I'd find another girlfriend. But then I had a sister here pretty soon.

Los Angeles was a large city but I adjusted to it real well. It didn't take me long to find a way about it. I knew how to get around, and I knew how to stay out of danger and not take too many chances. I read the *Eagle* and I still get the *Sentinel*[1] once in a while. I have to get it to keep up with what the black people are doing. I used to read those papers when I was a child back home. That's what give me a big idea. I used to read a little paper called the *Kansas City Call*, and they had a *Pittsburgh Courier* that all the Negroes read. . . .

---

1. ***Eagle* and . . . *Sentinel*:** The *California Eagle* and the *Los Angeles Sentinel*, two newspapers that catered to the African American community.

[She returns to Texas to get married.] I stayed there for about nine months until he [her husband] went into the service. Then I came to Los Angeles. I told my sister, "Well, I better get me a good job around here working in a hotel or motel or something. I want to get me a good job so when the war is over, I'll have it." And she said, "No, you just come on out and go in the war plants and work and maybe you'll make enough money where you won't have to work in the hotels or motels." . . .

I don't remember what day of the week it was, but I guess I must have started out pretty early that morning. When I went there, the man didn't hire me. They had a school down here on Figueroa and he told me to go to the school. I went down and it was almost four o'clock and they told me they'd hire me. You had to fill out a form. They didn't bother too much about your experience because they knew you didn't have any experience in aircraft. Then they give you some kind of little test where you put the pegs in the right hole.

There were other people in there, kinda mixed. I assume it was more women than men. Most of the men was gone, and they weren't hiring too many men unless they had a good excuse. Most of the women was in my bracket, five or six years younger or older. I was twenty-four. There was a black girl that hired in with me. I went to work the next day, sixty cents an hour.

I think I stayed at the school for about four weeks. They only taught you shooting and bucking rivets and how to drill the holes and to file. You had to use a hammer for certain things. After a couple of whiles, you worked on the real thing. But you were supervised so you didn't make a mess.

When we went into the plant, it wasn't too much different than down at the school. It was the same amount of noise; it was the same routine. One difference was there was just so many more people, and when you went in the door you had a badge to show and they looked at your lunch. I had gotten accustomed to a lot of people and I knew if it was a lot of people, it always meant something was going on. I got carried away: "As long as there's a lot of people here, I'll be making money." That was all I could ever see.

I was a good student, if I do say so myself. But I have found out through life, sometimes even if you're good, you just don't get the breaks if the color's not right. I could see where they made a difference in placing you in certain jobs. They had fifteen or twenty departments, but all the Negroes went to Department 17 because there was nothing but shooting and bucking rivets. You stood on one side of the panel and your partner stood on this side, and he would shoot the rivets with a gun and you'd buck them with the bar. That was about the size of it. I just didn't like it. I didn't think I could stay there with all this shooting and a'bucking and a'jumping and a'bumping. I stayed in it about two or three weeks and then I just decided I did *not* like that. I went and told my foreman and he didn't do anything about it, so I decided I'd leave.

While I was standing out on the railroad track, I ran into somebody else out there fussing also. I went over to the union and they told me what to do. I went back inside and they sent me to another department where you did bench work and I liked that much better. You had a little small jig that you would work on and you just drilled out holes. Sometimes you would rout them or you would scribe them and then you'd cut them with a cutters.

I must have stayed there nearly a year, and then they put me over in another department, "Plastics." It was the tail section of the B-Bomber, the Billy Mitchell Bomber.[2] I put a little part in the gun-sight. You had a little ratchet set and you would screw it in there. Then I cleaned the top of the glass off and put a piece of paper over it to seal it off to go to the next section. I worked over there until the end of the war. Well, not quite the end, because I got pregnant, and while I was off having the baby the war was over. . . .

Some weeks I brought home twenty-six dollars, some weeks sixteen dollars. Then it gradually went up to thirty dollars, then it went up a little bit more and a little bit more. And I learned somewhere along the line that in order to make a good move you gotta make some money. You don't make the same amount everyday. You have some days good, sometimes bad. Whatever you make you're supposed to save some. I was also getting that fifty dollars a month from my husband and that was just saved right away. I was planning on buying a home and a car. And I was going to go back to school. My husband came back, but I never was laid off, so I just never found it necessary to look for another job or to go to school for another job.

I was still living over on Compton Avenue with my sister in this small little back house when my husband got home. Then, when Beverly was born, my sister moved in the front house and we stayed in the back house. When he came back, he looked for a job in the cleaning and pressing place, which was just plentiful. All the people had left these cleaning and pressing jobs and every other job; they was going to the defense plant to work because they was paying good. But in the meantime he was getting the same thing the people out there was getting, $1.25 an hour. That's why he didn't bother to go out to North American [Aircraft Company]. But what we both weren't thinking about was that they did have better benefits because they did have an insurance plan and a union to back you up. Later he did come to work there, in 1951 or 1952.

I worked up until the end of March and then I took off. Beverly was born the twenty-first of June. I'd planned to come back somewhere in the last of August. I went to verify the fact that I did come back, so that did go on my record that I didn't just quit. But they laid off a lot of people, most of them, because the war was over.

It didn't bother me much — not thinking about it jobwise. I was just glad that the war was over. I didn't feel bad because my husband had a job and he also was eligible to go to school with his GI bill. So I really didn't have too many plans — which I wish I had had. I would have tore out page one and fixed it differently; put my version of page one in there.

I went and got me a job doing day work. That means you go to a person's house and clean up for one day out of the week and then you go to the next one and clean up. I did that a couple of times and I discovered I didn't like

2. **Billy Mitchell bomber:** B-25 bomber.

that so hot. Then I got me a job downtown working in a little factory where you do weaving—burned clothes and stuff like that. I learned to do that real good. It didn't pay too much but it paid enough to get me going, seventy-five cents or about like that.

When North American called me back, was I a happy soul! I dropped that job and went back. That was a dollar an hour. So, from sixty cents an hour, when I first hired in there, up to one dollar. That wasn't traveling fast, but it was better than anything else because you had hours to work by and you had benefits and you come home at night with your family. So it was a good deal.

It made me live better. I really did. We always say that Lincoln took the bale off of the Negroes. I think there is a statue up there in Washington, D.C., where he's lifting something off the Negro. Well, my sister always said—that's why you can't interview her because she's so radical—"Hitler was the one that got us out of the white folks' kitchen." . . .

[She recalled the discrimination faced by black workers at North American Aircraft.] But they had to fight. They fought hand, tooth, and nail to get in there. And the first five or six Negroes who went in there, they were well educated, but they started them off as janitors. After they once got their foot in the door and was there for three months—you work for three months before they say you're hired—then they had to start fighting all over again to get off of that broom and get something decent. And some of them did.

But they'd always give that Negro man the worst part of everything. See, the jobs have already been tested and tried out before they ever get into the department, and they know what's good about them and what's bad about them. They always managed to give the worst one to the Negro. The only reason why the women fared better was they just couldn't quite give the woman as tough a job that they gave the men. But sometimes they did. . . .

There were some departments, they didn't even allow a black person to walk through there let alone work in there. Some of the white people did not want to work with the Negro. They had arguments right there. Sometimes they would get fired and walk on out the door, but it was one more white person gone. I think even to this very day in certain places they still don't want to work with the Negro. I don't know what their story is, but if they would try then they might not knock it.

But they did everything they could to keep you separated. They just did not like for a Negro and a white person to get together and talk. Now I am a person that you can talk to and you will warm up to me much better than you can a lot of people. A white person seems to know that they could talk to me at ease. And when anyone would start—just plain, common talk, everyday talk—they didn't like it. . . .

And they'd keep you from advancing. They always manage to give the Negroes the worst end of the deal. I happened to fall into that when they get ready to transfer you from one department to the next. That was the only thing that I ever ran into that I had to holler to the union about. And once I filed a complaint downtown with the Equal Opportunity.

The way they was doing this particular thing—they always have a lean spot where they're trying to lay off or go through there and see if they can curl out a bunch of people, get rid of the ones with the most seniority, I suppose. They had a good little system going. All the colored girls had more seniority in production than the whites because the average white woman did not come back after the war. They thought like I thought: that I have a husband now and I don't have to work and this was just only for the war and blah, blah, blah. But they didn't realize they was going to need the money. The average Negro was glad to come back because it meant more money than they was making before. So we always had more seniority in production than the white woman.

All the colored women in production, they was just one step behind the other. I had three months more than one, the next one had three months more than me, and that's the way it went. So they had a way of putting us all in [the] Blueprint [department]. We all had twenty years by the time you got in Blueprint and stayed a little while. Here come another one. He'd bump you out and then you went out the door, because they couldn't find nothing else for you to do—so they said. They just kept doing it and I could see myself: "Well, hell, I'm going to be the next one to go out the door!"

So I found some reason to file a grievance.[3] I tried to get several other girls: "Let's get together and go downtown and file a grievance." I only got two girls to go with me. That made three of us. I think we came out on top, because we all kept our jobs and then they stopped sending them to Blueprint, bumping each other like that. So, yeah, we've had to fight to stay there. . . .

When I bought my house in '49 or '48, I went a little further on the other side of Slauson, and I drove up and down the street a couple of times. I saw one colored woman there. I went in and asked her about the neighborhood. She said there was only one there, but there was another one across the street. So I was the third one moved in there. I said, "Well, we's breaking into the neighborhood."

I don't know how long we was there, but one evening, just about dusk, here comes this woman banging on my door. I had never seen her before. She says, "I got a house over here for sale, you can tell your friends that they can buy it if they want to." I thought to myself, "What in the hell is that woman thinking about?" She was mad because she discovered I was there. Further down, oh, about two streets down, somebody burned a cross on a lawn.

Then, one Sunday evening, I don't know what happened, but they saw a snake in the yard next door to us. Some white people were staying there and the yard was so junky, I tell you. Here come the snake. We must have been living there a good little while, because Beverly was old enough to bring the gun. Everybody was looking and they had a stick or something. I don't know

---

3. **grievance:** A discrimination complaint that is filed with the Equal Employment Opportunity Commission.

how, but that child came strutting out there with the gun to shoot the snake. My husband shot the snake and from that point on, everybody respected us—'cause they knew he had a gun and could use it.

I was talking to a white person about the situation and he said, "Next time you get ready to move in a white neighborhood, I'll tell you what you do. The first thing you do when you pull up there in the truck, you jump out with your guns. You hold them up high in the air." He says, "If you don't have any, borrow some or rent 'em, but be sure that they see you got a gun. Be sure one of them is a shotgun and you go in there with it first. They going to be peeping out the window, don't you worry about it. They going to see you. But if they see those guns going in first, they won't ever bother you."

I did like he said, moved in here with some guns, and nobody come and bothered me. Nobody said one word to me.

Working at North American was good. I did make more money and I did meet quite a few people that I am still friends with. I learned quite a bit. Some of the things, I wouldn't want to go back over. If I had the wisdom to know the difference which one to change and which one not to, I would. I would have fought harder at North American for better things for myself.

I don't have too many regrets. But if I had it to do over again, if I had to tamper with page one, I would sure get a better education. I would never have stopped going to school. I took several little classes every so often—cosmetology, photography, herbs. For a little while, I did study nursing. I would have finished some of them. I would have went deeper into it.

We always talking about women's lib and working. Well, we all know that the Negro woman was the first woman that left home to go to work. She's been working ever since because she had to work beside her husband in slavery—against her will. So she has always worked. She knows how to get out there and work. She has really pioneered the field. Then after we've gotten out here and proved that it can be done, then the white woman decided: "Hey, I don't want to stay home and do nothing." She zeroed in on the best jobs. So we're still on the tail-end, but we still back there fighting.

41

BEN YORITA AND PHILIP HAYASAKA
Memories of the Internment Camp

During World War II, the United States was more careful about protecting the civil lib-erties of its citizens than it had been after its entrance into World War I. There was, however, one glaring exception: the internment of 110,000 Japanese Americans in camps euphemistically called "relocation centers." The military director of the internment pro-gram declared that the "Japanese race is an enemy race and while many second and third generation Japanese born on United States soil, possessed of United States Citizenship, have become Americanized, the racial strains are undiluted. . . . It, therefore, follows that along the vital Pacific coast over 112,000 potential enemies, of Japanese extraction, are at large today." These people, 70,000 of them native-born citizens of the United States, were forced to evacuate their homes within forty-eight hours (losing about $500 million in property along with their jobs) and made to live for long periods of time in tar-papered barracks behind barbed wire.

The U.S. Supreme Court, in two major decisions, supported the constitutionality of internment. In 1988 Congress, in recognition of the wrong the government had inflicted, appropriated compensation for internees.

This reading comes from interviews conducted by newspaperman Archie Satterfield in the 1970s. It documents the experiences of two Japanese Americans who suffered through this period of injustice.

QUESTIONS TO CONSIDER

1. What fears did internment arouse in Japanese Americans?
2. What did Japanese Americans lose because of their internment?
3. What were the psychological effects of internment?
4. Compare the treatment of Japanese Americans in the United States with that of Jews in Germany. What was similar? What was different?

BEN YORITA

"Students weren't as aware of national politics then as they are now, and Japanese-Americans were actually apolitical then. Our parents couldn't vote, so we simply weren't interested in politics because there was nothing we could do about it if we were.

Archie Satterfield, *The Home Front: An Oral History of the War Years in America, 1941–1945* (New York: Playboy Press, 1981), 330–38.

"There were two reasons we were living in the ghettos: Birds of a feather flock together, and we had all the traditional aspects of Japanese life—Japanese restaurants, baths, and so forth; and discrimination forced us together. The dominant society prevented us from going elsewhere.

"Right after Pearl Harbor we had no idea what was going to happen, but toward the end of December we started hearing rumors and talk of the evacuation started. We could tell from what we read in the newspapers and the propaganda they were printing—guys like Henry McLemore,[1] who said he hated all Japs and that we should be rounded up, gave us the idea of how strong feelings were against us. So we were expecting something and the evacuation was no great surprise.

"I can't really say what my parents thought about everything because we didn't communicate that well. I never asked them what they thought. We communicated on other things, but not political matters.

"Once the evacuation was decided, we were told we had about a month to get rid of our property or do whatever we wanted to with it. . . . Second-hand dealers and everybody else came in and bought our refrigerator, the piano, and I had a whole bunch of books I sold for $5, which was one of my personal losses. We had to sell our car, and the whole thing was very sad. By the way, it was the first time we had ever had a refrigerator and it had to be sold after only a few months.

"We could take only what we could carry, and most of us were carrying two suitcases or duffel bags. The rest of our stuff that we couldn't sell was stored in the Buddhist church my mother belonged to. When we came back, thieves had broken in and stolen almost everything of value from the church.

"I had a savings account that was left intact, but people who had their money in the Japanese bank in Seattle had their assets frozen from Pearl Harbor until the late 1960s, when the funds were finally released. They received no interest.

"They took all of us down to the Puyallup fairgrounds, Camp Harmony,[2] and everything had been thrown together in haste. They had converted some of the display and exhibit areas into rooms and had put up some barracks on the parking lot. The walls in the barracks were about eight feet high with open space above and with big knotholes in the boards of the partitions. Our family was large, so we had two rooms.

"They had also built barbed-wire fences around the camp with a tower on each corner with military personnel and machine guns, rifles, and search-lights. It was terrifying because we didn't know what was going to happen to us. We didn't know where we were going and we were just doing what we were told. No questions asked. If you get an order, you go ahead and do it.

"There was no fraternization, no contact with the military or any Cau-casian except when we were processed into the camp. But the treatment

1. **Henry McLemore:** Syndicated columnist for the Hearst newspapers who strongly sup-ported the mass evacuation of Japanese Americans from the West Coast to the interior.
2. **Camp Harmony:** Temporary assembly center in Puyallup, Washington.

in Camp Harmony was fairly loose in the sense that we were free to roam around in the camp. But it was like buffalo in cages or behind barbed wire.

"There was no privacy whatsoever in the latrines and showers, and it was humiliating for the women because they were much more modest then than today. It wasn't so bad for the men because they were accustomed to open latrines and showers.

"We had no duties in the sense that we were required to work, but you can't expect a camp to manage itself. They had jobs open in the kitchen and stock room, and eventually they opened a school where I helped teach a little. I wasn't a qualified teacher, and I got about $13 a month. We weren't given an allowance while we were in Camp Harmony waiting for the camp at Minidoka[3] to be finished, so it was pretty tight for some families.

"From Camp Harmony on, the family structure was broken down. Children ran everywhere they wanted to in the camp, and parents lost their authority . . .

"Eventually they boarded us on army trucks and took us to trains to be transported to the camps inland. We had been in Camp Harmony from May until September. There was a shortage of transportation at the time and they brought out these old, rusty cars with gaslight fixtures. As soon as we got aboard we pulled the shades down so people couldn't stare at us. The cars were all coaches and we had to sit all the way to camp, which was difficult for some of the older people and the invalids. We made makeshift beds out of the seats for them, and did the best we could.

"When we got to Twin Falls,[4] we were loaded onto trucks again, and we looked around and all we could see was that vast desert with nothing but sagebrush. When the trucks started rolling, it was dusty, and the camp itself wasn't completed yet. The barracks had been built and the kitchen facilities were there, but the laundry room, showers, and latrines were not finished. They had taken a bulldozer in the good old American style and leveled the terrain and then built the camp. When the wind blew, it was dusty and we had to wear face masks to go to the dining hall. When winter came and it rained, the dust turned into gumbo mud. Until the latrines were finished, we had to use outhouses.

"The administrators were civilians and they tried to organize us into a chain of command to make the camp function. Each block of barracks was told to appoint a representative, who were called block managers. Of course we called them the Blockheads.

"When winter came, it was very cold and I began withdrawing my savings to buy clothes because we had none that was suitable for that climate. Montgomery Ward and Sears Roebuck[5] did a landslide business from the camps because we ordered our shoes and warm clothing from them. The people who didn't have savings suffered quite a bit until the camp distributed

---

3. **Minidoka:** Relocation center in Idaho.
4. **Twin Falls:** Transfer city in Idaho.
5. **Montgomery Ward and Sears Roebuck:** Two mail-order catalog companies.

navy pea coats. Then everybody in camp was wearing outsize pea coats because we were such small people. Other than army blankets, I don't remember any other clothing issues.

"The barracks were just single-wall construction and the only insulation was tar paper nailed on the outside, and they never were improved. The larger rooms had potbellied stoves, and we all slept on army cots. Only the people over sixty years old were able to get metal cots, which had a bit more spring to them than the army cots, which were just stationary hammocks.

"These camps were technically relocation centers and there was no effort to hold us in them, but they didn't try actively to relocate us until much later. On my own initiative I tried to get out as soon as I could, and started writing letters to friends around the country. I found a friend in Salt Lake City who agreed to sponsor me for room and board, and he got his boss to agree to hire me. I got out in May 1943, which was earlier than most. In fact, I was one of the first to leave Minidoka.

"Of course I had to get clearance from Washington, D.C., and they investigated my background. I had to pay my own way from Twin Falls to Salt Lake City, but after I left, the government had a program of per diem for people leaving.

"I got on the bus with my suitcase, all by myself, my first time in the outside world, and paid my fare and began looking for a seat, then this old guy said: 'Hey, Tokyo, sit next to me.'

"I thought, Oh, my God, Tokyo! I sat next to him and he was a friendly old guy who meant well."

Yorita's friend worked in a parking garage across the street from the Mormon tabernacle, and the garage owner let them live in the office, where the two young men cooked their own meals. One nearby grocery-store owner wouldn't let them buy from him, and a barber in the neighborhood hated them on sight. Yorita parked a car once that had a rifle and pair of binoculars in the back seat, and he and his friend took the binoculars out and were looking through them when the barber looked out and saw them studying the Mormon tabernacle. He called the FBI, and two agents were soon in the garage talking to the young men.

Yorita wasn't satisfied with his job in Salt Lake City, and soon left for Cincinnati, then Chicago, which he enjoyed because most Chicago people didn't care what nationality he was. He and a brother were able to find good jobs and a good place to live, and they brought their parents out of the Idaho camp to spend the rest of the war in Chicago.

PHILIP HAYASAKA

Philip Hayasaka was a teen-ager when Pearl Harbor was attacked. Unlike most Japanese-Americans, his parents had been able to find a home in a predominantly Caucasian neighborhood because his father was a wholesale produce dealer and most of his business was conducted with Caucasians.

Consequently, when the family was interned, Hayasaka was a stranger to most of the other families.

Still, he and his family understood well the rationale of the Little Tokyos along the West Coast.

"If you could become invisible, you could get along. We were forced into a situation of causing no trouble, of being quiet, not complaining. It was not a matter of our stoic tradition. I've never bought that. We did what we had to do to survive.

"There was a lot of hysteria at the time, a lot of confusion, and the not knowing what was going to happen created such a fear that we became supercautious. We would hear that the FBI was going into different houses and searching, and we would wonder when they were coming to our house. We just knew that they were going to come and knock on the door and that we wouldn't know what to do when they came.

"A lot of people were burning things that didn't need to be burned, but they were afraid suspicion would be attached to those things. All those wonderful old calligraphies were destroyed, priceless things, because they thought someone in authority would believe they represented allegiance to Japan. One time I was with my mother in the house, just the two of us, and there was a knock on the door. My mother had those rosary-type beads that the Buddhists use for prayer, and she put them in my pocket and sent me outside to play and stay out until whoever was at the door left. . . .

"When this happened, my dad's business went to hell. Suddenly all his accounts payable were due immediately, but all the accounts receivable weren't. People knew the guy wasn't going to be around much longer, so they didn't pay him. I knew at one time how much he lost that way—we had to turn in a claim after the war—but I've forgotten now. But it was a considerable amount. Those claims, by the way, didn't give justice to the victims; it only legitimized the government. We got about a nickel on the dollar. . . .

"All the leaders of the community were taken away, and my dad was interned before we were and taken to the interrogation camp in Missoula. It was one of the greatest shocks of my life when the FBI came and picked him up. Here was a guy who had followed all the rules, respected authority, and was a leader in the company. And all of the sudden he was behind bars for no reason. He stayed there several months before they let him join us at Minidoka."

When the war ended and the camps were closed, about the only people left in them were young children and the elderly. All who could leave for jobs did so, and the experience had a scattering effect on the Japanese-American communities across the Pacific Coast. Several families settled on the East Coast and in the Midwest, and when those with no other place to go, or who didn't want to migrate away from the Coast, returned to their hometowns, they usually found their former ghettos taken over by other minority groups. Consequently, whether they wanted to or not, they were forced to find housing wherever it was available. It was difficult returning to the cities, however. Everybody dreaded it, and some of the elderly people with no place to go of their own were virtually evacuated from the camps. They had become accustomed to the life there and were afraid to leave.

Some Caucasians, such as Floyd Schmoe and the Reverend Emory Andrews, worked with the returning outcasts to help them resettle as smoothly as possible. A few farms had been saved for the owners, but four years of weeds and brush had accumulated. Schmoe was back teaching at the University of Washington by that time, and he organized groups of his students to go out on weekends and after school to help clear the land for crops again. Some people returning found their former neighbors had turned against them in their absence, and grocery-store owners who had become Jap-haters during the war would not sell them food.

The farmers who did get their crops growing again were often so discriminated against that they could not sell their produce, or get it delivered into the marketplace. Schmoe was able to solve this problem for one farmer by talking a neighbor, a Filipino, into taking the Japanese-American's produce and selling it as his own. Hayasaka's father was able to get back into the wholesale produce business by becoming partners with a young Japanese-American veteran of the famed 442d Regiment, the most highly decorated group in the war. The veteran put up a sign over the office saying the business was operated by a veteran, which made it difficult for buyers to avoid it.

BEN YORITA

"The older people never recovered from the camps. The father was the traditional breadwinner and in total command of the family. But after going into the camps, fathers were no longer the breadwinners; the young sons and daughters were. Most of them couldn't even communicate in English, so all the burdens fell on the second generation. And most of us were just kids, nineteen or twenty. Consequently there was a big turnover of responsibility and authority, and the parents were suddenly totally dependent on their children. When we returned to the cities after the war, it was the second generation again that had to make the decisions and do all the negotiating with landlords, attorneys, and the like."

42

OTTO APEL

Mechanized Angels in Korea

The Korean War is often described as "the forgotten war," possibly because the generation that fought it was fatigued—first from the privations of the Great Depression and the terrible sacrifices at home and abroad during World War II, and second from struggles to return to the tasks of peace, such as employment, housing, education, and building families. In 1950, when the United States government decided to send troops to the Korean peninsula to stop the spread of communism in Asia, there were few Americans who were enthusiastic enough about another foreign entanglement to either wholeheartedly support the war or oppose it. Although the U.S. military had been involved in the developing civil war in Korea since the day the Japanese Empire was defeated, the full-scale war involving American forces and the North Korean army began in June 1950 and ended in the summer of 1953. During that time, the United States sent almost 1.8 million troops to Korea and registered 54,000 fatalities. On the Korean side there were over two million killed or missing.

Many of the U.S. military personnel who served in Korea struggled with the fact that the U.S. army was fighting a new type of war for which it had little practical experience. While many historians speak of the American Civil War or World War I as the first modern wars due to new technologies that enabled mass killing, some historians argue that Korea was the first modern war due to the availability of technologies to save lives. The Mobile Army Surgical Hospital, or MASH, drew on such technologies, particularly helicopters and antibiotics. Suddenly, highly trained medical doctors were able to provide nearly state-of-the-art treatment only minutes from the battle. Wounds that had once meant amputation or death from infection were suddenly treatable and often minor.

The contributions of the doctors were immortalized in M*A*S*H, a 1970 feature film that was adapted to television in 1972 and became one of the most beloved and popular shows in U.S. history. It focused on a group of conscripted medical doctors, nurses, and army healthcare staff, struggling to retain their humanity and sanity amidst the brutality and bureaucratic stupidity of the war. Overtly antiwar and harshly critical of the U.S. Army, the show helped define the Korean War as unnecessary, unpopular, and wrong. However, the black humor, critical cynicism, and antiauthority/antiwar/antimilitary attitude of the show's hero, surgeon Hawkeye Pierce, was more an expression of America during the 1970s when the show was being produced and broadcast—a country torn apart by the conflict in Vietnam—than it was an accurate reflection of the young men and women who went to fight and heal in Korea.

Otto F. Apel and Pat Apel, *MASH: An Army Surgeon in Korea* (Lexington, KY: University Press of Kentucky, 1998), 66–89.

Otto Apel was a surgical resident with a wife and young children in Cleveland, Ohio, when he was called up for army service at the 8076th Mobile Army Surgical Hospital—the model for the 4077th that was memorialized in the television show. Though barely out of medical school, he rapidly rose to the position of chief surgeon. In 1998, Apel published his memoirs, in which he described many of the realities portrayed in the television show, including terrible working conditions, long hours, and irreverent fun, as well as the remarkable innovations made by MASH healthcare workers.

QUESTIONS TO CONSIDER

1. In what ways do you think that the rise of more sophisticated war technologies and advanced scientific breakthroughs, such as helicopters and battlefield medicine, may have changed what it means to have a career in the military?
2. Apel demonstrates in the passage how the helicopter greatly expanded access to the battlefield by noncombatants. How do you think this may have changed the information that the public receives about war?
3. Given the value of helicopters for both munitions resupply going in and medical evacuation going out, how might helicopters have changed the rules of war?
4. From what you have read in this passage, what impact do you think modern U.S. war technologies may have had on the Chinese soldiers?

The wounded came to us every way they possibly could. It was always a race. Some came in army ambulances driven helter-skelter the few miles over the hills and gullies and dusty roads. Some hitched rides on the backs of jeeps or trucks that had delivered cargo to the front and had been commandeered to backhaul the injured or the prisoners or those replaced for rest and recuperation (R&R). Some of the wounded scooted off the hills on litters lugged by weary, staggering comrades. Some walked under their own power or with improvised crutches or on the shoulder of a friend. All were bloody and in need of immediate surgical care.

When I got to MASH 8076 in 1951, there was another way that the wounded were transported to the hospital: they came by helicopter. We knew when they were arriving because we got a call first. Sometimes we were relaxing in the officers' tent or playing cards or passing the football. We might be in the midst of surgery or making rounds or in the mess hall. The Koreans were there, Choi and the others, and the nurses and doctors and the NCOs, and we would hear the helicopters coming. . . .

The *thump-thump* of the rotors broke the tension. The medics and the orderlies would leave the tents and scan the skies until they saw the helicopters, little specks in the clouds. The helicopters descended into MASH 8076 for touchdown at our landing zone. Sometimes, when the loads were heavy, Choi and the other Koreans helped carry the wounded from the helicopters to the in-processing tent for movement into surgery. It was always an exhilarating—if deadly solemn—experience to hear the wounded arrive. You became very still and your blood throbbed in your head and you wanted to do something, but you had to wait. And then they came, and the work began.

The use of the helicopter for medical evacuation was one of the major advances in emergency medical care pioneered in the Korean War. . . . Although the helicopter made its debut in World War II, it saw broader—if still limited by today's standards—action in Korea. Korea was helicopter country: the entire nation was marked by poor roads ruined by tank traffic, railroads with bombed-out track and bridges, mountainous terrain with ridges up to six thousand feet. Conditions deteriorated in rainy weather, which washed out roads, and winter weather, which covered roads with snow and iced over bridges. Tactical positions in those mountains became impassable for ground vehicles. The helicopter was the only solution. . . .

When I arrived in Korea in 1951, the 2d Helicopter Detachment was attached to the 8076th. Later, the 2d was replaced by the 8193d. Each detachment had four helicopter pilots and four mechanics, headquartered with us in the MASH. They moved when we did, they ate when we did, and they worked when we did. I must say that, for the most part, they were a remarkable collection of men. . . .

The morale factor was a major advantage of helicopter evacuation. Troops could be in the operating tent of a MASH within hours of being wounded. Dr. Elmer Henderson, president of the American Medical Association, toured the Korean theater and reported on the "President's Page" of the *Journal of the American Medical Association*, "I talked to many of the wounded, and all of them were outspoken in their praise of the medical treatment they were receiving." One lieutenant told Henderson, "Doctor, I was wounded when a mortar blew up. I was taken to the First Aid Station in 5 minutes, and within 55 minutes I was on a plane heading for a hospital. When they take care of you like that, a man doesn't mind fighting."

By contrast, local Korean villagers carried the Chinese wounded on litters from the battlefield. Medical supplies were extremely short. Given one day's rations, the Chinese wounded hoped that they could find a hospital before the locals dumped them and headed home. Often, the wounded were left on the battlefield without weapons or food or medical care. It seemed that when they went to the front, the Chinese were on their own to fight fatigue, hunger, and death. When the going got tough, as it did for both sides in Korea, lack of medical support weighed heavily on the minds and morale of the Chinese soldiers.

But for the American wounded, the hope and promise of immediate evacuation and medical treatment was incarnate in the helicopter. Like the MASH they served, the pilots became larger than life in the eyes of the soldiers. They not only served a specific function in the unit, but "their intrepid spirit" also constantly boosted the morale of the doctors and nurses and the wounded themselves. The pilots were the life of the party in the garrison and the cavalry on call for the wounded and dying. Tireless, they were always ready to go. . . .

Economy was the byword of helicopter evacuation: economy of time; economy of expense; economy of use; economy of personnel; economy of material and facilities; and as a result, economy of lives. Granted, the role of the helicopter was very limited when compared to its role in Vietnam or in the army today. In 1951 most of the pilots and helicopters were being used to help the tactical commanders carry the war to the enemy. They provided the eyes and the ears and the strong backs to see and maneuver about the battlefield. The tactical commanders themselves were just learning the benefits of the helicopter.

Ours were the pilots, few though they were, who would carry the wounded. From beginning to end, the medical evacuation by helicopter was, by necessity, designed for economy of time. It was time that was so precious, and it was time that the helicopter gave the surgeon, precious time to treat the wounds before the patient was too far gone. At places like Heartbreak Ridge, the terrain was so rugged and the fighting so intense that it took American medics hours to move the wounded down the ridge to a first aid station in preparation for transport by ambulance to the MASH. But the helicopter could bypass all that and cover miles in no time at all. On one occasion, a corps surgeon called the 8193d Helicopter Detachment with a message that a soldier had been seriously wounded and was expected to die within the hour. Because of the weather and the terrain, they could not move him by ambulance or litter. The unit called for copters, but the cloud ceiling was right down on the ground and all air traffic was socked in. The corps surgeon left the decision whether to fly to the pilots.

The pilots plotted the unit's location on their maps and knew that they would never make it through a pass just south of the pickup point. They directed the unit by radio to take the soldier through the pass to a point on the south side where the helicopter could land. Flying at an altitude of fifty feet, rotor blades in the clouds, they landed at the proposed location and awaited the delivery of the wounded soldier. When several soldiers arrived, they loaded the patient and the helicopter lifted off. The helicopter was on an incline, so instead of going up it eased down the road to gain speed (translational lift) to help gain altitude. But a wire had been stretched across the road. It caught the helicopter at bubble height, took out the radio antenna, slid up over the bubble, and hit the mast. The helicopter slowed as it stretched the wire until it snapped and the helicopter—as if shot by a slingshot—raced along the roadway and gained altitude. Without further complications, the crew made it back to the MASH. The entire mission took forty minutes. The patient lived. . . .

The copter pilot had to go to the front to pick up the wounded. Pilots selected landing zones, read markings for them, landed in live-fire areas, and coordinated with artillery and air strikes prior to entering a combat area. Audio and visual communication with ground units became especially important in combat operations. As the helicopter approached the battalion aid station to pick up the wounded, it was an easy target for the Chinese and the North Koreans. The pickup had to be synchronized and swift. The medics on the ground set out a flare of prearranged color when the helicopter approached. It had to be done quickly because the smoke would attract enemy guns.

When the helicopter arrived, the patients had to be ready for transport. The helicopter could not sit on the ground in a combat zone for very long without drawing enemy fire. Beyond that, we did not want to tie up helicopters waiting for personnel to be prepared for transportation. The helicopter could be carrying someone else who was ready to be evacuated. As soon as the helicopter hit the ground, the medics carried the wounded on a litter, placed the litter on the helicopter just above the skids, and strapped it down. The helicopter lifted off immediately. All this had to be done as quickly as possible and was often done under direct enemy fire. . . .

The helicopter provided economy of personnel by permitting the battalion surgeon to direct the wounded to the appropriate hospital and allowing the army to centralize medical personnel in specialized hospitals. Those in immediate need of surgery went directly to the MASH. Those whose injuries required immediate evacuation but did not require immediate surgery could be sent to other facilities. For example, psychiatric patients or patients dying of complications from illness could be sent directly to a field hospital of the battalion surgeon's choice, thus bypassing the MASH. Helicopters made all the hospitals in the combat zone available to the battalion surgeon.

On the other hand, the speed and flexibility of the helicopter permitted the Medical Corps to centralize doctors and nurses in specialized treatment facilities instead of scattering them to different places on the battlefields. At the beginning of the war, each MASH unit did general surgery. When I arrived, the 8076th took all comers. As time went on, each MASH began to specialize. MASH 8076 became known as the place to treat extreme vascular injuries. MASH 8055 was known for its treatment of head injuries. If a head injury came to us at MASH 8076, we would give immediate treatment, stabilize the patient, and transport him to 8055. The other MASH units did likewise with vascular injuries, and by late 1951 we were receiving the lion's share of vascular work. MASH 8063 was known for treating unusual conditions, particularly the mysterious ailment that swept Korea in 1951–52 called, for lack of a better name, hemorrhagic fever. In cases of suspected use of biological or chemical weapons, such as nerve gas, the wounded were taken to MASH 8209, later redesignated MASH 8225, a stable unit that did not move like the other MASH units. Others may have gone to an evacuation hospital. With the reduction in transit time from the battlefield to the MASH, the increase in range, and the flexibility of landing, the wounded could go to a specialized treatment facility where he could receive the best treatment available. . . .

In addition to the evacuations, the helicopters provided another advantage to the medical corps: we used the copters to make house calls. Often, in the heat of battle, the wounded swamped a beleaguered battalion surgeon or group of medics in an aid station. The battalion surgeon or the medic would cry "Help!" to the nearest MASH, and if possible, a surgeon would come forward with the helicopter. Many times I snatched a kit bag and hopped on the copter en route to the aid stations to provide immediate medical care and additional assistance in preparing seriously injured soldiers for the flight to the MASH. . . .

A few months after Triple Nickels was ambushed in the fifth Chinese offensive, MASH 8076 received a call for assistance from the field artillery battalion operating in the mountains west of us. We first recognized that something was wrong when we heard the frantic radio communications from several corps units calling for reinforcements, air support, artillery support, helicopter evacuation, and surgeons to assist with the wounded. We stood silently and somberly in the operations section and listened as the battle unfolded. The field artillery battalion was among those pleading for help. The radioman shouted over the small-arms fire and the static that the Chinese were in their perimeter. Grenade and mortar explosions drowned out the frenzied young voice. Bugles blared in the distance, and the deep and deafening roar of the American 105s fired at point-blank range broke into the transmissions.

"Send helicopters and doctors," the voice shouted. "We need them now."

We had been alerted for possible movement to the north, and the Koreans and enlisted personnel had begun to strike tents. Dayton Warren was one of our pilots, and although I had been with the 8076th only a month or so, he and I had come to be friends. We had flown together on several occasions and had many things in common. Dayton was tall and slender with short-cropped hair. He was conscientious, and his mind was always looking for ways to get things done.

He looked at me and said, "Ottie, you ready?" It was not a mission I was excited about. When we left the tent, we could hear the guns to the north and the west of us. Down in the aviation section, all the helicopters were warming up. In minutes we were airborne over the steep, dark mountains toward the reported location of the field artillery unit. Dayton contacted the unit by radio and asked for a more specific location. When we reached the area, we were unable to locate the unit. Circling the mountains, we searched but saw no signs of combat. We tried again to raise the unit by radio, but there was no answer.

We came over a mountaintop just as dawn was breaking and saw a green meadow near the crest of the mountain. One soldier sat in the field. There were bodies all over. When we landed, the blasts of a blazing firefight, the bugles of attacking Chinese, the thuds of mortars, the shouts of men in mortal combat, all had ceased. An eerie silence enveloped the field.

The soldier sat with arms wrapped around his knees and his head bowed between his legs. As we approached, I could see the man was near shock.

"Where are the wounded?" Dayton shouted.

With a slight nod of his head toward the slope of the mountain, the soldier said, "They're all gone. They're all gone." He dropped his head again between his knees and said, "They're all gone."

Dayton and I glanced at each other. That could mean several things: they had retreated, they had been captured, or they had been killed.

"I'll go look," Dayton said, and he pulled his pistol from his flight jacket. I followed him over the slope. There we found more bodies. The unit that fought there, judging by the bodies in the field, was an African American unit. It appeared to be a battery-sized element. I have no idea how many may have escaped or been captured. The soldiers were spread on the slopes beside the road where they had perhaps sought cover from an ambush, circled their unit, and defended to the death. In the center of the circle were flaming equipment and several charred and mangled artillery pieces that appeared to be 105s. Interspersed among the bodies were Chinese soldiers. They were all dead: the artillerymen, the Chinese, the medics, the cooks, the drivers, the mechanics, the ammo bearers, the radio operator, the officers, all had met their deaths in that field on a mountaintop in Korea. We returned to the meadow and the helicopter. I tended the young soldier in the field. We loaded him in the helicopter, lifted off from the meadow, and flew a course over the battlefield. All the soldiers were gone. We were no help on that day. We evacuated the young soldier to the 8076th and then back to the psychiatric section of a field hospital.

43

RING LARDNER JR.

Blacklisted: The Post–World War II Red Scare

Following each of the world wars of the twentieth century, American politics shifted from progressive to conservative and went through a "red scare," a heightened fear of communism. The administration of President Harry Truman conducted a rigid internal security program to weed out disloyal or potentially subversive federal employees (although it fired many more homosexuals than political activists). Truman also pursued a foreign policy of unparalleled aggressiveness against the Soviet Union. Despite these measures, the president was successfully attacked by Republicans as "soft" on communism.

The Red Scare after World War II affected the entertainment industry particularly. Both Hollywood and New York had been centers of political radicalism in the 1930s. Highly organized citizens' groups pressured the entertainment industry to blacklist writers, directors, and actors, among others. The blacklisting greatly influenced what Americans did and did not see on television and at the movies and left hundreds of industry workers unemployed.

Ring Lardner Jr. (1915–2000) was one of many such entertainment industry workers who suffered from the postwar Red Scare. An open member of the Communist Party, Lardner had contributed to writing the movie A Star Is Born *and won the 1942 Academy Award for Best Original Screenplay for* Woman of the Year *at the age of twenty-six. Five*

"Notes on the Blacklist: Lardner," interview by Barry Strugatz, *Film Comment*, September/ October 1988, 52–69.

years later, he was subpoenaed by the House Un-American Activities Committee (HUAC) and asked the infamous question, "Are you now or have you ever been a member of the Communist Party?" Knowing that answering would provide the legal opening for HUAC to ask many other questions and force him to "name names," Lardner replied, "I could answer it, but if I did, I would hate myself in the morning." He was subsequently cited for contempt of Congress, was blacklisted, and served one year in prison. The government, however, never took away Lardner's passport—as had happened to African American singer, athlete, actor, writer, and lawyer Paul Robeson—enabling Lardner to wait out the 1950s abroad, where he wrote under pseudonyms and through "fronts" (nonblacklisted people paid to pretend to have written scripts). When he finally returned to working under his own name, he won a second Oscar for writing the screenplay for the movie M*A*S*H. *During the 1970s, he wrote twenty-two episodes of the television adaptation of* M*A*S*H *and scripts for several movies, including* The Greatest, *about heavyweight boxing champion Muhammad Ali. In this excerpt from an interview conducted in 1988, Lardner details his experiences in the period leading up to and during his time on the blacklist.*

QUESTIONS TO CONSIDER

1. Are a screenwriter's politics a public or a private matter? Explain.
2. If you have seen any of Ring Lardner Jr.'s movies or television shows, can you find a connection between his beliefs, his experiences with the blacklist, and the scripts he wrote?
3. What issues today are similar to those that arose in the entertainment industry during the Red Scare of the post–World War II period? What comparisons and contrasts can you make between the two sets of issues?

When did you join the Party?
In 1936. . . .
What was the general political climate in Hollywood?
People were becoming quite political about the Spanish Civil War, which broke out in the middle of that year, and about what was going on in Germany. The most popular political organization in Hollywood at that time was the Hollywood Anti-Nazi League. . . .

Also, toward the end of 1936, the Screenwriters Guild, which had been effectively smashed a couple of years before, began to reorganize because of the Wagner Labor Relations Act,[1] and we were working toward a Labor Board election, which took place in the spring of 1937. There was also a strike going on, in '36–'37, of the various crafts, the non-IATSE-AFL[2] crafts—car-

---

1. **Wagner Labor Relations Act:** Officially known as the National Labor Relations Act, or Wagner Act, this law, enacted in 1935, established workers' right to join trade unions without fear of management reprisals.
2. **IATSE:** International Alliance of Theatrical Stage Employees; labor union representing technicians, artisans, and craftspeople in the entertainment industry. **AFL:** American Federation of Labor, known since its 1955 merger with the Congress of Industrial Organizations as the AFL-CIO; the largest federation of labor unions in the United States.

penters and painters—supported by the office workers and readers; and the Screen Actors Guild [SAG] was heading toward its first contract and, as an AFL union, was in a position where they had to decide whether to support the IATSE or this other AFL group. It was a very close battle, and there was a big political fight in SAG. At one point they actually passed a straw vote to support the strikers and respect picket lines, but when it came to an actual vote, they didn't.

What did it mean to be an active member of the Party? What do you think you accomplished by being a member? What do you think the Party accomplished?

What it meant to be an active member was mostly spending a lot of time at meetings of various sorts. . . . I had meetings of the Guild board once a week and usually a committee meeting another evening of the week, and there was a regular Party branch meeting about once a week, and very often a writers' faction—these were writers who were members of the Party, as well as a few who, for various reasons, were not but were very close to the Party. They would meet and would discuss policy in the Guild. With one thing and another, I found I was going to meetings five or six nights a week. And Sylvia, who joined some months after we were married, was going to a good many of those, too. . . .

We did play a part, I think, in most everything that was going on in the Hollywood scene. Organizations such as the Motion Picture Committee to Aid Spanish Democracy, the Hollywood Anti-Nazi League, and the League of American Writers would not really have functioned anywhere near to the extent that they did without the very active participation of Communists in their forefront; nor, I think, would the unions that were being formed or reformed at that time—the guilds of actors, writers, and directors, etc., and the emerging office workers union, etc.—have gotten as strong as fast as they did without the extra work that the Communists put into organizing and recruiting people for them.

The nature of the work we did changed twice during that period. Once in the fall of 1939, with the outbreak of the war in Europe and the Nazi-Soviet Pact, the Russian war against Finland, etc., when there was a very sharp division for a while between Communists and liberals—most of the latter being supporters of the British and French in the war and most of us remaining pretty skeptical about what the Allies were up to in the war. And then, of course, when Hitler invaded the Soviet Union, and when Pearl Harbor was attacked, there was another big shift, and with much more unity on the liberal and left side of things.

Why were you skeptical of the Allies in the beginning?

The basic skepticism was what I still think is a well-founded fear: That the people who were in charge of those governments—Neville Chamberlain in England and Deladier in France—were likely to, if they got a chance, make some kind of a deal with Hitler to turn the war against the Soviet Union, which was a very popular idea in British and French circles. . . .

How did you see your politics as they related to your writing?

It was pretty difficult to find much relationship between them, except to the extent that when I was able—after *Woman of the Year*—to make some selection in what I was doing, I tried to get assignments that had some potential for progressive content.

We had what was called a clinic within the Communist Party, where writers used to meet and discuss each other's problems with scripts and sometimes with other kinds of writing: books, etc. That was, I think, helpful to many individuals in just working out certain technical story problems and things in conjunction with their colleagues. But I can't say that it had much of a broad effect on the content of what was done in the movies.

Did the studios or the Party try to influence the political content of scripts?

When they finally came before the House Un-American Activities Committee in 1947, the heads of the studios maintained that there was never any real question about the content of pictures because they retained control of content. And largely this was true; they did. What things a few writers might have been able to sell them on or slip into a script were of minor consequence. . . .

When the war ended, did you detect a change in the political atmosphere—the beginning of the Cold War, etc.?

Yes, quite rapidly. I think it probably came quicker in Hollywood than in most other places because during the last six months of the war, most of the same group that had been involved in that strike back in the late Thirties under the leadership of a man named Herbert Sorrell started a strike against the studios. And it was the position of the Communist Party during the war that there should be no strikes and no support for strikes until the war was over. So we did not actively help. There was some money raised, because we were basically sympathetic with what was going on, but we thought they had called the strike prematurely.

And when the war ended in the summer of 1945, the strike was still going on, and that condition persisted for six months after that. As I recall, it was a long, drawn-out, and quite violent struggle, with a lot of violence taking place on picket lines. Many of us marched on those picket lines in '45 and '46. That strike divided Hollywood very much into a sort of liberal-left camp that supported the strike in varying degrees and the conservative element in the Screen Actors Guild, which, by the time it was over, I think included a new president, Ronald Reagan.

At the same time there was an organization called the Hollywood Independent Citizens Committee of the Arts, Sciences & Professions, or HICCASP. The New York office was called NICCASP; in Hollywood it was HICCASP. The members were very enthusiastic supporters of Roosevelt during his fourth election campaign, and many supported what Henry Wallace stood for subsequently. But there did arise a split between those who were more inclined toward Harry Truman's policies and those of us who thought Henry Wallace was the man who should run in 1948. . . .

On the national scene, we knew that there were big industrial conflicts going on. The United Electrical Workers Union and other unions that had a somewhat left orientation were trying to carry on strikes, and they were being opposed by the hierarchy in the AFL. I guess the AFL and the CIO were still separate at that time. This was the time when the so-called Truman Doctrine in regard to Greece and Turkey was promulgated, and when Winston Churchill made his Iron Curtain speech[3] in Fulton, Missouri, with President Truman seated alongside him. This was the time when we all seemed to be going in the wrong direction.

When were you served with a subpoena? Do you remember that moment?

It was in September, I think, of 1947. I remember it particularly because we had just bought a new house. I had been divorced and remarried to Frances, my present wife, who was the widow of my brother David, who was killed in the Spanish Civil War. . . .

Dalton Trumbo[4] and I had a couple of times discussed what we would do if it came up. We decided that it was not a good idea to deny membership in the Communist Party, although some of our colleagues had done that before the California State Un-American Activities Committee. We just felt that there were too many stool pigeons and various other ways to find out, and you could get yourself in a much worse situation for perjury; it would be very hard to organize any sympathy around that. On the other hand, we thought it would be a bad idea to answer "Yes" to the question because the studios would probably use it against us and also because it made it less feasible to refuse to answer further questions about other people.

You anticipated that they would proceed along those lines?

Yes. We therefore felt the most sensible policy was just not to answer questions and to challenge the right of the committee to ask any questions at all. The two of us had agreed that was the position we thought best to take.

It was only after it became known that there were 19 of us who had received subpoenas, known as "unfriendly" witnesses—as opposed to people who had received subpoenas who we believed were going to be cooperative witnesses—that we got together at meetings in Hollywood, all 19 of us, with the exception of Bertolt Brecht,[5] who was then in a considerably different position. He was an enemy alien all during the war; the rest of us were citizens.

We met with some lawyers, and Trumbo and I brought up this idea of not answering any questions. There were problems with that position. There were several people who wanted to say yes, they were Communists; they felt it was time to raise the face of the Party. But we raised the point—and the lawyers agreed with us—that it would then be very difficult to take a position against naming practically everybody they knew.

We discussed the Fifth Amendment, and there was some dispute as to whether that would really work. The Smith Act,[6] under which the Communist

---

3. **Iron Curtain speech:** This speech, given in 1946, is often considered the beginning of the cold war.
4. **Dalton Trumbo:** Novelist and screenwriter who was blacklisted as a communist after testifying before HUAC.
5. **Bertolt Brecht:** Germany's most famous twentieth-century playwright, poet, and theater director.
6. **Smith Act:** During the 1940s and 1950s, hundreds of communists were prosecuted under this act, which made it a criminal offense to be a member of any group that advised the overthrow of the U.S. government.

Party leaders were later convicted, had not been invoked against them at that time; it wasn't until the next year that they were arrested. So we would be saying: "It's a crime to be a Communist and therefore I plead 'self-incrimination.'" But beyond that, we thought that that position would not do anything to challenge the right of the committee to function.

In other words, it was a freedom of speech issue?

Yes. We were saying: "Under the First Amendment there is freedom of speech and freedom of the press—and that includes the movie business. Therefore Congress cannot legislate in this field—and Congress has no right to investigate where it cannot legislate."

What about the issue of political affiliation? Did that come under the First Amendment also?

Yes; that it was our business what political party we belonged to or believed in. And Alvah Bessie[7] at that time pointed out to the committee that Dwight Eisenhower was then refusing to say whether he was a Democrat or a Republican—and we should have the same rights as he did.

So gradually the policy of not answering questions and of challenging the committee was agreed upon: More or less, we all agreed that we were going to do that, although we didn't want to seem to be doing it by agreement. Our lawyers additionally advised us that it was a good idea to say we were answering the question, but in our own way, while never actually answering it.

And we went along with this last tactic, which actually turned out to be a bad idea and just made us seem to be more evasive than we were, and it didn't accomplish anything in the end.

Could you describe what it was like testifying? What was going through your head?

I was somewhat frightened, I guess, of the idea of appearing before this committee. . . .

I had no great confidence in my ability to be articulate before this committee or to make any great points at such a hearing. The experience of my colleagues who had preceded me—the way they were jumped on and shut up—made me less confident.

I just couldn't see any real good coming out of it and determined that I would try to make a couple of points about why I wasn't answering these questions; that that was about the maximum good you could accomplish—namely, to get in a phrase or two.

And that's what I tried to do.

Jumping ahead to after your sentence. What was your prison experience like? Were you scared?

Yes, that was really a considerable unknown, both as to what it would actually be like in prison and what it would be like with our particular offense. I faced that with a good deal of uncertainty and pessimism because I didn't think it was going to go well.

It turned out, on the whole, not to be nearly as bad as I anticipated. . . .

---

7. **Alvah Bessie:** Writer blacklisted during the anticommunist witch hunts of the 1950s.

Lester Cole[8] and I were both sent to Danbury, where my mother, who was only about 13 miles away, was able to visit once a week.

Were you put in the same cell?

No. In Danbury every new inmate went through an orientation course, which involved living in a segregated part of the prison in a kind of dormitory and spending a few days learning about prison life and discipline and so on. Then we were released into the general population and assigned jobs according to whether we were classified as maximum security or moderate security or light security. Those who were light security were allowed to have jobs working outside the prison walls. . . .

When did you first realize you were blacklisted?

We returned from the hearings in Washington not sure of what was going to happen. We thought we had a pretty good chance to win the case based on the court decisions so far, and we thought if we won the case, the studios would not take any action, would not get enough support to take any blacklisting action.

However, there was a meeting called the very next month in New York: The heads of companies in New York met and passed a resolution that ten of us would not work—and anyone else who took the same position couldn't work—until we had been cleared by the committee, and that they would not knowingly hire a Communist or anyone who refused to answer questions of a congressional committee. So that was then put into effect in varying degrees. Only five of the ten of us were actually working at studios then.

Where were you?

I was under contract at 20th Century-Fox. I was in kind of a special situation because after I came back from the hearing, Otto Preminger[9] asked if I would work on an adaptation of a book he had bought, and we started working on it. So they were giving me a new assignment after the hearing.

This later became an issue in a civil case when a jury decided that they had waived their right to fire me by giving me a new assignment. But a judge threw that out, and at a second trial we settled out of court for a relatively minor amount of money. Anyway, Darryl Zanuck[10] made a public statement that he wasn't going to fire anybody unless he was specifically urged to do so by his board of directors. But the 20th Century-Fox board got together and obliged him. I was the only person at the studio. . . .

How did they let you know?

I was in Otto's office—we were talking about the story—when a message came that Zanuck wanted to see me. And Otto said, "Not both of us?" [laughter], and the message was, "No, just Lardner."

---

8. **Lester Cole:** Screenwriter who cofounded the Writers Guild of America and was blacklisted as a communist.
9. **Otto Preminger:** One of the most famous film directors of the post–World War II period.
10. **Darryl Zanuck:** One of the legendary Hollywood studio chiefs.

And then when I went to Zanuck's office, I was shunted off and did not get to Zanuck himself but to his assistant, Lou Schreiber, who told me that my contract was terminated and I was supposed to leave the premises.

I told this to Otto. He was very distressed but couldn't think of anything to do about it.

What was the impact of the blacklist?

Well, the impact was to create intimidation in the motion picture business and in the emerging television business. It affected the content of pictures to some extent, because people avoided subjects they thought were controversial. The studios started making anti-Communist pictures, which the committee more or less specifically asked for, and, although they didn't do very well, there was a tendency to stay away from material that might be controversial. There was, I think, an increased kind of escapism in pictures. Certainly the impact was strongest on the 300 or more who were blacklisted. But it also threatened people who sort of got nervous about being revealed as entertaining dangerous thoughts.

Do you think this was an attack on freedom of speech?

Yes, I think it certainly had a limiting effect on freedom of expression in Hollywood.

44

Levittown: Making America Suburban

Until the late 1940s, suburbs, located just at the edge of major cities, were typically privileged enclaves of the elite. At the time, most Americans lived and worked in cities, small towns, or the countryside. Many did not have the money to own a home.

The end of World War II brought the return of sixteen million GIs, many of whom expected to start families. But there was no place to house them. The decade of economic depression during the 1930s and five years of war in the 1940s had left the country with a severe housing shortage, estimated at five million units or more. Returning soldiers and their families were sometimes compelled to live in barns, abandoned trolley cars, unheated bungalows, and toolsheds.

William Levitt (1907–1994), along with his father and brother, helped change all that in 1947 when they built Levittown, the first modern mass-produced suburb, on an abandoned Long Island potato farm just outside New York City. Helped by their low-interest GI loans, returning soldiers and their families could buy a Levittown home outfitted with a modern stove, a refrigerator, a washing machine, and an oil burner for just a $90 deposit and $58 a month. Levitt took advantage of the housing crisis to transform home construction, avoiding union labor, building on poured concrete slabs (in violation of laws requiring basements), and undermining traditional craftsmen by factory-cutting materials in his lumberyard and nail factory in California.

The growing car culture and affluent postwar consumers favored Levitt's creation, which was so popular that in 1950 he was featured on the cover of Time *magazine, having constructed more than fifteen thousand homes at the rate of thirty per day. Levitt and Sons determined early on to restrict their planned community to white people only. The federal government accepted this decision, marking a turning point in which tendencies toward residential segregation common in the first half of the twentieth century were amplified, hardened, and permanently written into the landscape of postwar American development. The 1950s saw running protests against this outcome by African Americans and whites who were committed to a more inclusive society, but Levittowns remain disproportionally white to this day. Many scholars lament the development of these planned communities as a lost opportunity for a more just America.*

QUESTIONS TO CONSIDER

1. What is most and least appealing to you about the homes shown in the two images?
2. Levittown has been criticized for homogenizing American housing and creating a wasteful suburban sprawl filled with cheap, ugly housing. What is your perspective?
3. Levitt agreed, in a newspaper interview, that segregated housing was a "racial problem." How do you think he might have justified keeping Levittown all white?

People wait in line outside a new Levittown house. Levittown, New York. *NGS Image Collection / The Art Archive at Art Resource, NY.*

Street in Levittown. © *Bettmann / Corbis.*

45

CHARLES DOUGLAS JACKSON

The *Sputnik* Crisis: The Beep Heard 'round the World

On October 4, 1957, the Soviet Union shocked the world by launching Sputnik 1, *the first artificial satellite. In a world captivated by the dream of space exploration, the Soviets' aeronautical milestone precipitated a national crisis of confidence for Americans. Across the United States, people listened to Sputnik's tracking signal as it was broadcast on the radio. The simple, repetitive "beep-beep-beep" symbolized for many a loss of power, prestige, and certainty for the country. Sputnik, which circled Earth every ninety minutes, also evoked profound fear in many Americans, who wondered what the*

Memorandum from C. D. Jackson regarding Soviet satellite, October 8, 1957. C. D. Jackson Papers, Box 69, Log-1957 (4).

hostile Soviet Union might be doing to them as the satellite cruised above their houses, schools, and farms.

For the administration of President Dwight D. Eisenhower, whose Project Vanguard had aimed to make the United States the first space power, the Soviets' triumph was a political humiliation. Republican congresswoman Clare Boothe Luce described Sputnik's tracking signal reverberating across the United States as "an intercontinental outer-space raspberry to a decade of American pretensions that the American way of life was a gilt-edged guarantee of our national superiority." Eisenhower, a five-star general in World War II, was a fiscal conservative who had reined in the military budget in the wake of the Korean War (1950–1953). The successful launch of Sputnik 1 *—and only a few weeks later* Sputnik 2, *which carried a dog named Laika into orbit—forced Eisenhower into a "space race" that would result in one of the largest spending sprees in U.S. history and culminate with a moon landing in 1969. A lasting effect of the* Sputnik *crisis was the National Defense Education Act (1958), which poured billions of dollars into the public schools and expanded secondary and tertiary education access to communities across the United States. This legislation inspired the contemporary phrase "a* Sputnik *moment," meaning a point when people realize that they have been left behind and must change their priorities to catch up.*

Charles Douglas Jackson (1902–1964), the author of the following memorandum, spent his working life moving among the media, the government, and what during the cold war came to be called the "national security apparatus." Starting his career in the 1930s, Jackson worked for Henry Luce (husband of Clare Boothe Luce), the owner of Time *magazine. When the United States entered World War II, Jackson joined the diplomatic corps in Europe and eventually found his way into the Office of Strategic Services (the predecessor of the Central Intelligence Agency) and the army, working in the emerging field of psychological warfare. After the war he rejoined Luce as managing director of Time-Life International and publisher of* Fortune *magazine. Jackson, however, continued his connection with the national security apparatus, participating in several CIA operations and taking various posts in the Eisenhower administration, including stints as speechwriter, special assistant to the president, and United Nations delegate. At the time of* Sputnik 1*'s launch, Jackson was not an official government employee, but his opinion on the national security implications of* Sputnik *was important to his employer Luce and to President Eisenhower, whose library later archived Jackson's personal papers.*

QUESTIONS TO CONSIDER

1. Why was Charles Douglas Jackson so alarmed by the launch of *Sputnik 1*?
2. According to Jackson, what should have been the United States' proper response to the launch?
3. Why did Jackson suggest to Henry Luce that he "be prepared for military action"? Do you think Jackson was overreacting to the Soviet space program? Explain.
4. What other actions might Jackson have proposed to defuse the situation and to prevent the United States from embarking on an arms

race with the Soviet Union that would become a major part of both countries' foreign policy for the next generation?

MEMORANDUM TO: Mr. Luce
FROM: C. P. Jackson

October 8, 1957

If I were still in Washington working for the President, this is what I think I would have told him Monday morning.

* * *

The successful launching of the Soviet satellite is an overwhelmingly important event—against our side. You know the military implications better than I do, and your scientific advisers can spell out the scientific implications better than I. And conceivably on these two points you may think my word "overwhelming" is too strong.

But from the standpoint of worldwide psychological warfare it is the correct word. In the Middle East, in Africa, in Asia, where it will be exploited to the hilt by the Communists, it will have tremendous impact. This will be the first time that they will have achieved a big scientific jump on us, ostensibly for peaceful scientific purposes, yet with tremendous military overtones. Up to now it has generally been the other way around.

In this country, it will not have the same jolting impact, and the Americans will undoubtedly do a slower "take." But it will certainly deepen the national malaise, and the inter-Services and partisan political bickering that is certain to develop will heighten the confusion and make a further continuing contribution to the malaise.

For some time, I have used the word "orchestration"[1] to try to describe the way we should conduct our psychological or political warfare. Orchestration as opposed to one-shot spectaculars. . . .

Within the past thirty days we have been treated to as skillfully executed an example of psychological warfare orchestration as I have ever seen.

The first note was the arrival of the Soviet jet airliner.[2] The second was the announcement of the successful testing of their ICBM.[3] The third was the earth satellite. The fourth was the announcement of their setting off a hydrogen device "at great height."[4] The fifth will be another bigger and bet-

---

1. **orchestration:** The process of organizing a series of events and incidents designed to confuse, anger, or embarrass one's enemy.
2. **arrival of the Soviet jet airliner:** The Soviets built and successfully flew their first intercontinental strategic bomber in 1947.
3. **ICBM:** Intercontinental ballistic missile.
4. **setting off a hydrogen device "at great height":** A reference to the Soviets' detonation, on August 12, 1953, of their first hydrogen bomb, whose explosive force was roughly twenty-six times more powerful than that of the U.S. atomic bomb dropped on Hiroshima on August 6, 1945.

ter earth satellite to be launched on the 40th anniversary of the Russian Revolution.[5]

You will notice the skillful alternation of war and peace—coexistence and atomic blackmail. You will also notice that all these items convey either Soviet "firsts" or Soviet success where the U.S. has either failed or not yet succeeded.

To repeat, all of this adds up to "overwhelming."

We already know from all over the world that the impact has been unusually great, and in favor of Russia—and no comfort should be derived from the fact that it has shoved Little Rock[6] off the front pages of the world. . . .

I should add that the successful impact of the Soviet orchestration is considerably heightened by the U.S. backdrop in front of which the Russians are playing—Little Rock, two unsuccessful Atlas launchings,[7] eleventh-hour Defense Department cuts and stretchouts by departing Secretary [of Defense Charles] Wilson, non-resolution of the whole U.S. missiles program and consequent public inter-Services bickering, etc.

You badly need a little U.S. orchestration right now, and unfortunately you have very little to work with at the moment, so little that most of the recommendations have to be negative rather than positive.

• For instance, although you will doubtless want to speed up our own satellite program as much as possible, it should not be speeded up in such a way that it looks like a crash program. If we are indeed geared to the IGY[8] and have a schedule, the important thing is to stick to the schedule but make sure that when our satellite goes up, it goes all the way—and if not bigger than the Russians' let it be unmistakably better.

• For instance, you would not only immeasurably help [the new secretary of defense] Neil McElroy but the whole U.S. cause if, on the first day that McElroy is in office, you were to summon the Joint Chiefs and the civilian Service Secretaries to a meeting in your office with McElroy, and lay down the law on inter-Service behavior for the coming months. This is no time for fooling, and on both Defense Department cuts and the missiles program the Administration must speak soon and with one voice.

• For instance, over the weekend I read a mystery story, the international intrigue type. At one point the Central European Master Mind, explaining to the simple Britisher who has stumbled into the middle of "the situation," says, "Your phrase 'psychological warfare' is all wrong. You don't really use

5. **bigger and better earth satellite . . . Russian Revolution:** The Soviets launched *Sputnik 2* on November 3, 1957, to coincide with the official anniversary date of the Russian Revolution, November 3, 1917.
6. **Little Rock:** A reference to white citizens' massive resistance toward the admission of black students to the all-white Central High School in Little Rock, Arkansas, in September 1957 and to the Supreme Court's 1954 desegregation order in *Brown v. Board of Education*.
7. **unsuccessful Atlas launchings:** The failed launchings of the Atlas missile, the first U.S. intercontinental ballistic missile, on June 11, 1957, and September 25, 1957.
8. **IGY:** International Geophysical Year, July 1957–December 1958; a period during which, as proposed by the International Council of Scientific Unions, scientists worldwide took part in coordinated observations and experiments of different geophysical events.

psychology, and from what I have been able to observe you will go to any lengths (Munich,[9] plus) to avoid warfare. Therefore the only way in which you can be effective is for you to understand and help us in what we are trying to do. And the name for that is 'interference.' The Soviet appearance of strength and omniscience depends on their functioning without interference. That is why they have their Iron Curtain,[10] their NKVD,[11] their monolithic media of communication. As soon as any real interference arises, their whole apparatus gets out of kilter."

I recommend some quick and possibly drastic interference.

There are quite a few things that can be done in Poland, many of them quite benign, that would constitute interference. Middle East is another area for interference, but not panic-switch type à la Jordan two months ago. Maybe this is the moment to start thinking about Albania again.[12] Certainly this is the moment for U.S. diplomacy and the U.S. Treasury to join hands in exploiting targets of opportunity.

• For instance, it is none too soon for you personally to start a series of public appearances in which by reasoned argument you start to restore U.S. prestige. But this too will require its own sub-orchestration, because you will not only have to make sure that the normal organs of U.S. information abroad correctly interpret and amplify your statements, but you should also insure that a small bipartisan group of prominent Americans steps up and supports your thesis.

You should be prepared for military action, and it might be better to have it on a small scale before the U.S. back is to the wall.

I have been through quite a few of the ups and downs of this game, and have always been able in a "down" to know that it would pass.

This is the first time I have seen so many important options in Soviet hands.

9. **Munich:** The Munich Pact, signed in September 1938 by the major European powers, permitted Nazi Germany's annexation of Czechoslovakia's Sudetenland and became widely viewed as a misguided act of craven appeasement toward Germany.
10. **Iron Curtain:** Phrase referring to the post–World War II ideological, political, and military divisions between communist Eastern Europe and the democratic nations of the West.
11. **NKVD:** The People's Commissariat for Internal Affairs of the Soviet Union, the public and secret police who enforced the laws and power of the Soviet leadership.
12. Poland and Albania were communist states at the time. Much of the Middle East was vacillating between forming a partnership with the United States or with the USSR; this wavering brought instability and a series of political coups, one of which U.S. ally King Hussein of Jordan survived in April 1957.

PART SIX

Awakenings

Authority and Liberty in the Modern Age

In the twentieth century, an American national culture came to dominate all regions of the country and much of the world. Consumerism ruled national markets, the mass media shaped people's most personal aspirations, and federal and state governments provided services and regulations that were both desired and distrusted. The United States took on the role of global policeman and became an immense military superpower.

The African American freedom struggle intensified in the 1960s, giving rise to social unrest. Young people were inspired to action by a political idealism reflected in the letters sent home by student civil rights workers during the Freedom Summer of 1964. As the middle class was greatly enlarged and became more mobile and vocal, new political movements arose on both the right and the left. Catalyzed by the struggle of African Americans to regain many of the rights they had lost when Reconstruction was reversed in 1877, other groups long facing discrimination began to protest in large numbers, including Puerto Rican youths who mobilized as the Young Lords, Mexican American farmworkers led by César Chávez, and gays who rebelled against aggressive police tactics in New York City. And as had happened during the antislavery movement in the nineteenth century, women became frustrated at being denied, by their male colleagues, the respect and equality these various groups claimed to fight for. This frustration led to a revival of the women's rights movement as women across the United States began publicly to question the political and personal aspects of gender inequality. Female scientists like Naomi Weisstein had to fight to be recognized for their academic achievements and to get the jobs they were qualified to perform but were denied by the male-dominated academic establishment. On the other side of the debate, Phyllis Schlafly argued that women's liberation went too far, and she campaigned against the Equal Rights Amendment in the 1970s.

Overshadowing all American lives during this period was the Vietnam War—the nation's longest war. The massacre at My Lai in 1968 became a potent symbol of what the war—and, many feared, the nation—had become. By 1979, when Islamic militants seized the American embassy in Iran and held personnel hostage for more than a year, the United States had been defeated on the battlefield by Vietnamese Communists, the years of protest had largely passed, and a sizable segment of society was calling for the restoration of order and traditional values.

POINTS OF VIEW
The My Lai Massacre and Its Aftermath (1968–1970)

46

RONALD L. RIDENHOUR ET AL.

Disbelief and Corroboration

Throughout the twentieth century, civil wars led to atrocities, and Vietnam was no exception. Such wars rarely obey the international rules of warfare, and combatants often control areas through deliberate terror. When the Vietcong (Vietnamese Communists, or VC) captured the ancient city of Hue during the Tet Offensive of 1968, they murdered hundreds, perhaps thousands, some of whom were buried alive. The attempt to eradicate guerrillas from among a population, any member of which might be a friend, an enemy, or simply a poor peasant wanting to be left alone, usually produces episodes of indiscriminate killing of civilians. One U.S. "pacification" effort in a Mekong delta province in 1969, for example, produced an official body count of eleven thousand Vietcong killed. That only 748 weapons were captured makes it likely that very many of the dead were noncombatants.

The massacre at My Lai on March 16, 1968, was the most notorious atrocity committed by U.S. soldiers in Vietnam. The episode caused many around the world to forget

---

Peers Report, vol. 1, 1–7 to 1–11; "My Lai File," Army Crimes Records Center, Fort Belvoir, Virginia; *Peers Report*, vol. 4, 299–300; *Peers Report*, vol. 4, exhibit M-21, 111.

the discipline and restraint of countless other American troops since the beginning of the intervention. After a particularly forceful briefing in which the men of Company C (Charlie) of Task Force Barker, part of the American Division, were reminded of previous casualties they had suffered at the hands of the VC, they attacked the village of My Lai, known to be a VC stronghold. Finding no enemy forces there, they opened fire on the old men, women, and children who remained in the hamlet, killing between two hundred and four hundred. Rapes preceded several of the killings.

However awful the war in Vietnam and however frequent the atrocities on all sides, the men of Charlie Company and those who heard about My Lai knew that they had done something far out of the ordinary. Neither they nor their superiors wanted to talk about what had happened. The standard press release, though written by an eyewitness, made no reference to the atrocities. A cover-up had begun that lasted for an entire year, until Ronald L. Ridenhour (1946–1998), a former infantryman, wrote a letter to Congress, forcing an investigation that made available the pertinent documents, some of which are reproduced here.

QUESTIONS TO CONSIDER

1. Why did Ronald L. Ridenhour write his letter? Does the letter convincingly present the need for an investigation? Explain.
2. Are there any indications in the documents that military personnel present during the raid objected to what was happening?

LETTER TO CONGRESS FROM RON RIDENHOUR

Mr. Ron Ridenhour
1416 East Thomas Road #104
Phoenix, Arizona
March 29, 1969

Gentlemen:

It was late in April, 1968 that I first heard of "Pinkville"[1] and what allegedly happened there. I received that first report with some skepticism, but in the following months I was to hear similar stories from such a wide variety of people that it became impossible for me to disbelieve that something rather dark and bloody did indeed occur sometime in March, 1968 in a village called "Pinkville" in the Republic of Viet Nam. . . .

In late April, 1968 I was awaiting orders for a transfer from HHC, 11th Brigade to Company "E," 51st Inf. (LRP), when I happened to run into Pfc "Butch" Gruver, whom I had known in Hawaii. Gruver told me he had been assigned to "C" Company 1st of the 20th until April 1st when he transferred to the unit that I was headed for. During the course of our conversation he told me the first of many reports I was to hear of "Pinkville."

---

1. **"Pinkville":** Army slang for the vicinity around My Lai.

"Charlie" Company 1/20 had been assigned to Task Force Barker in late February, 1968 to help conduct "search and destroy" operations on the Batangan Peninsula, Barker's area of operation. The task force was operating out of L. F. Dottie, located five or six miles north of Quang Nhai [Ngai] city on Viet Namese National Highway 1. Gruver said that Charlie Company had sustained casualties; primarily from mines and booby traps, almost everyday from the first day they arrived on the peninsula. One village area was particularly troublesome and seemed to be infested with booby traps and enemy soldiers. It was located about six miles northeast of Quang Nhai city at approximate coordinates B.S. 728795. It was a notorious area and the men of Task Force Barker had a special name for it: they called it "Pinkville." One morning in the latter part of March, Task Force Barker moved out from its firebase headed for "Pinkville." Its mission: destroy the trouble spot and all of its inhabitants.

When "Butch" told me this I didn't quite believe that what he was telling me was true, but he assured me that it was and went on to describe what had happened. The other two companies that made up the task force cordoned off the village so that "Charlie" Company could move through to destroy the structures and kill the inhabitants. Any villagers who ran from Charlie Company were stopped by the encircling companies. I asked "Butch" several times if all the people were killed. He said that he thought they were, men, women and children. He recalled seeing a small boy, about three or four years old, standing by the trail with a gunshot wound in one arm. The boy was clutching his wounded arm with his other hand, while blood trickled between his fingers. He was staring around himself in shock and disbelief at what he saw. "He just stood there with big eyes staring around like he didn't understand; he didn't believe what was happening. Then the captain's RTO (radio operator) put a burst of 16 (M-16 rifle) fire into him." It was so bad, Gruver said, that one of the men in his squad shot himself in the foot in order to be medivac-ed out of the area so that he would not have to participate in the slaughter. Although he had not seen it, Gruver had been told by people he considered trustworthy that one of the company's officers, 2nd Lieutenant Kally (this spelling may be incorrect) [Calley] had rounded up several groups of villagers (each group consisting of a minimum of 20 persons of both sexes and all ages). According to the story, Kally then machine-gunned each group. Gruver estimated that the population of the village had been 300 to 400 people and that very few, if any, escaped.

After hearing this account I couldn't quite accept it. Somehow I just couldn't believe that not only had so many young American men participated in such an act of barbarism, but that their officers had ordered it. There were other men in the unit I was soon to be assigned to, "E" Company, 51st Infantry (LRP), who had been in Charlie Company at the time that Gruver alleged the incident at "Pinkville" had occurred. I became determined to ask them about "Pinkville" so that I might compare their accounts with Pfc Gruver's.

When I arrived at "Echo" Company, 51st Infantry (LRP) the first men I looked for were Pfc's Michael Terry, and William Doherty. Both were veterans of "Charlie" Company, 1/20 and "Pinkville." Instead of contradicting "Butch"

Gruver's story they corroborated it, adding some tasty tidbits of information of their own. Terry and Doherty had been in the same squad and their platoon was the third platoon of "C" Company to pass through the village. Most of the people they came to were already dead. Those that weren't were sought out and shot. The platoon left nothing alive, neither livestock nor people. Around noon the two soldiers' squad stopped to eat. "Billy and I started to get out our chow," Terry said, "but close to us was a bunch of Vietnamese in a heap, and some of them were moaning. Kally (2nd Lt. Kally) had been through before us and all of them had been shot, but many weren't dead. It was obvious that they weren't going to get any medical attention so Billy and I got up and went over to where they were. I guess we sort of finished them off." Terry went on to say that he and Doherty then returned to where their packs were and ate lunch. He estimated the size of the village to be 200 to 300 people. Doherty thought that the population of "Pinkville" had been 400 people.

If Terry, Doherty and Gruver could be believed, then not only had "Charlie" Company received orders to slaughter all the inhabitants of the village, but those orders had come from the commanding officer of Task Force Barker, or possibly even higher in the chain of command. Pfc Terry stated that when Captain Medina (Charlie Company's commanding officer Captain Ernest Medina) issued the order for the destruction of "Pinkville" he had been hesitant, as if it were something he didn't want to do but had to. Others I spoke to concurred with Terry on this.

It was June before I spoke to anyone who had something of significance to add to what I had already been told of the "Pinkville" incident. It was the end of June, 1968 when I ran into Sargent Larry La Croix at the USO in Chu Lai. La Croix had been in 2nd Lt. Kally's platoon on the day Task Force Barker swept through "Pinkville." What he told me verified the stories of the others, but he also had something new to add. He had been a witness to Kally's gunning down of at least three separate groups of villagers. "It was terrible. They were slaughtering the villagers like so many sheep." Kally's men were dragging people out of bunkers and hootches and putting them together in a group. The people in the group were men, women and children of all ages. As soon as he felt that the group was big enough, Kally ordered an M-60 (machine-gun) set up and the people killed. La Croix said that he bore witness to this procedure at least three times. The three groups were of different sizes, one of about twenty people, one of about thirty people, and one of about forty people. When the first group was put together Kally ordered Pfc Torres to man the machine-gun and open fire on the villagers that had been grouped together. This Torres did, but before everyone in the group was down he ceased fire and refused to fire again. After ordering Torres to recommence firing several times, Lieutenant Kally took over the M-60 and finished shooting the remaining villagers in that first group himself. Sargent La Croix told me that Kally didn't bother to order anyone to take the machine-gun when the other two groups of villagers were formed. He simply manned it himself and shot down all villagers in both groups.

This account of Sargent La Croix's confirmed the rumors that Gruver, Terry and Doherty had previously told me about Lieutenant Kally. It also convinced me that there was a very substantial amount of truth to the stories that all of these men had told. If I needed more convincing, I was to receive it.

It was in the middle of November, 1968 just a few weeks before I was to return to the United States for separation from the army that I talked to Pfc Michael Bernhardt. Bernhardt had served his entire year in Viet Nam in "Charlie" Company 1/20 and he too was about to go home. "Bernie" substantiated the tales told by the other men I had talked to in vivid, bloody detail and added this. "Bernie" had absolutely refused to take part in the massacre of the villagers of "Pinkville" that morning and he thought that it was rather strange that the officers of the company had not made an issue of it. But that evening "Medina (Captain Ernest Medina) came up to me ("Bernie") and told me not to do anything stupid like write my congressman" about what had happened that day. Bernhardt assured Captain Medina that he had no such thing in mind. He had nine months left in Viet Nam and felt that it was dangerous enough just fighting the acknowledged enemy.

Exactly what did, in fact, occur in the village of "Pinkville" in March, 1968 I do not know for *certain*, but I am convinced that it was something very black indeed. I remain irrevocably persuaded that if you and I do truly believe in the principles of justice and the equality of every man, however humble, before the law, that form the very backbone that this country is founded on, then we must press forward a widespread and public investigation of this matter with all our combined efforts. I think that it was Winston Churchill who once said "A country without a conscience is a country without a soul, and a country without a soul is a country that cannot survive." I feel that I must take some positive action on this matter. I hope that you will launch an investigation immediately and keep me informed of your progress. If you cannot, then I don't know what other course of action to take.

I have considered sending this to newspapers, magazines, and broadcasting companies, but I somehow feel that investigation and action by the Congress of the United States is the appropriate procedure, and as a conscientious citizen I have no desire to further besmirch the image of the American serviceman in the eyes of the world. I feel that this action, while probably it would promote attention, would not bring about the constructive actions that the direct actions of the Congress of the United States would.

Sincerely
/s/ Ron Ridenhour

TESTIMONY OF ROBERT T'SOUVAS

Q: Have you ever heard of Pinkville?

A: Yes. As far as I remember Pinkville consisted of My Lai (4), My Lai (5), and My Lai (6), and maybe some other Hamlets. The Pinkville area was mostly our area of operation, to my knowledge.

Q: Is there one operation in the Pinkville area that stands out in your mind?

A: Yes. In March 1968 we went on an operation to My Lai (4) which is in the Pinkville area. This area stands out in my mind because there was so many women, children, and men killed.

I do not remember the name of my Platoon Leader or my Platoon Sergeant. After we got out of the helicopters, we organized. As soon as I got out the helicopter threw a smoke bomb and I and my Squad were told to look for the Viet Cong in the vicinity where the helicopter had dropped the smoke bomb. Names are hard to remember and I do not know at this time who the soldiers were that accompanied me. We searched for the Viet Cong, but we could not find them until the helicopter radioed and hovered at a certain spot right over the Viet Cong. Personnel in our Company went to the busy area and found a weapon. I do not know if they found the Viet Cong. I was there with my machine gun. After this my Platoon moved into the Hamlet and we just had to search and destroy mission. I seen people shot that didn't have weapons. I've seen the hootches burn, animals killed—just like saying going to Seoul and start burning hootches and shooting—a massacre wherein innocent people were being killed, hootches being burned, everything destroyed. They had no weapons and we were told that they were VC sympathizers. To come right to the point, we carried out our orders to the very point—Search and Destroy. In my mind, that covered the whole situation.

Q: How many people do you think was shot by C Company in My Lai (4)?

A: This is hard to say—from my personal observation I would say 80 that I have seen myself.

Q: What did the people that you saw shot consist of?

A: Women, men, children and animals.

Q: Did you at anytime receive hostile fire?

A: I was told that we were fired upon, but I myself did not receive direct fire.

Q: Were there still any people living in the Hamlet when you came through?

A: When we got there there was still people alive in the Hamlet and the Company was shooting them, however, when we left the Hamlet there was still some people alive.

Q: Did you see a trail in the village with a pile of dead women and children?

A: I seen dead women, children and men in groups and scattered on the trails and the rice paddies. I seen people running and just innocently being shot.

Q: Did you shoot 2 wounded children laying on the trail outside of My Lai (4)?

A: I opened up on people that were running. I do not remember that I shot at 2 children that were laying down on the trail. However, I do remember I did shoot a girl that was sitting there amongst 5 or more people, sitting there completely torn apart. She was screaming. I felt just as if it was my mother dying. I shot her to get her out of her misery. She was around 15. This happened inside the hamlet. However, I do not remember about the 2 children laying on the trail. I also shot 5 wounded villagers because they did not give them medical aid. They refused to give them medical aid. . . .

Q: Was the combat assault on My Lai (4) different than any of the others you were on?

A: Yes, I never heard anything so stupid as to search and destroy and to kill all those people.

Q: Is there anything else you would like to say?

A: I wanted to talk about this for a long time—and am glad now that it is off my chest—it is wrong. Even before it was investigated, I wanted to write about it to my Senator, but I didn't know how to go about it. This is all that I know about the incident. It is such a long time ago and it is hard to remember the exact sequence of events and I am not too good a map reader and I will not be able to draw a sketch of the Hamlet and show how we went through the Hamlet.

JOURNAL OF THOMAS R. PARTSCH

Mar. 16 Sat.

Got up at 5:30 left at 7:15 we had 9 choppers. 2 lifts first landed had mortar team with us. We started to move slowly through the village shooting everything in sight children men and women and animals. Some was sickening. There legs were shot off and they were still moving it was just hanging there. I think there bodies were made of rubber. I didn't fire a round yet and didn't kill anybody not even a chicken I couldn't. We are [now] suppose to push through 2 more it is about 10 A.M. and we are taken a rest before going in. We also got 2 weapons M1 and a carbine our final destination is the Pinkville suppose to be cement bunkers we killed about 100 people after a while they said not to kill women and children. Stopped for chow about 1 P.M. we didn't do much after that. . . .

Mar. 17 Sun.

Got up at 6:30 foggy out. We didn't go to Pinkville went to My Lai 2, 3, and 4 no one was there we burned as we pushed. We got 4 VC and a nurse. . . .

Mar. 18 Mon.

We got with company and CA out to Dottie [their base] there is a lot of fuss on what happened at the village a Gen was asking questions. There is going to be an investigation on MEDINA. We are not supposed to say anything. I didn't think it was right but we did it at least I can say I didn't kill anybody. I think I wanted to but in another way I didn't.

CAPTAIN BRIAN LIVINGSTON'S LETTER TO HIS WIFE

Saturday 16 March 68

Dear Betz,

Well its been a long day, saw some nasty sights. I saw the insertion of infantry-men and were they animals. The[y] preped the area first, then a lot of women and kids left the village. Then a gun team from the shark[s], a notorious killer of civilians, used their minny guns, people falling dead on the road. I've never seen so many people dead in one spot. Ninety-five percent were women and kids. We told the grunts on the ground of some injured kids. They helped them al[l-]right. A captain walked up to this little girl, he turned away took five steps, and fired a volly of shots into her. This Negro sergeant started shooting people in the head. Finally our OH23 [a helicopter] saw some wounded kids, so we acted like medivacs. Another kid whom the grunts were going to "take care of" was next on our list. The OH23 took him to Quang Nai [Ngai] hospital. We had to do this while *we* held machine guns on our own troops—American troops. I'll tell you something it sure makes one wonder why we are here. I can also see why they hate helicopter pilots. If I ever [hear] a shark open his big mouth I'm going to shove my fist into his mouth.

We're trying to get the captain and sergeant afore mentioned reprimanded. I don't know if we will be successful, but we're trying. Enough for that.

Brian

47

GENERAL WESTMORELAND, PRESIDENT NIXON ET AL.

Cover-Up and Outcome

The period spanning March 1968, when the massacre at My Lai occurred, and December 1969, when the New York Times *and* Life *magazine broke the story, was tumultuous. The Reverend Martin Luther King Jr. and Robert Kennedy were assassinated; ghettos across the country erupted in riots; the Democratic National Convention degenerated into*

Peers Report, vol. 4, 245; *Peers Report*, vol. 4, exhibit M-22, 113; *Peers Report*, vol. 4, 401–5; *Peers Report*, vol. 4, 264–65; *Peers Report*, vol. 3, 261–62; *Peers Report*, vol. 2, bk. 24, 44–50; William C. Westmoreland, *A Soldier Reports* (New York: Doubleday, 1976), 377–78; Richard M. Nixon, *RN: The Memoirs of Richard Nixon* (New York: Grosset & Dunlap, 1978), 449–50.

violence; Alabama governor George Wallace ran a divisive presidential campaign; antiwar demonstrations escalated enormously; and despite a strategy of "disengagement" (that was being renamed Vietnamization), U.S. casualties were greater in 1969 than in any previous year.

With so much wrong, it became difficult to assign responsibility for the massacre. A thorough and careful investigation, directed by the highly respected general William R. Peers, recommended charges against fourteen officers: two generals, two colonels, two lieutenant colonels, four majors, two captains, and two first lieutenants. In the end, only Lieutenant William Calley was found guilty of killing. He was convicted of the deaths of "at least" twenty-two people and sentenced to life in prison. Several higher officers suffered administrative penalties: demotions, lost decorations, and letters of censure placed in their files for covering up the incident, although according to military law, they could have been held responsible for criminal acts of which they should have been aware. The documents included here present evidence of the cover-up and some of the reasons why it occurred.

Calley's conviction stirred intense controversy. Some regarded him as a scapegoat for higher-ranking officers; others argued that amid the confusion over who was a friend and who was an enemy in Vietnam, his acts could not be considered criminal. Jimmy Carter, then governor of Georgia, thought it unfair to single out Calley for punishment. President Richard Nixon reduced his sentence, and in March 1974 Calley was paroled. When hearing of Calley's parole, General Peers told reporters, "To think that out of all those men, only one, Lieutenant William Calley, was brought to justice. And now, he's practically a hero. It's a tragedy." In My Lai, Nyugen Bat, a hamlet chief who was not a Vietcong before the massacre, later recalled, "After the shooting, all the villagers became Communists."

QUESTIONS TO CONSIDER

1. Why did the Barker report and the Henderson investigation cover up the events at My Lai? What light does the Vietcong document throw on this question?
2. How does the testimony of Herbert L. Carter help you to understand why participants and observers at My Lai did not reveal what had happened?
3. How did General William Westmoreland explain the My Lai incident? How persuasive do you find his explanation?
4. Why did President Richard Nixon reduce Calley's sentence? Was that the right thing to do? Explain.

SERGEANT JAY ROBERTS, PRESS RELEASE ON MY LAI, 1968

CHU LAI, Vietnam—For the third time in recent weeks, the American Division's 11th Brigade infantrymen from Task Force Barker raided a Viet Cong stronghold known as "Pinkville" six miles northeast of Quang Ngai, killing 128 enemy in a running battle.

The action occurred in the coastal town of My Lai where, three weeks earlier, another company of the brigade's Task Force Barker fought its way out of a VC ambush, leaving 80 enemy dead.

The action began as units of the task force conducted a combat assault into a known Viet Cong stronghold. "Shark" gunships[1] of the 174th Aviation Company escorted the troops into the area and killed four enemy during the assault. Other choppers from the 123d Aviation Battalion killed two enemy.

"The combat assault went like clockwork," commented LTC Frank Barker, New Haven, Conn., the task force commander. "We had two entire companies on the ground in less than an hour."

A company led by CPT Ernest Medina, Schofield Barracks, Hawaii, killed 14 VC minutes after landing. They recovered two M1 rifles, a carbine, a short-wave radio and enemy documents.

CAPTAIN BRIAN LIVINGSTON'S LETTER TO HIS WIFE

19 March 68

Dear Betz,

. . . You remember I told you about the massacre I witnessed, well I read a follow-up story in the paper. The article said I quote "The American troops were in heavy combat with an unknown number of V.C. Two Americans were killed, seven wounded, and 128 V.C. killed." Thats a bunch of bull. I saw four V.C., that is, those with weapons, and the amazing thing about that, is two of them got away. It made me sick to watch it.

Brian

LIEUTENANT COLONEL FRANK A. BARKER JR., "COMBAT ACTION REPORT" ON MY LAI

28 March 1968

8. *Intelligence:* Enemy forces in the area of operation were estimated to be one local force battalion located in the vicinity of My Lai, BS 728795 as shown in Inclosure 1. This information was based upon previous combat operations in this area, visual reconnaissance, and PW and agent reports. During the operation it was estimated that only two local force companies supported by two to three local guerrilla platoons opposed the friendly forces. The area of operation consisted of six hamlets to varying degree of ruin, each separated by rice paddies which were bounded by a series of hedge rows and tree lines. The area was also honeycombed with tunnels and bunkers. . . .

9. *Mission:* To destroy enemy forces and fortifications in a VC base camp and to capture enemy personnel, weapons and supplies.

1. **"Shark" gunships:** Helicopters.

10. *Concept of Operation:* Task Force Barker conducts a helicopter assault on 160730 Mar 68 on a VC base camp vicinity BS 728795 with Company C, 1st Battalion, 20th Infantry landing to the west and Company B, 4th Battalion, 3d Infantry landing to the southeast of the VC base camp. Company A, 3d Battalion, 1st Infantry moves by foot to blocking positions north of the base camp prior to the helicopter assault. . . .

11. *Execution:* The order was issued on 14 March 1968. Coordination with supporting arms reconnaissance and positioning of forces was conducted on 15 Mar 68. On 160726 Mar 68 a three minute artillery preparation began on the first landing zone and at 0730 hours the first lift for Co C touched down while helicopter gunships provided suppressive fires. At 0747 hours the last lift of Co C was completed. The initial preparation resulted in 68 VC KIA's [killed in action] in the enemy's combat outpost positions. Co C then immediately attacked to the east receiving enemy small arms fire as they pressed forward. At 0809H a three minute artillery preparation on the second landing zone began and the first lift for Co B touched down at 0815 hours. At 0827 the last lift of Co B was completed and Co B moved to the north and east receiving only light enemy resistance initially. As Co B approached the area of the VC base camp, enemy defensive fires increased. One platoon from Co B flanked the enemy positions and engaged one enemy platoon resulting in 30 enemy KIA. Throughout the day Co B and Co C received sporadic sniper fire and encountered numerous enemy booby traps. . . . At 1715 hours Co C linked-up with Co B and both units went into a perimeter defense for the night in preparation for conducting search and destroy operations the next day. With the establishment of the night defensive position at 161800 March 1968 the operation was terminated.

12. *Results:*
   A. Enemy losses:
      (1) Personnel:
         128 KIA
         11 VCS CIA
      (2) Equipment captured:
         1 M-1 rifle
         2 M-1 carbines
         10 Chicom hand grenades
         8 US M-26 hand grenades
         410 rounds small arms ammo
         4 US steel helmets with liners
         5 US canteens with covers
         7 US pistol belts
         9 sets US web equipment[2]

---

2. **web equipment:** Belts for carrying supplies.

> 2 short wave transistor radios
> 3 boxes of medical supplies
>   (3) Equipment and facilities destroyed:
>   16 booby traps
>   1 large tunnel complex
>   14 small tunnel complexes
>   8 bunkers
>   numerous sets of web equipment
> B. Friendly losses:
>   2 US KHA [killed by hostile action]
>   11 US WHA [wounded by hostile action] . . .

15. *Commander Analysis:* This operation was well planned, well executed and successful. Friendly casualties were light and the enemy suffered heavily. On this operation the civilian population supporting the VC in the area numbered approximately 200. This created a problem in population control and medical care of those civilians caught in fires of the opposing forces. However, the infantry unit on the ground and helicopters were able to assist civilians in leaving the area and in caring for and/or evacuating the wounded.

A VIETCONG LEAFLET ON MY LAI

Since the Americans heavy loss in the spring they have become like wounded animals that are crazy and cruel. They bomb places where many people live, places which are not good choices for bombings, such as the cities within the provinces, especially in Hue, Saigon, and Ben Tre. In Hue the US newspapers reported that 70% of the homes were destroyed and 10,000 people killed or left homeless. The newspapers and radios of Europe also tell of the killing of the South Vietnamese people by the Americans. The English tell of the action where the Americans are bombing the cities of South Vietnam. The Americans will be sentenced first by the Public in Saigon. It is there where the people will lose sentiment for them because they bomb the people and all people will soon be against them. The world public objects to this bombing including the American public and that of its Allies. The American often shuts his eye and closes his ear and continues his crime.

In the operation of 15 March 1968 in Son Tinh District the American enemies went crazy. They used machine guns and every other kind of weapon to kill 500 people who had empty hands, in Tinh Khe (Son My) Village (Son Tinh District, Quang Ngai Province). There were many pregnant women some of which were only a few days from childbirth. The Americans would shoot everybody they saw. They killed people and cows, burned homes. There were some families in which all members were killed.

When the red evil Americans remove their prayer shirts they appear as barbaric men.

When the American wolves remove their sheepskin their sharp meat-eating teeth show. They drink our peoples blood with animal sentimentalities.

Our people must choose one way to beat them until they are dead, and stop wriggling.

COLONEL FRANK HENDERSON, REPORT OF INVESTIGATION OF MY LAI INCIDENT

24 April 1968

Commanding General
Americal Division
APO SF 96374

1. (U) An investigation has been conducted of the allegations cited in Inclosure 1. The following are the results of this investigation.

2. (C) On the day in question, 16 March 1968, Co C 1st Bn 20th Inf and Co B 4th Bn 3rd Inf as part of Task Force Barker, 11th Inf Bde, conducted a combat air assault in the vicinity of My Lai Hamlet (Son My Village) in eastern Son Tinh District. This area has long been an enemy strong hold, and Task Force Barker had met heavy enemy opposition in this area on 12 and 23 February 1968. All persons living in this area are considered to be VC or VC sympathizers by the District Chief. Artillery and gunship preparatory fire were placed on the landing zones used by the two companies. Upon landing and during their advance on the enemy positions, the attacking forces were supported by gunships from the 174th Avn Co and Co B, 23rd Avn Bn. By 1500 hours all enemy resistance had ceased and the remaining enemy forces had withdrawn. The results of this operation were 128 VC soldiers KIA. During preparatory fires and the ground action by the attacking companies 20 noncombatants caught in the battle area were killed. US Forces suffered 2 KHA and 10 WHA by booby traps and 1 man slightly wounded in the foot by small arms fire. No US soldier was killed by sniper fire as was the alleged reason for killing the civilians. Interviews with LTC Frank A. Barker, TF Commander; Maj Charles C. Calhoun, TF S3; CPT Ernest L. Medina, Co Co C, 1–20 and CPT Earl Michles, Co Co B, 4–3 revealed that at no time were any civilians gathered together and killed by US soldiers. The civilian habitants in the area began withdrawing to the southwest as soon as the operation began and within the first hour and a half all visible civilians had cleared the area of operations.

3. (C) The Son Tinh District Chief does not give the allegations any importance and he pointed out that the two hamlets where the incident is alleged to have happened are in an area controlled by the VC since 1964. CC Toen, Cmdr 2d ARVN [Army of the Republic of Vietnam] Div reported that the making of such allegations against US Forces is a common technique of the VC propaganda machine. Inclosure 2 is a translation of an actual VC propaganda message targeted at the ARVN soldier and urging him to shoot Americans. This message was given to this headquarters by the CO, 2d ARVN

Division o/a 17 April 1968 as matter of information. It makes the same allegations as made by the Son My Village Chief in addition to other claims of atrocities by American soldiers.

4. (C) It is concluded that 20 non-combatants were inadvertently killed when caught in the area of preparatory fires and in the cross fires of the US and VC forces on 16 March 1968. It is further concluded that no civilians were gathered together and shot by US soldiers. The allegation that US Forces shot and killed 450–500 civilians is obviously a Viet Cong propaganda move to discredit the United States in the eyes of the Vietnamese people in general and the ARVN soldier in particular.

5. (C) It is recommended that a counter-propaganda campaign be waged against the VC in eastern Son Tinh District.

TESTIMONY OF HERBERT L. CARTER

Q: Did you ever hear anything about an investigation into the My Lai incident?

A: Yes.

Q: What did you hear?

A: I heard that they said if anybody asks around or any questions about what happened at My Lai, to tell them that we were fired upon and say that a sniper round had come in or something.

Q: Whom did you hear this from?

A: I was in the hospital at this time at Qui Nhon, and a couple of guys from the company came over. I'm not bragging, but most of the guys in that company liked me. I didn't bother nobody. I did my job and they did their job. We drank together.

Q: They came to see you in the hospital?

A: Yes. A lot of guys came over. You know, when they came back through, they would come over.

Q: Captain MEDINA told us that soon after this operation he got the company together and told them that there was an investigation and it would be better if nobody talked about it while the investigation was underway. Did your friends say anything about this?

A: No. The way they ran it down to me was like somebody was trying to cover something up or something, which I knew they were. They had to cover up something like that.

Q: I think you know that it took a long time for the story of My Lai to get out. What is your opinion as to why this wasn't reported right at the time? You did mention about some of your friends coming and telling you to keep quiet. Do you know anything else?

A: Like a lot of people wondered how come I didn't say something. Now, who would believe me. I go up to you with a story like that and you would call me a nut. You would tell me I am a nut and that there was nothing like this going on. You would think that nothing like this goes on in the United States.

Just like I was in a bar a couple of weeks ago, and there was a drunk in there. He was standing there reading a paper and he was asking me if I believed that things like that actually went on, and I said, "I wouldn't know, pal." It was kind of weird. This happened three different times. One time I was sitting up there with a friend of mine, and my partner told me to be quiet about the whole mess. Some people want to talk that talk all day long, and they just don't know this and that about what they are talking about.

Q: Did you or the other members of the company ever think about these killings as a war crime?

A: Not at that time. No. I didn't want to think about anything at the time.

Q: In your statement to Mr. CASH you spoke of it as murder?

A: Yes.

Q: You looked at it as being murder, but you didn't think about it as being a war crime?

A: That's right. I thought it was just the poor misfortunes of war.

GENERAL WILLIAM C. WESTMORELAND

In the criminal cases, acquittal resulted in all but that of a platoon leader, First Lieutenant William L. Calley Jr. Charged with the murder of more than a hundred civilians, he was convicted on March 29, 1971, of the murder of "at least" twenty-two. He was sentenced to dismissal from the service and confinement at hard labor for life, but the latter was reduced by judicial review to twenty years and further reduced after my retirement by Secretary of the Army Howard Callaway to ten years, an action that President Nixon sustained. The case was subsequently and for a long time under judicial appeal in the federal courts.

Lieutenant Calley was legally judged by a jury whose members all were familiar with the nature of combat in Vietnam and well aware that even the kind of war waged in Vietnam is no license for murder. The vast majority of Americans in Vietnam did their best to protect civilian lives and property, often at their own peril. That some civilians, even many, died by accident or inevitably in the course of essential military operations dictated by the enemy's presence among the people was no justification or rationale for the conscious massacre of defenseless babies, children, mothers, and old men in a kind of diabolical slow-motion nightmare that went on for the better part of a day, with a cold-blooded break for lunch. I said at the time of the revelation: "It could not have happened—but it did."

Although I can in no way condone Lieutenant Calley's acts—or those of any of his colleagues who may have participated but went unpunished—I must have compassion for him. Judging from the events at My Lai, being an officer in the United States Army exceeded Lieutenant Calley's abilities. Had it not been for educational draft deferments, which prevented the Army from drawing upon the intellectual segment of society for its junior officers, Calley probably never would have been an officer. Denied that usual reservoir of talent, the Army had to lower its standards. Although some who became officers under those conditions performed well, others, such as Calley, failed.

An army has a corps of officers to insure leadership: to see that orders are given and carried out and that the men conduct themselves properly. Setting aside the crime involved, Lieutenant Calley's obvious lack of supervision and failure to set a proper example himself were contrary to orders and policy, and the supervision he exercised fell far short.

In reducing standards for officers, both the United States Army and the House Armed Services Committee, which originated the policy of deferments for college students, must bear the blame. It would have been better to have gone short of officers than to have accepted applicants whose credentials left a question as to their potential as leaders.

PRESIDENT RICHARD M. NIXON

On March 29, 1971, just days after the withdrawal of ARVN troops from Laos, First Lieutenant William Calley Jr. was found guilty by an Army court-martial of the premeditated murder of twenty-two South Vietnamese civilians. . . .

It was in March 1968, ten months before I became President, that Calley led his platoon into My Lai, a small hamlet about 100 miles northeast of Saigon. The village had been a Vietcong stronghold, and our forces had suffered many casualties trying to clear it out. Calley had his men round up the villagers and then ordered that they be shot; many were left sprawled lifeless in a drainage ditch.

Calley's crime was inexcusable. But I felt that many of the commentators and congressmen who professed outrage about My Lai were not really as interested in the moral questions raised by the Calley case as they were interested in using it to make political attacks against the Vietnam War. For one thing, they had been noticeably uncritical of North Vietnamese atrocities. In fact, the calculated and continual role that terror, murder, and massacre played in the Vietcong strategy was one of the most underreported aspects of the entire Vietnam War. Much to the discredit of the media and the antiwar activists, this side of the story was only rarely included in descriptions of Vietcong policy and practices.

On March 31 the court-martial sentenced Calley to life in prison at hard labor. Public reaction to this announcement was emotional and sharply divided. More than 5,000 telegrams arrived at the White House, running 100 to 1 in favor of clemency.

John Connally and Jerry Ford[3] recommended in strong terms that I use my powers as Commander in Chief to reduce Calley's prison time. Connally said that justice had been served by the sentence, and that now the reality of maintaining public support for the armed services and for the war had to be

3. **John Connally and Jerry Ford:** Connally was Secretary of the Treasury under Richard Nixon; Gerald Ford (Republican) was U.S. House of Representatives minority leader and later president.

given primary consideration. I talked to Carl Albert and other congressional leaders. All of them agreed that emotions in Congress were running high in favor of presidential intervention.

I called Admiral Moorer on April 1 and ordered that, pending Calley's appeal, he should be released from the stockade and confined instead to his quarters on the base. When this was announced to the House of Representatives, there was a spontaneous round of applause on the floor. Reaction was particularly strong and positive in the South. George Wallace, after a visit with Calley, said that I had done the right thing. Governor Jimmy Carter of Georgia said that I had made a wise decision. Two days later I had Ehrlichman[4] announce that I would personally review the Calley case before any final sentence was carried out.

By April 1974, Calley's sentence had been reduced to ten years, with eligibility for parole as early as the end of that year. I reviewed the case as I had said I would but decided not to intervene. Three months after I resigned, the Secretary of the Army decided to parole Calley.

I think most Americans understood that the My Lai massacre was not representative of our people, of the war we were fighting, or of our men who were fighting it; but from the time it first became public the whole tragic episode was used by the media and the antiwar forces to chip away at our efforts to build public support for our Vietnam objectives and policies.

FOR CRITICAL THINKING

1. Why did the My Lai massacre occur? Does the response to it, including both the cover-up and the outcome, suggest how it happened?
2. What responsibility did higher-ranking officers bear for the massacre? What policies encouraged such atrocities?
3. Should William Calley have been required to serve a larger part of his sentence, or were the actions of President Richard Nixon and other officials appropriate? Explain.
4. General William Westmoreland claimed that "the vast majority of Americans in Vietnam did their best to protect civilian lives and property, often at their own peril," while President Nixon argued strenuously that My Lai "was not representative of our people, of the war we were fighting, or of our men who were fighting it." Judging from these documents and what else you may know about the Vietnam War, do you agree with these statements? Would Ronald Ridenhour have agreed with them? What about Captain Brian Livingston? Why or why not?

---

4. **Ehrlichman:** John Ehrlichman, one of President Nixon's closest advisers.

48

NAOMI WEISSTEIN

The Adventures of a Woman in Science in the 1960s

During the twentieth century, America led a revolution in educational access. In 1900, only the most privileged 6 percent of the population had a high school degree and less than 1 percent had finished at least four years of college. By the 1950s earning a high school diploma was the norm. This was as much the case for women as it was for men. When Naomi Weisstein (1939–2015) started her PhD in psychology in the early 1960s men still outnumbered women in colleges by almost two to one, and women rarely attended graduate school. Men received their doctorates at a rate that was over 800 percent higher than that of women, and employment prejudices further winnowed out women at professional levels.

This vast expansion of educational access for both sexes during the mid-twentieth century collided with neo-traditionalist beliefs criticizing women who worked outside the home. A generation of women growing up after World War II found they were being offered new opportunities with one hand only to have old ones taken away with the other. During the 1960s a generation of highly educated young women whose ambitions at school and work were being blocked by sexism rose up to confront the inequality and discrimination they faced in their personal and professional lives. They began to challenge the male domination of work, education, and domestic life. This movement came to be called the women's movement *or* feminism.

While women continue to earn about 20 percent less than men do for the same work, they outperform men at every level of education and in all academic subjects. They also outnumber men at the college level. Researchers and policymakers no longer question girls' and women's academic abilities, even in fields such as mathematics and science; the issue now is how to keep men in school and help them achieve educational outcomes that are equal to those of women.

In the following passage Weisstein describes her early feminist journey through the scientific world during the difficult days for women in the 1960s before the women's liberation movement. She went on to become an internationally known scientist, an American feminist leader, the director of a major research institute, and the founder of the first women's liberation rock band.

Naomi Weisstein, " 'How can a little girl like you teach a great big class of men?' the Chairman Said, and Other Adventures of a Woman in Science," in Sara Ruddick and Pamela Daniels, eds., *Working It Out: 23 Women Writers, Artists, Scientists, and Scholars Talk About Their Lives and Work* (New York: Pantheon Books, 1977), 242–50.

QUESTIONS TO CONSIDER

1. It took much longer for women to catch up to men in science and mathematics than in other academic fields. What do you think Naomi Weisstein would say was the reason for that?
2. Naomi Weisstein went to a women's college. In what ways do you think that benefited her? In what ways did it make things more difficult?
3. Do you think that any of the problems she describes exist today? If so, which ones?
4. Elizabeth Blackwell, the United States' first woman doctor, described being warmly welcomed into medical school by 150 male students in 1847. What might have been different for women like Naomi Weisstein over 100 years later?
5. Weisstein argues that her professional survival depended on feminism. What do you think she means?

I am an experimental psychologist. I do research in vision. At the time I entered graduate school in the early sixties, I was not prepared for the discovery that women were not welcome in science, primarily because nobody had told me. I graduated from the Bronx High School of Science in New York City where gender did not enter very much into intellectual pursuits.

I ended up at Wellesley: the women faculty at Wellesley were brilliant. (I learned later on that they were at Wellesley because the schools that had graduated them,—the "very best" schools where you were taught to do the very best research—couldn't, or didn't care to, place them in similar schools, where they could continue their research.) So they are our brilliant unknowns, unable to do research because they labor under enormous teaching loads, unable to obtain the minimal support necessary for scholarship—graduate students, facilities, communication with colleagues.

So my discovery that women were not welcome in psychology began when I got to Harvard, on the first day of class. That day, the entering graduate students had been invited to lunch with one of the star professors in the department. After lunch, he leaned back in his chair, lit his pipe, began to puff, and announced: "Women don't belong in graduate school."

The male graduate students, as if by prearranged signal, then leaned back in their chairs, puffed on their newly bought pipes, nodded, and assented: "Yeah."

"Yeah," said the male graduate students. "No man is going to want you. No man wants a woman who is more intelligent than he is. Of course, that's not a real possibility, but just in case. You are out of your *natural* roles; you are no longer feminine."

My mouth dropped open, and my big blue eyes (they have since changed back to brown) went wide as saucers. An initiation ceremony, I thought. Very funny. Tomorrow, for sure, the male graduate students will get it.

But the male graduate students never were told that they didn't belong. They rapidly became trusted junior partners in the great research firms at

Harvard. They were carefully nurtured, groomed, and run. Before long, they would take up the white man's burden and expand the empire. But for me and for the other women in my class, it was different. We were shut out of these plans; we were *shown* we didn't belong. For instance, even though I was first in my class, when I wanted to do my dissertation research, I couldn't get access to the necessary equipment. The excuse was that I might break the equipment. This was certainly true. The equipment was eminently breakable. The male graduate students working with it broke it every week; I didn't expect to be any different.

I was determined to collect my data. I had to see how the experiment I proposed would turn out. If Harvard wouldn't let me use its equipment, maybe Yale would. I moved to New Haven, collected my data at Yale, returned to Harvard, and was awarded my Ph.D. in 1964, and afterward could not get an academic job. I had graduated Phi Beta Kappa from Wellesley, had obtained my Ph.D. in psychology at Harvard in two and one half years, ranked first in my graduate class, and I couldn't get a job. Yet most universities were expanding in 1964, and jobs were everywhere. But at the places where I was being considered for jobs they were asking me questions like—

"How can a little girl like you teach a great big class of men?" At that time, still unaware of how serious the situation was, I replied, "Beats me. I guess I must have a talent."

and

"Who did your research for you?" This last was from a famous faculty liberal at another school, who then put what I assume was a fatherly hand on my knee and said in a tone of deep concern, "You ought to get married."

Meanwhile, I was hanging on by means of a National Science Foundation postdoctoral fellowship in mathematical biology, at the University of Chicago, and attempting to do some research. Prior to my second postdoctoral year, the University of Chicago began negotiations with me for something like a real job: an instructorship jointly in the undergraduate college and the psychology department. The negotiations appeared to be proceeding in good faith, so I wrote to Washington and informed them that I would not be taking my second postdoctoral year. Then, ten days before classes began, when that option as well as any others I might have taken had been closed, the person responsible for the negotiations called to tell me that, because of a nepotism rule—my husband taught history at the University of Chicago— I would not be hired as a regular faculty member. If I wanted to, I could be appointed lecturer, teaching general education courses in the college; there was no possibility of an appointment in psychology. The lectureship paid very little for a lot of work, and I would be teaching material unconnected with my research. Furthermore, a university rule stipulated that lecturers (because their position in the university was so insecure) could not apply for research grants.

I took the job, and "sat in," so to speak, in the office of another dean, until he waived the restriction on applying for research grants. Acknowledging my presence, he told a colleague: "This is Naomi Weisstein. She hates men."

I had simply been telling him that women are considered unproductive precisely because universities do their best to keep women unproductive through such procedures as the selective application of the nepotism rule. I had also asked this dean whether I could read through the provisions of the rule. He replied that the nepotism rule was informal, not a written statute—flexibility being necessary in its application.

Lecturers at major universities are generally women. They are generally married to men who teach at these major universities. And they generally labor under conditions which seem almost designed to show them that they don't belong. In many places, they are not granted faculty library privileges; in my case, I had to get a note from the secretary each time I wanted to take a book out for an extended period. Lecturers' classrooms are continually changed; at least once a month, I would go to my assigned classroom only to find a note pinned to the door instructing me and my class to go elsewhere: down the hall, across the campus, out to Gary, Indiana.

In the winter of my first year, notices were distributed to all those teaching the courses I was teaching, announcing a meeting to discuss the next year's syllabus. I didn't receive the notice. As I was to learn shortly, this is the customary way a profession that prides itself on its civility and genteel traditions indicates to lecturers and other "nuisance personnel" that they're fired: they simply don't inform them about what's going on. A little while later, Loyola University in Chicago offered me a job.

I was awarded the research grant and found the Psychology Department at Loyola at first very supportive. The chairman, Ron Walker, was especially helpful and especially enlightened about women at a time when few academic men were. I was on my way, right? Not exactly. There is a big difference between a place like Loyola and a place with a heavy commitment to research—any large state university, for example—a difference that no amount of good will on the part of an individual chairman could cancel out. The Psychology Department was one of the few active departments at Loyola. The other kinds of support one needs to do experimental psychology—machine and electrical shops, physics and electrical engineering departments, technicians, a large computer—were either not available or were available at that time only in primitive form.

When you are a woman at an "unknown" place, you are considered out of the running. It was hard for me to keep my career from "shriveling like a raisin" (as an erstwhile colleague predicted it would). I was completely isolated. I did not have access to the normal channels of communication, debate, and exchange in the profession—those informal networks where you get the news, the comment and the criticism, the latest reports of what is going on. I sent my manuscripts to various people for comment and criticism before sending them off to journals; few replied. I asked others working in my field to send me their prepublication drafts; even fewer responded. Nobody outside Loyola informed me about special meetings in my area of psychology, and few inside Loyola knew about them. Given the snobbery rife in academic circles (which has eased lately since jobs are much harder to find and thus even "outstanding" young male graduates from the "best" schools may now be found at places formerly beneath their condescension), my being at Loyola almost automatically disqualified me from the serious attention of professional colleagues.

The "inner reaches" of the profession, from which I had been exiled, are not just metaphorical and intangible. For instance, I am aware of two secret societies of experimental psychologists in which fifty or so of the "really excellent" young scientists get together regularly to make themselves better scientists. The ostensible purpose of these societies is to allow these "best and brightest" young psychologists to get together to discuss and criticize each other's work; they also function, of course, to define who is excellent and who is not, and to help those defined as excellent to remain so, by providing them with information to which "outsiders" in the profession will not have access until much later (if at all).

But the intangibles are there as well. Women are treated in ways men hardly ever experience. Let me give you one stunning example. I wrote up an experiment I thought was really good and its results, which were fascinating, and sent the paper to a journal editor whose interests I knew to be close to what was reported in my paper. The editor replied that there were some control conditions that should be run, and some methodological loose ends, so they couldn't publish the paper. Fair enough. He went on to say that they had much better equipment over there, and they would like to test my ideas themselves. Would I mind? I wrote them back, told them I thought it was a bit unusual, asked if they were suggesting a collaboration, and concluded by saying that I would be most happy to visit with them and collaborate on my experiment. The editor replied with a nasty letter explaining to me that by suggesting that they test my ideas themselves, they had merely been trying to help me. If I didn't want their help in this way, they certainly didn't want mine, that is, they had had no intention of suggesting a collaboration.

In other words, what they meant by "did I mind" was: Did I mind if they took my idea and did the experiment themselves? As we know, instances of taking someone else's idea and pretending it's your own are not at all uncommon in science. The striking thing about this exchange, however, was that the editor was arrogant enough, and assumed that I would be submissive enough, so that he could openly ask me whether I would agree to this arrangement. Would I mind? No, of course not. Women are joyful altruists. We are happy to give of ourselves. After all, how many good ideas do you get in your lifetime? One? Two? Why not give them away?

Generally, the justification for treating women in such disgraceful ways is simply that they are women. Let me give another spectacular example. I was promised the use of a small digital laboratory computer, which was to be purchased on a grant. The funds from the grant would become available if a certain job position entailing administration of this grant could be filled. I was part of the group which considered the candidates and which recommended appointing a particular individual. During the discussions of future directions of this individual's work, it was agreed that he would of course share the computer with me. He was hired, bought the computer, and refused me access to it. As justification for his conduct, the man confessed to the chairman that he simply couldn't share the computer with me: he has difficulty working with women. To back this up, he indicated that he'd been "burned twice." Although the chairman had previously been very helpful and not bothered in the least about women, he accepted that statement as an explanation. Difficulty in working with women was not a problem this man should work out. It was *my* problem. Colleagues thought no worse of him for this problem; it might even have raised him in their estimation. He obtained tenure quickly, and retains an influential voice in the department. Yet if a woman comes to *any* chairman of *any* department and confesses that she has difficulty working with men, she is thought pathological.

What this meant for me at the time was that my research was in jeopardy. There were experimental conditions I needed to run that simply could not be done without a computer. So there I was, doing research with stone-age equipment, trying to get by with wonder-woman reflexes and a flashlight, while a few floors below, my colleague was happily operating "his" computer.

Perhaps the most painful of the appalling working conditions for women in science is the peculiar kind of social-sexual assault women sustain.

This harassment is especially clear at conventions. Scientific meetings, conferences, and conventions are harassing and humiliating for women because women, by and large, cannot have male colleagues. Conversations, social relations, invitations to lunch, and the like are generally viewed as sexual, not professional, encounters if a woman participates in them. It does not cross many men's minds that a woman's motivation may be entirely professional.

I have been at too many professional meetings where the "joke" slide was a woman's body, dressed or undressed. A woman in a bikini is a favorite with past and perhaps present presidents of psychological associations. Hake showed such a slide in his presidential address to the Midwestern Psychological Association, and Harlow, past president of the American Psychological Association, has a whole set of such slides, which he shows at the various colloquia to which he is invited. This business of making jokes at women's bodies constitutes a primary social-sexual assault. The ensuing raucous laughter expresses the shared understanding of what is assumed to be women's primary function—to which we can always be reduced. Showing pictures of nude and sexy women insults us: it puts us in our place. You may think you are a scientist, it is saying, but what you really are is an object for our pleasure and amusement. Don't forget it.

I could continue recounting the horrors, as could almost any woman who is in science or who has ever been in science, but I want to stop now and ask: What conclusions can we draw from my experience? What does it all add up to?

Perhaps we should conclude that persistence will finally win out. Or that life is hard, but cheerful struggle and a "sense of humor" may make it bearable. Or perhaps we should search back through my family, and find my domineering mother and passive father or my domineering father and passive mother, to explain my persistence. Perhaps, but all these conclusions are beside the point. The point is that none of us should have to face this kind of offense. The point is that we must change this man's world and this man's science.

How will other women do better? One of the dangers of this kind of narrative is that it may validate the punishment as it singles out the few survivors. The lesson appears to be that those (and only those) with extraordinary strength will survive. This is not the way I see it. Many have had extraordinary strength and have *not* survived.

Much of the explanation for my professional survival has to do with the emergence and growth of the women's movement. I am an experimental psychologist, a scientist. I am also a feminist. I am a feminist because I have seen my life and the lives of women I know harassed, dismissed, damaged, destroyed. I am a feminist because without others I can do little to stop the outrage. Without a political and social movement of which I am a part— without feminism—my determination and persistence, my clever retorts, my hours of patient explanation, my years of exhortation amount to little. If the scientific world has changed since I entered it, it is not because I managed to become an established psychologist within it. Rather, it is because a women's movement came along to change its character.

Science, knowledge, the search for fundamental understanding is part of our humanity. It is an endeavor that seems to give us some glimpse of what we might be and what we might do in a better world. To deny us the right to do science is to deny us our humanity. We shall not have our humanity denied.

49

PHYLLIS SCHLAFLY

The Limits of the Women's Movement

Phyllis Schlafly (b. 1924) answered the cry of the women's rights movement with a resounding "STOP," an acronym for Stop Taking Our Privileges. An attorney and conservative Republican activist, she spearheaded a successful grassroots campaign to block the ratification of the Equal Rights Amendment in the 1970s. Schlafly interpreted the feminist movement as a misguided effort to empower the federal government to mandate false ideals of "equality." She claimed that it ignored women's natural facility and moral responsibility to care for families and raise children, as well as the deep-seated sense of happiness

Phyllis Schlafly, "The Radical Goals of the Feminists," *Phyllis Schlafly Report*, December 1991, http://www.eagleforum.org/psr/1991/dec91/psrdec91.html.

and comfort that comes from performing these tasks. Through the Eagle Forum, a political interest group that she founded in 1972 and that still flourishes today, Schlafly created networks of conservative policymakers and maintained a steady protest against what she called the excesses of the civil rights movement.

One of Schlafly's nemeses was the National Organization for Women (NOW). Begun in 1966 as a liberal organization originally dedicated to erasing discrimination on the basis of sex, NOW soon became a leader in the political effort to expand women's right to reproductive freedom and to oppose racism and homophobia. In the following excerpts from an article written in 1991, Schlafly surveys and strongly criticizes NOW as an institution bent on forcing its officers and supporters to adopt a radical political agenda that contradicts the will of most Americans. At times bombastic (as when she wrongly states that NOW advocates the legalization of prostitution), this article demonstrates the range of opinions surrounding the women's rights movement.

QUESTIONS TO CONSIDER

1. Why was Phyllis Schlafly so upset by NOW's actions?
2. What strategy did Schlafly use to counter the civil rights movement?
3. How could Americans support the black freedom struggle, with its stress on equal rights and opportunities for all citizens, and still support Schlafly?

The American people [have] tended to forget how radical the feminists are—and the media [have] helped the feminists by not reporting their radical goals, their disgusting tactics, or their vulgar language. When you see feminists on television, they usually wear dresses, clean up their language, and sanctimoniously advocate "women's rights."

It is important to realize that, when the feminists talk about "women's rights," they don't mean fair treatment for women in jobs, school, or home. When feminists talk about "women's rights," they mean a radical restructuring of society, with government using its power to force feminist goals on all the rest of us.

What are those goals? The best way to find out is to read the resolutions passed by NOW at its annual convention. NOW's resolutions document what is meant by "feminism," namely, the Equal Rights Amendment, abortion on demand at any time during pregnancy and financed by the taxpayers, homosexual and lesbian privileges, affirmative action quotas for women, government child care, legalization of prostitution, assigning women to military combat duty, and political action at every level of government to achieve these goals.

In order to carry out its political objectives, NOW has two political action committees [PACs].[1] NOW/PAC endorses in federal elections, and NOW

---

1. **political action committees [PACs]:** Private voluntary organizations seeking to influence the election or appointment of a public official or the enactment or amendment of a piece of legislation.

Equality PAC endorses in state and local races. NOW's newspaper, called *National NOW Times* (Summer 1990), stated how NOW chooses the candidates it endorses:

> Criteria for endorsement include support for the Equal Rights Amendment; reproductive freedom including Medicaid funding for abortions and young women's rights; civil rights for all—including lesbian and gay rights; and legislation to decrease the feminization of poverty. Candidates for executive offices are also asked to support gender balance laws or commit to making appointments on a gender basis where there is no existing law. While NOW's PACs use the same standards when evaluating male and female candidates, it is NOW policy that women be given preference as candidates whenever possible.

Here is a translation of the NOW jargon used in the above criteria:

reproductive freedom means abortion on demand throughout nine months of pregnancy for any reason whatsoever;

Medicaid funding means taxpayer funding of abortions;

young women's rights means abortion for minor girls without parental consent;

civil rights for all means quota hiring for minorities and women;

lesbian and gay rights means the entire homosexual agenda, including privileges to teach in the classroom, adopt children, be Boy Scout leaders, etc.;

legislation to decrease the feminization of poverty means the entire feminist-liberal economic-social agenda, including federally financed and regulated daycare, Comparable Worth (that means government wage fixing), Federally Mandated Parental Leave (that means forcing employers to skew employee benefits in favor of feminist demands), Glass Ceiling (that means government forcing businesses to promote women to executive positions), the United Nations Treaty on Discrimination Against Women (that means an "Equal Rights Amendment" enforced on Americans by a commission of international busybodies), and repeal of all laws that exempt women from combat duty in the U.S. military;

gender balance laws or appointments on a gender basis means a candidate's commitment to appoint women—because they are women—instead of men to all government positions. (The goal is to humiliate men and put women in all positions of power and authority.)

Any candidate who is endorsed by NOW can be assumed to have endorsed all these positions.

The [full] resolution . . . uses the expression "consciousness raising." This is essentially a cult-type technique of indoctrinating vulnerable women with the message that women are oppressed victims, that men are the oppressors, and that a small cadre of bitter women should work together to demand power over men in order to "remedy centuries of oppression."

In consciousness-raising sessions, women exchange their horror stories about men and, with this kind of mutual sharing and encouragement, little slights are magnified into grievances, small grievances are transformed into bigger grievances, and women are able to blame "society" or "all men" for their own failures, mistakes, and disappointments. These women are falsely led to believe that a constitutional amendment called ERA is the key to whatever they want, whether it is a raise, a promotion, a husband, a divorce, child custody payments, or simply revenge against men for real or imagined grievances. This is the psychology of producing bitter—but dedicated—women activists.

50

STUDENT WORKERS
Mississippi Freedom Summer

In the summer of 1964, after nearly a decade of civil rights demonstrations, more than a thousand people, most of them Northern white college students, volunteered to travel to Mississippi to aid the movement. Their mission was to help African Americans register to vote and to teach black children African American history in "freedom schools." The Mississippi Freedom Summer project was a high point and nearly the end of the integrated, nonviolent civil rights movement of the 1950s and 1960s. Although twelve hundred new African American voters registered in the state, it was a hard summer. Consider this macabre score: at least one African American and two white civil rights workers were killed, not including an uncertain number of African American Mississippians who died mysteriously; more than eighty volunteers were wounded and more than a thousand were arrested; thirty-five African American churches were burned; and thirty homes and other buildings were bombed.

But another score also can be calculated. Mississippi Freedom Summer contributed to the success of the Voting Rights Act of 1965, which prohibits discrimination in voting practices because of race or color. This landmark legislation quickly secured the right to vote for millions of Southern blacks. Furthermore, the murders of James Chaney, Michael "Mickey" Schwerner, and Andrew Goodman forced federal authorities to infiltrate and destroy the Ku Klux Klan in Mississippi. These letters home from participants in the project (some supplied without attribution) testify to the intensity of the volunteers' experiences.

Elizabeth Sutherland, ed., *Letters from Mississippi* (New York: McGraw-Hill, 1965), 83, 93–94, 108–10, 172–73, 217–24.

QUESTIONS TO CONSIDER

1. What did the student workers learn about African Americans' lives in Mississippi in the 1960s?
2. What difficulties did they encounter there, and what were their rewards?
3. What did David Dennis argue in his eulogy for the murdered civil rights workers? Do you think his accusations were fair? Explain.

Mileston, August 18

Dear folks,

One can't move onto a plantation cold; or canvas a plantation in the same manner as the Negro ghetto in town. It's far too dangerous. Many plantations—homes included—are posted, meaning that no trespassing is permitted, and the owner feels that he has the prerogative to shoot us on sight when we are in the house of one of *his* Negroes.

Before we canvas a plantation, our preparation includes finding out whether the houses are posted, driving through or around the plantation without stopping, meanwhile making a detailed map of the plantation.

We're especially concerned with the number of roads in and out of the plantation. For instance, some houses could be too dangerous to canvas because of their location near the boss man's house and on a dead end road.

In addition to mapping, we attempt to talk to some of the tenants when they are off the plantation, and ask them about conditions. The kids often have contacts, and can get on the plantation unnoticed by the boss man, with the pretense of just visiting friends.

Our canvassing includes not only voter registration, but also extensive reports on conditions—wages, treatment by the boss man, condition of the houses, number of acres of cotton, etc. Much more such work needs to be done. The plantation system is crucial in Delta politics and economics, and the plantation system must be brought to an end if democracy is to be brought to the Delta. . . .

Love,
Joel

July 18

. . . Four of us went to distribute flyers announcing the meeting. I talked to a woman who had been down to register a week before. She was afraid. Her husband had lost his job. Even before we got there a couple of her sons had been man-handled by the police. She was now full of wild rumors about shootings and beatings, etc. I checked out two of them later. They were groundless. This sort of rumor-spreading is quite prevalent when people get really scared. . . .

At 6 P.M. we returned to Drew for the meeting, to be held in front of a church (they wouldn't let us meet inside, but hadn't told us not to meet outside). A number of kids collected and stood around in a circle with about

15 of us to sing freedom songs. Across the street perhaps 100 adults stood watching. Since this was the first meeting in town, we passed out mimeoed song sheets. Fred Miller, Negro from Mobile, stepped out to the edge of the street to give somebody a sheet. The cops nabbed him. I was about to follow suit so he wouldn't be alone, but Mac's[1] policy was to ignore the arrest. We sang on mightily "Ain't going to let no jailing turn me around." A group of girls was sort of leaning against the cars on the periphery of the meeting. Mac went over to encourage them to join us. I gave a couple of song sheets to the girls. A cop rushed across the street and told me to come along. I guess I was sort of aware that my actions would get me arrested, but felt that we had to show these girls that we were not afraid. I was also concerned with what might happen to Fred if he was the only one.

    . . . The cop at the station was quite scrupulous about letting me make a phone call. I was then driven to a little concrete structure which looked like a power house. I could hear Fred's courageous, off-key rendition of a freedom song from inside and joined him as we approached. He was very happy to see me. Not long thereafter, four more of our group were driven up to make their calls. . . .

                                                        Holly Springs

Dear Mom and Dad:

The atmosphere in class is unbelievable. It is what every teacher dreams about—real, honest enthusiasm and desire to learn anything and everything. The girls come to class of their own free will. They respond to everything that is said. They are excited about learning. They drain me of everything that I have to offer so that I go home at night completely exhausted but very happy. . . .

    I start out at 10:30 teaching what we call the Core Curriculum, which is Negro History and the History and Philosophy of the Movement, to about fifteen girls ranging from 15 to 25 years of age. I have one girl who is married with four children, another who is 23 and a graduate from a white college in Tennessee, also very poorly educated. The majority go to a Roman Catholic High School in Holly Springs and have therefore received a fairly decent education by Mississippi standards. They can, for the most part, express themselves on paper but their skills in no way compare to juniors and seniors in northern suburban schools.

    In one of my first classes, I gave a talk on Haiti and the slave revolt which took place at the end of the eighteenth century. I told them how the French government (during the French Revolution) abolished slavery all over the French Empire. And then I told them that the English decided to invade the island and take it over for a colony of their own. I watched faces fall all around

1. **Mac:** Charles McLaurin, the project director and a member of the Student Nonviolent Coordinating Committee (SNCC), a civil rights group.

me. They knew that a small island, run by former slaves, could not defeat England. And then I told them that the people of Haiti succeeded in keeping the English out. I watched a smile spread slowly over a girl's face. And I felt the girls sit up and look at me intently. Then I told them that Napoleon came to power, reinstated slavery, and sent an expedition to reconquer Haiti. Their faces began to fall again. They waited for me to tell them that France defeated the former slaves, hoping against hope that I would say that they didn't. But when I told them that the French generals tricked the Haitian leader Toussaint to come aboard their ship, captured him and sent him back to France to die, they knew that there was no hope. They waited for me to spell out the defeat. And when I told them that Haiti did succeed in keeping out the European powers and was recognized finally as an independent republic, they just looked at me and smiled. The room stirred with a gladness and a pride that this could have happened. And I felt so happy and so humble that I could have told them this little story and it could have meant so much.

We have also talked about what it means to be a Southern white who wants to stand up but who is alone, rejected by other whites and not fully accepted by the Negroes. We have talked about their feelings about Southern whites. One day three little white girls came to our school and I asked them to understand how the three girls felt by remembering how it feels when they are around a lot of whites. We agreed that we would not stare at the girls but try to make them feel as normal as possible. . . .

Every class is beautiful. The girls respond, respond, respond. And they disagree among themselves. I have no doubt that soon they will be disagreeing with me. At least this is one thing that I am working towards. They are a sharp group. But they are under-educated and starved for knowledge. They know that they have been cheated and they want anything and everything that we can give them.

I have a great deal of faith in these students. They are very mature and very concerned about other people. I really think that they will be able to carry on without us. At least this is my dream. . . .

Love,
Pam

Ruleville

To my brother,

Last night, I was a long time before sleeping, although I was extremely tired. Every shadow, every noise—the bark of a dog, the sound of a car—in my fear and exhaustion was turned into a terrorist's approach. And I believed that I heard the back door open and a Klansman walk in, until he was close by the bed. Almost paralyzed by the fear, silent, I finally shone my flashlight on the spot where I thought he was standing. . . . I tried consciously to overcome this fear. To relax, I began to breathe deep, think the words of a song, pull the sheet up close to my neck . . . still the tension. Then I rethought why

I was here, rethought what could be gained in view of what could be lost. All this was in rather personal terms, and then in larger scope of the whole Project. I remembered Bob Moses[2] saying he had felt justified in asking hundreds of students to go to Mississippi because he was not asking anyone to do something that he would not do. . . . I became aware of the uselessness of fear that immobilizes an individual. Then I began to relax.

"We are not afraid. Oh Lord, deep in my heart, I do believe. We Shall Overcome Someday" and then I think I began to truly understand what the words meant. Anyone who comes down here and is not afraid I think must be crazy as well as dangerous to this project where security is quite important. But the type of fear that they mean when they, when we, sing "we are not afraid" is the type that immobilizes. . . . The songs help to dissipate the fear. Some of the words in the songs do not hold real meaning on their own, others become rather monotonous—but when they are sung in unison, or sung silently by oneself, they take on new meaning beyond words or rhythm. . . . There is almost a religious quality about some of these songs, having little to do with the usual concept of a god. It has to do with the miracle that youth has organized to fight hatred and ignorance. It has to do with the holiness of the dignity of man. The god that makes such miracles is the god I do believe in when we sing "God is on our side." I know I am on that god's side. And I do hope he is on ours.

Jon, please be considerate to Mom and Dad. The fear I just expressed, I am sure they feel much more intensely without the relief of being here to know exactly how things are. Please don't go defending me or attacking them if they are critical of the Project. . . .

They said over the phone "Did you know how much it takes to make a child?" and I thought of how much it took to make a Herbert Lee[3] (or many others whose names I do not know). . . . I thought of how much it took to be a Negro in Mississippi twelve months a year for a lifetime. How can such a thing as a life be weighed? . . .

With constant love,
Heather

Tchula, July 16

Yesterday while the Mississippi River was being dragged looking for the three missing civil rights workers, two bodies of Negroes were found—one cut in half and one without a head. Mississippi is the only state where you can drag a river any time and find bodies you were not expecting. Things are really much better for rabbits—there's a closed season on rabbits.

2. **Bob Moses:** Robert P. Moses, a young African American high school teacher from New York who organized SNCC workers to join other civil rights workers in Mississippi that summer.
3. **Herbert Lee:** Mississippi farmer killed by a local white politician after registering to vote in a SNCC campaign in 1961.

Meridian, August 4

Last night Pete Seeger was giving a concert in Meridian. We sang a lot of free-dom songs, and every time a verse like "No more lynchings" was sung, or "before I'd be a slave I'd be buried in my grave," I had the flash of understand-ing that sometimes comes when you suddenly think about the meaning of a familiar song. . . . I wanted to stand up and shout to them, "Think about what you are singing—people really have died to keep us all from being slaves." Most of the people there still did not know that the bodies had been found. Finally just before the singing of "We Shall Overcome," Pete Seeger made the announcement. "We must sing 'We Shall Overcome' now," said Seeger. "The three boys would not have wanted us to weep now, but to sing and under-stand this song." That seems to me the best way to explain the greatness of this project—that death can have this meaning. Dying is not an everpresent possibility in Meridian, the way some reports may suggest. Nor do any of us want to die. Yet in a moment like last night, we can feel that anyone who did die for the Project would wish to be remembered not by tributes or grief but by understanding and continuation of what he was doing. . . .

As we left the church, we heard on the radio the end of President John-son's speech announcing the air attacks on Vietnam. . . . I could only think "This must not be the beginning of a war. There is still a freedom fight, and we are winning. We must have time to live and help Mississippi to be alive." Half an hour before, I had understood death in a new way. Now I realized that Mississippi, in spite of itself, has given real meaning to life. In Missis-sippi you never ask, "What is the meaning of life?" or "Is there any point to it all?" but only that we may have enough life to do all that there is to be done. . . .

Meridian, August 5

At the Freedom school and at the community center, many of the kids had known Mickey [Schwerner] and almost all knew Jimmy Chaney. Today we asked the kids to describe Mickey and Jimmy because we had never known them.

"Mickey was a big guy. He wore blue jeans all the time." . . . I asked the kids, "What did his eyes look like?" and they told me they were "friendly eyes" "nice eyes" ("nice" is a lovely word in a Mississippi accent). "Mickey was a man who was at home everywhere and with anybody," said the 17-year-old girl I stay with. The littlest kids, the 6, 7, 8 years olds, tell about how he played "Frankenstein" with them or took them for drives or talked with them about Freedom. Many of the teen-age boys were delinquents until Mickey went down to the bars and jails and showed them that one person at least would respect them if they began to fight for something important. . . . And the grownups too, trusted him. The lady I stay with tells with pride of how Mickey and [his wife] Rita came to supper at their house, and police cars circled around the house all during the meal. But Mickey could make them feel glad to take the risk.

People talk less about James Chaney here, but feel more. The kids describe a boy who played with them—whom everyone respected but who never had to join in fights to maintain this respect—a quiet boy but very sharp and very understanding when he did speak. Mostly we know James through his sisters and especially his 12-year-old brother, Ben. Today Ben was in the Freedom School. At lunchtime the kids have a jazz band (piano, washtub bass, cardboard boxes and bongos as drums) and tiny Ben was there leading all even with his broken arm, with so much energy and rhythm that even Senator Eastland[4] would have had to stop and listen if he'd been walking by. . . .

Laurel, August 11

Dear Folks,

. . . The memorial service began around 7:30 with over 120 people filling the small, wooden-pew lined church. David Dennis of CORE,[5] the Assistant Director for the Mississippi Summer Project, spoke for COFO.[6] He talked to the Negro people of Meridian—it was a speech to move people, to end the lethargy, to make people stand up. It went something like this:

"I am not here to memorialize James Chaney, I am not here to pay tribute—I am too sick and tired. Do YOU hear me, I am S-I-C-K and T-I-R-E-D. I have attended too many memorials, too many funerals. This has got to stop. Mack Parker, Medgar Evers, Herbert Lee, Lewis Allen, Emmett Till, four little girls[7] in Birmingham, a 13-year-old boy in Birmingham, and the list goes on and on. I have attended these funerals and memorials and I am SICK and TIRED. But the trouble is that YOU are NOT sick and tired and for that reason YOU, yes YOU, are to blame. Everyone of your damn souls. And if you are going to let this continue now then you are to blame, yes YOU. Just as much as the monsters of hate who pulled the trigger or brought down the club; just as much to blame as the sheriff and the chief of police, as the governor in Jackson who said that he 'did not have time' for Mrs. Schwerner when she went to see him, and just as much to blame as the President and Attorney General in Washington who wouldn't provide protection for Chaney, Goodman and Schwerner when we told them that protection was necessary in Neshoba County. . . . Yes, I am angry, I AM. And it's high time that you got angry too, angry enough to go up to the courthouse Monday and register—everyone of you. Angry enough to take five and then other people with you. Then and only then can these brutal killings be stopped. Remember it is your sons and your daughters who have been killed all these years and you have done nothing about it, and if you don't do nothing NOW baby, I say God Damn Your Souls." . . .

4. **Senator Eastland:** James Eastland, a U.S. senator from Mississippi from 1943 to 1978 and an outspoken supporter of segregation.
5. **CORE:** Congress of Racial Equality, a civil rights group.
6. **COFO:** Council of Federated Organizations, an organization of the civil rights groups operating in Mississippi that summer.
7. **Parker . . . four little girls:** African American victims of racial murders.

Mileston, August 9

Dear Blake,

. . . Dave finally broke down and couldn't finish and the Chaney family was moaning and much of the audience and I were also crying. It's such an impossible thing to describe but suddenly again, as I'd first realized when I heard the three men were missing when we were still training up at Oxford, [Ohio,] I felt the sacrifice the Negroes have been making for so long. How the Negro people are able to accept all the abuses of the whites—all the insults and injustices which make me ashamed to be white—and then turn around and say they want to love us, is beyond me. There are Negroes who want to kill whites and many Negroes have much bitterness but still the majority seem to have the quality of being able to look for a future in which whites will love the Negroes. Our kids talk very critically of all the whites around here and still they have a dream of freedom in which both races understand and accept each other. There is such an overpowering task ahead of these kids that sometimes I can't do anything but cry for them. I hope they are up to the task, I'm not sure I would be if I were a Mississippi Negro. As a white northerner I can get involved whenever I feel like it and run home whenever I get bored or frustrated or scared. I hate the attitude and position of the Northern whites and despise myself when I think that way. . . . I asked my father if I could stay down here for a whole year and I was almost glad when he said "no" that we couldn't afford it because it would mean supporting me this year in addition to three more years of college. I have a desire to go home and to read a lot and go to Quaker meetings and be by myself so I can think about all this rather than being in the middle of it all the time. But I know if my emotions run like they have in the past, that I can only take that pacific sort of life for a little while and then I get the desire to be active again and get involved with knowing other people. I guess this all sounds crazy and I seem to always think out my problems as I write to you. I am angry because I have a choice as to whether or not to work in the Movement and I am playing upon that choice and leaving here. I wish I could talk with you 'cause I'd like to know if you ever felt this way about anything. I mean have you ever despised yourself for your weak conviction or something. And what is making it worse is that all those damn northerners are thinking of me as a brave hero. . . .

Martha

51

Protest Movements of the 1960s and 1970s

In 1957, President Dwight D. Eisenhower sent troops to Little Rock, Arkansas, to back up a court order for the integration of the city's public schools. The decision was not of his choosing—the defiance by a federal judge acting under the court of the state of Arkansas forced it on him—but it initiated a process of federal military and police intervention in protection of constitutional rights for black Southerners that had been absent since Reconstruction's end. But especially in the aftermath of the Supreme Court's condemnation of segregation in the 1954 decision Brown v. Board of Education of Topeka, *black communities in the South had acted on their own to topple white supremacy, most notably in the boycott of segregated busing in Montgomery, Alabama, led by Martin Luther King Jr. in 1956.*

Large-scale and sweeping demonstrations for civil rights intensified during the 1960s. Heeding King's plea for nonviolence, sit-ins were staged across the segregated South at various public places long denied to African Americans. The photo below shows sit-in protesters Professor John R. Salter, Joan Trumpauer, and Anne Moody at a lunch counter in Jackson, Mississippi, in the spring of 1963.

QUESTIONS TO CONSIDER

1. Who do you think the people in the crowd are? Why do you think they are so angry?
2. Can you think of any situations or protests you have read or heard about lately that remind you of this confrontation?

Sit-in protesters at a Jackson, Mississippi, lunch counter, May 28, 1963. *Photographed by Fred Blackwell / photograph provided by the Wisconsin Historical Society, image ID number 2381*

52

PABLO GUZMÁN

The Young Lords

The Young Lords Party, founded in 1969, was one of the many left-wing urban youth organizations that developed out of the political turmoil of the late 1960s. Modeled on the Black Panthers, the Young Lords were a loose confederation of Puerto Rican youth groups exhibiting elements of a civil rights organization, a street gang, and a third-world

Pablo Guzmán, "*La Vida Pura*: A Lord of the Barrio," in Andrés Torres and José E. Velázquez, eds., *The Puerto Rican Movement: Voices from the Diaspora* (Philadelphia: Temple University Press, 1998), 155–58, 164–67.

anticolonial liberation army. The organization attracted a remarkable mix of Puerto Ricans, from upwardly mobile "college kids" to street toughs, prostitutes, and recent immigrants from the island. The Young Lords, along with the Black Panthers and other minority youth organizations that sprang up around the same time, articulated the political voice of a generation of nonwhite teenagers that had been shaped by growing up on the excluded margins of the greatest economic boom in world history.

Heavily influenced by the Marxist revolutions in Cuba, Vietnam, and China, the Young Lords attempted to weld traditional ethnic community organizations to their politics of revolution through neighborhood study groups, educational meetings, and the kind of confrontational, direct political action that had made the black power movement so frightening to the authorities. Like the Black Panthers, they often carried guns and used paramilitary tactics borrowed from third-world guerrilla movements to gain attention. Their political banditry included commandeering a hospital van to provide free mobile medical services to their communities. They also established a free breakfast program for schoolchildren and produced a weekly radio program and newspapers.

The New York Police Department and the FBI eventually managed to destabilize the group, but for six years the Young Lords captured the imagination of many in urban America, particularly in New York City with its sizable Puerto Rican community. A large number of the group's leaders went on to become successful journalists, television and radio personalities, union organizers, academics, and authors. Pablo Guzmán, the author of the memoir excerpted here, became a television reporter after his time in the Young Lords.

QUESTIONS TO CONSIDER

1. What were the main objectives of the Young Lords?
2. Why do you think the Young Lords gained support from their community?
3. What does Pablo Guzmán reveal about how he later felt about his involvement with the Young Lords?

RAÍCES/ROOTS

We called ourselves the Young Lords Organization [YLO]. In June 1969, two small groupings from Spanish Harlem and one from the Lower East Side, consisting overwhelmingly of guys between seventeen and twenty-two, decided to merge. I was in the Sociedad de Albizu Campos, named for the leader of the old Nationalist Party of Puerto Rico. Primarily college students, we had begun meeting three months before. I had just returned from a semester of study in Cuernavaca, Mexico, completing the required "in-the-field" half of my freshman year at the State University at the brand-new Old Westbury. I left as Paul Guzman, a nervous only child of a Puerto Rican–Cuban mother and a Puerto Rican father, both of whom were born "here"—stateside. I came back to the states as Pablo Guzmán. The other East Harlem group consisted mostly of high-school dudes who met in an after-school photo workshop run by Hiram Maristany. The Lower East Side group was a mix of college and high-school aged guys who we later found out had already been penetrated by two or three NYPD Red Squad agents.

Immediately after the merger, Mickey, David, and I drove in Mickey's Volkswagen Beetle to Chicago. We didn't know at the time about the Brown Berets or La Raza Unida among the Chicanos and the Mexicans of the West and Southwest. But Mauricio and I had read in that week's *Guardian*[1] about what the Chicago Panthers called a "Rainbow Coalition" they had put together. The Panthers had turned (or were trying to turn) two Chicago gangs, the Young Patriots (poor Whites with Appalachian roots) and the Young Lords (Puerto Ricans and Mexicans), away from 'banging and toward something more constructive. If there was already a Latino group in action, we reasoned, why not throw in together? The Lords' chairman, Cha Cha Jiménez, breezily gave us permission to organize as the New York chapter of the YLO. The affiliation with Chicago was where we got our purple berets—even though they claimed to be moving away from street life, the Lords weren't giving up their colors.

This whole gang thing was fairly jolting. Although to this day people think the New York group was a gang because of that name, we never were, and except for Felipe Luciano (one of the few New Yorkers who had been in a gang himself), we walked lightly around the Chicago boys. Nevertheless, it was a Mexican member of the Chicago Lords, Omar López, who came up with our slogan, *"Tengo Puerto Rico en Mi Corazón"*—"I Have Puerto Rico in My Heart." We loved it, and it soon spread throughout Puerto Rican circles. Only years later did we learn that it contained a slight grammatical error, a testimonial to the bad Spanish most of us "spoke." We were truly examples of Ricans raised in the states.

I wasn't yet nineteen. My folks would have freaked if they'd known what their only child—the altar boy from Our Lady of Pity who was supposed to use his Bronx science diploma and college scholarship to bust out of the ghetto—was really doing on his summer vacation. But it didn't come from nowhere—my parents and my grandparents, after all, had first instilled in me a sense that there was far too long a history of injustice in this society. "Only," as my father would say later at my trial, "your mother and I never thought you would actually try to do something about it. Not on such a scale, anyhow."

By the time of that trial, the Young Lords Party—we split from Chicago in April 1970 because we felt they hadn't overcome being a gang—had been targeted by [J. Edgar] Hoover's FBI as the Latino version of the Panthers and the Weather Underground.[2] Although we never kept a roster, I tallied our New York membership at the end of 1970, and we had grown to more than a thousand, with storefront offices in *El Barrio*, the Lower East Side, and the South

---

1. **Guardian:** New York City–based radical news weekly published between 1948 and 1992.
2. **Weather Underground:** Radical direct action organization that split from Students for a Democratic Society.

Bronx. We had branches in Newark-Hoboken, Bridgeport, Philadelphia, and Puerto Rico, active supporters in Detroit, Boston, Hawaii, in the military and in the prisons. We published a weekly newspaper, *Pa'lante*. We had organized workers, including medical professionals, in the city's hospitals and had a sizeable following on campuses across the country, where we often spoke. . . .

"WHERE ARE THE DAMN GUNS!"

In early October 1970, two of our members, Bobby Lemus and Julio Roldán, were arrested basically for drinking beer and hanging out with some guys on a stoop one night. This was 1970, remember. The next morning, Julio was found hung in his cell at the "Tombs" (Manhattan House of Detention), the latest in a series of controversial "suicides" in jails and police precincts, often with autopsies returned that did not indicate unassisted death. We had been covering the issue in *Pa'lante*. Julio was a quiet, unassuming little guy of about thirty who joined mainly because he believed in independence. His main contribution was cooking at one of our communal apartments at East Harlem.

Surrounded by five thousand demonstrators, we carried his casket from the González Funeral Home on Madison Avenue and marched to the church on 111th that we had taken over a year before. We took it over again, suddenly, posting armed guards at the entrance and at either side of the casket. The standoff would continue, we said, until conditions in the prisons changed. It was the first time we had ever been connected with weapons. We caught even most of our own organization by surprise. Given the risk involved, and the infiltration we took as a given, we had to. The police, already at war with the "soft" Lindsay[3] administration, were furious, but the mayor did not want a confrontation, and so he negotiated. The cops vented their frustration in other ways.

Very soon after the takeover, the Central Committee received reports from inmates in cells next to Julio indicating that he may have taken his own life. This created a debate that split the leadership. My view was that we should admit to doubts and cut our losses immediately. By this time Felipe was not part of the leadership, and indeed, soon he would be gone altogether. Meanwhile, a hard-liner named Gloria Fontanez, recruited from Gouverneur Hospital in the Lower East Side, had risen rapidly through the ranks. She argued that we should stick with our issue regardless of its actual truth, and the majority went along so as not to undermine the months of work we'd put into the UN march scheduled for October 1970. Because I continued to argue, I was suspended. In five and a half years of hard work, that is the only episode of which I am not proud—that and not doing more to get Gloria tossed out.

The march to the UN came off spectacularly, as it probably would have had we left the church earlier. But when the march was over with, we were

---

3. **Lindsay:** John Lindsay, mayor of New York City from 1966 to 1973, famous for being a left-leaning "Rockefeller Republican."

still there. Negotiations were ongoing, however, and by God they budged: The Board of Corrections would institute sweeping reforms, and José Torres would get a seat on the board.

So now there was the matter of getting out of the church. Past the ring of cops waiting to bust us for the guns. The deal with the city included an amnesty clause that the city was sure would backfire on us. The cops would be allowed in to make sure there were no guns, and only upon their OK could we walk with no charges against us. Because the police had the place surrounded and had infiltrators inside, they were sure they were going to catch us sneaking guns out. And then, all bets would be off. On the appointed day, the police arrived, and at the front door I had the captain and his escort put up against the wall and frisked. "Sorry, Captain," I said, "but we agreed: no weapons. And that includes you. We don't want to say anybody planted anything, right?" The captain acquiesced, and because this occurred within view of reporters covering the "surrender," the image of the Young Lords telling a police captain to assume the position spread. The PBS (Policemen's Benevolent Association) and indignant editorialists called for his head, on a stake right next to ours.

The cops searched thoroughly and found nothing. To this day, I have had police veterans ask me how we pulled it off. Later that day, I had to break policy and get the story from the Lord in charge, David Pérez. "Never underestimate the power of the people," he said laughing. "The cops stopped everybody they thought looked like a Young Lord a block from the church. 'Where are the damn guns?!' one cop yelled at me. But we've spent the last year and change organizing this whole community, not just a part of it. They've been stopping everyone under thirty-five. We broke the weapons down and hid them under the coats of *las viejitas*, the little old ladies who look like your grandmother. Hey, those little old ladies were down."

GERALDO RIVERA SAVES MY ASS

In April 1970, a seven-month effort by Juan González was to culminate in the takeover of Lincoln Hospital. Juan and his team had organized doctors, nurses, other health-care providers, and patients in Manhattan and the Bronx in revealing exposés of just how poorly the system works for poor folks. From lead poisoning and tuberculosis, we had gone on to report the wave of unnecessary hysterectomies performed on Latin women, organized disgruntled rank-and-file workers within 1199,[4] "liberated" an X-ray truck, promoted preventive medicine, and tried to show the links between the pharmaceutical companies, the AMA [American Medical Association] establishment, hospitals, and insurance outfits that made up the multibillion-dollar health-care industry. But our immediate plan was to take over Lincoln Hospital in the South Bronx and run it with the help of staff who were fed up with rats in

---

4. **1199:** Health Care Workers Union.

the emergency room, antiquated equipment, meager supplies, and chronic personnel shortages.

Lincoln was a mess. For twenty-five years it awaited demolition, and for twenty-five years the city never funded the construction of its replacement. Getting spics a better hospital was the last thing on their agenda. I was from the South Bronx, and growing up I had heard the stories of a stabbing victim crawling two blocks to the catchment zone where the ambulance would take him to Morrisania (which would eventually be shut down as well). Apocryphal, perhaps, but it reflected Lincoln's street rep.

At dawn, we moved in, sneaking through windows and doors opened by doctors and nurses working with us. From inside, we told the guards they could go on a "lo-o-o-ng" break. A huge Puerto Rican flag was flown from the roof. The city was notified, and acute-care patients were transferred, but all other patients were treated by a reenergized staff. A phalanx of cops in riot gear sealed off the area outside, and the standoff was on. We held a news conference in the hospital auditorium, me in an Afro and white lab coat, and made our case against the city. Deputy Mayor [Richard] Aurelio sent Sid Davidoff and Barry Gottehrer and their Latino "liaison," Arnie Segarra (who went on to become Dinkins's[5] appointment aide). Negotiations began. By late afternoon, we had won: A new Lincoln would be built. And, of course, the participants would receive amnesty.

The cops were not going for this amnesty bullshit. And they could give a f—— that Lindsay was their boss—he was as hated as Dinkins. So a few blocks from the hospital, I was chased by four detectives in an unmarked car. I thought I had given them the slip, but a dog, a goddamn dog, came nipping after me and slowed me down, and I was collared. Just before they got the cuffs on, I pulled my beret from my back pocket and waved it to the onlookers. "Call the Young Lords!" I vainly cried out. Then my wrists got pinched tight, and my head was slammed on the car roof before I was thrown inside.

They gave me a few more shots, but I knew I was in for a serious beating back at the precinct. As spokesmen, Felipe and I were the biggest targets. On two occasions, cops arrested guys they mistook for me, breaking one's leg and another's arm. In Chicago, I spoke at a rally at the start of the Chicago 7 trial,[6] and as I was finishing, word came that the cops were going to bust me. I managed to escape but learned later that once again the cops grabbed a look-alike and beat the shit out of him. I had been shot at by cops and nearly run over by a squad car in both Chicago and New York. And now my charmed existence had come to an end.

At the 40th Precinct, I was put in a "bing," or holding cell. Louie Perez, who had been assigned as my security when he left Lincoln, was already there. This Negro detective put on a show for his White comrades. They had taken

5. **Dinkins:** David Dinkins, the first African American mayor of New York City, 1990–1993. He was widely hated by police, who famously blocked City Hall, shouting racist slogans during a police protest in 1992.
6. **Chicago 7 trial:** Trial of seven well-known activists who led the protests that disrupted the Chicago Democratic Party convention in 1968.

Louie's nunchakus, the "karate sticks" many Lords used. "So, this is what you use against cops, huh?" the lackey said. "Well, let's see how it stands up against this"—and he patted one of the three guns he was visibly packing. His boys laughed, and I knew we were goners. "This is America, c—— s—— ." He was leaning in close through the bars. His hand was at the lock. "And you oughta be taught what happens to punks who want to mess it up for the rest of us." He was going for the key. Louie and I braced ourselves.

Suddenly, there was a commotion. Bustling sounds from below. Shouting, growing louder. Gerry Rivera materialized, with what seemed like half the precinct coming up the stairs behind him, Keystone Kops–style. He dodged a cop, leaped over a railing, dodged another, and got to our cell. "You OK?" he asked. I was ready to kiss his feet. "Yeah, yeah," I panted. "You just made it. Behind you, watch out!" He turned just before the first cop could grab him. "I'malawyerthesearemyclientsyoutouchanyoneofusI'lltakeallyourbadges." Cops froze in mid air.

From an office, a supervisor emerged looking down at some paper. "Jesus! I just got off the phone with headquarters. Do we have some Young Lord here for the hospital thing, they're getting all kinds of calls from the media—" He finally looked up and took the scene in. "What the f—— is all this?" Gerry waded through fifty or so cops and glibly explained. I had to laugh; he was a piece of work.

Gerry burst into our collective lives soon after we had opened the first office, interrupting a meeting with our lawyers to charge that we had no Latino representation, like, for instance, him, even though one of our attorneys was a Puerto Rican he knew personally. Appalled though we were, we admired his chutzpah. But when he tried to join we drew the line. "This is an adventure for you, bro," he was told. "You're not really into the ideology." Still, he had a lot of heat, and he loved the street battles—and the press conferences. Eventually he took advantage of a scholarship to the Columbia School of Journalism that I had turned down because it would have meant leaving the Lords. We wished him well. Once out of Columbia, he got a gig with WABC-TV and hit the ground running. And that's how the Young Lords Party unleashed Geraldo Rivera on an unsuspecting universe. . . .

By our sixth year, it was over. Partly because of destabilization by arrest and government infiltration but mainly because we were young and prone to mistakes—mistakes of leadership, of vulnerability to betrayal, and of the same movement infighting that we had once so despised. But before we dissolved, the Young Lords Party had left its mark:

- A new Lincoln Hospital was built in the South Bronx after we seized a facility that the city had run out of a condemned building for twenty-five years.
- We forced the city to use the lead-poisoning and tuberculosis detection tests gathering dust in some agency's basement after we liberated them and exposed epidemics in both diseases—which are now making comebacks.

- We pushed the Board of Corrections into reforming prison conditions just before the Attica uprising[7]—which our sixteen-year-old chief of staff, Juan "Fi" Ortíz, witnessed as our representative on the negotiation team.
- We encouraged schools to teach Puerto Rican history. Some, at least, now do.
- We created a climate for the start of bilingual education. Never intended as a parallel track, but as a way of mainstreaming Spanish-dominant kids to English proficiency, it has since been sabotaged by educators who were against it from the beginning.
- We produced the first radio show by a New York–born Latino (myself, over WBAI).
- Ask any Latino professional in Nueva York who advanced in government or the corporate world between, say, 1969 and 1984, and you'll be told they owe part of their opportunity to the sea change in perception that the Young Lords inspired.
- We helped raise the understanding, first among Latinos and then the society at large, that Puerto Ricans possessed a culture on a par with anyone's.

7. **Attica uprising:** 1971 prison riot in upstate New York in which thirty-nine people were killed.

53

CÉSAR CHÁVEZ

Toward Mexican American Civil Rights

César Chávez (1927–1993) was a Mexican American farmworker who played a key role in organizing migrant farmworkers in the South and Southwest and especially in California. Building on the success and visibility of the African American freedom struggle and of scattered efforts of Mexican agricultural laborers to better their working conditions, he founded the National Farm Workers Association in 1962. Dedicated to protecting and promoting the civil rights of all farmworkers, the organization enrolled tens of thousands of laborers, mostly Mexican Americans. It led grape and lettuce pickers in a series of successful strikes against their employers—large landowning companies—in

César Chávez, "César Chávez Talks in New York, 1968," César Chávez Research Center, California Department of Education, http://chavez.cde.ca.gov/researchCenter/default.aspx.

the late 1960s and 1970s, securing higher wages and stricter environmental safeguards against the widespread use of toxic pesticides.

During his career as a labor organizer, Chávez gave many speeches whose core themes were the dignity of labor and the evils of unregulated enterprise. In these excerpts from a June 1968 speech given at an interfaith luncheon of clergy and laypeople at Calvary Episcopal Church in Manhattan, New York, he refers to a long-running boycott of grapes grown by a large-scale agricultural corporation, Giumarra of southern California, as an effort to win civil rights for all workers.

QUESTIONS TO CONSIDER

1. Why did César Chávez link the struggles of the National Farm Workers Association to a history of discrimination against all workers?
2. How were the demands of the National Farm Workers Association similar to the goals of the African American civil rights movement? How were they different?
3. In what ways did Chávez broaden the scope of the civil rights movements of the 1960s and 1970s?

We are not in the age of miracles, and yet it is surprising that we can attract, and keep, and increase the type of support that is needed to keep our economic struggle going for 33 months. It is a struggle in which the poorest of the poor and weakest of the weak are pitted against the strongest of the strong. We are fighting not against the family farm, not against agriculture, but against agribusiness.

When we think of powerful interests, we think of General Motors and other great corporations. But we must turn our minds to the power of the land. It is hard to think that agribusiness could have such tremendous power as it has in California — it is worth five billion dollars in our state alone. We must see it as it is, a similar situation to Latin America. The interests can control not only the land but everything that moves, everyone that walks in the land. They control even the actions of the Congress of the United States, even some church groups.

One thing was necessary to the success of the exploitation of California land: workers. The whole cry to get poor people to do the work of the land is a story in itself. When the Southern Pacific and Union Pacific railroads were completed, the Chinese were left without work to do. They went to the cities. The growers who needed workers dealt with contractors who supplied the Chinese. The contractors, who were Chinese themselves, began to sell their brothers for profit. When the Chinese wanted to own their own land, we had the Chinese Exclusion Act. The Chinese land workers could not own land nor could they marry Caucasian women, so they left agriculture for the cities.

The growers went to Congress for special legislation. Tailor-made immigration laws made it possible for them to recruit labor from Japan. When the Japanese used the slow-down (they had no unions and could not strike) to get better conditions, the growers began to get rid of them. The Japanese could not own land, either, but began to rent it. In time they began to exploit the laborers.

The growers even went to India for labor, and in the early twenties they were recruiting in the Philippines. When they saw that many Mexicans were leaving their country because of the Revolution, they saw an opportunity. One grower explained that Mexicans were good for California land work because they were short and close to the ground.

The growers went further than they ever went before. During World War II, our own government became the recruiter for laborers, "braceros." Even today, as I stand here talking to you, we cannot choke off production on the great farms for one simple reason. The regulations on immigration are not being enforced. Our own government is the biggest strikebreaker against the union. The biggest weapon in the hands of the growers is the "green card" commuter.

You can live in Mexico and come in to work for a season and then go back home. This is not like the regulations covering immigrants from Europe. Hundreds of thousands of people are recruited and put into employers' camps. We cannot reach them there. They are like concentration camps. If the laws were enforced, we would not have to boycott.

Employers are not supposed to recruit workers while labor disputes are in progress. We have to play the game without any rules or procedures. In New York, the rights of unions are enforced, but in our case, 95% of the workers were signed up with the union but the producer of table grapes, Giumarra, refused to sit down with us for representation procedures. We were willing to abide by the results of the election [for local union leaders]. The employers would not talk to us. The only approach left to us is the strike and the boycott.

People raise the question: Is this a strike or is it a civil-rights fight? In California, in Texas, or in the South, any time you strike, it becomes a civil-rights movement. It becomes a civil-rights fight.

The local courts say we have no right to use an amplifier to reach strikebreakers who are a quarter of a mile away. In every case, the growers get an injunction against us immediately. Then we go up to the Appellate Court and up to the Supreme Court. Justice is very expensive sometimes.

We go further. We take advantage of modern technology. I even went up in a plane with two priests to broadcast to the strikebreakers from seven hundred feet up. As soon as we came down, the growers were there to protest.

The three most important issues at this time are these. First, union recognition by the employers. We have certain rights as human beings. Every law is for this recognition—except when it comes to farm workers. Recognizing the union is recognizing us as human beings. Second, an increase in wages is important. Third, in my opinion and in the opinion of the workers, is safety. The whole question of pesticides and insecticides must be met. The men who work to apply these poisons should have protection. Two or three weeks after working with pesticides a man begins to have trouble with his sight. In some cases, he begins to lose his fingernails. It does not happen immediately. Someday our government will have to undertake real research to determine the effects of these poisons, not only on the workers who are in direct contact with them, but on the consumers. Millions of dollars are spent in the research on the effectiveness of the poisons in destroying pests and insects on plants. This is from the business angle. Millions must also be spent on the effects of the same poisons on human beings.

There is a fine dust that nature puts on grapes. It is called bloom. The contamination from the insecticides remains in this fine dust. I don't eat grapes because I know about these pesticides. You can stop eating grapes for your safety as well as for the boycott. Even our strongest supporters are afraid of the boycott of table grapes. The key to the success of this boycott is right here in New York. Action is necessary. If you don't do anything, you are permitting the evil. I would suggest that labor take a page in the largest newspaper and make the issue clear to all, and I would suggest that the clergy also take a page. The message of the clergy should be different, bringing out the morality of our struggle, the struggle of good people who are migrants, and therefore the poorest of the poor and the weakest of the weak.

54

ROBERT AMSEL ET AL.

The Gay Rights Movement

Sex has not changed much over the course of American history. As far as we can tell from diaries, underground publications, and soldiers' passionate letters home to their wives and girlfriends, the things people do have remained pretty much the same. However, sexuality, or the social meanings, situations, and types of relationships that individuals attach to their sexual acts, has changed profoundly—and probably nowhere more so than in regard to homosexuality.

In early America, it seems that despite a variety of social sanctions against it, sodomy was considered a sinful act, one among many relatively ordinary transgressions, rather than a mental illness, a social identity, or a biological destiny. It was typically treated like many other sins—through some combination of punishment and forgiveness. Not until the mid- to late nineteenth century was any notion of a durable and lifelong sexual identity, either homosexual or heterosexual, imagined. As the idea of a homosexual identity developed, so did the prejudices, restrictions, persecutions, and debates that we recognize today. After World War II a civil rights movement emerged in response to these new strictures that, for roughly one hundred years, presented homosexuality as a crime or disease that required prevention, cure, or extirpation from the social body.

Robert Amsel, "Back to Our Future? A Walk on the Wild Side of Stonewall," *Advocate*, September 15, 1987.

Among the many civil right movements that emerged in the post–World War II era, there may be none that has remained as well organized, active, and successful as the gay rights movement. John D'Emilio, a historian of the gay rights movement, observes that World War II "plucked millions of young men and women, whose sexual identities were just forming, out of their homes, out of towns and small cities, out of the heterosexual environment of the family, and dropped them into sex-segregated situations. For men and women already gay, it provided an opportunity to meet people like themselves. Others could become gay because of the temporary freedom to explore sexuality that the war provided." This occurred in the military and on the homefront, where millions of women moved away from home for employment (see Document 40, Fanny Christina Hill, Rosie the Riveter). As gay communities sprang up in center cities, especially around ports where soldiers were returning from war such as San Francisco and New York, there was a rise in prejudice, intolerance, and discrimination against gays and lesbians. President Eisenhower imposed a total ban on gays and lesbians in federal employment, the military purged many from the ranks, and police forces across the United States started using little known and rarely enforced sodomy laws to clear out gay bars and meeting places, and even arrested people in their homes.

The Mattachine Society (see photo on page 301), founded in Los Angeles in 1950, responded to this rise in intolerance by promoting civil rights for sexual minorities. Within a few years there were chapters in most major U.S. cities. In 1955, in San Francisco, a group of lesbian activists founded their own group, the Daughters of Bilitis. The two groups worked together for roughly fifteen years, trying to effect nonviolent political reform in discriminatory laws and social practices. However, as young, politically active homosexuals were often drawn to other, more glamorous and "mainstream" movements like African American civil rights and the fledgling antiwar movement, the Mattachines and Daughters of Bilitis went into decline.

The raid on the Stonewall nightclub in New York in the early hours of the morning of June 28, 1969, changed the trajectory of the gay rights movement. At Stonewall several hundred gay men said "Enough!" to police arrests, raids, beatings, and forced mental health treatment. They fought back, and in so doing set an example that was followed across the nation and around the world. A new chapter of the gay rights movement began—one that made the older, more closeted homosexuals of the Mattachine Society seem stodgy. Young gays were drawn to seemingly more militant and confrontational organizations like the Gay Liberation Front. In honor of their achievement, the Stonewall anniversary was made into a day of marching and parading called Gay Pride Day, which is now celebrated worldwide.

At the time of the Stonewall riots, Robert Amsel (b. 1946) worked for the Mattachine Society in New York City and would soon become its president. He wrote the article excerpted here eighteen years after Stonewall, to "set the record straight—or gaily forward" as he put it.

QUESTIONS TO CONSIDER

1. What types of nonviolent resistance did homosexuals practice prior to Stonewall? How did their tactics compare and contrast with the

nonviolent resistance used by demonstrators in the African American freedom struggle?

2. In what ways did the Stonewall riots change gay men's and lesbians' attitudes and feelings about their sexual orientation?

3. How was the movement for gay and lesbian rights strengthened by Stonewall?

4. Why do you think the Mattachine Society and Daughters of Bilitis dressed the way they did for this protest? How do you think homosexuals after Stonewall might have felt looking at this picture?

For whatever strange reason, the police that summer decided to launch an all-out attack on illegal clubs throughout the city. They did not limit themselves to gay clubs—straight black and Hispanic clubs were also raided. They did, however, seem to specialize in places frequented by members of minorities. Prior to the Stonewall, there had been raids on other gay after-hours clubs, the Sewer and the Snake Pit, both aptly named. The Tele-Star and the Checkerboard had closed down not long before. By the time the cops hit the Stonewall [on Saturday/Sunday, June 27/28], the customers were angry, frustrated, and, more important, running out of places to go. Deputy Inspector Seymour Pine led eight plainclothes officers (including two women) into the Stonewall at 3 A.M. It was a hot night and a full moon was shining over Sheridan Square. The employees were arrested for selling liquor without a license. The customers were allowed to leave, one at a time. They waited outside for their friends. Many had been in such raids before, some in the past few weeks.

One straight observer referred to the gathering as "festive," with those exiting the club striking poses, swishing and camping. Then he noted a sudden mood change when the paddy wagon arrived and the bartender, doorman, three drag queens and a struggling lesbian were shoved inside. There were catcalls and cries to topple the paddy wagon. Pine hurriedly told the wagon to take off, drop the prisoners off at the Sixth Precinct and rush back. The crowd threw coins at the police and shouted "Pigs!" Coins progressed to bottles. The crowd was closing in. Pine and his detectives moved quickly back into the Stonewall and locked themselves in.

The "mood change" reported was not a mood change at all. Camping it up had long been a way of passive resistance. By joking and being "outrageous," one could somehow neutralize the reality of harassment. Suddenly, watching the prisoners as they were roughly shoved into the wagon, the crowd felt a surge of reality rushing in. Their turf had been invaded; camping was not deterring their callous persecutors. The hidden anger exploded. There were many witnesses to report what happened outside the Stonewall. Fortunately, there was also one witness to report what happened inside. *Village Voice* reporter Howard Smith, sniffing a good story, was hot on the scent as he rushed into the building. The police bolted the door. The Stonewall front was mostly brick, except for windows, boarded within by plywood. Part of Smith's account:

Inside we hear the shattering of windows, followed by what we imagine to be bricks pounding on the door, voices yelling. The floor shudders at each blow. "Aren't you guys scared?" I say.

"No." But they look uneasy.

The door crashes open, beer cans and bottles hurtle in. Pine and his troop rush to shut it. At that point the only uniformed cop among them gets hit with something under his eye. He hollers, and his hand comes away scarlet. It looks a lot more serious than it really is. They are all suddenly furious. Three run out in front to see if they can scare the mob from the door. A hail of coins. A beer can glances off Deputy Inspector Smyth's head. . . .

[Pine] leaps out into the melee, and grabs someone around the waist, pulling him downward and back into the doorway. They fall. Pine regains hold and drags the elected protester inside by the hair. The door slams again. Angry cops converge on the gay, releasing their anger on this sample from the mob. The victim was Dave Van Ronk, a popular Village folk singer. Van Ronk admitted to throwing a few coins.

Again, from Howard Smith's report:

The cop who was cut is incensed, yells something like, "So you're the one who hit me!" And while the other cops help, he slaps the prisoner five or six times very hard and finishes with a punch to the mouth. They handcuff the guy as he almost passes out. . . .

The door is smashed open again (with an uprooted parking meter). More objects are thrown in. The detectives locate a fire hose, the idea being to ward off the madding crowd until reinforcements arrive. They can't see where to aim it, wedging the hose in a crack in the door. It sends out a weak stream. We all start to slip on water and Pine says to stop. . . .

A door over to the side almost gives. One cop shouts. "Get away from there or I'll shoot!" It starts shaking. The front door is completely open. One of the big plywood windows gives, and it seems inevitable that the mob will pour in. A kind of tribal adrenalin rush bolsters all of us; they all take out and check pistols. . . . Pine places a few men on each side of the corridor leading away from the entrance. They aim unwavering at the door. One detective arms himself in addition with a sawed-off baseball bat he has found. I hear, "We'll shoot the first motherf——er that comes through the door." . . .

I can only see the arm at the window. It squirts liquid into the room, and a flaring match follows. Pine is not more than 10 feet away. He aims his gun at the figures.

He doesn't fire. The sound of sirens coincides with the whoosh of flames where the lighter fluid was thrown. . . . It was that close. . . .

The first riot lasted 45 minutes. *The New York Times* claimed that 400 youths participated. They claimed the same number for the next evening's riot. Gay observers estimated in the thousands, at least for the second one.

Police reinforcements had arrived en masse, extinguished the fire and cleared the area. Howard Smith went outside and took more notes. He returned inside to discover that the police had vented their anger by smashing all the mirrors, juke boxes, phones, toilets, and cigarette machines. No one but the police had been inside, but the courts would later find them innocent of vandalism.

Stonewall management found it difficult to keep their customers inside Saturday night, since all the action was outside. Shouts of "Gay Power!" and "Liberate Christopher Street!" echoed along Sixth and Seventh avenues, and Greenwich Avenue (where incarcerated lesbians in the House of Detention shouted support from their barred windows). The battle cry raged the length of Christopher Street.

There was a strong feeling of gay community and a strong fighting spirit, an intoxicating sense of release. It was "us against them, and by God, we're winning." Crowds were growing, as if from the pavement. There was kissing, hugging, fondling. Tanned bodies merged together like some orgy scene in a Cecil B. DeMille epic. Craig Rodwell, owner of a gay bookstore in the Village, reported that some gay men were barricading the streets and not allowing heterosexual drivers to pass. A car of newlyweds was half lifted before the open-mouthed bride and groom were allowed to drive on.

New York's Tactical Police Force (TPF) arrived on the scene. They were helmeted and carried clubs. They had rescued Pine and his men the morning before, but were unprepared for the guerrilla warfare that awaited them.

These streets were gay territory. Gay people knew every doorway, alley and side street and where they would lead. They knew how to split up the TPF and run them in circles. Men on roofs or in rooms overlooking Christopher Street hurled bottles at the cops. When the cops looked up, no one could be seen.

Two TPF men chased a gay guy down a side street. Gay bystanders started running with their brother. Before long a large group was running. A man at the head of the group suddenly held out his arms and yelled, "Stop!" The group stopped. "There are two pigs and how many of us?" A moment of meaningful silence. The two cops had also stopped, were looking at one another and then at the crowd. The group leader grinned. "Get the bastards!" About face. The cops were now running at full gallop, a lynch mob on their heels. "Catch 'em! F—— 'em!"

The crowd dispersed by 3 A.M.

Sunday night was quiet. Monday and Tuesday nights[,] crowds started to gather again, but outbreaks were few and often funny. Dick Leitsch and I were covering the story for the newsletter of the Mattachine Society and reported the following:

Some of the police maintained enormous 'cool,' but others deliberately tried to provoke trouble. 'Start something, faggot, just start something,' one cop kept telling people. 'I'd like to break your ass wide open.' After saying that to several dozen people, one man turned and said[,] 'What a Freudian comment, officer!' The cop started swinging. . . .

There were also two cops in a car cruising the streets, yelling obscenities at passers-by and trying to start a fight. Another stood on the corner of Christopher and Waverly. He swung his nightstick and made nasty cracks to pedestrians. Again, from our newsletter report:

> A wildly 'fem' queen sneaked up behind him, lit a firecracker and dropped it between his feet. It exploded and he jumped into the air in a leap that Villella[1] would have envied, landing on a part of his anatomy that one queen called a 'money-maker.' The queen tossed another firecracker under him, and when it went off a melee followed, during which the cop's badge was lifted. The next day, the badge turned up hanging on a tree in Washington Square Park, stuck into a string of pickled pigs' feet.

This may have been the first gay riot ever, but we certainly did it with panache. The next night, Wednesday, July 2, events took a brutal turn. The TPF men used their nightsticks indiscriminately. "At one point," Leitsch wrote, "7th Avenue from Christopher to West 10th looked like a battlefield in Vietnam. Young people, many of them queens, were lying on the sidewalk, bleeding from the head, face, mouth, and even the eyes. Others were nursing bruised and often bleeding arms, legs, backs and necks."

Another problem, *The Voice* article had appeared that afternoon. It attracted to the area Black Panthers, Yippies, crazies and street gangs. Looting was rife and shops sympathetic to gay people were hit. Village gays were outraged and blamed the looting on outside exploiters. . . .

After Wednesday the riots petered out and the politicizing began. Gay Liberation Front (GLF) was a new group of young male and female homosexuals, which formed in late July under the Mattachine umbrella. . . .

Many smaller groups sprang up as well. All the groups suffered from infighting, out-fighting and egos in conflict. But age-old barriers were breaking down. Gay people in other parts of the country were starting to emerge from their closets. California's heavily gay cities of San Francisco and Los Angeles had their own gay renaissance. New organizations spread throughout the land. A year later, diverse gay groups and independent gays marched in brotherhood and sisterhood. Annual gay pride days would follow.

---

1. **Villella:** Edward Villella, popular American ballet dancer and choreographer of the time.

Mattachine Society picket line in front of the White House, 1965. *Photo by Kay Tobin Lahusen / © Manuscripts and Archives Division, The New York Public Library*

Gay Liberation Front. *Photo by Diana Davies/Manuscripts and Archives Division, The New York Public Library*

PART SEVEN

Between History and Tomorrow

Into a New Century

In 1979 the United States was a country plagued by uncertainty. The economy was into its sixth year of crisis, the army had recently been defeated by Vietnamese communists, and citizens were divided over various social issues. In the face of the widespread unease, a sizable segment of society called for the restoration of order and traditional values.

Onto the national stage strode former movie actor Ronald Reagan, who was elected president in 1980 on a promise to make the United States strong and confident again. Reagan's legacy, however, is uneven. He projected strength but used the military most effectively against tiny nations like Grenada and Nicaragua. He slashed school breakfast programs for children from poor families at the same time that most Americans found themselves working long hours for less pay—conditions that underlay a strike by unionized air traffic controllers early in Reagan's first term. He promised fiscal conservatism but ran up the biggest deficit in U.S. history and raised taxes several times to try to pay for his increased spending.

Yet when Reagan declared in his campaign ads, "It's morning in America," he captured the soaring hopes of Americans for a better day. The president bolstered spirits by providing amnesty for three million excluded and undocumented immigrants with one stroke of his pen and by shoring up financial markets. Reagan's optimism was such that at the close of his second term, his vice president, George H. W. Bush, was swept into office.

Domestically Bush struggled. He continued with Reagan's often painful social and economic policies but had little of the folksy charm that had enabled "the Gipper" to manage the explosive contradictions of a nation increasingly divided between haves and have-nots. Rates of homelessness and poverty mounted. Racial tensions simmered and occasionally boiled over, as in the case of rioting in April 1992 following the acquittal of four white Los Angeles police officers who were videotaped viciously beating an African American motorist named Rodney King. Bush, who stayed in the White House during the rioting, was ultimately seen as weak and out of touch with everyday Americans. A souring economy doomed his reelection bid in 1992. He lost his job to Democrat Bill Clinton, governor of Arkansas and a man who was far more comfortable with ordinary people, particularly African Americans.

Clinton's election ushered in a new era of relative social peace. Americans still fought over social issues like abortion, religion in the schools, immigration, race, and the death penalty. Bias attacks like the one that killed gay college student Matthew Shepard also continued, but the widespread support for Shepard's family, as well as Clinton's public appearance with Shepard's mother to announce new hate crimes laws, suggested a growing consensus over tolerance, social liberalism, and civil rights. The economy boomed as trillions of dollars flowed into the stock market from around the world. The information superhighway created a "new economy," producing overnight "dot-com" millionaires, software billionaires, and millions of CEOs, MBAs, and workplace "day traders." This was also the period of "emerging markets," as globalization and free-trade policies ended protectionist tariffs and forced the sale of state-owned industries across the planet. These liberalization policies, which came to be known in the developing world as "the Washington consensus," drew new capital into aging industries, modernized inefficient production facilities and forced the layoff of redundant workers, while opening new opportunities for entrepreneurial individuals in countries around the world.

Most of the world's population missed the boom, however, experiencing it instead as displacement, poverty, and blocked ambition. Many took the traditional path out of misery, leaving home and family to migrate to a wealthier region. Mexico lost millions of people as the 1994 devaluation of the peso greatly increased the migration stream, bringing landless peasants, laid-off workers, and suddenly impoverished professionals to the United States.

As the excesses of the 1990s ended, ominous changes were set in motion. In 1999 antiglobalization protesters outside a World Trade Organization meeting demanded the return to a time when the economy was more local and when global warming did not threaten the planet. The new century saw an economic bust, bringing down not just dot-com millionaires but also countless ordinary people who had invested in tech stocks whose value plummeted. Then, on September 11, 2001, coordinated suicide attacks by nineteen fundamentalist Muslims in hijacked jetliners killed almost three thousand people and destroyed one of the great symbols of America, the twin towers of the World Trade Center in New York City.

Americans were forced into a world of difficult ethical, political, and historical choices that divided people at home and made the nation unpopular abroad. Newly elected president George W. Bush declared a "war on terror" involving a significant abrogation of civil liberties, "extraordinary renditions," assassinations, and, most notoriously, the open-ended detention without trial of suspected enemies of America at the U.S. military base in Guantánamo Bay, Cuba.

In 2007 the arrival of the worst economic crisis since the Great Depression of the 1930s, combined with increasing pessimism about the wars in Iraq and Afghanistan and scandals surrounding the behavior of the U.S. military, made George W. Bush among the most unpopular presidents in more than a century. In the 2008 presidential race, Democratic senator Barack Obama of Illinois prevailed over Republican senator John McCain of Arizona, becoming the first nonwhite president in American history. In his concession speech from Phoenix, Senator McCain saluted the African American struggle for equality and the "special pride that must be theirs tonight." There were tears of joy and dancing through the night as African Americans and whites alike took to the streets to celebrate what McCain described as a nation that "is a world away from the cruel and prideful bigotry" of its racially divided past.

There were clearly changes in the American understanding of race and ethnicity. A new cohort of respected nonwhite political leaders seemed to be emerging on the national stage and the United States suddenly appeared to be more ethnically democratic. However, there were many commentators who started to come around to Stanley Crouch's concern that Obama was the president of a new and more cosmopolitan nation, but not a more racially democratic one. Many of the same old problems between blacks and whites seemed to continue: the urban uprisings in undercapitalized cities with large numbers of underemployed African Americans, mass incarceration of African Americans out of proportion to their numbers, and the often rancorous national debate about racially biased urban policing that Ahmir Questlove Thompson references in his discussion of growing up black in Philadelphia.

Inner-city African Americans were not the only population facing frustrated socioeconomic and political aspirations, though. After nearly four decades of rising inequality and declining intergenerational socioeconomic mobility, middle-class rebellions were emerging on the left, like debt resisters, and on the right among "tea party" activists. As new candidates were lining up for the 2016 presidential campaign, the nation wondered if Obama's promises of "change we can believe in" and a rejection of the unilateralism of the Bush administration had had any substantive meaning.

A Public Debate between Somalis in Lewiston, Maine, and Their Mayor (October 1, 2002 – January 29, 2003)

55

MAYOR LAURIER T. RAYMOND ET AL.

The Letter That Sparked the Debate and Supporters of It

America has always depended on immigrants to conquer new frontiers and revitalize old ones. The "manifest destiny" to "overspread the continent allotted by providence" and create a "boundless future . . . comprising hundreds of happy millions" that John L. O'Sullivan talked about in the 1840s has always involved the arrival of people from other places in search of a better life. The period since 1965 when post–World War I immigration controls were loosened is not really so different. Though many Americans think of immigrants working in low-wage jobs in big teeming cities like Los Angeles, New York, and Miami, immigrants from Iraq work in meatpacking on the Great Plains, Cambodians run grocery stores in Minnesota, Mexicans have revitalized post-industrial cities and towns in upstate New York, and South Asians have renovated abandoned 1960s motels in small towns across the nation. According to researchers at the University of Michigan, America saw a rural renaissance in the 1990s, and it was partly driven by immigrants.

In particular, the need of new arrivals for housing and space for small business start-ups has increased real estate values in undercapitalized downtowns, forgotten small towns, and dying neighborhoods across the country. Not only have these immigrants provided cheap labor for existing local businesses, especially farming and food processing, but they also have contributed vast amounts of "sweat equity," repopulating fallow communities across the country, pulling boards off shuttered windows, patching holes in leaking roofs, and filling the streets with new life and a new vitality. Even in the U.S./Mexican border region, where neither legal nor illegal immigrants are likely to stay for long, the impact of these "new immigrants" has been felt in the form of a huge expansion of well-paid border patrol jobs that has led to the gentrification of old mining towns and border stations like Bisbee and Douglas in Arizona.

Laurier T. Raymond, "A Letter to the Somali Community," *Portland Press Herald*, October 1, 2002; Gary Savard, "Our Mayor," Sunjournal.com, January 18, 2003.

However, there are problems and challenges that such immigration poses both for immigrants and for receiving communities. Among them is the provision of social services, schooling, public infrastructure, and municipal administration for new arrivals, who may not earn enough money or pay enough taxes at first to offset their use of public resources; the changing ethnocultural or religious makeup of longstanding communities that are not accustomed to outsiders or newcomers; new political alliances in town councils; fear of overpopulation and crime; and potential interracial dating and marriage between the children of longtime community members and newcomers.

Many of these challenges and problems emerged in the conflict over the letter sent by the mayor of Lewiston, Maine, Laurier T. Raymond, to the Portland Press Herald *in October 2002 asking the roughly 1,100 Somali refugees who had arrived in the previous two years to discourage more of their countrymen from coming to the city of roughly 35,000. The letter immediately sparked a nationwide controversy. The press described a "Somali invasion" and, in January 2003, white supremacists descended on the town to organize a demonstration in defense of the mayor and against the Somalis. Few in the community came out to support the white supremacists, who managed to bring together roughly one hundred demonstrators. Many, including the mayor, avoided the confrontation entirely. However, a large crowd of four thousand people, more than ten percent of the entire population of Lewiston, came out in the middle of a Maine winter to show that they welcomed the newcomers, displaying signs like the one carried by a small white girl in Syrian immigrant filmmaker Ziad Hamzeh's documentary* The Letter: An American Town and the "Somali Invasion". *The sign reads: "My best friend is from another country."*

The documents in this section, including the original letter written by Mayor Raymond, are a small representative sample of the many letters to the editor that appeared in the local news media relating to Somali immigration to the Lewiston area.

QUESTIONS TO CONSIDER

1. Should communities have the right to restrict how many immigrants come?
2. What personal and political reasons do you think the mayor may have had for sending this letter?
3. Do you think that the people who supported the mayor and his letter are racist or anti-immigrant? Explain.

MAYOR LAURIER T. RAYMOND

A Letter to the Somali Community, October 1, 2002

For some number of months, I have observed the continued movement of a substantial number of Somalis into the downtown area of our community. I have applauded the efforts of our city staff in making available the existing services and the local citizenry for accepting and dealing with the influx.

I assumed that it would become obvious to the new arrivals the effect the large numbers of new residents has had upon the existing staff and city finances and that this would bring about a voluntary reduction of the number of new arrivals—it being evident that the burden has been, for the most part, cheerfully accepted, and every effort has been made to accommodate it.

Our Department of Human Services has recently reported that the number of Somali families arriving into the city during the month of September is below the approximate monthly average that we have seen over the last year or so. It may be premature to assume that this may serve as a signal for future relocation activity, but the decline is welcome relief given increasing demands on city and school services.

I feel that recent relocation activity over the summer has necessitated that I communicate directly with the Somali elders and leaders regarding our newest residents. If recent declining arrival numbers are the result of your outreach efforts to discourage relocation into the city, I applaud those efforts. If they are the product of other unrelated random events, I would ask that the Somali leadership make every effort to communicate my concerns on city and school service impacts with other friends and extended family who are considering a move to this community.

To date, we have found the funds to accommodate the situation. A continued increased demand will tax the city's finances.

This large number of new arrivals cannot continue without negative results for all. The Somali community must exercise some discipline and reduce the stress on our limited finances and our generosity.

I am well aware of the legal right of a U.S. resident to move anywhere he/she pleases, but it is time for the Somali community to exercise this discipline in view of the effort that has been made on its behalf.

We will continue to accommodate the present residents as best as we can, but we need self-discipline and cooperation from everyone.

Only with your help will we be successful in the future—please pass the word: We have been overwhelmed and have responded valiantly. Now we need breathing room. Our city is maxed-out financially, physically and emotionally.

I look forward to your cooperation.

Laurier T. Raymond Jr.
Mayor, City of Lewiston

GARY SAVARD

Our Mayor, January 18, 2003

I am writing to express my support for the city's mayor, Laurier T. Raymond Jr.

Mayor Raymond's October letter to the Somali elders was not a request that they leave Lewiston, but rather a request that they slow down the influx to allow the city to assimilate their existing population and have some time to assess its impact on schools, housing and services.

This has been blown completely out of proportion over the past few months by a very vocal minority with a holier than thou attitude. Groups of people that seem to require a cause to champion in order to justify their own self worth. Every cause, worthy or not, has such a group at its core.

Now it seems, in the natural progression of this cause, the inevitable calls for Mayor Raymond's resignation are being piped into the system.

Mayor Raymond chose not to attend the Many and One rally at Bates College. I didn't attend either, nor it seems, did about 36,000 other Lewiston residents.

Does this mean we are racist or that we don't care? I don't think so.

I think that the majority of Lewiston's residents are, like myself, very willing to allow any minority population of this city every opportunity to take root and succeed. In the same sense, I also think that, as citizens and taxpayers, we are entitled to an honest accounting of the impact, financial and otherwise, on our community that these ongoing changes have. Our city officials should not keep us in the dark, elected or otherwise.

In closing, I will submit that any citizen of Lewiston has the right to ask the mayor to step down. Conversely, we also have the right to ask him not to bend to these pressures, but to continue on with his elected office.

I urge Lewiston residents to exercise that right. Non-residents need not apply.

Gary Savard, Lewiston, ME

56

ELDERS OF THE SOMALI COMMUNITY ET AL.

Letter in Support of the Somali Community

War may tear regions and countries apart and destroy countless lives, but it also brings people together. Since America ended its flirtation with isolationism in the 1930s by entering World War II, the nation has intervened in numerous domestic disputes and regional conflicts. Each intervention brings new social and political connections, some as intimate as mixed marriages and babies and others as abstractly instrumental and professional as recruiting native academics to teach foreign languages and area studies in American universities or bringing locals to American corporate headquarters to help identify and take advantage of business opportunities in the region.

In the seven decades since the end of World War II, the United States has become a giant force in world politics, often absorbing political refugees and dissidents from around the globe when U.S. actions have helped shape the outcome of political conflicts

---

Elders of the Somali Community, "Somalis in Lewiston," *Portland Press Herald*, October 8, 2002.

in the refugees' home countries. From the millions of people from dozens of communist countries who were given political asylum during America's cold war conflict with the U.S.S.R. to the many allies granted visas during the numerous Middle Eastern crises over the past sixty years, one commitment the government has made is to provide a haven for those who have lost their homes in conflicts involving the United States. Though the policy is not always successful, the question of what happens to displaced allies is always on the agenda. Somalia was no exception.

In 1991, after many decades as a cold war flash point on the strategically important Horn of Africa, Somalia pitched into civil war. In 1993, the U.S. Army led a United Nations force into Somalia with a stated purpose of ending a famine and wresting the country from the war lords who were said to be making life unbearable. Though the U.S. Army lost only nineteen soldiers—a relatively small toll compared to the hundreds lost in Lebanon in the 1980s and the two thousand plus killed in the recent conflict in Iraq—the conflict spun out of control for President Bill Clinton, who woke up one morning to the front cover of American newspapers displaying photos of a dead American soldier being dragged through the streets of Mogadishu. These dramatic images shocked the nation and, in combination with a lack of strategic goals and bad coordination with other U.N. partners, each of whom had its own allies on the ground, made the intervention in Somalia one that most Americans would prefer to forget. Such were the difficult conditions under which Somali Muslims made their way to the United States.

People displaced by war and politics, like the Somalis, are a tiny percentage of the total immigration flow to the United States. However, despite their presence being connected to highly charged foreign policy debates, many of the challenges that they faced were similar to those of the more common migration stream: people in search of economic opportunity. Like most immigrant groups in the American past, upon arriving the Somali generally sought homes in places where there was available employment and ties to friends, immediate family, clans, villages, and political or professional affiliations. This brought the majority of them, estimated at 50,000, to the Minneapolis/St. Paul twin city area and eventually to the small towns and cities of neighboring Wisconsin, where many have found work in meatpacking plants. They also took up residence in cities and towns from Texas to Maine. The terror attacks of September 11, 2001, came as a terrible blow to their adjustment to their new homes. None of the terrorists had been Somali, but to foreigners and Muslims, the country suddenly seemed less friendly and homelike.

The next year was a disaster for Somali immigrants. British filmmaker Ridley Scott released Black Hawk Down *(2001), which graphically, represents the downing of a U.S. Army helicopter in Somalia and the fighting between American soldiers and nameless, somewhat faceless Somalis who were loyal to various war lords. The movie focuses on the struggle of the Americans to make their way out of the confusing and terrifying battles of urban Mogadishu. Critics have disparaged the movie for many things, including rushing release to take advantage of post–9/11 jingoism, ignoring the far greater loss of Somali life and the courage of poorly armed Somalis fighting an invading modern army, and not hiring any of the Somali immigrants as actors. In light of the movie's success, Somali immigrants came to be seen by some as movie villains who popped out from behind buildings with automatic weapons, like targets in a shooting gallery.*

In late 2002, the Midwestern Somali community found itself the victim of a series of violent race bias incidents, and distrust grew between Somalis and their neighbors as Somalis felt increasingly unwanted in their new home. Lewiston, Maine, is one of the many places across the United States that became home to Somali refugees. One of the "whitest" cities in what might be the "whitest" state in the United States, Lewiston is home to Bates College and was probably chosen by Somali migrants because of its relatively affordable real estate, low crime and drug rates, and proximity to Portland, which was the initial point of arrival for Somalis in Maine. Through much of 2002, the national news media did stories about this migration of African Muslims to this small, white Maine college town.

Though there were many in the community who welcomed the Africans, there were many who were concerned about the potential drain on municipal resources and the potential changes to the character of the community. On October 1, 2002, the mayor of Lewiston, Laurier T. Raymond, sent a letter to the Portland Press Herald requesting that the Somalis who were living in Lewiston make an effort to discourage further settlement by their countrymen. There was a national media scandal that emerged from this letter and its implication that some people have more right to live in a place than others. However, for many Somalis, the letter ultimately proved positive by bringing some of the tensions surrounding their arrival into the open, forcing them to organize in their own defense, and showing them and their new countrymen, through the January 11, 2003, Many and One rally, how many of their neighbors they could already call friends.

The following document is the original response from a council of Somali elders to Mayor Raymond's letter.

QUESTIONS TO CONSIDER

1. Do you think that the Somali elders responded in the right way? Why or why not?
2. Why do you think so many people came out to support the Somalis?
3. Do you think that the makers of *Black Hawk Down* had any obligation to the Somali American community? Should they have approached the film differently?

October 6, 2002

Mr. Laurier Raymond
Mayor, City of Lewiston

Re: Your letter dated October 1, 2002, Somalis in Lewiston

This letter is in response to your above referenced letter in regard to the move of Somali refugees/immigrants to the city of Lewiston. First of all, with due respect, we would like to indicate that your letter is not only untimely but is also inflammatory and disturbing, to say the least. Your letter is untimely because it is written and released at a time when the movement of Somalis to Lewiston has naturally dropped and as per records no Somali moved to Lewiston since the end of August 2002. The letter is also inflammatory and disturbing as we are dismayed to see such a letter from an elected official and leader who is supposed to show good leadership, co-existence and harmony among the residents of this humble city.

We react to your letter in mixed feelings ranging from dismay, astonishment and anger. This is because of the fact that you have never given us a chance to meet with you and discuss our future plans with you during your term in office. Your predecessor Mayor Kalleigh Tara perfectly understood us and was working with us as new additions to a city where she was the mayor. We also had and were given opportunities to meet with and discuss our future with elected and non-elected local and state officials. Most recently, such meetings included those we had with Governor Angus King on September 17 and with the gubernatorial candidate, Congressman John Baldacci on September 27th, among others.

During all such meetings, the officials indicated their satisfaction with our coming to live here in the state, they say, [that] is sparsely populated and needs to attract more residents as both manpower and future electorates. Those officials, after listening to us, applauded our efforts to try and "Fit in" as much as we can. While we have had contacts with other leaders as stated above, you have never given us a chance to meet and explain ourselves to you. The first contact, which you ever had with us, is through your recent letter, which prompted this response; something which we never thought would happen and feel unwarranted at this time.

For your information therefore, our coming to Lewiston and living here have revitalized this city in certain ways. Our presence has turned Lewiston into a multi-ethnic, multi-racial city, which has embraced diversity and change. A city of thirty-six thousand people, in the middle of the "whitest" state in the country has suddenly become an international city. Lewiston's name appeared in papers and news clips around the country. We portrayed the facts about this place and its humble people who we consider, by and large, as generous Americans who understand our plight and are ready to help in our initial days of settling down. Our presence here has also attracted hundreds of thousands of dollars in state and federal funds to boost existing social services for all residents of Lewiston. This particular point was not stated in your letter.

Apartment units located in the Lewiston downtown area which were abandoned many years ago, were suddenly refurbished and made livable as the arrival of Somalis generated funds and put money in the pockets of landlords. This also raised the market value of real estate. Somalis were hired to work in businesses and plants making them to be able to contribute to the local economy as taxpayers. Back in April 2002, there were 249 able-bodied Somali men and women who could work. Forty people worked at the time. Today out of the 416 able bodied men and women 215 persons are currently employed. This is over 50% of adults who could work. Also, there are three Somali businesses in Lewiston which opened in less than a year.

While we thank the city of Lewiston, and the general public for their understanding and accepting us in their midst, we would nevertheless like to bring to your attention and to the attention of others in your line of thinking, that we are citizens and/or legal residents of this country. Although we originally hail from the Eastern African state of Somalia, we renounced our

Somali citizenship and taken U.S. citizenship. Over 80% of our children are Americans by birth. Therefore, we believe we have every right to live anywhere in this country. So do other Somalis or any other legal residents who choose to come and live in Lewiston or in Alaska for that matter.

In view of the above, and with due respect we consider your letter Mr. Mayor, as the writing of ill-informed leader who is bent towards bigotry. Therefore, by a copy of this letter we ask both the state government and law enforcement to guarantee our safety here. If any harm in form of an attack happens to any Somali-American man, woman or child in the wake of your letter, we hold you squarely responsible for any such acts. We think your letter is an attempt to agitate and incite the local people and a license to violence against our people physically, verbally and emotionally.

Hope this is clear and let God show all of us what is right.

Sincerely,
Elders of the Somali Community

cc: Office of Governor Angus King
William Welch, Lewiston Police Chief
Lewiston/Auburn Community Task Force
Pierrot Rugaba, State Refugee Coordinator
Jim Bennet, Administrator: City of Lewiston

FOR CRITICAL THINKING

1. Do you think the Somalis could have approached settling in Lewiston in a different way that might have avoided this conflict? How would you have advised them?
2. What responsibilities do immigrants have to their receiving communities? What responsibilities do receiving communities have to immigrants?

57

CATHY LANGSTON

When PATCO Went on Strike

In August 1981, in one of Ronald Reagan's first major acts as president, he used the U.S. military to break an air traffic controllers' strike led by the Professional Air Traffic Controllers Organization (PATCO). Although PATCO had endorsed Reagan during his campaign for president, thanks to his professed support for their demands for safer and better working conditions, Reagan ordered all striking workers to return to work in forty-eight hours or be terminated. Then, when less than 10 percent of them returned, he took action, firing more than eleven thousand air traffic controllers, jailing key PATCO leaders, and banning all strikers from future work for the federal government.

With no other unions supporting the strike or stopping work in sympathy, supervisors and military controllers joined the two thousand nonstriking PATCO members to ensure that air travel continued, albeit at reduced levels, until the Federal Aviation Administration's flight school could train permanent replacements. PATCO quickly became isolated and neutralized. By the end of October, it was officially decertified by the government.

Reagan had shown strong leadership and put a decisive end to a half century of growing trade union power and rising standards of living for workers, particularly in blue-collar fields. While national union membership had been slowly declining from its peak in the 1950s, probably due to the growth of nonunionized white-collar and service sector jobs, Reagan put a chill on organized labor, and union membership dropped during his time in office from more than 20 percent to around 12 percent of the national workforce.

At the time of the strike, Cathy Langston was the mother of two young children and the wife of one of the strike leaders, Randy Langston. It was not until 2010—almost thirty years after the terminations—that she recorded her recollections of those difficult days, excerpted here, and revealed the depth of the confusion and betrayal experienced by workers at the hands of President Reagan.

QUESTIONS TO CONSIDER

1. Many people have argued that Ronald Reagan's firing of the PATCO workers was overkill. What evidence do you find that his actions were unexpected?
2. The PATCO strike is often seen as a major moment of change in the history of American labor that permanently tilted power toward em-

Cathy Langston, *What It Means When God Goes on Strike* (N.p.: published by author, 2010), 2–8, 22, 30, 34–36, 57–60.

ployers, even at nonunion sites. What evidence do you find in this document for that change?
3. How might Cathy Langston have told the story differently back in the 1980s, at the time of the firings?

The headlines screamed . . .

11,500 AIR TRAFFIC CONTROLLERS FIRED!

However, to me they were only a whisper. I knew it was only a façade. "Within days they would be right back at work, right?" I kept questioning. PATCO had outlined to all of us exactly how it would go.

You're fired!

Harsh words to ever have to hear, but especially from the President of the United States. August 3, 1981, is the official date of the air traffic controllers strike. It is now a date in the history books. College students are assigned term papers to write to analyze it.

We lived through it. It is more than just history to us. It is pain, heartache, denial, tragedy, and finally, triumph.

I could not believe what was happening. My husband, along with 11,500 other air traffic controllers, was saying no to the President. Of course, they expected to go back to work at some point, but not until some negotiations had taken place. The leadership of PATCO (Professional Air Traffic Controllers Organization) had promised that the salary of anyone fired would be paid from a million dollar strike fund. So it didn't seem like a tremendous financial risk at the time.

I am a true Southern girl and I did not even believe in unions and strikes. Nonetheless, since my husband, Randy, was the vice-president of the local Raleigh-Durham unit, I knew I had to support him and what he was backing.

For a federal employee to strike is illegal. However, they convinced the rank and file of controllers that all 13,000 who went on strike could not be fired. There were 11,500 who were refusing to go back when ordered to do so. The head of PATCO was then arrested. Several presidents of local unions were put in shackles when they were arrested; one from Virginia was paraded in front of the TV cameras in his shackles and chains as if he were a danger to society.

The reasons behind the strike had to do with improving the safety for the traveling public. The controllers had to use outdated equipment, work too many hours with not enough personnel. They had worked a year and a half with no contract. Also, every time there were negotiations, they were asked to give up benefits they had already garnered. This was definitely unfair.

Air traffic controllers have one of the most stressful jobs that exist. It affects both their health and families. Randy would be so stressed when he came home from a shift that he would immediately have to go to sleep in order to decompress. Some controllers turned to alcohol to unwind, which then caused more stress at home, in addition to their intense workday. Their careers are short-lived. They often retire in their forties with disability.

In relation to pay being equal to the job, a pilot is responsible for 100 to 200 passengers and crew, while a controller is responsible for 10 to 12 times that number at any given moment. An air traffic controller's salary is 4 to 5 times less than that of a pilot.

To insure the public safety, it was felt that a controller should not be overworked. PATCO thought a shorter work week was needed to accomplish this. The FAA (Federal Aviation Administration) seemingly would not listen. Drastic measures were called for, PATCO concluded.

The FAA was aware a strike was being planned. They had known for over a year and had been making alternate arrangements to handle the work load of the striking controllers.

Although Ronald Reagan had promised in a letter to PATCO before he was elected that he would assist in easing the working conditions of the controllers if they helped elect him, he chose to do the very opposite of that.

He chose to renege in true political fashion.

The following is a copy of the letter written to Robert Poli, PATCO president, from Ronald Reagan. This was dated October 20th 1980, before Reagan was elected as President of The United States of America:

Dear Mr. Poli:

I have been briefed by members of my staff as to the deplorable state of our nation's air traffic control system. They have told me that too few people working unreasonable hours with obsolete equipment has placed the nation's air travelers in unwarranted danger. In a[n] area so clearly related to public safety the Carter administration has failed to act responsibly.

You can rest assured that if I am elected President, I will take whatever steps are necessary to provide our air traffic controllers with the most modern equipment available and to adjust staff levels and work days so that they are commensurate with achieving a maximum degree of public safety.

I pledge to you that my administration will work very closely with you to bring about a spirit of cooperation between the President and the air traffic controllers.

Sincerely,
Ronald Reagan

I had just given birth to our second child in March [1981]. Nikki was only five months old when Randy went on strike. Our son, Steve, had just turned eleven. Randy was the vice-president of the local union and chose to be the spokesman to the media to protect our local president. His outgoing personality made him a natural for the role. Later he would regret this since his face became synonymous with the aftermath. He was constantly interviewed. At one point, to humanize the plight, the camera crew and reporters even held an interview at the bowling alley, where Randy was attempting to spend quality time with his only son. Furthermore, he was quoted daily in the *News and Observer*, which at the time was the most read newspaper in North Carolina. We even had Nikki in her stroller on the picket line. Our family was whole-heartedly in this strike for the "greater good."

Every day we woke up with renewed hope that the government would relent and the controllers would be allowed to return to work. Regardless of what we saw or heard, we just knew a deal was being worked out in the background to get everyone back to work. Days turned into weeks, weeks turned into months. No end. No deal. PATCO had been dissolved. "Who was looking out for us, now?" I thought.

Those cocky controllers were beginning to crumble. Nothing like this had ever happened before in the history of unions. The loyal obedient soldiers who were fighting to make their world better soon came to realize they had been grossly misled.

The courts became a battlefield—seemingly our only means of returning to air traffic control. We expected any day to hear that the controllers had won their jobs back with back pay. . . .

We were so naïve and innocent to believe no hurt was possible. The hurt and pain that followed that walk-out was unbelievable: suicides, failed marriages, nervous breakdowns, severe depressions, foreclosures, heart attacks, bankruptcies. I wondered if any of us would survive this. Surely no one involved would ever be the same.

Within a couple of weeks of the strike I could see families already falling apart. We had been over to [controller] Tim Sanford's house to discuss the walk-out a couple of days before it was scheduled to take place. He and his wife, Sandy, had just moved in and were not quite straightened out. The wife was attractive and looked the professional she was. She had apparently landed a good paying job and they were having a heated argument about what might happen after the strike. Sandy did not want to leave the area if the strike lasted for any length of time or if Tim were fired. Several days after the strike and some violent arguments, Tim left, strung out on drugs. Randy and several other controllers were asked to help his wife move to a less expensive place.

The morning after the move, I drove to the convenience store with my children to get a Pepsi. A haggard-looking woman, lined face, and hair pulled straight back came over to the car to speak to me. I soon realized it was Sandy Sanford, who, only a couple of weeks before looked youthful and well-kept. What had this precious individual gone through in such a short time? I had never seen anyone age so fast in all my life.

Another family heartbreak involved a striking controller named Matt Burnette. He was able to put up a good front for about a year. He was in business for himself, selling insurance. Of course, he had to drive a luxurious car to look successful in order to recruit others to sell for him. That is part of the strategy for directors or managers. His car was a brand new Cadillac de Ville. Few people knew it was only leased.

One day, his wife, Patsy, came home to find a tape recording and a power of attorney from him. Matt had recorded a message that said he could no longer continue living the lies and maintaining the charade. Bills had been piling up and he was not making a lot of money. They would need to sell the house. No one knew where he was. He had just disappeared. Patsy sold the house and was quite distraught afterward. About nine months later he returned and said he had had to get away from the bill collectors.

We read in the newspaper not long after this that a controller (who we did not know) and his wife had placed all their bills on the kitchen table and hung themselves.

Oh, the guilt we felt, especially Randy. Not only had we done this to our family, but as an officer, Randy had tried to convince other controllers to join the strike. Who knew?

Then, when a person is in a crisis situation that he caused himself, he is subject to disdain, rather than sympathy. And who could blame others for feeling this way?

The government had told us "Good-bye" and now they were handing out retirement checks. I knew this meant finality. I wanted to say, "Take ours back!"

Some controllers tried to start businesses with their retirement money. More than not, these were not successful. . . .

Uncertainty is petrifying. Since striking federal employees can not draw unemployment benefits, my teaching salary was all the income we had. That would not cover our living expenses since we were still living on the same level as before. That meant taking money out of savings to cover what Randy normally brought home. No one knows the agony I felt every time we did that. Our next home was dissolving with every dollar we spent.

Everything that was happening was taking a tremendous emotional toll on me. As long as Randy and I had been married, he had had a paycheck on a regular basis. Also, I was accustomed to being self-sufficient without depending on others. I had no idea what the future held. I was very frightened. I remember crying and being nervous all the time. In fact, my nerves were so bad, I felt like all my skin had been pulled off my body to expose bare nerves. Raw! Oh, so raw! I was irritated and agitated. I wanted to be in the bed whenever I could. That was my solace.

Randy knew we had unknowingly sabotaged our lives. It's hard to face reality when you really don't know what reality is. Aren't there talks behind closed doors that will settle this mess, give Randy back the career he loved with back-pay? A lawyer in Fayetteville agreed to take the case. "Surely, we have a chance, now," I thought.

Meanwhile as weeks turn into months, hope turns into a dark depression for Randy. With each day and no resolution, the chances of his return diminished.

He began to write his life story with the anticipation of the last chapter ending in tragedy. I was very upset that he was not working, not bringing in any money for our bills and our savings was dwindling. I was extremely angry with him, but I was afraid to say anything to him in his state of mind.

I thought a new career would be good for him, because it would alleviate the stress that had been so difficult for him. Nonetheless, I had not anticipated how difficult it would be for him to leave air traffic control and move on.

First of all, no future employers would even talk to someone who was a fired controller. The ex-controllers were all black-listed. It was hard to even pickup a part-time job.

Furthermore, Randy didn't want a new career. He wanted the one he loved so much. It was challenging and invigorating to him, as well as many of the other controllers, in spite of the difficulties and stress of it. . . .

We had begged God to end the strike, put the controllers back to work and give them their back pay. Apparently God was on strike also. He would not budge.

58

The Wall

In August of 1961 the East German government (DDR) erected a wall dividing the city of Berlin between the communist East and the capitalist West. It was the first inkling for many that the communist Eastern Bloc might be a weaker opponent than strategists in the West believed. The Soviet Union had launched the world's first satellite into space in 1957, and, only months before the wall went up, they had decisively beaten the United States into space, sending Soviet cosmonaut Yuri Gagarin into orbit and safely bringing him home. Soviet allies in China had taken the world's most populated country into the communist bloc, most of southeastern Europe had gone communist at the end of World War II, communists in North Korea had recently fought the United States to a draw, Vietnam was sliding away from capitalism, and the Cuban revolutionaries who had seized power in 1959 were, at the time, also flirting with communism. For many in the West there was a genuine fear that Marx's prediction that capitalism would create its own gravediggers was correct. And then there was the Berlin Wall, which divided families and neighborhoods in the same city. To those who supported communism, it was a shock that a wall was necessary to keep people in, and for those who supported capitalism it was a confirmation that they were right about the bankruptcy of a system built around the idea that people should be equal.

For twenty-eight years this wall stood as a symbol of a world divided by political philosophy and by the two camps supporting these different visions of the greatest good. Called the Cold War, both sides mobilized proxy wars across the globe, spent unimaginably large sums of money building weapon systems designed to threaten each other, and sometimes ran to the brink of nuclear war. Everyday life on both sides was radically reconfigured around this battle. Individuals, both innocent and guilty, were rooted out of their lives in political purges and witch hunts, as little children huddled under their school desks in air raid drills and studied Cold War curriculum like the Florida public school system's Americanism vs. Communism.

Then suddenly, with only a little warning, on November 9, 1989, seventy-two years after the Russian Revolution that had started the communist Soviet Union and twenty-eight years after the Berlin Wall was erected, political changes in the Eastern Bloc and protests in Europe forced East German authorities to open the border. Parties, celebrations, and dancing in the streets ensued. Soon, an open border was not enough for the millions of Europeans who had long been kept separate by the wall and its two economic systems. On November 12, 1989, they decided to begin to remove the border itself, by opening up a large gate through which Westerners and Easterners could easily and freely pass without the approval of authorities. This was the fall of the Berlin Wall, the end of the communist Eastern Bloc, and the start of a radical change in how the United States and its allies viewed world security.

QUESTIONS TO CONSIDER

1. Why do you think these people are on top of the wall?
2. What events in your life remind you of this public moment in Germany?
3. How do you think such a big change occurred without rioting or police violence?
4. At the time the Berlin Wall went up, "separation barriers" between nations were very rare and generally viewed as unacceptable. Since the fall of the Berlin Wall, they have become more common. How would you explain the difference between the Berlin Wall and, for instance, the wall that currently separates the United States and Mexico?

Berliners celebrate the fall of the Berlin Wall.
© *Regis Bossu/Sygma/Corbis.*

59

DENNIS W. SHEPARD

Homophobia in the Heartland

On October 12, 1998, Matthew Shepard, a twenty-one-year-old University of Wyoming student, died from injuries suffered five days earlier in a gay-bashing incident. Lured

Dennis W. Shepard, victim impact statement, November 4, 1999, www.wiredstrategies.com/mrshep.htm.

into a truck by two men he had met at the campus bar, Shepard believed he was going with them to discuss gay liberation politics. Once inside the truck, the men told the five-foot-two, 102-pound Shepard that they were not gay. They robbed and beat him and tied him to a split-rail fence. He was found there eighteen hours later—barely breathing, with a crushed skull, and with blood covering his face, except in those spots where his tears had washed it away. The image of the gentle and delicate Shepard tied to a fence post and left for dead became a national symbol in the fight against intolerance.

The outrage over the attack and the outpouring of sympathy for Shepard's parents suggested how far most of the country had come in its tolerance of sexual minorities. The trial prosecutor sought the death penalty for Shepard's murderers, despite its unpopularity in Wyoming and pressure from the Roman Catholic Church. People organized tributes and memorial services for Shepard. President Bill Clinton held a press conference at the White House, where he and Judy Shepard, Matthew's mother, spoke out in support of federal hate crimes legislation. Many states have since passed their own hate crimes laws.

There were, however, reminders that homosexuality remained far from universally accepted. At Shepard's funeral, members of a Kansas City Baptist congregation disrupted the occasion with signs that read "God hates fags" and "No fags in heaven." Although the trial judge disallowed a "gay panic" defense—that one of the killers had been compelled to commit the crime because he had been humiliated as a child by homosexual experiences—the compromise defense, that Shepard's sexual advances had triggered a murderous rage, struck a chord with many Americans who believed homosexuality to be immoral and wrong. Additionally, many people objected to the new hate crimes laws, arguing that they created a two-tier justice system and punished ideas as well as actions.

The following selection comes from a statement by Dennis Shepard, Matthew's father, that he read to the court after the second of his son's killers, Aaron McKinney, received two life sentences without parole.

QUESTIONS TO CONSIDER

1. Why did this case become so important to so many people?
2. Why do you think Dennis Shepard read this statement in court?
3. Do you think hate crimes laws might have prevented the death of Matthew Shepard? Explain.

Your Honor, Members of the Jury, Mr. Rerucha,

I would like to begin my statement by addressing the jury. Ladies and gentlemen, a terrible crime was committed in Laramie thirteen months ago. Because of that crime, the reputation of the city of Laramie, the University of Wyoming, and the state of Wyoming became synonymous with gay bashing, hate crimes, and brutality. While some of this reputation may be deserved, it was blown out of proportion by our friends in the media. Yesterday, you, the jury, showed the world that Wyoming and the city of Laramie will not tolerate hate crimes. Yes, this was a hate crime, pure and simple, with the added ingredient of robbery. My son Matthew paid a terrible price to open the eyes of all of us who live in Wyoming, the United States, and the world to the unjust and unnecessary fears, discrimination, and intolerance that members of the gay community face every day. Yesterday's decision by you showed true courage and made a statement. That statement is that Wyoming is the Equality State, that Wyoming will not tolerate discrimination based on sexual orientation, that violence is not the solution. Ladies and gentlemen, you have the respect and admiration of Matthew's family and friends and of countless strangers around the world. Be proud of what you have accomplished. You may have prevented another family from losing a son or daughter.

Your Honor, I would also like to thank you for the dignity and grace with which this trial was conducted. Repeated attempts to distract the court from the true purpose of this trial failed because of your attentiveness, knowledge, and willingness to take a stand and make new law in the area of sexual orientation and the "gay panic" defense. By doing so, you have emphasized that Matthew was a human being with all the rights and responsibilities and protections of any citizen of Wyoming.

Mr. Rerucha took the oath of office as prosecuting attorney to protect the rights of the citizens of Albany County as mandated by the laws of the state of Wyoming, regardless of his personal feelings and beliefs. At no time did Mr. Rerucha make any decision on the outcome of this case without the permission of Judy and me. It was our decision to take this case to trial just as it was our decision to accept the plea bargain today and the earlier plea bargain of Mr. [Russell] Henderson. A trial was necessary to show that this was a hate crime and not just a robbery gone bad. If we had sought a plea bargain earlier, the facts of this case would not have been known and the question would always be present that we had something to hide. In addition, this trial was necessary to help provide some closure to the citizens of Laramie, Albany County, and the state. . . .

My son Matthew did not look like a winner. After all, he was small for his age—weighing at the most 110 pounds and standing only 5'2" tall. He was rather uncoordinated and wore braces from the age of thirteen until the day he died. However, in his all too brief life, he proved that he was a winner. My son, a gentle, caring soul, proved that he was as tough as, if not tougher than, anyone I have ever heard of or known. On October 6, 1998, my son tried to show the world that he could win again. On October 12, 1998, my first-born son, and my hero, lost. On October 12, 1998, my first-born son, and my hero, died. On October 12, 1998, part of my life, part of my hopes, and part of my dreams died, fifty days before his twenty-second birthday. He died quietly, surrounded by family and friends, with his mother and brother holding his hand. All that I have left now are the memories and the mementos of his existence. I would like to briefly talk about Matt and the impact of his death.

It's hard to put into words how much Matt meant to family and friends and how much they meant to him. Everyone wanted him to succeed because he tried so hard. The spark that he provided to people had to be experienced. He simply made everyone feel better about themselves. Family and friends were his focus. He knew that he always had their support for anything that he wanted to try.

Matt's gift was people. He loved being with people, helping people, and making others feel good. The hope of a better world, free of harassment and discrimination because a person was different, kept him motivated. All his life he felt the stabs of discrimination. Because of that, he was sensitive to other people's feelings. He was naïve to the extent that, regardless of the wrongs people did to him, he still had faith that they would change and become "nice." Matt trusted people, perhaps too much. Violence was not a part of his life until his senior year in high school. He would walk into a fight and try to break it up. He was the perfect negotiator. He could get two people talking to each other again as no one else could.

Matt loved people and he trusted them. He could never understand how one person could hurt another, physically or verbally. They would hurt him and he would give them another chance. This quality of seeing only good gave him friends around the world. He didn't see size, race, intelligence, sex, religion, or the hundred other things that people use to make choices about people. All he saw was the person. All he wanted was to make another person his friend. All he wanted was to make another person feel good. All he wanted was to be accepted as an equal.

What did Matt's friends think of him? Fifteen of his friends from high school in Switzerland, as well as his high school advisor, joined hundreds of others at his memorial services. They left college, fought a blizzard, and came together one more time to say goodbye to Matt. Men and women coming from different countries, cultures, and religions thought enough of my son to drop everything and come to Wyoming—most of them for the first time. That's why this Wyoming country boy wanted to major in foreign relations and languages. He wanted to continue making friends and, at the same time, help others. He wanted to make a difference. Did he? You tell me.

I loved my son and, as can be seen throughout this statement, was proud of him. He was not my gay son. He was my son who happened to be gay. He was a good-looking, intelligent, caring person. There were the usual arguments and, at times, he was a real pain in the butt. I felt the regrets of a father when he realizes that his son is not a star athlete. But it was replaced with a greater pride when I saw him on the stage. The hours that he spent learning his parts, working behind the scenes, and helping others made me realize he was actually an excellent athlete, in a more dynamic way, because of the different types of physical and mental conditioning required by actors. To this day, I have never figured out how he was able to spend all those hours at the theater, during the school year, and still have good grades.

Because my job involved lots of travel, I never had the same give-and-take with Matt that Judy had. Our relationship, at times, was strained. But, whenever he had problems, we talked. For example, he was unsure about revealing to me that he was gay. He was afraid that I would reject him immediately so it took him a while to tell me. By that time, his mother and brother had already been told. One day, he said that he had something to say. I could see that he was nervous so I asked him if everything was all right. Matt took a deep breath and told me that he was gay. Then he waited for my reaction. I still remember his surprise when I said, "Yeah? Okay, but what's the point of this conversation?" Then everything was okay. We went back to being a father and son who loved each other and respected the beliefs of the other. We were father and son, but we were also friends.

How do I talk about the loss that I feel every time I think about Matt? How can I describe the empty pit in my heart and mind when I think about all the problems that were put in Matt's way that he overcame? No one can understand the sense of pride and accomplishment that I felt every time he reached the mountaintop of another obstacle. No one, including myself, will ever know the frustration and agony that others put him through, because he was different. How many people could be given the problems that Matt was presented with and still succeed, as he did? How many people would continue to smile, at least on the outside while crying on the inside, to keep other people from feeling bad?

I now feel very fortunate that I was able to spend some private time with Matt last summer during my vacation from Saudi Arabia. We sat and talked. I told Matt that he was my hero and that he was the toughest man that I had ever known. When I said that I bowed down to him out of respect for his ability to continue to smile and keep a positive attitude during all the trials and tribulations that he had gone through, he just laughed. I also told him how proud I was because of what he had accomplished and what he was trying to accomplish. The last thing I said to Matt was that I loved him and he said he loved me. That was the last private conversation that I ever had with him.

Impact on my life? My life will never be the same. I miss Matt terribly. I think about him all the time—at odd moments when some little thing reminds me of him; when I walk by the refrigerator and see the pictures of him and his brother that we've always kept on the door; at special times of the year like the first day of classes at UW or opening day of sage-chicken hunting. I keep wondering almost the same thing I did when I first saw him in the hospital. What would he have become? How would he have changed his piece of the world to make it better?

Impact on my life? I feel a tremendous sense of guilt. Why wasn't I there when he needed me most? Why didn't I spend more time with him? Why didn't I try to find another type of profession so that I could have been available to spend more time with him as he grew up? What could I have done to be a better father and friend? How do I get an answer to those questions now? The only one who can answer them is Matt. These questions will be with me for the rest of my life. What makes it worse for me is knowing that his mother and brother will have similar unanswered questions. . . .

Matt officially died at 12:53 A.M. on Monday, October 12, 1998, in a hospital in Fort Collins, Colorado. He actually died on the outskirts of Laramie, tied to a fence that Wednesday before when you beat him. You, Mr. McKinney, with your friend Mr. Henderson, killed my son.

By the end of the beating, his body was just trying to survive. You left him out there by himself but he wasn't alone. There were his lifelong friends with him—friends that he had grown up with. You're probably wondering who these friends were. First, he had the beautiful night sky with the same stars and moon that we used to look at through a telescope. Then he had the daylight and the sun to shine on him one more time—one more cool, wonderful autumn day in Wyoming. His last day alive in Wyoming. His last day alive in the state that he always proudly called home. And through it all, he was breathing in, for the last time, the smell of Wyoming sagebrush and the scent of pine trees from the Snowy Range. He heard the wind—the ever-present Wyoming wind—for the last time. He had one more friend with him. One he grew to know through his time in Sunday school and as an acolyte at St. Mark's in Casper as well as through his visits to St. Matthew's in Laramie. He had God. I feel better, knowing that he wasn't alone.

Matt became a symbol—some say a martyr—putting a boy-next-door face on hate crimes. That's fine with me. Matt would be thrilled if his death would help others. On the other hand, your agreement to life without parole has taken yourself out of the spotlight and out of the public eye. It means no drawn-out appeals process, [no] chance of walking away free due to a technicality, and no chance of a lighter sentence due to a "merciful" jury. Best of all, you won't be a symbol. No years of publicity, no chance of a commutation, no nothing—just a miserable future and a more miserable end. It works for me. . . .

Matt's beating, hospitalization, and funeral focused worldwide attention on hate. Good is coming out of evil. People have said, "Enough is enough." You screwed up, Mr. McKinney. You made the world realize that a person's lifestyle is not a reason for discrimination, intolerance, persecution, and violence. This is not the 1920s, '30s, and '40s of Nazi Germany. My son died because of your ignorance and intolerance. I can't bring him back. But I can do my best to see that this never, ever happens to another person or another family again. As I mentioned earlier, my son has become a symbol—a symbol against hate and people like you; a symbol for encouraging respect for individuality, for appreciating that someone is different, for tolerance. I miss my son but I'm proud to be able to say that he is my son. . . .

. . . Every time you celebrate Christmas, a birthday, or the Fourth of July, remember that Matt isn't. Every time that you wake up in that prison cell, remember that you had the opportunity and the ability to stop your actions that night. Every time that you see your cell mate, remember that you had a choice, and now you are living that choice. You robbed me of something very precious, and I will never forgive you for that. Mr. McKinney, I give you life in the memory of one who no longer lives. May you have a long life, and may you thank Matthew every day for it.

Your Honor, Members of the Jury, Mr. Rerucha, Thank you.

60

U.S. Security Policy after 9/11

On the mild autumnal morning of September 11, 2001, a group of militants hijacked four airplanes and intentionally crashed two of them into the twin towers of the World Trade Center in New York. Another plane was flown into the Pentagon, destroying a section of the building, and a final plane crashed in a field in Pennsylvania. While the roughly 2,600 people who died in these attacks was far fewer than the 20,000 who died in the Gujurati earthquake of the same year or the 250,000 who died in the 2004 Indian Ocean tsunami, the political nature of the crime and the response on the part of the U.S. government made this a moment of world historic importance that is remembered as 9/11 or September 11th.

Among the many responses to 9/11 were the U.S. invasion of Afghanistan, the war in Iraq, the intensification of counterinsurgency against Muslim militants in the Philippines, and a whole new approach to international security. The increased screening and inspection at airport security checkpoints changed the way people travel; however, this was largely uncontroversial and has mostly been memorialized in everyday travel stories. More controversial were the changes in laws and practices governing civil liberties and jurisprudence. In January of 2002 the U.S. government set up Camp X-Ray in Guantánamo Bay, Cuba, where suspected terrorists were indefinitely detained without trial and outside the jurisdiction of courts or international treaties governing the treatment of prisoners of war. For many Americans this was a small price to pay for security from terrorism. For others this denial of the basic right to a trial, combined with increased surveillance of citizens, suggested a dark new world of unchecked state power. Harvard law professor Alan Dershowitz distilled the debate for the nation with his "ticking time bomb" scenario, in which a terrorist knew where a giant bomb was. Dershowitz asked if it was right to use torture to find out where it had been placed. For many people, including former president Bill Clinton, the answer was an obvious yes. Dershowitz proposed "torture warrants" that would take the form of presidential approval for enhanced interrogation. Throughout the Bush presidency, suspected terrorists were regularly brought to Guantánamo or "black sites" through "extraordinary rendition," or abduction, and subjected to "enhanced interrogation."

There had been much debate, at first, for and against torture, using Dershowitz's ticking time bomb scenario, but as the public became increasingly disgusted by the abuse and seemingly unending scandal connected to detention without trial and enhanced interrogation, and as the prisoners at Camp X-Ray became increasingly disconnected to the struggles going on outside the camp, cooler voices emerged. The discovery, capture, and execution of Osama Bin Laden—the man believed to have masterminded 9/11—in 2011, which drew on clever interrogation rather than force, brought to the fore some of the problems with Dershowitz's either-or thought problem. Suddenly other choices seemed to emerge, such as those suggested by psychologist Saul Kassin, whose *groundbreaking research suggests that innocent people are more likely to confess than guilty ones, and that the more pressure is exerted to obtain a confession, the more likely incorrect information will drive out real discovery.*

Though prison camps continue to exist at Guantánamo, the Obama administration radically reduced their population and largely eliminated enhanced interrogation, preferring to pose security as less of an either-or thought problem and more of an everyday set of practices. The picture reprinted depicts one of the early prisoners at Camp X-Ray who was caught in the initial struggle between Americans who supported "security" and those who supported "legal rights."

QUESTIONS TO CONSIDER

1. The army allowed journalists to publish only a few photos of Camp X-Ray. Why do you think they might have chosen to release this one?
2. Imagine you are debating with a classmate whether or not Camp X-Ray should exist. List the arguments you might make for and against its existence based on what you see in this picture.
3. How do you think Americans might have seen a different story in this photo than people abroad?

U.S. Army military police escort a prisoner at Camp X-Ray, Guantánamo Bay, Cuba. *U.S. Navy iPhoto Inc./Newscom.*

61

AHMIR QUESTLOVE THOMPSON

Walking While Black: The Unhappy Marriage of Race and Criminal Justice

Concerns about unequal justice for blacks and whites have been a part of American life since the eighteenth century, and many of the urban uprisings of the past fifty years have been in direct response to an incident involving police. In August of 2014, a young African American man, Michael Brown, who was accused of theft and assaulting a police officer, was shot to death by police in Ferguson, Missouri. The incident touched off days and nights of running battles between the nearly all-white police force and protesters. As similar incidents occurred in towns and cities that did not have such racially skewed police hiring patterns, the national discussion expanded to the bigger problem of unequal policing and what many African Americans refer to as "walking while black."

First and foremost among these other incidents was the strangulation death of a middle-aged father of six who was caught illegally selling cigarettes on the street in Staten Island, New York. Captured by a cellphone video, Eric Garner's last dying pleas of "I can't breathe" were played on computer screens across the country. Shortly after this incident, two Cleveland, Ohio, policemen were captured on a security video shooting twelve-year-old Tamir Rice to death for carrying a plastic toy gun. Adding to the national dialogue was the fact that instead of attempting to administer first aid to the dying child, they tackled and arrested his teenage sister. Critics and defenders of the police across America disagreed about who was at fault, but most Americans seemed to recognize that there was a larger problem between police and African Americans. President Barack Obama, the United States' first nonwhite president, also joined the national debate, seemingly struggling to balance his expressed concern for the high rates of African American incarceration and death in police custody with his concern for law, order, safety, and the law enforcement apparatus that he was charged with leading.

Ahmir "Questlove" Thompson is an African American musician, journalist, writer, and record producer who was born in Philadelphia in 1971. He grew up during a previous generation of conflict between police and African American communities that culminated in the 1985 police bombing of a house inhabited by the black liberation organization MOVE. Drawing on his childhood experiences in Philadelphia and later engagements with the police, he became an influential part of the discussion that emerged in 2014 around racialized policing.

Ahmir Questlove Thompson, interview, *Democracy Now!* August 14, 2013. http://www
.democracynow.org/2013/8/14/questlove_on_police_racial_profiling_stop.

QUESTIONS TO CONSIDER

1. Thompson recalls his own experience with racial discrimination in this interview. Why do you think that he talks about his father's advice about how to act when confronted by the police? Why does Thompson tell the story of the police officer suggesting he is driving the wrong type of car?
2. Thompson compares himself to Trayvon Martin. Do you agree with this comparison? In what ways do you think Thompson is similar to Martin and in what ways is he different?
3. Thompson argues that police treat him differently because he is black. Do you think his evidence is convincing? Why or why not?

There was a point where I was coming home from—from Bible study, like teen Bible study on a Friday night, and there was a Tower Records on South Street. And a friend of mine wanted to purchase U2's *The Joshua Tree* album, which just came out. And they were coming to Philly at RFK Stadium, so he wanted to, like, study the record and know all the material before they came, and so we went and purchased *The Joshua Tree*. And we were driving home, and then, seconds later, on Washington Avenue in Philly, like, cops stopped us. And he was holding a gun on us.

And there's nothing like the first time that a gun is held on you. Like, we're 16, mind you, like 16, 17 years old. And, you know, I just remember the protocol. I remember my father telling me, like, "If you're ever in this position, you're to slowly keep your hands up." I mean, he did it in sort of a humorous way that Richard Pryor did. You know, Richard Pryor told a joke of, whenever you're stopped, "Yes, officer, my hands are on the steering wheel." You know, it was that type of thing. I remembered that lesson. So, my friends didn't know that, so they just thought that it was normal. And I was like, "Yo! Get your hands up! Get your hands up!" Like, how I knew that was the protocol at that young age, I mean, it's probably a sad commentary, but it was also, you know, a matter of survival. . . .

I mean just two, three weeks ago—I mean, I wasn't frisked, but I was—I definitely know that was I stopped for, you know, unknown reasons, that I was just the wrong person in the wrong automobile. . . .

I was leaving my Thursday night residency. I do a regular DJ night at Brooklyn Bowl in Williamsburg, and right before we got on the Williamsburg Bridge, we got pulled over. They walked up, asked to see license and registration. And it was like four of them with flashlights everywhere. And I played a risky card: I was like—I pulled this [the book he is author of] out of my backseat and was like, "This is me," you know, hoping. And nine times out of 10 when I'd play that card, it never works. . . . so I showed them the book, and they looked, and they kind of had a meeting for five minutes. And then, it was like, "Oh, OK, you can go." And phew, you know, but this happens all the time. . . .

Probably, in my lifetime, I've been stopped—one, two, three—I mean, the memorable ones are probably six times. But it's definitely in the twenties and thirties. I mean, probably, since 1994, twenties and thirties. The worst one was after Super Tuesday in Orange County. I was campaigning for Super Tuesday. . . . For Obama. And after it was over, a friend of mine, Jurnee Smollett, who's an actress on *True Blood*, she and I were done campaigning, and we decided to see a movie. After the movie, we went to Borders to get—I wanted to get a housewarming gift for my manager. And we pulled over. I pulled over to take a phone call from my manager, because, you know, I thought, being a law-abiding citizen, you're not supposed to drive and talk. So I pulled over, talked, finished the conversation, pulled off. Five cars stopped us, and pretty much that was like the—that was the most humiliating experience, because, like, we had to get out the car. They made us spread on, you know, the car. They searched the car. We sat in the back of . . . their car. And the whole time I was thinking, like, "God, please don't look in the trunk." Like, first of all, I felt like a criminal already, like, OK, I've got stuff in the trunk. But the stuff I had in the trunk were psychology books and some Scrabble games. And in my head, I was like, there's no way that they're going to believe that that stuff belongs to me. Like, there's no way that they're—and so, the whole time I was just like, "God, please don't. Please don't." She was trying to get like her camera phone. She's like, "This is unconstitutional! They're not—this is an illegal search. They're supposed to have a protocol for"—you know, so that—you know, I've been—this is like the night before the Grammys, the night before the Grammys in 2010, when I won. So, it's like, this happens all the time. . . .

It is absolutely probably the most humiliating, lowest, lowest feeling a human being can have. Twice this happened in front of dates. And all I kept thinking about was like, man, like, nothing's more emasculating than to be emasculated in front of a girl that you like. You know, like there's just no coming back from that. And it's sort of like an unspoken thing, like I always felt like, even afterwards, like there's this unspoken cloud of the question of my manhood, because—you know, that's why I'm often shocked when I see footage of people and they talk back to cops. Like, I want to do that, but it's like—you know, even watching *Fruitvale*, like I was like, "No, don't—don't—like, just get on your knees! Just don't—you know, you can die." And that's—it's the most humiliating, emasculating feeling I've ever had. That's—I only feel low when that happens, you know, even—even if it's playful.

In Philly, whenever we finish a Roots album, I give it the car test. So, even driving up and down Broad Street in Philadelphia, I once got stopped three times. And, you know, the first two times, they were just like—they looked, they were just like, "Oh, it's you." They let me go. Third time, this guy, "Oh, man, it's you!" And then I felt safe enough to sort of have casual banter with him. I was like, "This is the third time I've been stopped. Like, what's going on here?" And he was like, "Well, you know, I mean, you're kind of in Temple University's neighborhood." And I was like, "Yeah? And?"

He's like, "Well, look at the car you're in." I drive a Scion. And my logic for getting a Scion was like don't get a flashy—like, I come from the '80s, so in the '80s, when you saw someone in a BMW, in a Mercedes, they automatically got pulled over, because they were a drug dealer. So I thought, OK, I'll get a Scion—well, first of all, it was free; it was given to me. And it was boxy; it was afro-friendly, like it didn't smoosh my afro down, and so it's a comfortable car. I like it. He said, "You know, in this, you kind of look like you stole it from a college student." And I was like, "Oh, well, OK, I get it." So, in even choosing the car in my mind that would sort of not put me in that position, I actually wound up putting me in that position by driving that car, because he said, "If you were in a SUV, we would have just thought you were one of the Philadelphia Eagles or something." Like, oh, OK, that's the car you belong in. . . .

[M]ost people, when they finish their records, they try and find a really good speaker system. When you mix your records, you do it on horrible speakers, so that way, if it sounds great on horrible speakers, it'll sound great elsewhere. So when you finish your record, the first place you want to take it to is to a good car system. I mean, mine is not—I mean, it's satisfactory, but, you know, I just wanted to drive around with it. I always do it, with every Roots album. I just drive around for five hours, making sure that I like the mix and I'm fine with it. I just happen to drive between the hours of 2:00 A.M. and 4:00 A.M., and, you know, that was another unfortunate circumstance I found myself in. But even then, it's just like, what do you do? Do you—I mean, how much more can I play it safe? Like, I'm already like taking—purposely taking myself out of situations because I want to avoid that. But I don't know how much more I can—I can suppress myself to not seem like a threat or be a threat. . . .

I think there's just a bit of our soul that sort of just melts away when things like this happen. I mean, first of all, you internalize it. Like, as I watched the case, I mean, I identified with Trayvon Martin, like I felt like, OK, that would have been me in that situation. I mean, there's definitely been times where I've been watching either a sporting event or the Grammys or any sort of television event, and then I'd be the person that would run to the store to get something. Like, that could have easily been me. I live in hoodies. I opened a hoodie shop. I have a hoodie shop that sells nothing but hoodies. Like, I love hoodies, because it gives me anonymity, like I get to go to movies, and no one bothers me. . . .

And so, when the verdict was handed down, you know, I just felt like—half of me, I instantly felt like, well, yeah, I knew that was going to happen. But then the other half of me was upset that I had just resigned to that fact. And, you know, because I was on an international flight—I was in Holland the day that the verdict was handed down, so that whole eight-hour trip on the plane, I just felt like, oh, well, you know, nothing matters anymore, like this really—life doesn't matter, like you're guilty no matter what, and you just now have to figure out a way just to make everyone feel safe and everyone feel comfortable, even if it's at the expense of your own soul. . . .

<h1 style="text-align:center">62</h1>

RYAN J. DOWNEY AND HANNAH APPEL

<h2 style="text-align:center">Personal and Social Debt</h2>

In 2008 the world economy plunged into the worst crisis since the 1930s. Coinciding with the subprime mortgage crisis of 2007–2009 in which massive unpayable home mortgage debts threatened to put major international banks out of business, the ensuing crisis came to be called "the Great Recession." Debt became one of the key political and social issues for a generation of Americans who faced economic crisis and declining real incomes. Talk show hosts, bloggers, and pundits threw around statistics like "77 percent of Americans are in debt" and "one in seven Americans is being pursued by a collection agency," while ordinary Americans worried about maxed-out credit cards, "underwater mortgages" (where more is owed than a home is worth), and the impossibility of paying off massive student loan debt.

While some of it proved to be fear and hype, expanding consumer debt was a reality that negatively impacted millions of Americans. For over thirty years since 1985 the ratio of debt to personal disposable income and personal savings increased dramatically. In that same period, the cost of a year at college had increased over 500 percent—all of this during a period of low inflation; student loan interest rates were often two or three times higher in the United States than in other wealthy countries, many of which provide a free college education. By 2010 the Federal Reserve Bank reported that American consumers owed $11.74 trillion in debt, of which $882.6 billion was to credit card companies, $8.14 trillion was for mortgages, and $1.13 trillion was for student loans. The United States was drowning in debt, much of which likely would never be repaid.

Both the Bush and Obama administrations developed programs to address crushing debt, but the debt was too big for these policies to cover more than a small percentage of citizens. A generation of Americans continued to find that debt was defining their life decisions about home, security, education, and participation in society. The two selections that follow suggest the differing ways that individuals thought about the debts they had incurred and some of the solutions that they were able to envision—both in their individual lives and in the communities in which they found a sense of belonging and home.

Ryan J. Downey, "How to Walk Away." *The Huffington Post*, October 8, 2011. http://www.huffingtonpost.com/ryan-j-downey/mortgage-walk-away-what-happens-_b_993756.html; Hannah Appel, interview. *Tavis Smiley*, September 26, 2014. http://www.pbs.org/wnet/tavissmiley/interviews/economic-anthropologist-hannah-appel/.

QUESTIONS TO CONSIDER

1. Whom do these two authors blame for the debt crisis?
2. How would you contrast the solutions that these documents offer individuals with crushing debt?
3. Hannah Appel describes her approach to the debt crisis as a "social hack." What do you think she means?
4. How are the policy changes suggested by these two authors different?

RYAN J. DOWNEY

How to Walk Away

I made my last mortgage payment on November 1, 2009.

Bank of America changed the locks on my house on September 29, 2011.

What happens when you walk away? Are you arrested? Are you shunned? Do your kids decide they hate you?

When I signed a mountain of loan documents to purchase my first home in 2006 I had the same attitude as most people. "Do whatever you can to pay your mortgage: run up credit cards, work out payment plans with the IRS, eat Ramen noodles. But pay your mortgage, every month, always. Because when you miss a few payments, a sheriff shows up with a cardboard box and throws you and your family onto the sidewalk. Or maybe if he's friendly he'll give you a lift to a shelter." . . .

This is what happened when I decided to walk away. And it's not nearly as nightmarish as you might think.

I purchased a brand new home in Riverside County, California in April, 2006 for $422,000. As I write this more than five years later, Zillow.com estimates the home's value at $253,000. I had an interest only, nothing down loan with an adjustable rate mortgage through a lender called First Franklin. (Yeah, I'm one of those guys you've been reading about.) I had a 711 FICO score when I bought my house but the woman who worked out the mortgage assured me that because I'm self-employed, I would never get anything better than an interest only, nothing down adjustable rate mortgage.

When the housing bubble burst I had some friends who purchased new houses—which they told their banks were "investment properties"—only to move into them while letting the first "underwater" house slip voluntary into foreclosure. At first I thought this was bananas. . . . I spent eight months trying to get a loan modification. I faxed close to a hundred pages of documents to them. . . . the bank told me in no uncertain terms that they were denying my request because, well, I hadn't ever missed a mortgage payment and therefore I wasn't viewed as an "imminent risk of foreclosure." That's right. They wouldn't help me because I was paying them every month and on time. . . .

The same month I made my last mortgage payment I read an article about an Arizona law professor who was advising people to do exactly what I had decided I must do. Two months after that, I read about how investors in the largest residential real estate deal in U.S. history had walked away from 11,232 properties at once.

The banks call it "writing off a bad investment." But when a private citizen does it, we're scum? Please . . .

THE SCARY NOTICE TAPED TO YOUR DOOR. PFFT!

The bank first taped up the scary "your home is going to be sold at auction in three weeks" papers on my door in March, 2010. The actual auction didn't take place until August, 2011. But of course, at the time, I was sweating bullets.

What's interesting was that I never really formally requested postponements of the auction dates. I would call in to get updates throughout my third attempt at a loan modification and they would tell me in ominous tones, "Mr. Downey, I see here you have an auction date for April 29. That's in a week. What are you going to do about this today?" I would call back the next day and a different person would tell me in the same manner, "I see here you have an auction date of May 5."

This continued all the way until September when I got a letter from Bank of America politely informing me they had become my new mortgage servicer. It turns out First Franklin had "charged off" my second mortgage and sold my first mortgage to Bank of America, or so I think . . . Who knows really? They don't seem to know themselves. . . . Then on August 9, 2011 they finally took my house to auction. Nobody bought it and it went back to the bank.

WHAT HAPPENS AFTER THE AUCTION?

I'm told that if investors buy it they will eventually show up on your porch, give you a call or write you a letter. They'll tell you they've purchased your home and they are prepared to offer you some "moving expenses" cash to get outta Dodge. If the bank takes your house it's more or less the same thing. A realty company came by my place on BOFA's behalf.

In either case the bank or the investors could evict you, which you can fight. This process will cost them money and give you even more time in the house—anywhere from thirty to ninety days, I've heard. It makes more sense to them to give you cash to get out faster so they can be sure you won't trash the place on the way out or let the lawn turn brown. If you decide to stay this extra bit of time, be aware that an eviction looks much worse than a foreclosure to a landlord.

In my case it took the realty company a few days to show up and (surprise, surprise) they had to wait on Bank of America to finish up some details before they could work everything out with me. I'm not saying I worked out a "cash-for-keys" agreement. I'm pretty sure those agreements have a non-disclosure mechanism. But I hear they're offering about $5,000. I handed Bank of America's representatives the keys nearly two months after the day they took the house to auction.

BUT WHAT ABOUT MY CREDIT SCORE?

American Express lowered my spending limit for a few months when I stopped paying my mortgage. A few months later they raised it again. I kept all of my credit cards and auto loans current. When it came time to rent a house I was accepted by the first landlord at the first rental property I looked at with the only application I turned in. I simply explained the entire situation to him in our first conversation. He wanted to see my bank statements and ran a credit report. That was it.

It's my suspicion that a foreclosure is going to be much less detrimental when it comes time to getting credit to do anything—including buying another house—than it used to be. Think about it. If people won't rent to folks who've lost their homes, who will they rent to? It would be McDonald's deciding they won't sell food to people who are out of shape.

The place I'm renting is costing me less than half my monthly mortgage and property tax bill used to be.

WHAT WILL THE KIDS SAY?

My three-year-old daughter loves our bigger house and our nicer neighborhood. She announced recently that, "One time I saw an ant sleeping on my bike in the garage so we had to get a new house." Our dog loves the new house, too.

FINALLY, WHAT WILL THE NEIGHBORS SAY?

The honest ones will ask you for advice. The proud ones will probably end up with papers taped to their doors, too.

HANNAH APPEL

Interview

. . . the Rolling Jubilee is something we could think of as a social hack, right? It's an action that allows us, that in fact forces us, to rethink, to reimagine what we thought we knew about debt.

In the past, debtors experienced debt as isolating, shameful, a reason to be afraid, a reason not to open the mail, a reason not to pick up the phone. And the Rolling Jubilee and Strike Debt work more broadly in saying what if debt was not about individual isolation, shame, fear? What if debt was a platform for collective action?

So the Rolling Jubilee, by buying up what's called distressed debt for pennies on the dollar and then sending a letter to the debted that says, hey, we have forgiven this debt. We don't try to collect the debt. We abolish it. It asks people to rethink that, to look at it and say, wait a minute. First of all, you can buy debt for pennies on the dollar?

Most people think that, if their debt is $1,000, they owe $1,000. They don't know that it circulates on secondary markets for mere pennies on the dollar, that debt collectors are making hundreds of percent profit by forcing me to pay the full amount when in fact the debt collector bought it for only pennies on the dollar.

So we really—in part, it's really about public education. It's really about asking people to step back and to rethink that just as you introduced it in the beginning of the show as a systemic problem and not as a problem of the failure of individuals.

And, of course, in the Rolling Jubilee project, we're able to help thousands of debtors along the way and that's wonderful, but it really is about asking the entire nation and beyond to rethink debt as a political platform. . . .

Certainly medical care and, at this point, student debt, and that really has been over the last three decades when there hasn't been as much public funding and people are having to go into radical debt just to send a kid to college. Kids are currently graduating with about $30,000 worth of debt on average from all schools in the country. . . .

Student debt right now is approaching $1.3 trillion dollars. So we could turn that adage and say, if I owe the bank $25,000 for my student loans, then the bank owns me. But if we as student debtors owe the bank $1.3 trillion dollars, then we actually have a tremendous amount of power, an untapped power, in our hands.

Millions of students are defaulting on their loans every year already, but we're not doing so in an organized fashion. We're not doing so in a way that brings the sort of collective power of that figure whether as student debtors, whether as mortgage debtors, whether as medical debtors, to begin to have power to actually negotiate terms with creditors.

On September 17, which was the third anniversary of Occupy Wall Street, we announced that we had bought and abolished $4 million dollars of student debt for students at a college called Everest, which is for-profit college, national chain under the Corinthian Colleges, Inc. corporation. And I feel like that's a really good example of how we can start to mobilize because that has actually attracted a lot of media attention. . . .

Given how many of us are in debt and given where public opinion is in this country about the banks right now, I actually think we could have a tremendous amount of legal decisions on our side. I think a lot of the media will be on our side. In other words, I feel like public pressure against the banks, public pressure to get us out of what we might call odious debt, of what we might call exploitative debt, and into reimagining how we fund social services in this country, working class kids, low income kids, middle class kids, should not graduate from "public schools" with $30,000 worth of debt.

I actually think the vast majority of this country across the political spectrum would agree with that. And that kind of unity is not something the banking lobby can fight easily. We are out to be kind of a new labor movement in certain ways. We work alongside the labor—the idea is not to replace the labor movement, but to say the way that the labor movement changed working conditions for working people, we would like to be that same movement for indebted people, especially because in certain ways so many more people are indebted than have good jobs.

63

STANLEY CROUCH

Barack Hussein Obama: Black Like Whom?

Although President Obama is the first African American to be president of the United States, other African Americans before him have served in elected office. Wentworth Cheswell became the first African American elected official in the United States when he was elected town constable in 1768 in Haymarket, New Hampshire. During the period of Reconstruction (1865–1877) many African Americans were elected to offices at the national, state, and local levels, including one governor, several U.S. congressmen, and one congressman who was briefly Speaker Pro Tempore of the House of Representatives. However, the presidency was the domain of white male Christians until the 2008 election of Barack Hussein Obama, the son of a white American mother and an immigrant African father from Kenya.

From the day that Obama first appeared as a legitimate candidate for the Democratic Party ticket, Americans began debating what his election might mean for race relations in the United States. Some argued that it was the harvest of the civil rights movement, demonstrating the possibility for racial democracy; others dismissed it as tokenism for an Ivy League graduate at the top. For a few it signaled the newest version of a longstanding process, described by anthropologist Karen Brodkin as "becoming white," in which immigrants, this time from Latin America, Asia, and even Africa,

Stanley Crouch, "What Obama Isn't: Black Like Me on Race," *New York Daily News*, Thursday, November 2, 2006. http://www.nydailynews.com/archives/opinions/obama-isn -black-race-article-1.585922.

find acceptance, success, and belonging in America, often by climbing over the backs of African Americans. Black journalist Stanley Crouch, the author of the following commentary, was probably the first public commentator to suggest this last interpretation in a column written in 2006, long before most Americans had any idea who Obama was.

During the early days of his campaign against Hillary Clinton for the Democratic Party nomination, African Americans struggled to warm to Obama, confirming some of Crouch's criticisms. However, after Clinton began to court conservative white rural voters in the South, Obama became increasingly popular among black voters. When he won, African Americans celebrated an unprecedented milestone for one of their own. But the honeymoon did not last. As he journeyed deeper into the presidency it become increasingly apparent to African Americans that whether he was black like them or not, his presidency was not the sea change many had hoped for. As the children of new immigrants like South Asian Bobby Jindal and Hispanics like Marco Rubio, Susana Martinez, and Ted Cruz took the national stage in this same period, it seemed that Crouch's concerns had been prescient. Instead of signaling a new era in relations between black and white, the election of Barack Obama may have reflected an age in which Latin Americans, Asians, and even Africans might become white. However, for those who were black like Stanley Crouch, and born into the American caste color system, most of the longstanding inequalities and frustrations remained.

QUESTIONS TO CONSIDER

1. Stanley Crouch talks about a distinction between a black American politician and Obama, whom he describes as an African American. Why does Crouch think this is significant?
2. Crouch says that "Obama is being greeted with the same kind of public affection" that General Colin Powell, the son of Jamaican immigrants, received when he was considered a presidential candidate. What do you think Crouch means?
3. Do you think Crouch is right that Americans might be more accepting of a candidate who has black skin, but does not "share a heritage with the majority of black Americans, who are descendants of plantation slaves"? Why?
4. What do you think that Crouch means by the phrase coming into the White House "through a side door"?

If Barack Obama makes it all the way to becoming the Democratic nominee for President in 2008, a feat he says he may attempt, a much more complex understanding of the difference between color and ethnic identity will be upon us for the very first time. Back in 2004, Alan Keyes made this point quite often. Keyes was the black Republican carpetbagger chosen by the elephants to run against Obama for the U.S. Senate seat from Illinois. The choice of Keyes was either a Republican version of affirmative action or an example of just how dumb the party believes black voters to be, since it was obvious that Keyes came from the Southeast, not the Midwest. That race was never much of a contest, but one fascinating subplot was how Keyes was unable to draw a meaningful distinction between himself as a black American and Obama as an African-American. After all, Obama's mother is of white U.S. stock. His father is a black Kenyan. Other than color, Obama did not—does not—share a heritage with the majority of black Americans, who are descendants of plantation slaves.

Of course, the idea that one would be a better or a worse representative of black Americans depending upon his or her culture or ethnic group is clearly absurd. Even slavery itself initially came under fire from white Christians—the first of whom to separate themselves from the institution were Quakers. The majority of the Union troops were white, and so were those who have brought about the most important civil rights legislation. Why then do we still have such a simple-minded conception of black and white—and how does it color the way we see Obama?

The naive ideas coming out of Pan-Africanism are at the root of the confusion. When Pan-African ideas began to take shape in the 19th century, all black people, regardless of where in the world they lived, suffered and shared a common body of injustices. Europe, after all, had colonized much of the black world, and the United States had enslaved people of African descent for nearly 250 years. Suffice it to say: This is no longer the case. So when black Americans refer to Obama as "one of us," I do not know what they are talking about. In his new book, *The Audacity of Hope*, Obama makes it clear that, while he has experienced some light versions of typical racial stereotypes, he cannot claim those problems as his own—nor has he lived the life of a black American. Will this matter in the end? Probably not.

Obama is being greeted with the same kind of public affection that Colin Powell had when he seemed ready to knock Bill Clinton out of the Oval Office. For many reasons, most of them personal, Powell did not become the first black American to be a serious presidential contender. I doubt Obama will share Powell's fate, but if he throws his hat in the ring, he will have to run as the son of a white woman and an African immigrant. If we then end up with him as our first black President, he will have come into the White House through a side door—which might, at this point, be the only one that's open.

ACKNOWLEDGMENTS *(continued from p. iv)*

Bracketed numbers indicate selection numbers.

[1] "Victory 3at Greasy Grass." *Lakota and Cheyenne: Indian Vviews of the Great Sioux War, 1876–1877* by GREENE, JEROME A. Reproduced with permission of UNIVERSITY OF OKLAHOMA PRESS in the format Republish in a book via Copyright Clearance Center.

[3] "African Americans during Reconstruction." From B.A. Botkin, ed., *Lay My Burden Down: A Folk History of Slavery,* pp. 65–70, 223–24, 242–42, 246–47. Copyright © 1945 by B. A. Botkin. Reprinted by permission of Curtis Brown, Ltd.

[23] "A Bintel Brief." From Isaac Metzler, *Bintel Brief: Sixty Years of Letters from the Lower East Side to the Jewish Daily Forward* (New York: Doubleday, 1971). Used by permission of Isaac Metzer/Black Star.

[29] "Down and Out in the Great Depression." From *DOWN AND OUT IN THE GREAT DEPRESSION: LETTERS FROM THE FORGOTTEN MAN* by Robert S. McElvaine. Copyright © 1983 by the University of North Carolina Press. Foreword © 2008. Used by permission of the publisher. www.uncpress.unc.edu.

[30] "On the Road during the Great Depression." From *Morey Skaret: Riding the Rails in the 1930s,* the autobiography of Morest L. "Morey" Skaret, June 15, 2001, courtesy HistoryLink.org.

[32] "In Defense of the Bible." From *Monkey Trial: The State of Tennessee vs. John Thomas Scopes,* edited by Sheldon Norman Grebstein. Copyright © 1960 by Sheldon Norman Grebstein. Reprinted by permission.

[33] "The Harlem Renaissance." Excerpts from "Harlem Literati," "Parties," and "When the Negro Was in Vogue" from *The Big Sea* by Langston Hughes. Copyright © 1940 by Langston Hughes. Copyright renewed 1968 by Arna Bontemps and George Houston Bass. Reprinted by permission of Hill and Wang, a division of Farrar, Straus and Giroux, LLC.

[34] "My Fight for Birth Control." From *My Fight for Birth Control* by Margaret Sanger, pp. 46–56, 152–60. Copyright © 1931 by Margaret Sanger. Reprinted with permission of Sanger Resources and Management, Inc.

[36] "Mexican Migrants and the Promise of America." From *The Mexican Immigrant: His Life Story, Autobiographic Documents Collected by Manuel Gamio.* University of Chicago Press, 1931. Reprinted by permission of the University of Chicago Press.

[37] "Taking a Stand: The Sit-Down Strikes of the 1930s." From *Diary of a Sit-Downer* by Francis O'Rourke, December 30, 1936–January 10, 1937. Reprinted courtesy of Mrs. Mary O'Rourke.

[39] "To Use an Atomic Bomb." From "One Hell of a Bang," by Studs Terkel, *The Guardian,* August 6, 2002; Paul Weller, published with permission of Anthony Weller, Gloucester, Massachusetts, through Dunow & Carlson Literary Agency, New York via Tuttle-Mori Agency, Inc., Tokyo.

[40] "Rosie the Riveter." From *Rosie the Riveter Revisited,* edited by Sherna Berger Gluck. (Boston: Twayne, 1987), pp. 28–33, 35–38, 40–45, 48–49. Reprinted by permission of Sherna Berger Gluck.

[41] "Memories of the Internment Camp." From Archie Satterfield, *The Home Front: An Oral History of the War Years in America, 1941–1945,* pp. 330–38. © 1981 by Archie Satterfield. Used by permission. Published by Playboy Press.

[42] MASH: an army surgeon in Korea by APEL, OTTO F.; APEL, PAT. Reproduced with permission of UNIVERSITY PRESS OF KENTUCKY in the format Book via Copyright Clearance Center.

[43] "Blacklisted: The Post–World War II Red Scare." From "Notes on the Blacklist: Lardner," interview by Barry Strugatz, *Film Comment,* September/October 1988, 52–69. Reprinted by permission of Barry Strugatz.

[48] "The Adventures of a Woman in Science in the 1960s." From Naomi Weisstein, *"How can a little girl like you teach a great big class of men?" the Chairman Said, and Other Adventures of a Woman in Science.* Reprinted by permission of Jesse Lemisch.

[49] "The Limits of the Women's Movement." From Phyllis Schlafly, *The Eagle Forum,* http://www.eagleforum.org/psr/1991/dec91/psrdec91.html. Reprinted by permission of Phyllis Schlafly.

[50] "Mississippi Freedom Summer." Excerpt from *Letters from Mississippi,* edited by Elizabeth Sutherland Martínez, pp. 83, 93–94, 108–110, 172–173, and 217–224. Original edition copyright © 1965 and renewed 1993 by Elizabeth Sutherland Martínez. New edition copyright © 2002 by Elizabeth Sutherland Martínez. Reprinted with the permission of The Permissions Company, Inc. on behalf of Zephyr Press, www.zephyrpress.org.

[52] "The Young Lords." From Pablo Guzmán, "La Vida Pura: A Lord of the Barrio," in Andrés Torres and José E. Velázquez, eds., *The Puerto Rican Movement: Voices from the Diaspora* (Philadelphia: Temple University Press, 1998), 155–58, 164–67. Originally appeared in the *Village Voice,* March 21, 1995. Reprinted by permission of Pablo Guzmán.

[53] "Toward Mexican American Civil Rights." César Chávez, "César Chávez Talks in New York, 1968" from *The Catholic Worker.* Reprinted by permission of The Catholic Worker.

[54] "The Gay Rights Movement." From "Recalling the Stonewall Uprising," originally published as "Back to the Future? A Walk on the Wild Side of Stonewall," by Robert Amsel, *The Advocate,* September 15, 1987. Reprinted by permission of Robert Amsel.

[55] "The Letter That Sparked the Debate and Supporters of It." Letter from Lewiston Mayor Larry Raymond to the Somali Community, *Portland Press Herald,* October 1, 2002. Used by permission.

[55] "The Letter That Sparked the Debate and Supporters of It." Letter from Gary Savard, January 18, 2003. Posted online at www.sunjournal.com/. Reprinted by permission of Gary Savard.

[56] "Letters in Support of the Somali Community." Letter from the Elders of the Somali Community, October 6, 2002. Used by permission of the *Portland Press Herald.*

[56] "Letters in Support of the Somali Community." Letter from the Elders of the Somali Community, October 6, 2002. Used by permission.

[57] "When PATCO Went on Strike." From Cathy Langston, *What It Means When God Goes on Strike* (self-published by author, 2010), pp. 2–8, 22, 30, 34–36, 57–60. Reprinted by permission of Cathy Langston.

[61] "Walking While Black: The Unhappy Marriage of Race and Criminal Justice." Ahmir Questlove Thompson, interview. *Democracy Now!* August 14, 2013. Used by permission of *Democracy Now!* Democarcynow.org

[62] "Personal and Social Debt." Ryan J. Downey, "How to Walk Away." *The Huffington Post,* October 8, 2011. Used by permission of Ryan J. Downey.

[62] "Personal and Social Debt." Hannah Appel, interview. Tavis Smiley, September 26, 2014. http://www.pbs.org/wnet/tavissmiley/interviews/economic-anthropologist -hannah-appel/.

[63] "Barack Hussein Obama: Black Like Whom?" Stanley Crouch, "What Obama Isn't: Black Like Me on Race." *The New York Daily News,* Thursday, November 2, 2006. © Daily News, L.P. (New York). Used by permission.